T0285007

MAKING SOCIAL SPENDING WORK

Peter H. Lindert

CAMBRIDGE
UNIVERSITY PRESS

University Printing House, Cambridge CB2 8BS, United Kingdom

One Liberty Plaza, 20th Floor, New York, NY 10006, USA

477 Williamstown Road, Port Melbourne, VIC 3207, Australia

314–321, 3rd Floor, Plot 3, Splendor Forum, Jasola District Centre, New Delhi – 110025, India

79 Anson Road, #06–04/06, Singapore 079906

Cambridge University Press is part of the University of Cambridge.

It furthers the University's mission by disseminating knowledge in the pursuit of education, learning, and research at the highest international levels of excellence.

www.cambridge.org
Information on this title: www.cambridge.org/9781108478168
DOI: 10.1017/9781108784467

First published 2021

Printed in the United Kingdom by TJ Books Limited, Padstow Cornwall

A catalogue record for this publication is available from the British Library.

ISBN 978-1-108-47816-8 Hardback

To Natasha, Sophie, Izzy, Nadia, Carson, Alex, Kailani, and Kiara

Contents

APPENDICES

Available online at www.cambridge.org/Lindert

Figures

Tables

APPENDICES

Available online at www.cambridge.org/Lindert

PART I

OVERVIEW

CHAPTER 1

Enduring Issues

THIS BOOK INTERPRETS A NEARLY GLOBAL HISTORY OF social spending up through the year 2020, drawing lessons for the years up to 2050. In the long history covered here, what most enriches the record has been harvested within the last twenty years – twenty years of experience, and twenty years of accelerating scholarship.[1] The new knowledge extends far beyond the usual tales of the North Atlantic community, inviting new interpretive forays into Latin America, East Asia, and the formerly communist Eastern Europe.[2] While much of the best evidence is recent, the underlying social issues have endured for millennia.

ALWAYS NEEDED, JUST NOW ARRIVED

Human societies have always needed safety nets to catch those who end up in need, whether by unlucky endowments, by past mistakes, or by the arrival of hard times. The risks are not new. They have always been there. Yet for most of human history, we have lacked the means, or the political will, to prevent or cushion them.

With each wave of expansion in the economic base, humans did what little they could to cut risk at the local level, yet serious risks remained. Prehistoric fortunes were never stabilized by hunting and gathering. The arrival of agriculture tens of thousands of years ago initially helped to diversify humanity's economic portfolio, yet brought new vulnerabilities to weather and pests once it had expanded. More recently, as the spread of commerce diversified our sources of supply and allowed a further expansion of population, our risks were reduced a bit further, though they remained. Still more recently – in a mere blink of an eye lasting less than three hundred years – industrialization and the ever-growing reliance on skilled services once again cut our risks somewhat yet have not eliminated them. Our world is risky, but not increasingly so.

A common error in the way we view history, and the way it is taught in school, is to believe that an unprecedented economic insecurity was ushered in by the Industrial Revolution and by the rise of a new greedy market mentality around 1750. Marx and Engels said so. The gentler reformists of the Fabian Society agreed that the age of dark satanic mills brought new urgency to finding ways of providing social insurance and social assistance to the needy. Karl Polanyi's *The Great Transformation* (1944) agreed. While their landmark writings contained great insights, they were mistaken in believing that the industrial era and the rise of a market mentality brought a transformational rise of risk and a brand-new need for social security. The risks were at least as great before the Industrial Revolution. As for the rise of a market mentality, it did not happen. There was no modern dawn of market exchange, nor of self-interest, nor of "greed," because all of these are at least as old as the human species itself.

The risk of mortality, even more than economic risk, has also been dropping over the centuries. There has been a great convergence in human life spans, thanks mainly to the elimination of death from childbirth and infant mortality. In the 2020s, people will naturally share the fear that our vulnerability to mortality shocks is greater than ever, as witnessed by the coronavirus pandemic. Not so. Horrible as it is, the latest pandemic will not match the introduction of smallpox and malaria into the Western Hemisphere, which killed a majority of its population. The Black Death of the fourteenth century killed perhaps a quarter or half of the European population, which the coronavirus will not do. And Chinese history recorded frequent epidemics stretching back at least three thousand years. Life has always been filled with risks as least as great as those we face today, underlining the point that our need for safety nets was at least as great in the past.

Given that humanity's exposure to risks seems eternal, it is puzzling that societies have only very recently built effective safety nets for containing such risks.

Defining Some Terms

- **Social spending** in this book will usually refer to public (tax-based) spending on:
  - education,
  - old-age support,
  - incapacity and disability,
  - health care and health insurance,
  - family assistance,
  - labor-market assistance (retraining, unemployment compensation, etc.), and
  - housing.

In practice, the official measures of social spending only partially cover tax breaks, sector subsidies, public infrastructure, etc., which could arguably be included in the definition if there had been sufficient data coverage of these transfers. The tax breaks and sector subsidies excluded here (e.g. subsidies to the energy sector or the agricultural sector) are often more pro-rich than the social spending covered in this book.

Social spending here excludes private social spending aimed at the same targets, even when the private spending is mandated by government. To be sure, private social spending can make important contributions toward a host of social goals. But the real controversies center on the government's increasingly dominant role, and this book will stay focused accordingly.

- **Safety nets** are society's many supports to keep people from falling too low economically. They consist of both **social assistance** expenditures for those whose needs may be life-long, and **social insurance** expenditures for cushioning temporary falls. In this book, the term "safety nets" is thus broader than just social assistance for the poorest, or "welfare." It covers all of the egalitarian uplift provided by social spending, both short-

(cont.)

run and long-run. Basically, safety nets are what social spending is for.

- **Selfish generations**: The book will use the convenient shorthand *Selfish Generations* borrowed from David Thomson's (1996) fine book on how New Zealand governments had redistributed resources between age groups.

  The **selfish** is a shorthand for "advantaged by inter-generational redistribution." The advantaged "selfish" ones are not the whole generation, but just those of its members who have political voice. In many cases, the selfish generation's poor were not helped. To further clarify, a **generation** in this phrase and in Thomson's book refers to an age group, as in the common parlance about "the older generation" or "the younger generation." It does not strictly refer to a birth cohort, as a demographer might prefer.

BASIC QUESTIONS

The recent global surge of government social spending, after millennia without it, poses some natural questions, each of which is pursued in this book.

(1) Why did social spending arrive so late in human history?
(2) Why has Northwest Europe always led the way?
(3) Did the task of providing safety nets to cushion us against life's many risks really have to fall to government, instead of to private charity and the extended family?
(4) How does a large tax-based social budget affect our livelihoods over our life spans?
(5) For any given size of the government social budget, which countries have been spending it on the wrong things?
(6) What threatens social programs between now and mid-century?

To lighten the burden of carrying so many questions at once into the coming chapters, I will offer two immediate spoiler alerts:

- The answer to the third question is yes. Yes, safety nets had to be administered mainly by government. Private charity and family supports have never been up to the tasks of eliminating poverty or educating the whole population. The forces behind government social programs came together only in the last two hundred years, with almost all their advance coming in the last sixty years. Government social spending has now become worldwide, absorbing around 10 percent of world product.
- A partial answer to the fifth question: The tendency to get the mix wrong is as great among the world's low-spending governments as it is among those who spend more. Thus, the fourth and fifth questions can be studied separately.

A striking pattern will also emerge as to which countries got social spending wrong, either at low levels or at high levels: The clearest mistakes are myopic ones. The errors have tended to be errors of "selfish generations," in which those in office have deprived future generations by appeasing those whose lobbying power is here and now.

AS CONTROVERSIAL AS EVER

The fourth question, whether large "welfare-state" social budgets are better or worse for incomes and wellbeing than smaller budgets, has always been the main fight. The combatants in the debate over the size of social budgets need introductions here, deferring the final verdict until a preview in Chapter 2 and a fuller empirical update in Chapters 8 and 9.

To report on the battle between small-government free-market capitalism and the tax-based social spending, recently dubbed the war between "cutthroat" and "cuddly" capitalism,[3] let us begin by reviewing the classic arguments over the economic effects of social spending versus an imagined free-market alternative. The debate has raged for at least eight centuries. The words have changed, but the opposing positions have not.

TRADITIONAL ARGUMENTS AGAINST GOVERNMENT SOCIAL SPENDING. Each side of the debate sends a respectable signal along with ideological noise. To pick up the signal worth hearing in the critiques of social spending, one must first mute out the noisy demonizing images of welfare queens, welfare bums, and bureaucrats, and the sneers about a nanny state.

For centuries now, the core argument against tax-based social spending, or all civilian government spending, has warned of perverse incentives. The incentive argument has economic plausibility and deserves careful testing. Basically, if the government taxes the incomes or wealth of productive people and gives the money to less productive people in need, the incentives work badly on both sides. The productive lose the incentive to produce, or innovate, or take risks. The less productive are rewarded for being in a bad state, and are likely to respond by staying longer in that bad state and not producing.

The incentives critique has been leveled at all four main forms of social spending – anti-poverty "welfare," public pensions, public health, and public education, in roughly that order of emphasis. The archetypal prediction, since the twelfth century or earlier, is that welfare spending will kill the work incentive. Public pensions are faulted for crowding out private savings, and for killing the work incentive by inviting earlier retirement. Public subsidies to health-care provision or health insurance may have subtler incentive problems referred to as "moral hazard": inviting people to adopt lifestyles with greater health risk or to see the doctor too often, and inviting doctors and hospitals to overcharge. The case against public education is the most muted: Paying for public schools, but not for private schools, may make parents accept lower-quality education and may lower the public schools' incentives to become more efficient.

All of these respectable criticisms deserve careful testing.

TRADITIONAL ARGUMENTS FOR GOVERNMENT SOCIAL SPENDING. The respectable signals in favor of social spending have also had to contend with ideological noise from advocates of greater public assistance. The noise includes demonizing images of greedy and insensitive billionaires, robber barons, and corporations. "Privatization" is used as a pejorative, defined as handing the people's public assets over to the fat cats.

The respectable signals strike notes that are replayed in today's economics textbooks. For basic welfare spending – that is, assistance to poor families and unemployment compensation, the incentives critique is not rejected altogether. Rather, it is rebutted by denying that poor people lost work by choice, or that working more is a valid option without government help.

Public pensions help to smooth consumption over the life cycle, and can insure people against a bad consequence of something good: outliving the wealth they had saved up for retirement. As for the familiar criticism that people should self-save and purchase private old-age insurance, proponents of public pensions counter that people, especially poor people, often save little for the future because shorter-run needs look larger to them, and they cannot borrow at reasonable rates of interest. As for the argument that people could be forced to save in the form of government-mandated paycheck deductions, we return to its complexities in Chapter 13.

Public health care and public health insurance are defended largely on grounds of positive externalities, or spillovers. For example, as a taxpayer, I should help to pay for your vaccinations and good health, lest you pass on infections and over-use my hospital's emergency room. Believers in tax-based health insurance deny that there is much moral hazard, claiming that people do not take big health risks just because taxpayers will cover some or all of their out-of-pocket costs. The alternative of leaving all health insurance to the private marketplace is rejected on the grounds that voluntary private health insurance leads to a "death spiral": The insurers want to cover only those with lower health risks than the premiums will cover; so the insurance will be bought only by those who know they are likely to have health problems, not by healthier individuals; this adverse selection threatens the insurers with higher costs, which they then try to cover by charging still-higher premiums; so even more healthy people drop the insurance; and the cycle repeats, crippling the market for private health insurance.

The argument for public education also rests on a belief in positive externalities, in this case from the knowledge and civic responsibility that schools are supposed to instill. The benefits from a child's education are not captured only by the child and the child's family. All of society benefits from the knowledge, therefore all of society should help pay for it with taxes.

WHY THE CONTROVERSY ENDURES. If the debate is so ancient, why does it persist? A partial excuse is that it takes a lot of effort to dig out the facts, and to run convincing tests. Fortunately, an accelerating volume of economic studies has been delivering the necessary effort, as summarized in the chapters that follow.

More fundamentally, the conflict of self-interests is what generates controversy forever. Any solid research finding can be challenged by those whose self-interest it seems to threaten. Nonetheless, as has been argued several years ago,

> new facts can raise the level of the debate. They can arm all sides with an awareness of how tax-based social spending would affect collective goods that all profess to care about – social peace and the size of the economy. The competitiveness of the intellectual marketplace, and of the political marketplace in electoral democracies, allows new facts to exert pressure toward these collective goods. At the very least, new facts can speed up society's rejection of bad arguments.[4]

Eventually, despite the noise, true signals do come through, and far-sighted societies heed them.

CHAPTER 2

Findings and Lessons

SO WHAT DO WE NOW KNOW ABOUT THE ROLE OF SOCIAL spending in the economy and society? This chapter summarizes ten main findings supported by global experience and fresh research in the early twenty-first century. Documenting these findings yields three clear policy lessons, and an international scorecard on the far-sightedness or myopia of different countries' approaches to social spending.

TEN MAIN FINDINGS

> **Finding #1**. A country's government social spending takes off only after the country has both the fiscal capacity and the political will to build safety nets. This is why the world had only negligible social spending before 1800, and why it emerged first in Northwest Europe after that.

The main reasons why social spending has spread all over the world is the mirror image of what prevented social spending outside of Europe before the last century: Having the government spend on the poor, the sick, the elderly, and school children requires fiscal capacity plus political pressure from below (Chapters 3 and 4).

Within the last sixty years, government social spending has grown to absorb more than a quarter of GDP in over a dozen countries, mainly in Europe. The demand for such tax-based programs was raised by a diversity of forces: the shocks of world wars, revolutions, hyperinflations, and the Great Depression; the continuing rise of political voice for middle- and lower-income groups; rising trust in government; improvements in medicine; and population aging (Chapters 5 and 6).

Finding #2. A major barrier to growth and equality has been the refusal of those with power to devote taxes to universal education. Government funding for mass education has always been the main driver of adults' years of schooling, building human skills and productivity. The leading countries passed up chances to capture these gains in the eighteenth century and part of the nineteenth. Once tax-based schooling took off, it became more equal. The Americans were leaders in the quantity of primary and secondary schooling, but never leaders in its quality.

No country has ever delivered primary and secondary education to the majority of its children without financing it mainly through taxes.

In the eighteenth century and part of the nineteenth, the leading countries passed up chances to capture the gains from public schooling of the masses. In Britain and the Netherlands, the payoffs from basic schooling already promised high rates of return, privately and socially, partly by interacting with the rise of commerce. Yet these two leaders delayed for at least a century and a half, partly because of church-school issues and more fundamentally because those with political voice resisted paying taxes for educating the children of others.

Once the political will was mustered to launch universal primary education, adults' years of school not only grew, but became more equal. So say the data on years of school worldwide since 1870. This growth and leveling of schooling was, again, dominated by the rise of tax-based public schools (Chapter 5).

Starting around 1850, the Americans were leaders in the quantity of education, as measured by years of enrollment and of adults' accumulated education. Yet as best one can tell from indirect and circumstantial evidence, the United States never led the world in the quality of primary and secondary schooling (Chapter 5).

Finding #3. Since around 1910, there has been a long mission shift in social spending, toward support for the powerful and elderly, at the expense of assisting the young and the poor. This mission shift in social targeting has offset part of the pro-growth and pro-equality effects of the overall expansion of safety-net spending.

Over the last hundred years, many countries' social spending shifted missions, toward public pensions for the non-poor and away from progressive policies like mass schooling and aid to the poor. This mission shift has not been reversed since. It probably compromised both income equality and income growth. The global mission shift toward public pensions may have been due in large part to improvements in life expectancy, which allowed longer life past work and contributed to political "gray power." The inference about gray power springs from the fact that public pension spending rose even *per elderly person*, and not just at the rate of population aging. Its per person generosity rose faster than the rise in educational spending per child of school age.

The rising demand for government pensions was probably also linked, in addition, to a quiet global change in the role of intra-family transfers. Career and family developments may have raised public pressure for more tax-based support of the elderly (Chapter 6).

Finding #4. Larger social-spending budgets have not produced any net loss of GDP, or in skills, or in work. Without any such costs, Europe's welfare states have produced greater equality, cleaner government, and even longer life. There are good economic explanations for this "free lunch puzzle."

So says the international evidence for any decade or combination of decades back to 1880, before which there was little social spending at all.

None of these decades, or any longer periods, showed any significantly negative correlation between the share of GDP channeled into social spending and the level (or growth) of GDP itself. The lack of any significant negative correlation is all the more remarkable because shocks to GDP should have biased the results in favor of seeing a negative relationship (Chapter 8).

Behind this statistical outcome lie some sound reasons suggested by recent history. One can find at least *four positive features* of the real-world welfare-state bundle of policies, features that have cancelled any anti-growth effects. One consists of those economies of scale in delivering social insurance: the more universal the coverage, the smaller the administrative, or bureaucratic, costs of raising tax revenues and allocating transfers. A second is that the large welfare states raise their tax revenues through broad consumption taxes and sin taxes, the type of taxation that conventional theory predicts will favor growth the most. Third, the welfare-state policies of parental leave and pre-school child development foster better human productivity for both the child and the career-interrupting parent, usually the mother. Fourth, single-payer public health insurance is more cost-efficient than voluntary private insurance (Chapters 9 and 14).

The claim that greater social spending must somehow shrink the size of the economic pie is in deep trouble, and has already retreated in the slump of 2020.

Finding #5. Governments around the world have shifted toward equalizing incomes since 1910. This tide has not been reversed, not even by the conservative movements since 1980. The usual measures of fiscal redistribution understate the rise of progressivity, by missing the delayed equalizing effects of public education expenditures.

Over the last hundred years, government redistribution of income has become more "progressive," shifting income from richer households to poorer ones in the Robin Hood tradition. Retreats toward the opposite "regressive" redistribution have been rare and limited. For all that has been written about a shift of political sentiments and government policy away from progressivity since the late 1970s, no such trend is clear yet in how overall taxes or social spending are distributed. Among democratic welfare states, the closest thing to a demonstrable reversal against Robin Hood is the slight retreat in Sweden since the 1990s. Globally, the most dramatic swing since the late 1970s has been Chile's record-setting return toward progressivity after the regressivity of Pinochet.

Finding that redistribution has continued to march slowly toward progressivity carries a strong implication for our interpretation of the rise in income inequality since the 1970s, so firmly established by the World Top Incomes Project and by Thomas Piketty (2014). That rise may owe nothing to a net shift in government redistribution toward the rich, despite the lowering of top tax rates. If so, it is all the more important to explore what non-fiscal forces have widened gaps in market incomes around the world (Chapter 10).

Finding #6. A short-run threat to the future of social spending looms from waves of refugees and the nationalist reactions to these waves. Of four policy options facing rich destination countries, politics will probably favor the option that protects national goals, including social programs, at the expense of international growth and equality. The likely favorite policy, Chapter 11's "Option 4," will add more cherry-picking restrictions favoring skilled immigrants.

An open humanitarian acceptance of refugees ("Option 1") would serve global growth and global equality. It could also serve domestic growth, and is fiscally sustainable. Yet it is politically unsustainable, because it threatens domestic equality, domestic political harmony, and social programs. The backlash against this option will be around for a while. The opposite option, "Option 2," would slam the immigration door shut, catering to nativist reaction, but at a cost in terms of economic growth. The recently discussed option of "welfare chauvinism" ("Option

3"), admitting all sorts of immigrants but denying them access to social assistance and social insurance is unsustainable. The cherry-picking Option 4 seems to win by default (Chapter 11).

Finding #7. The most durable threat to the future of social spending and the welfare state is posed by the upward march of senior life spans. Something has to give, for financial sustainability. Five countries are clearly keeping their total public pension costs under control, while protecting their basic anti-poverty pensions, but at least seven others are not.

The aging of human populations will continue, at least until 2050. By then, the number of persons over 65 for each person of prime working age (18–64) will have doubled.

In the face of this aging, balancing pension budgets requires that benefits per year must grow more slowly than wages and salaries per member of the working-age population. Something has to give. Indeed, the same adjustment to longevity would be called for even if individuals self-financed all of their old age privately. If the share of your adult life spent earning income drops, with each generation living more of adulthood beyond work than did its ancestors, then your lifelong annual consumption must drop relative to your annual earnings. The problem faces us all, with or without government pensions (Chapter 12).

Finding #8. To be sustainable, average public pension spending per elderly person should not, and need not, rise as a share of peak GDP. The annual public support per elderly person can rise with average income growth, but should fall behind income growth as the population ages.

The logic governing how public pension budgets must behave in the long run produces this necessary rule for sustainability. Some countries have already built something like it into official policy rules. The notional defined contribution (NDC) system fixes the share of GDP (or earnings) to be paid out in yearly pension benefits. The simple rule stated in Finding #8 indexes pensions not to the latest GDP or earnings, but to the real value of *peak* GDP or earnings. Pension institutions need to retain this safeguard, to avoid having yearly pensions sink as fast as GDP in a short-run recession or depression like the one triggered by the coronavirus pandemic of 2020 (Chapters 12–14).[1]

Finding #9. The "second pillar" of government social insurance, the job-based kind that intervenes in the workplace, has shown various flaws. In many countries, it has redistributed in favor of top occupations. The famous second-pillar compulsory paycheck-deduction systems of Chile since 1980 and Singapore since 1965, while promoting financial stability, do not function as their proponents claim. Far from being "privatized," they have become slightly regressive instruments of state taxation and control. Universal first-pillar provision better protects transparency and equity.

The practice of linking social security to one's job or occupation should be cut back (Chapters 12 and 13).

Why should social security have anything to do with one's workplace? The two are mismatched, aside from the narrow cases of workplace accidents and experience-related unemployment compensation, where the job itself is the focus. If the benefits of social insurance (e.g. pensions, health) are shared by society as a whole and the covered individuals, the usual principles of public goods say that the insurance costs should be shared between the same two parties, i.e. society as a whole and the covered individuals, job or no job.

A further violation of economic principles arises as soon as linking the insurance to one's current job imposes a net cost on the employment relationship, a cost shared by employers and employees. Why should the employment of labor bear such a cost, when employing capital bears no such insurance cost?

Worse, many countries have had top-heavy pension practices, in which the general population bears a net fiscal burden of providing generous pensions to those in the well-paid formal-sector occupational groups, including civil servants, the military, and the courts. This book spotlights such regressive practices in a global South, here meaning Latin America, Africa, the Middle East, and South Asia (Chapters 7 and 12).

Chapter 13 reinterprets two mandatory-payroll-deduction pension systems, those of Chile since 1980 and Singapore since 1965. Both became famous as "privatized" pension systems, yet both are systems of central government taxation. Thinking of them as tax systems fits both common intuition and the official Organization for Economic Cooperation and Development (OECD) practice of defining mandatory payroll deductions as taxes.

Finding #10. The younger the person, the greater the long-run social return on society's investments in them, both on the average and at the still-unexploited margin. For any given total public social spending, investing in child development, not least pre-school children, is more pro-growth and pro-equality than spending the same amount on public pensions for the well-off (or on transfers favoring the rich). Generations of powerful groups in many countries have selfishly failed to heed this lesson from history.

An invest-early consensus that has emerged among micro-economists in this century can now be backed up by international and historical comparisons.[2] The new finding gained momentum in two stages. First, in the late twentieth century, empirical studies came to an earlier-pays-more conclusion for the traditional levels of schooling: the average social rate of return on education was respectable for higher education, but greater for secondary schooling, and still greater for primary schooling, as previewed in Finding #2. Then early in this century, numerous studies based on a variety of micro-level interventions, mostly in the United States, concluded that the payoff to inputs into children before age 6 probably paid even higher returns. Those returns could come from greater parenting time and/or from expenditures on pre-primary education programs. The earlier the expenditure, the better.

Policymakers have been moving toward the same earlier-is-better conclusion. First the communist countries took the lead in government-run child care and parental leave on a modest scale. Among democracies, substantial support arose in the late 1960s and 1970s in response to the rise in women's labor-force participation, with Sweden leading the way. A pro-natal wave of supports has arrived since the 1990s, in response to concerns about low fertility rates (Chapter 9).

THREE POLICY LESSONS FROM WORLD HISTORY

Findings #8–#10 imply three global lessons for government social-spending policies, namely

- *Index annual pension benefits*, both negatively to changing senior life expectancy and positively to peak GDP per adult. That will prevent any positive trend in the share of GDP that taxpayers spend on public pension benefits without any absolute pension cuts.
- As much as possible, *uncouple the funding of social insurance from the workplace*, reducing reliance on the second pillar of social insurance. Shift toward funding universal safety-net pensions and universal health care, with voluntary supplements.
- *Invest more in the young*, with a "cradle to career" strategy.

The final chapter returns to these three lessons, illustrating how a country can apply them, guided by its own history and by worldwide experience (Chapter 14).

THE MOST FAR-SIGHTED AND THE MOST MYOPIC

Which countries and which generations have shown far-sighted investment in the young, as opposed to the more myopic transfers to the current elderly? The historical listing should start with the selfish refusal of the *whole world's politically empowered adults* to pay taxes for universal primary schooling *before the mid-nineteenth century*. The generational sin was clearest in the eighteenth and early nineteenth centuries, when investing in basic education in the richest countries could have repaid the older generations almost immediately, as previewed in Finding #2 above.

Among the currently living generations, which countries have overcome, and which have failed to overcome, the anti-growth selfishness with the right mix of social spending? Several advanced countries have got it right, with a greater educational support per child relative to support per elderly person (Chapter 7, especially Figure 7.3). The worst performers – among countries for which we have usable data – have been India, Turkey, Greece, Latin America, and the global South more generally. These countries' underinvestment in the young shows up in their lower international test scores, lower GDP per person, and higher inequality.

To enrich this world geography with some history, we should ask *which recent generations* have been successfully selfish in their political influence? The generational timing of each country's redistributions is unique, of course. Yet, in most cases, it has been only certain powerful groups that have reaped the inter-generational harvest. Here is a quick alphabetical roll call of some cases in which a particular generation has recently benefited at the expense of others.

- In *Brazil*, overly generous pensions have been enjoyed by every generation of pensioners between the passage of the stakeholder-defending Constitution of 1988 and the modest pension reform of 2019. Within these generations of pensioners, the gains have been disproportionately captured by the high-income civil servants, judges, and the military. Even without the coronavirus pandemic of 2020, the pension system was projected to run far beyond its reserves by 2022.
- In *Chile*, those who held formal-sector jobs in the period 1960–1973 extracted considerable social security transfers from the rest of society. Their unearned gains were both sanctioned by, and capped by, the military government's pension reform of 1980–1981 (Chapter 13).
- In mainland *China* since the reforms launched by Deng Xiaoping, the inter-generational favoritism has been the reverse of what has happened in most other countries. In the super-growth since the 1980s, the government short-changed those who were born before 1925, who

suffered through their working life before 1990, while heaping health and education benefits on the generations born since 1970 in the east-coast provinces.

- In *Greece* between 1982 and 2014, pensioners in the public and formal private sectors received unsustainable gains paid for largely by others, contributing to the country's debt crisis.
- In *Japan*, despite a tradition of saying that the elderly should be able to count on their adult children for support, the elderly population has instead been supported by the taxpayers of their children's generation, ever since a jump in taxpayer support from 1974 to 1983. The support is only moderate per year of an elderly person's retirement, but becomes a huge aggregate burden on younger workers in such an aged population (Chapters 12 and 14).
- In *Singapore*, the main beneficiaries will be the first future generation to benefit from a shift in government policy away from capital accumulation toward public social spending (Chapter 13).
- *Turkey*'s pensioners have captured increasingly unsustainable benefits at the expense of the rest of society, at least for the period 1980–2017. The beneficiaries are again those near the top of society, as in Greece and several Latin American countries (Chapters 7 and 12).
- In the *United States*, the generation becoming 65 years old between 1967 and 2002 (born 1902–1937) benefited at the expense of other generations from the arrival of age-restricted Medicare and the shift toward more generous non-contributory Social Security benefits. Also since 1967, the United States has lost its lead in public education, and has been particularly remiss about having the nation's taxpayers provide paid work-leave for the parents of newborns (Chapters 9, 12, and 14).

In the long run, while all public safety nets have helped to stabilize people's purchasing powers, the strongest safety net has been the one woven by investing more in the young.

PART II

THE LONG RISE, AND ITS CAUSES

CHAPTER 3

Why Poor Relief Arrived So Late

DID SAFETY NETS FOR THE NEEDIEST HAVE TO WAIT FOR government to build them with taxes? If so, why did it take so long for any government in the world to channel a significant share of national income to those with needs based on inability to produce? Why did tax-based social spending then appear only in the forms of poor relief and public elementary schooling, and primarily in Northwest Europe? Why did the taxpayers start paying for poor relief before they started paying for education?

This chapter locates and explains the delayed arrival of tax-based help for those in poverty, and the next chapter does the same for tax-based mass education. The following historical changes dominated both the timing and the Northwest European location of the emergence of government social spending:

- Private safety-net mechanisms existed for millennia, both as social assistance and as social insurance. Yet for fundamental reasons, they never came close to curing poverty, either today or in centuries past.
- The rise of government revenue-raising capacity had to precede the emergence of social spending. This fiscal capacity arrived in Northwest Europe first.
- The extra revenue was not converted into poor relief until elites were threatened by disorder, and later when political voice had diffused far down the socio-economic ranks, breaking up the inertial power of vested interests. Northwest Europe led these two developments, though not until the late eighteenth century (for disorder) and the late nineteenth (for mass suffrage).

The latter change, the spread of political voice to lower social ranks, introduces a theme that recurs throughout this book: The importance of overcoming the inertial power of coalitions that block popular and efficient changes. Basically, the ultimate answer to the question "why so late?" lies in the delay in the arrival of a political will for safety nets. In this respect, what has held back the rise of government social spending is the same inertia of vested interests that retarded technological innovations and economic growth. The story unfolding here thus resembles the story of retarding forces, in Mancur Olson's emphasis on distributional coalitions against change, in Joel Mokyr's emphasis on both political and intellectual vested interests, and in the tale of anti-progressive extractive powers as told by Daron Acemoglu and James Robinson.[1]

FIGHTING POVERTY WITHOUT TAXES

It would be surprising indeed if humans had not devised any safety nets to protect themselves, and each other, against the risk they faced. Historians have convincingly documented humans' institutional ingenuity. To deal with economic risks, Europeans had already developed some local safety nets at least as far back as the middle ages. Even within the confines of traditional agriculture, and even without effective governments, illiterate villagers devised an array of mechanisms providing both social insurance and social assistance for the poorest. One such mechanism was the plot scattering emphasized by Dierdre McCloskey (1976, 1991): Peasants and their manor lords agreed that an individual peasant household's plots should be scattered spatially, partly in order to diversify that household's risks and stabilize their incomes (the arrangement also made for efficient plowing and harvesting). If the household got a bad return on one plot but did well on another, it would still have enough to survive from all of its plots put together. Other scholars rightly argued that if peasants could figure out that advantage of diversification, like modern portfolio managers, then surely they could have worked out other ways of protecting against risk. Indeed, they did, much like modern farmers forming cooperatives. So did their contemporaries in non-agricultural pursuits. Medieval and early modern history is replete with examples of informal mutual-aid arrangements among villagers, plus formal guilds, fraternities, and friendly societies, all of which served to insure members and their families.[2]

Households, villages, and guilds were not left entirely to fend for themselves in the face of terrible risks. Religious institutions also shared their concerns to some extent, and confronted the problem of designing proper safety nets.

THE MEDIEVAL DEBATE OVER POOR RELIEF. As early as the twelfth century, canonists grappled with the task of determining who was eligible for relief. Determining eligibility involved two main practical concerns that still challenge policymakers today: The incentives problem and the information problem. First, how to incentivize the able poor to support themselves, while giving relief to those who were unable to do so? The twelfth-century writers overwhelmingly rejected giving aid to the "valiant," "lusty," and "sturdy," who could and should support themselves. The image most invoked here was that of a healthy young adult male. Yet Christian teaching consistently called for aid, either individual or collective, to the "impotent," as typified by a disabled person or an elderly widow. As a further parallel to more modern debates, the twelfth-century writers even distinguished between "hospitality," which in the nineteenth century became "indoor relief" à la Dickens' *Oliver Twist*, and "liberality" or almsgiving, which became the nineteenth century's "outdoor relief."[3]

The second concern, the information problem, was magnified by the growth of population of migrant poor from the fifteenth century through the sixteenth: How to get information on poor strangers, in order to know which group they belonged to? To twelfth-century writers,

> the primary distinction was between those poor who were known to the administrator of charity and those who were strangers. Among those who were known, the more deserving cases were to be preferred to the less deserving. As for the strangers, a man claiming support as a priest [or mendicant friar] was to be examined, while any who asked only food for the love of God were to be helped. But the author[s] made one significant exception to this rule. A man capable of working with his hands was not to be given anything but corrected and told to go to work.[4]

Thus had Europeans grappled, centuries ago, with today's issues of workfare and of keeping tabs on the poor.

EARLY MODERN ALTERNATIVES TO POOR RELIEF. The sixteenth through eighteenth centuries brought the solidification of legal institutions for social insurance and social assistance in Northwest Europe, most prominently in the Netherlands and in England. The new institutions were a mix of aid and punishment. They were initially not governmental, not collecting "taxes" as such, but drifted in that direction over these three centuries.

An early formalization of poor relief swept through the Low Countries (and some of the German states) in the 1520s. Formal poor relief institutions happened to emerge when and where the Reformation was taking place, though the leaders were not always Protestant. The new policy outlook called for a shift from relying on voluntary individual charity to a more secular "common chest" of resources administered by government.[5] At the same time, however, it still called for harsh policing and stigmatizing of able-bodied beggars (Michielse 1990). The city of Ypres, after seeking the advice of the renowned writer Juan Luis Vives, assigned to four *dischmeesters* (distributors of alms) in every parish the task of investigating the state of the poor, their occupations, age, number of children, illnesses, income, whether they were well behaved, and whether they were drunkards or beggars. Ypres thus may deserve the title of pioneer in data-based social monitoring of the poor.

In the seventeenth century and the early eighteenth, the task of monitoring the poor was increasingly formalized into settlement laws, in the Netherlands as elsewhere in Europe. These were an interim negative response to the increasing arrival of immigrants, rather than a rise in generosity of relief. In the Netherlands, they took the form of letters of surety showing one's place of usual recent residence. If you had the letter from the current parish, you could stay (and perhaps receive relief). If not, you were evicted to your home parish or, if you lacked any such letter, to some exit point of the new parish's choosing.[6]

What rose in the Netherlands around 1750, and in England thereafter, was not only the generosity of poor relief, but also the development of formal institutions for social insurance. A recent study by Bas van Bavel and Auke Rijpma (2016) sifts through the evidence on both the amount

TABLE 3.1. *Poor relief from formal institutions, local taxes, and charity, four European countries, 1427–1868 (roughly estimated percentages of GDP)*

(A) Italy

	Northern and central Italy 1427	Northern and central Italy 1640	Northern and central Italy 1790	Italy 1868
Formal institutions	1.0	1.8	1.1	0.8
Direct bequests	[0.1]	[0]	[0]	[0]
Total % of GDP	1.0-[1.1]	1.8-[2.0]	2.0-[2.3]	2.1-[2.3]

(B) Netherlands

	Western Netherlands 1530	Western Netherlands 1760	Netherlands 1820
Formal institutions	1.2	2.9	1.3
Direct bequests	[0.1]	[0.3]	[0.1]
Total % of GDP	1.2-[1.3]	2.9-[3.3]	1.3-[1.8]

(C) England

	England 1500	England 1700	England 1790	England 1850
Formal institutions	1.1	0.4	0.4	0.1
Direct bequests	0.2	[~0]	[~0]	[~0]
Access to commons	[0.3]	[0.3]	0.3	[0.2]
Gleaning	[0.1]	[0.1]	0.1	[0.1]
Taxes or poor rates	~0	0.8	1.5	1.1
Total % of GDP	1.4-[1.8]	1.2-[1.6]	2.1-[2.3]	1.2-[1.5]

(D) France

	France 1764	France 1790	France 1833
Formal institutions	0.5	0.5	
Taxes or poor rates		0.63	
Total % of GDP	0.5	0.5	0.63

Sources and notes: See Appendix A, www.cambridge.org/Lindert.

of relief and the share of it delivered by formal institutions. Table 3.1 shows their compilation of the eclectic evidence on all sources of income assistance to the poor. Their study reaches out beyond the usual formal institutions to consider what the poor may have gained from post-harvest gleaning, from access to common fields, and from individuals' direct bequests to them. Table 3.1's estimates establish that the key movements over time, and the differences between countries, were dominated by the history and geography of formal institutions.

Let us focus on the context that probably delivered the greatest share of aggregate income to the poor, namely the western Netherlands around 1760.[7] In this setting the poor were given perhaps 3.3 percent of GDP – with almost all of it (2.9 percent) coming from formal institutions, mainly orphanages, hospitals, almshouses and private foundations. To what extent should we think of these organizations as "Church," spending past donations, and to what extent were they "government," spending tax revenues? In fact, they were arguably both, since local donations-or-taxes were often disbursed through religious institutions under town government rules, and the donations often were as compulsory as taxes.[8]

This mixed nature of the formal relief-giving institutions invites either or two interpretations. If one chooses to view them as private religious charity, then the western Netherlands around 1760 stands out as the peak in private charity of all data-supplying countries before the twentieth century. If one chooses to view these institutions as local government units, then the Dutch stand out as early leaders in generous public relief. Perhaps the best compromise is that they stood out in their generosity, and were midwives in the birth of the public poor relief institutions of the nineteenth century.

One way or another, private charity retreated after the mid-eighteenth century. The share of GDP transferred by "formal institutions" in Table 3.1 failed to rise in Italy and France, and it declined in the Netherlands and England. Why?

Economists and historians have long noted some limitations in the ability of private charity to respond to a rise in need. A chief limitation has always been the free rider problem: "Why should I give more than a pittance when my contribution can't be crucial in the aggregate? And shouldn't I hold back and hope that other, bigger, donors will provide what is needed?" Another limitation is that the impulse to give responds more to the giver's self-identity than to changes in the needs of the distant poor. Historically, the well-off have always given more to people like themselves, such as co-religionists, or fellow alumni of a university *alma mater*, and only smaller amounts to the poor. In addition, whatever "warm glow" or personal salvation the act of giving conveys is subject to sharply diminishing returns: What we seek is to be able to assure ourselves and others that "we gave" – meaning that we gave *at least something*, with less psychic or spiritual return to having given more. Thus, the history of charities shows a vast miscellany of pittances, with little aggregate transfer.[9]

The Netherlands in the eighteenth century perhaps stands as a local peak in this history of private charity, which remained meager until larger-budget governments began to subsidize private charity more heavily, with tax breaks in the twentieth and twenty-first centuries. The eighteenth-century summit in Dutch relief ended for reasons specific to the Low Countries' history. Poor relief plummeted when the Low Countries were taken over, militarily and politically, during the Batavian Republic and the French Empire, 1795–1813.[10] Let us instead turn to the other leading rise in poor relief before 1820, namely the rise of the Old Poor Law's relief in England.

England was not far behind the Low Countries in developing poor relief, and borrowed ideas from the continental leaders. In the sixteenth century, English scholars and officials under the Tudors were familiar with the works of Juan Luis Vives, who migrated from Bruges to become tutor to England's Princess Mary and a resident of Corpus Christi College, Oxford. As William Ashley wrote in 1893, "English statesmen, at every step of their action in the matter, moved in an atmosphere of European discussion, of which they must have been aware."[11]

Yet English poor relief policy did have a unique feature from the sixteenth century on: Leadership was exercised more by the national government, and less by local authorities, than on the continent. The throne passed laws about beggars and the poor as early as 1388 for England and 1425 for Scotland. The pressure for the national government (throne) to deal with poverty and beggars became much greater after Henry VIII seized monastic properties and dissolved religious charities in the 1530s and 1540s.

With the Tudor wave of centralization came a new harshness toward the poor. In England, as in most other countries, the greater the economic and political inequalities between the elite and the rest of the population, and the greater the share of the population in poverty, the less deserving the poor were considered and the more harshly they were treated. Under the assertive reign of Henry VIII in particular, England's Tudor "Poor Laws" started out harshly. The Beggars Act of 1531 offered nothing to the disabled "impotent" population, yet came down hard on the "able" ones:

> if any man or woman being whole and mighty in body and able to labour having no land, master, nor using any lawful merchandise, craft, or mystery, whereby he might get his living ... be vagrant and can give no reckoning how he does lawfully get his living, that then it shall be lawful [that the] Justice of Peace .... Shall cause every such idle person ... to be tied to the end of a cart naked and be beaten with whips ... till his body be bloody by reason of such whipping [etc.].[12]

A further Beggars Act of 1536 softened the punishment, yet still decreed that the local governments were to "compel all ... sturdy vagabonds and valiant beggars to be set and kept to continual labour, in such wise as by their said labours they and every one of them may get their own livings with the continual labour of their own hands."[13] The 1601 Act for the Relief of the Poor, the most famous of the Elizabethan Poor Laws, softened these requirements further. It called on parishes to offer relief, usually featuring outdoor relief, funded by local property taxes. Yet the 1601 Poor Law was largely what we now call an "unfunded mandate." The central government did not offer to pay for the relief. Nor did local parishes offer much relief at their own expense until the second half of the eighteenth century – indeed, we should not expect them to have sacrificed much in response to an order from a central government that was not willing to dig into its own pockets for this worthy cause. Instead, the 1601 Poor Law was hardened by the Settlement Act of 1662 into a system primarily charged with evicting unwanted immigrants, including those seeking relief. The settlements system continued to be in force for two more centuries, but it was combined with rising generosity up to the 1820s – thanks to the arrival of tax-based funding.

THE RISE OF FISCAL CAPACITY

A recent literature on "fiscal capacity" emphasizes the greater revenue-raising capacity that could have been achieved by centralization into nation-states. Table 3.2 reveals some wide variations in the tax revenues Eurasian rulers ended up raising in the early modern era. Its Panel (A) shows each nation's average tax rate, and Panel (B) supplements this with some conversions of annual government revenues per capita into days of unskilled labor, in order to include some countries and periods where Panel (A)'s tax rate cannot be calculated for want of even a rough measure of national product in the prices of that time. The two panels agree on which large nations raised greater revenues.

TABLE 3.2. *Eurasian central government revenues, c. 1600–1870*

Panel (A) Nominal revenues, as a percentage of GDP

	c. 1600	1650-1699	1700-1749	1750-1799	1800-1850	1850-1869
Japan			12.3[a]			10.9
China			4-8		6.5	
India (Mughal)	17.7					
Ottoman Empire	2.5	2.8	3.0	3.5	4.5	6.5
Russia						12.4
Spain		10.0				
Netherlands				13.5		11.5
England/UK	2.2	4.2	7.4	9.0	7.5	

Panel (B) Nominal revenues, in days of unskilled labor per capita

	c. 1600	1650-1699	1700-1749	1750-1799	1800-1849	1850-1899
Japan			6.1[a]		7.1	
China			2.3	1.3	1.2	2.0
India (Mughal/Brit.)	22.7					1.1
Ottoman Empire		1.7	2.6	2.0		
Russia			6.4	8.3		
Spain	2.8	7.7	4.6	10.0		
France	2.8	7.6	6.7	11.4		
Netherlands		13.6	24.1	22.8		
England/UK	2.4	4.2	8.9	12.6	17.2	19.4

[a] Refers only to the parts of Japan controlled directly by the shogunate.
Sources and notes: See Appendix A, www.cambridge.org/Lindert.

Before 1800, no nation raised revenues as high as 20 percent of GDP, a common achievement today. Yet some raised more than 10 percent, an amount that could have helped growth and development if invested wisely. Tokugawa Japan was one such case. So was Mughal India around 1595–1600, during the height of Akbar's reign. These two cases displayed as much fiscal capacity as in Western Europe. By contrast, China, the Ottoman Empire, and Russia – and India itself, once the British took over – imposed lower average tax rates and raised only smaller revenues per capita.

The reasons for the low revenue-raising in China, British India, Russia, and the Ottoman Empire are complex and unique to each of those countries.[14] The summary explanations offered for government penury are a mixture of "They didn't have the administrative capacity," "They didn't dare raise more, for fear of rebellion and overthrow," and "They could have raised more but didn't need to, because their administration was simply more efficient, less costly, than others." This last, most optimistic, interpretation founders on the fact that each of these countries was so much poorer than their European counterparts. All things considered, these four large states were simply unable to raise revenues at modern rates of taxation. Yet Japan and Mughal India did raise impressive amounts, as did the Western Europeans, posing the next question: How did such fiscally capable countries spend their revenues in those days?

It is a second force, the rulers' priorities, that delayed the onset of social spending, even long after some of them were raising ample revenues. Indeed, beyond blocking social spending, the same narrowness of priorities also blocked productive developmental investments. In particular, we know from their budgetary allocations that the shogunate in Tokugawa Japan and the Mughal emperors in India placed too high a priority on military security and buying domestic allies to invest in civilian safety nets and economic development.[15]

The main European cases having ample revenues and lower shares spent on the military and central administration, and thus the most leeway for civilian spending, were the Netherlands and the United Kingdom.[16] Why Northwest Europe, and why in the sixteenth to eighteenth centuries? Economic historians and political scientists have converged on an explanation for the early modern rise of fiscal capacity. The key to its historical geography can be summarized in the phrase "limited governments, powerful states."[17] The literature converging on this formula springs largely from the classic article by Douglass North and Barry Weingast (1988), which argued that Britain's Glorious Revolution, by subordinating the throne to Parliamentary control of the budget, actually made the state stronger by insuring its tax base. Indeed, while the original interpretation of the North–Weingast study is that Parliamentary control over the ruler lowered all interest rates and fostered private investment, Gregory Clark has shown evidence that it eased only the one kind of credit that is most relevant here: It allowed the Crown itself to borrow at lower rates (Clark 1996). The extra government creditworthiness, helped further by Britain's rising efficiency of collecting indirect taxes at low and predictable rates (Brewer 1989), allowed for lower military and administrative spending in peacetime, and more civilian investments by government.

The link between limitations on the autocrat and the fiscal power of the state has since been confirmed by many international comparisons. These comparisons now cover all continents, and some even trace today's government revenue capacities back to monarchs' degree of deference to representative assemblies in the middle ages.[18] While the assemblies holding sway over the throne's access to tax money were invariably restricted to small elites, at least until the nineteenth century, their having political power over the autocrat was a harbinger of the later rise of broader democracy, another major factor shaping the rise of social spending.

TAX-BASED POOR RELIEF UNDER ELITE RULE IN ENGLAND

The long gradual rise of English tax-based poor relief, from the mid-eighteenth century through the 1820s, can be viewed largely as the response of a landed elite to rising poverty, the shift from agriculture toward commerce and industry, and the French Revolution.[19] The landed aristocracy dominated poor relief policy in Parliament, and more importantly in parish vestries, before the 1834 Reform centralized poor relief. The progressive decision to raise outdoor relief needed the approval of the rate-paying owners and tenants of large holdings. That they faced conditions of rising poverty in the countryside around them is suggested by all the real-wage indicators for 1770–1815 and the loss of cottagers' access to commons.

The landed interests that dominated Parliament and rural parish politics so thoroughly before 1832 had much to fear from the prevailing economic and political trends. The relative prices of staple foods were rising, for at least three reasons. Two well-known reasons were the acceleration of population growth and Britain's loss of access to Eastern European grains during the French Wars. A third reason was that Britain's own policy, the infamous Corn Laws, had artificially raised food prices between 1765 and 1793, presumably in order to raise the value of land. Food scarcity and rioting became increasingly frequent. Britain's upper classes could also (figuratively) hear the sound of the guillotine from across the channel during France's Terror of 1793–1794.

Hastily, Britain's Corn Laws were suspended in 1793, and remained suspended until 1815. Then, after the poor harvest of 1795–1796, many parishes in southern England quickly set up "Speenhamland" relief scales, fixing poor relief to the price of bread. At the same time, the accelerating rise of London and the new industrial centers was siphoning off agricultural laborers, causing rural landed interests to raise the generosity of poor relief. In response, the labor-hiring farmers and landlords of the declining rural south and east used wintertime poor relief in such a way as to keep the labor force within their own parishes. By supporting living standards across the agricultural passive winter months, they could inhibit migration to the cities and industrial centers, thereby keeping a labor force available across spring and summer and at harvest time. They succeeded in getting those who did not hire farm laborers to share in the local tax burdens of keeping the laborers nearby (Boyer 1990).

Did those at the top of English society succeed in quieting down violent rebellion with the extra poor relief under the Old Poor Law? Apparently so, according to some suggestive econometric analysis of the experiences of thirty-nine English counties from 1650 to 1815 by Avner Greif and Murat Iyigun (2013). Greif and Iyigun were able to relate the county-level occurrence of food riots and similar disturbances to the preceding generosity of poor relief, using county-level Parliamentary returns on relief in the years 1685, 1750, 1776, 1784, 1803, and 1815. Their results suggest that counties where the parish-level authorities offered more generous relief payments had fewer and shorter outbreaks of rioting in the seventeenth and eighteenth centuries.

By the early nineteenth century, however, opposition to generous poor relief grew among those in power, especially after the defeat of Napoleon had reduced the perceived threat of rebellion. Fanned by the writings of Malthus and Ricardo, leading politicians increasingly asserted that generous poor relief caused extra babies, who would further burden the taxpayers. Their premise that generous poor relief bred babies has received support from two statistical studies: George Boyer (1989) and Greif and Iyigun (2013) found that more generous poor relief raised fertility and accelerated population growth. All these factors set the stage for a monumental crackdown on poor relief, especially but not solely in England.

England's Poor Law Reform of 1834 slashed poor relief, and the older generosity was not regained for half a century.[20] The cuts and stagnation over that half century, and the modesty of the rise after the 1880s, are evident for Britain and also for several countries in Table 3.3 and Figure 3.1. Why? What kept poor relief in check from the end of the French Wars until the 1880s? Were similar forces at work in all these countries?

Any reading of the debates from that long era show a return of the tense struggle over the issue of getting the work incentives right for the "underserving poor" and the "deserving poor" – the same issue that dominated those church debates in the twelfth century, and dominates "welfare" debates today. In the nineteenth century, when incomes, voting rights, and social respect were all more unequally distributed than in the twentieth, those in power saw most of the poor as able-bodied and undeserving. The insistence on workfare was even stronger in the nineteenth century than it is today. The deserving poor, those widows and orphans and cripples who obviously could not work their way out of poverty, were given a minimum of aid, but these were a relatively small share of the poor population.

Why this shift toward toughness? Did the long-established elites change their minds, or were new voices heard? While one might credit the new intellectual wave led by Malthus, Ricardo, and Bentham, with its

TABLE 3.3. *The growth of government social spending, other than for education, 1820–1910 (percentage shares of GDP)*

Panel (A) Poor relief spending

	1820	1830	1840	1850	1860	1870	1880	1890	1900	1910
Argentina	0	0	0	0	0	0	0	0	0	0
Australia	0	0	0	0	0	0	0	0	0	0.14
Belgium	1.03	0.34	0.28				0.11	0.11	0.09	0.16
Denmark					0.66	0.80	0.85	0.81	0.57	0.67
Eng-Wales/UK	2.66	2.00	1.12	1.07	0.86	0.85	0.73	0.67	0.71	0.68
Finland						0.43	0.42	0.43	0.52	0.43
France	0.63	0.63	0.46	0.47	0.49	0.50	0.21	0.25	0.30	0.29
Germany							0.50	0.50	0.50	0.50
Ireland, UK						0.91				
Japan	0	0	0	0	0	0	0.02	0.04	0.07	0.08
Netherlands	1.36			1.38	1.24	1.18	0.29	0.30	0.39	0.39
New Zealand							0	0	0	0
Norway						0.97	0.81	0.79	0.91	0.86
Russia						0.59	0.59	0.59	0.58	
Scotland						1.11				
Spain				0.84	0.98	1.17	0.87	1.02	1.06	1.00
Sweden		0.02			0.60		0.60	0.69	0.66	0.72
USA	0.10	0.12	0.12	0.13	0.20	0.31	0.38	0.30		

Panel (B) All social spending other than public education spending

	1820	1830	1840	1850	1860	1870	1880	1890	1900	1910
Argentina	0	0	0	0	0	0.05	0.08	0.02	0.05	0.04
Australia	0	0	0	0	0	0	0	0	0	1.12
Belgium	1.03	0.34	0.28				0.17	0.22	0.26	0.43
Denmark					0.66	0.80	0.96	1.11	1.41	1.75
Eng-Wales/UK	2.66	2.00	1.12	1.07	0.86	0.85	0.86	0.83	1.00	1.39
Finland						0.66	0.76	0.78	0.90	0.66
France	0.63	0.63	0.46	0.47	0.49	0.50	0.46	0.54	0.57	0.81
Germany							0.50	0.53	0.59	0.60
Ireland, UK						0.91				
Japan	0	0	0	0	0	0	0.05	0.11	0.17	0.18
Netherlands	1.36			1.38	1.24	1.18	0.29	0.30	0.39	0.39
New Zealand							0.17	0.39	1.09	1.35
Norway						0.97	1.07	0.95	1.24	1.18
Russia						0.59	0.59	0.59	0.58	0.59
Scotland						1.11				
Spain				0.84	0.98	1.17	0.87	1.02	1.06	1.00
Sweden		0.02			0.60		0.72	0.85	0.85	1.03
USA			0.10	0.12	0.12	0.13	0.29	0.45	0.55	0.56

Sources and notes: See Appendix A, www.cambridge.org/Lindert.

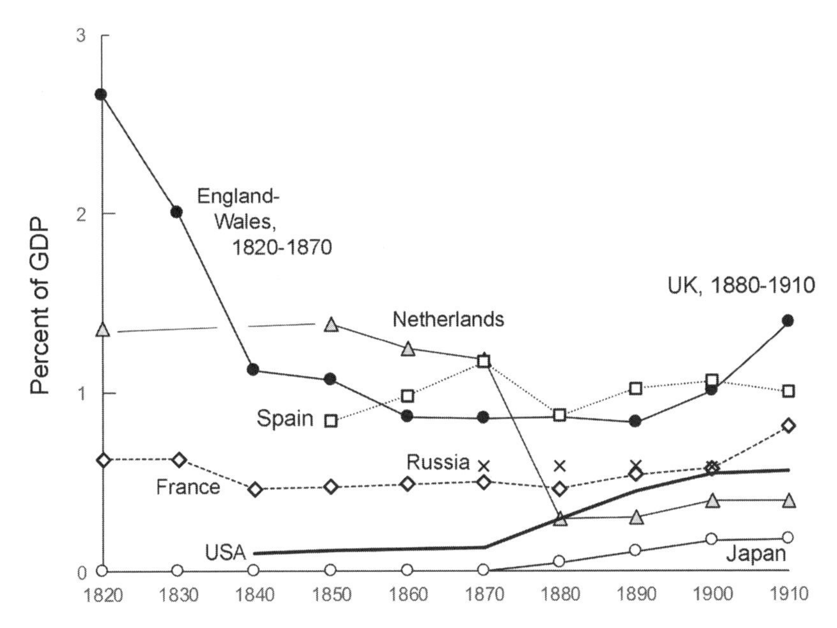

Figure 3.1. The growth of government social spending, other than for education, 1820–1910
Sources and notes: See Appendix A, www.cambridge.org/Lindert.

emphasis on individualism and self-help, these thoughts were not new. As already noted, medieval scholars wrestled with the same issues, yet the eighteenth-century Dutch and English shifted toward more generous relief even in the face of centuries-old fears that more relief would make the poor work less and have more babies. What we need to explain is why the balance of power shifted toward groups whose self-interests would have made them take a tougher stance in England in 1834, and why the toughness lasted for decades thereafter, both in England and on the continent.

When exploring possible explanations, it helps to begin with the obvious. The absence of any strong moves toward assistance to the poor or social insurance between 1820 and 1910 must have been due in large part to the absence of major wars, major revolutions, or any Great Depression. Inertia often prevails in political history, and it was not overturned by any huge shocks in this era.

THE SPREAD OF POLITICAL VOICE

Beyond the absence of shocks, was the nineteenth-century inertia made more stable by other causal forces? Without attempting any mono-causal explanation, or a complete explanation, I shall emphasize one of the potentially many forces that had different effects in the nineteenth century, versus either the late eighteenth or the twentieth. The stagnation in Table 3.3 and Figure 3.1 prevailed in part because political voice was shifting toward upper-middle-income groups whose interests were better served by forcing the poor to seek employment in rising cities and rising sectors of the economy. While there are hints of this shift in several countries, let us focus here on Britain's nineteenth-century shift in the electoral franchise, and in political voice.[21]

From the eighteenth century to the early twentieth, the share of households headed by someone with voting rights marched from a small elite share to universality of voting rights for adult males. The early twentieth century also recognized women's voting rights. This march toward democracy is illustrated for males in the United Kingdom in the left-hand column of Table 3.4. The new voting rights were not distributed at random. In fact, the progression of voting rights to more and more men took the form of a march down the property scales, and thus down the income scales. Before the First Reform Act of 1832, a principal condition entitling a man to vote was the "forty-shilling freehold," i.e. he had to be the owner of real estate assessed as generating at least forty shillings (£2) of annual rental value, a tight restriction in a country where only one household in seven owned any real estate. Each reform bill further relaxed the insistence on property ownership or taxpayer status.

The empowerment of the lower orders was reinforced by the arrival of the secret ballot in 1872, which made it harder for powerful landlords and employers to know which tenants and employees were voting against their preferred candidates, thus reducing intimidation. As the franchise extending down the income ranks, the median voter became less rich relative to the median household head, as shown for several years in the right-hand column of Table 3.4. Voting power thus spread downward,

TABLE 3.4. *The exclusiveness of the British franchise, 1688–1918*

	Estimated percentage of household heads (HHs), or of men, having the right to vote	Franchised voters' relative income (median household income of the franchised / median income of all households)
1688, England-Wales HHs	15.3	2.75
1759, England-Wales HHs	20.0	2.40
1803, England-Wales HHs	13.5	2.73
1831, United Kingdom men	8.6	
First Reform Act, 1832		
1835, United Kingdom men	13.4	
1866, United Kingdom men	18.0	
1867, United Kingdom HHs	17.8	1.46
1867, England-Wales HHs	19.0	1.37
Second Reform Act, 1867–1868		
1868, United Kingdom men	31.4	
1883, United Kingdom men	36.0	
Third Reform Act, 1883–1884		
1886, United Kingdom men	63.0	
1910, United Kingdom men	62.4	
1911, United Kingdom HHs	74.2	1.13
1918, United Kingdom men	88.6	

Sources and notes: See Appendix A, www.cambridge.org/Lindert.

from just the substantial and landed before 1832 to a large share of even manual laborers by the eve of World War I.[22]

The franchise marched down the income ranks in other democracies as well. Voting rights did not reach "the other half" of adult males until after 1880 in the majority of countries covered in Table 3.5. Given that the growing franchise share generally took the form of lowering wealth and income requirements in all these countries, the evidence sketched in Tables 3.4 and 3.5 implies that until the eve of World War I democracy had empowered the middle classes, but not yet the lower-income groups, especially not in the UK and the Netherlands.

A working hypothesis is therefore that the effect of fuller democracy on social assistance to the poor and needy was non-linear: Extending votes down through the middle classes did not raise tax efforts on behalf of the unfortunate, and these efforts were only forthcoming when lower-income groups themselves were given

TABLE 3.5. *Adult male suffrage in twelve countries before 1914*

	Voting rights first exceed 50% for men in this election year	Last pre-1914 share of men enfranchised to vote	
Australia	1857	100.0	(100% already in 1857)
Belgium	1894	91.6	in 1912
Denmark	1849	87.8	in 1913
Finland	1907	88.5	in 1913
France	1848	91.5	in 1910
Italy	1913	89.3	in 1913
Netherlands	1897	67.0	in 1913
New Zealand	1871	100.0	(100% already in 1871)
Norway	1900	70.3	in 1912
Sweden	1911	77.9	in 1914
UK	1885	62.1	in 1910
USA	before 1850	88.2	in 1912

Sources and notes: See Appendix A, www.cambridge.org/Lindert.

a voice, in the twentieth century. Would middle-class unwillingness to pay for the poor help to explain the post-1820 stagnation of poor relief and social spending that we saw in Table 3.3 and Figure 3.1?

Nineteenth-century British experience led off with what might appear to have been a smoking gun in the hands of the newly enfranchised urban middle classes when the Old Poor Law was effectively killed in the Poor Law Reform of 1834. Just two years earlier Parliament had enfranchised the urban middle classes in many boroughs, in the Reform Act of 1832, and simultaneously launched the Poor Law enquiry, which was written largely by Nassau Senior and Edwin Chadwick and released in less than a year. There may indeed be a smoking gun here, it was not the only one. As several scholars have emphasized, the newly enfranchised urban interests still lacked sufficient voting power in 1834 to have been decisive. Rather, they were joined by already powerful landed interests who had also given up on the relatively generous paternalism of the Old Poor Law. Their abandonment of paternalism was in part a reaction to the Captain Swing riots against farmers and landlords in 1830–1831. These outbreaks undermined the paternalistic belief that the relief offered under the Old Poor Law would continue to purchase gratitude and social peace.[23]

Upper-class disenchantment with paternalism, plus ascendant toughness of the newly franchised, also shaped a harsh and controversial design feature built into the 1834 Poor Law Reform. Just as representatives of all the ruling groups wanted to force the work ethic onto able-bodied males by forcing them to choose between the workhouse and supporting themselves, so too the same groups decided that the only solution to the problem of illegitimate births was to force unmarried women, a particularly low-income group, to choose between the workhouse and chastity. Those with voting power who renounced the old paternalism and believed in self-help were not only affluent but also male.

Under the Old Poor Law, local administrators had struggled to allocate the financial burden of "bastardy" fairly among six potentially responsible parties: the unwed mother, her parents, the ratepayers of her parish, the actual father of the baby, the accused father, and the ratepayers of the accused father's parish. They settled on a variety of compromises, none of which succeeded in checking the visible rise in the share of children born out of wedlock. The 1834 Poor Law's infamous Bastardy Clauses tried to check the rise of illegitimacy by heaping all the responsibility on the first party of the six, the young woman. The reformers had convinced themselves and many others that bastardy could be checked only if she faced a severe disincentive to risk pregnancy, knowing that naming a father would not save her from the workhouse. In the Report's words, bastardy would never decline until a bastard was "what Providence appears to have ordained that it should be, a burthen on its mother, and, where she cannot maintain it, on her parents."[24] The Bastardy Clauses drew immediate criticism. As many pointed out, the woman's disincentive for consent was offset by the new positive seduction incentive given to men, now freed from financial risk by the same Bastardy Clauses, which some dubbed "the philanderer's charter." The criticism never let up, and was eventually supported by aggregate evidence that the rate of illegitimate births continued to rise. Finally, in 1872, the clauses were effectively revised out of existence.[25]

The 1872 retreat from the Bastardy Clauses was not matched by any simultaneous retreat from the tough "Principles of 1834." On the contrary, the 1860s and 1870s saw a resurgent faith in using the workhouse as a stick to force self-reliance. Ever since 1834, the toughness of the national reform faced local resistance, from local authorities who preferred to continue giving outdoor relief, especially in the north and in working-class districts of London.[26] To clamp down on such insubordination, Parliament tried to centralize control further with the (Poor Law) Union Chargeability Act of 1865 and the Metropolitan (London) Poor Act of 1867. These brought little change by themselves, and were followed in the 1870s by the "crusade against outdoor relief" led by the Local Government Board and the Charity Organisation Society. Once again, the rhetoric found most of the poor unworthy, and sought to push a greater share of them into the workhouse.

And yet, the 1870s crusade against outdoor relief, with its reliance on the workhouse test, had self-checking effects. The crackdown did succeed in forcing the low-skilled and the poor to choose between incarceration in the workhouse or no relief at all. From 1871 to 1881, the share of the population getting any relief at all dropped by 27 percent. However, the harsher indoor relief was more expensive per relieved person, because indoor relief required expenditures on the workhouse itself and on employing supervisors and caregivers. In 1872, according to a Parliamentary Report by the Local Government Board, a family on indoor relief cost the taxpayers 10 shillings a week, whereas a family allowed to receive outdoor relief cost them only 4 shillings a week.[27] Not surprisingly, when one totes up the change in aggregate poor relief expenditures from 1871 to 1881, they declined by only 1 percent in nominal terms. The aggregate amount spent actually rose by 7.3 percent in real terms over those years, though slightly slower than total population. The result: a decade of throwing poor people out of relief without saving the taxpayers money.[28]

Thus in the English experience, the extension of the franchise down the income ranks may have contributed first to the passage of the 1834 Poor Law Reform, and then to stagnation in the generosity of relief until the 1880s. However, as already emphasized, the newly franchised would not have produced the 1834 Reform itself without the support of many who were landed, long-franchised, and disenchanted with the workings of the Old Poor Law. Still, the continuation of the tough emphasis on the workhouse until the 1880s probably owed something to the fact that the lower half of the income ranks was still denied the vote, while middle- and upper-income men had it.

The suspicion that vote shares influenced poor relief does not rest simply on the fact that poor relief remained stingy while voting rights trickled downward across the upper middle classes between 1820 and the 1880s. When voting rights began to reach further down across the lower half of the income ranks after 1890, poor relief and other social spending began to respond, breaking through the formidable barriers of political inertia. One way to see this is to compare the experiences of twenty-one countries over the six decadal years 1880, 1890, . . . , 1930. This fifty-year span includes a great deal of variation, both in democratic countries' documented right-to-vote shares and in their generally rising shares of social spending in national income. That comparative experience seems to confirm that the extension of the right to vote down the income ranks had a non-linear effect. As long as the franchised share was low, poor relief and social budgets were meager, as Table 3.3 and Figure 3.1 have shown. Yet once the voting share rose had passed 50 percent, social spending began to respond. Raising the voting shares still had little effect on poor relief itself, but it was increasingly supplemented by the sum of public health expenditures, public pensions, and public housing. Indeed, the progress "predicted" by the voting share variable happens to resemble Figure 3.1's upward turn of the spending curves between 1890 and 1910.[29]

Fresh international evidence now underlines the non-linear effect of voting rights on social spending within democracies, with little positive stimulus coming from extending the vote until the voting rights have become more equal, more universal. Ben Ansell and David Samuels (2014, pp. 141–170) have expanded the number of countries covered for 1880–1930, with additional measures and additional statistical tests, showing strong patterns in the relationship of social spending to the interaction of "democracy" and "inequality." In their baseline tests, democracy is proxied by the degree of inter-party competition and the constraints on the head of state (Polity index). They use two crude measures of economic inequality for the 1880–1930 era, namely inequality of agricultural land holdings and inequality of income, the latter having been guesstimated by François Bourguignon and Christian Morrisson (2002). They use these economic inequality measures to represent the inequality of political strength.

Armed with larger numbers of countries, Ansell and Samuels are able to compare the share of social spending in GDP not only between autocracies and democracies, but between more elitist democracies and fuller democracies. All of their tests yield the same result: elite democracies, with power concentrated among the wealthiest, spend less on social programs than even the average autocracy, whereas fuller democracies spend more, relative either to the elite democracies or to the average autocracy. Furthermore, the effect of greater equality of political voice shows up clearly *at the margin*: i.e. the slope of extra democracy keeps rising, as in the switch from Figure 3.1's stagnation 1820–1880 to a positive upslope correlated with the spread of democracy. So say the numbers from the 1880–1930 era, whether democracy is measured by the Polity index, or by the voting share of the adult population, or by the share of votes captured by left-wing parties. All of their tests imply that the spread of political voice to lower and lower-income groups raised the transfers of taxpayers' money to the poor, the sick, and the elderly.

It would help if one could confirm the non-linear influence of increasing enfranchisement of lower and lower-income ranks not just in a statistical panel but also in the deeper narrative histories covering the same era. Such histories have been written. Some boldly compare the social-spending and political behaviors of many countries.[30] A particularly clear picture of a political turning point on the issue of social spending is George Boyer's recent summary of how the spread of the franchise contributed to the arrival of Britain's shift toward more generous social insurance and social assistance in the early twentieth century.[31] Once the Third Reform Act in 1884 had extended the franchise to 63 percent of adult males, now including even farm workers and coal miners, one would have expected new agenda favorable at least to organized labor, if not to the truly destitute. Momentum began to build: Booth and Rowntree caught considerable attention with their disturbing studies of the poor, and Parliamentary commissions began reporting on proposals for public pensions, improved unemployment compensation, and children's health. The Conservatives were under threat, and the Liberal Party won by a landslide in 1906. As Boyer notes, there was a momentary disconnect between the Liberal Party's program and the agenda that would appeal to the newly franchised classes. The Liberals had not campaigned for social-welfare policies, yet the newly formed Labour Party had done so.

Even before the election itself, new "social Liberals" like Lloyd George and the young Winston Churchill saw the handwriting on the wall, and proposed a broad set of programs that same year (1906). Particularly popular was their Old Age Pension Act, passed in 1908. It was non-contributory, to be financed by the taxpayers rather than the workers' earlier contributions from their earnings. Compulsory health insurance followed in 1911. It was less popular with workers because it passed only 22 percent of the cost of health benefits on to the taxpayers, making the workers and their employers pay for the other 78 percent, yet it too bore political fruit. The whole package left Conservative leader Austen Chamberlain to fume: "Confound Ll. George. He has strengthened the government again. His sickness scheme *is* a good one and he is on the right lines this time."[32] Nonetheless, the strategy could not stop the continued rise of the Labour Party, the one most clearly based in the newly franchised classes.

Thus did public social assistance to the poor, the sick, and the elderly finally emerge in Northwest Europe on the eve of World War I, once the early modern rise of government revenue capacity was finally re-directed toward serving the needs and interests of the newly empowered lower half of the income ranks.

CHAPTER 4

The Dawn of Mass Schooling before 1914

WHY DID TAX-BASED PUBLIC ELEMENTARY SCHOOLING EMERGE SO LATE IN NORTHWEST EUROPE?

THE FOLLOWING HISTORICAL CHANGES DOMINATED both the timing, and the Northwest European location, of the emergence of tax-based schooling for the masses:

- As with poor relief, the rise of government revenue-raising capacity had to precede the emergence of social spending, starting in Northwest Europe.
- The sectoral shift from agriculture toward literate occupations raised parents' private demand for education. If those in power had had the political will to fund public schools and allow open access to literate occupations, mass public education could have reaped high returns as early as the onset of the commercial revolution in the sixteenth century.
- Yet the extra revenue was only converted into public education when political voice began to diffuse down the socio-economic ranks. Northwest Europe's overseas offshoots led this development, though not until after the middle of the nineteenth century.

THE INITIAL RISE OF PUBLIC SCHOOLING

WHY DID IT COME SO LATE?. The other main kind of government social spending before 1914 developed only later than poor relief – and curiously so. Spending on public schools especially lagged behind poor relief in the Netherlands and England, the two richest countries in

TABLE 4.1. *Public education expenditures, for all levels of education, 1820–1910 (percentages of GDP in current prices)*

	1820	1830	1840	1850	1860	1870	1880	1890	1900	1910
Australia									1.09	0.95
Belgium				0.38		0.62	1.10			
France	0.08	0.12	0.28	0.35	0.33	0.40	0.79	1.02	0.92	1.01
Germany					0.82	0.96	1.47	1.42	1.80	2.27
Italy					0.17	0.15	0.26	0.37	0.36	0.52
Japan							0.22	0.69		
Netherlands				0.29	0.41	0.69	1.14	1.30	1.64	2.13
New Zealand									1.42	1.77
Norway							0.56	0.58	0.77	0.79
United Kingdom				0.07	0.18	0.17	0.29	0.37	0.59	0.74
England-Wales						0.23	0.28	0.37	0.61	1.45
United States				0.33	0.48	0.73	0.74	1.10	1.24	1.42

Sources and notes: See Appendix A, www.cambridge.org/Lindert.

Northwest Europe. The delay can be seen by comparing the expenditures on public education in Table 4.1 with the corresponding expenditures on poor relief that we examined in Table 3.3. As of 1850, for example, local governments in the Netherlands were spending 1.38 percent of GDP on poor relief, even after the retreat from the higher share a century earlier, yet spent only 0.29 percent on public education. In England and Wales that year, local governments spent 1.07 percent on poor relief, yet less than 0.10 percent on public education.[1] That poor relief exceeded education in government budgets might have been partly due to the holdover from the late eighteenth-century attempt at using poor relief to prevent insurrection. Educating the poor was not then viewed as a way to prevent insurrections – often quite the contrary, as we shall soon note. A further curiosity about the Dutch and English tax-based education around 1850 or 1860 is that these two countries lagged behind not only the clear leader, Prussia (Germany), but also France, North America, and possibly even Belgium. Why?

HISTORIC BARRIERS TO PUBLIC EDUCATION. Three main forces held back the rise of public education through most of history:

(1) Insufficient government revenue devoted to the sum of non-military uses.
(2) Low economic payoff from the education of children, and thus low demand for it.
(3) Resistance of the politically powerful to paying taxes for educating the children of others, and to removing barriers to their entry into skilled occupations.

I shall argue here that for the Netherlands and Britain, the first two barriers had been removed by the end of the seventeenth century, if not earlier. With public education, as with assistance to the poor, it was the third constraint that continued to hold back progress until the mid-nineteenth century, even in countries that led the world in most other respects.

The first barrier had been removed by 1688 or 1700 for the Netherlands and England – and for that matter, for Spain, France, and the part of Japan ruled directly by the shogun. These countries could have afforded to spend a sizeable share of the national income on public education in peacetime, as was suggested by the numbers in Chapter 3.

PRIMARY EDUCATION WOULD HAVE PAID, BOTH PRIVATELY AND PUBLICLY. The second barrier was also removed, for Northwest Europe, by the late seventeenth century. By, say, 1688 or 1700 there was already a strong private demand for literacy in the Netherlands and in Britain, even in that poorer era, when most parents and students could not afford to borrow and got no help at all from the taxpayers. Literacy rates were highest in Northwest Europe, especially in the Netherlands. Measuring literacy by the share able to sign their marriage registers, Dutch literacy among grooms rose from 57 percent back in 1630 to 85 percent in 1780, and the number of book publishers and sellers was above 500 from the year 1600 on.[2] The Dutch lead in literacy began early, helped by the pre-Reformation foundation of the Brethren of Common Life (BCL) by Geert Groote in 1374. The BCL emphasized the understanding, writing, and preaching of the written word in the vernacular. It diffused to many cities throughout the Netherlands, with private backing. İ. Semih Akçomak, Dinand Webbink, and Bas ter Weel (2016) have recently exploited the historical geography of where the BCL was or was not established to show that it made a sizeable contribution to literacy, the production and distribution of books, and local city growth. This put the Netherlands a step ahead of the populations of Protestant Europe where the emphasis on reading the written word in the vernacular waited until after the Reformation. The literacy of the Dutch was noticed by cosmopolitan observers in the early sixteenth century. Erasmus concluded that "[n]owhere else does one find a greater number of people of average education," and Spanish visitors "noted that 'almost everyone' knew how to read and write, even women."[3]

Britain was not far behind the Netherlands in developing literacy in the absence of a public-school system, being another country with Protestant emphasis on the written word and a relatively early shift from agriculture toward commerce and other literacy-using service sectors. For Great Britain before 1850, the main occupational shift out of agriculture and into both industry and services came sometime between 1522 and 1700, a bit later than in the Netherlands. In that interval, the share of the labor force employed in agriculture dropped from 56 percent to 39 percent, while industry's share rose from 24 percent to 34 percent, and that in services rose from 21 percent to 27 percent. Of course, each sector's employment was a mixture of skilled and unskilled occupations. Nonetheless, the skilled pursuits, the kinds of work requiring literacy and numeracy, were a larger share of the total in the service sectors. And within the growing service sector, the share of England's household heads that were employed in literacy-intensive commerce and the professions was already as high as 12 percent by 1688.[4]

What would a strong private attainment of literacy imply about a region's likelihood of raising taxes to fund primary education for a large share of the population? On the negative side, one might conjecture that the literate and their parents would oppose tax-based schools as unnecessary, except perhaps for the very poorest. That view was indeed present in the early debates. On the positive side, however, there was a strong demand, already expressed by those who could pay for it. Also on the positive side, high literacy meant an abundant supply of teachers, a potential supplier lobby seeking tax support for themselves. A final positive implication is that a more literate society would be more persuaded that there were external benefits to be gained from paying for schooling the children of others. Such externalities have become "well known," both as a shared theory and as something now documented statistically.[5]

Indeed, leading thinkers at the time had already come down on the side of tax-based schools on the grounds of externalities. Consider what Adam Smith, Robert Malthus, and Thomas Jefferson wrote about tax-based mass public schooling even before it happened. Smith felt that a society at large should be ready to pay taxes for education's externalities, the part of its societal benefits that were not captured by the private providers or the students: "The expence of the institutions for education and religious instruction is [like the expense of maintaining good roads and communications] beneficial to the whole society, and may, therefore, without injustice, be defrayed by the general contribution of the whole society."[6] His recommendation might have been applied either to targeted tax-based education for those families that could not pay for it themselves, or to universal public education, which every leading country has since embraced.

Robert Malthus, for all his harshness toward poor relief, also favored tax-based education, at least for poor children. In 1807, when Samuel Whitbread, MP for Bedford, had introduced a bill in Parliament calling for free education for the poor funded by local taxation, Malthus backed him in an open letter:

> I wish you success in your plan of extending the benefits of education to the poor. There are at this time, I believe, few countries in Europe in which the peasantry are so ignorant as in England and Ireland; and if you are instrumental in removing this reproach, you will have just reason to be proud of your exertions. Our formidable neighbor [Napoleon] certainly does not think that education is likely to impede his subjects either in fighting or working; and the conduct of the conscripts, a large portion of whom is taken from a superior class of society to that which forms the mass of modern armies, clearly justifies his opinion. The principal objections which I have ever heard advanced against the education of the poor would be removed if it became general.[7]

Thomas Jefferson held a similar view of tax-based schooling. In 1779, Jefferson introduced his *Bill for the More General Diffusion of Knowledge* in the Virginia assembly, calling for a statewide system of free public elementary schools to be paid for by local taxpayers. Like Smith, the main author of the Declaration of Independence felt that everybody, and not just the parents of school-age children, was better off if all (white) persons had an equal maximum chance to achieve a liberal education at public expense. At the secondary level, he proposed, the burden should be shifted more to parents and away from taxpayers, though he called for full tax-based aid to the top-scoring students from elementary school. At the university level, Jefferson again saw a case for tax-based education. Unhappy with the performance of the private College of William and Mary, he called for state administration, state taxpayer funding, and secularization. Yet each time he introduced a taxes-for-education bill in Virginia – in 1779, in the 1790s, and again in 1817 – it was defeated by those whose self-interest would be compromised by property taxes that would pay for common schools.[8]

The returns from tax-based basic schooling would have been high in the eighteenth and nineteenth centuries, not only for the educated individual, but for society as a whole – and, in some cases, even for the government's own budget.

Confirming evidence comes through the availability of micro-studies of education in Victorian England, studies that now make it possible to quantify the returns on primary-school investments in England. David Mitch's work allows us to convert his extensive data on occupational rewards and school costs into rates of return on three years' schooling in the 1820s leading to literacy in adulthood, and Jason Long's matching of children in the 1851 census with adults in 1881 provides a similar view of the returns to completing primary school around mid-century. Table 4.2 presents my estimates of the returns, estimates that are conservative in that they are likely to understate some of the gains or overestimate some of the costs.[9] The estimates do not even take account of externalities, for example. Even with this tilt toward underestimation, the returns are high enough to make some suggestions. The direct costs and opportunity costs of schooling did not loom large enough to choke off the case for investing in formal primary education. Yes, there was sufficient demand for literacy, despite the likelihood that the demand for child labor held back the progress of schooling in the industrial North for a few decades.

TABLE 4.2. *Internal rates of return on schooling sons of laborers, Victorian England (percentage per annum)*

Population group	Private family	Social (all parties)	Fiscal (gov't)	Public (gov't + donors)	Yield on British gov't consol securities at start of schooling	
(1) Three years' schooling, achieving signature literacy						
Grooms 1840	19.5	19.0	21.2	13.6	4.4	in 1821
Grooms 1868	11.0	9.9	6.5	6.3	3.4	in 1842
(2) Six years of elementary school						
Students of 1851	14.0	12.1	7.4	5.8	3.1	in 1851

Sources and notes: See Appendix A, www.cambridge.org/Lindert.

The main innovation in Table 4.2, however, is the fiscal rate of return. Even with estimates that are probably too pessimistic, it was well above the rate of interest at which Parliament could borrow. Why, then, did Parliament decline to subsidize mass schooling if it would have repaid Her Majesty's government itself? Indeed, the fiscal indictment stands even when we reintroduce the fact that a grown-up child's labor-force participation would have been only partial, especially for females.[10] The British government appears to have left money on the sidewalk by not investing more in primary education before the Elementary Education Act of 1870 and the more decisive Fees Act of 1891. Passing up something that would have paid for itself was not confined to Victorian Britain: as we shall see in later chapters, recent scholarship suggests that in the twenty-first century, the United States has lowered its net revenue by under-investing in children's education and health.

The British public education failure may have extended back to 1688–1700. The returns and costs of primary education in the eighteenth century should have yielded rates of return at least as high as those in Table 4.2, given what we know about tax rates, interest rates, and the wage structure. The tax rates paid by laborers were thought by Joseph Massie to be 8 percent, similar to the Victorian rates.[11] Government could also borrow cheaply: The consol rate was below 5 percent as early as 1717, the fourth Hanoverian year. So at least as early as 1717, the government could have reaped a significant fiscal return for itself just by investing in universal primary education. Finally, the wage structure did not reward education any less in the eighteenth century than later, given the indirect evidence on the skilled/unskilled wage ratio. Thus, given the history of tax rates, interest rates, and wage rates, the rates of return back to about 1688–1700 should have been as high as those Victorian rates shown in Table 4.2. The operative constraint that held up the advance of schooling must have been the collective unwillingness to supply taxes.[12]

If the returns were so high after 1688 or 1700, why would society leave such free money lying on the sidewalk? Why did society not heed the wisdom of Smith, Malthus, and Jefferson, and pay taxes to make citizens more civilized and productive?

ELITE RESISTANCE. The third barrier was the only formidable one for Northwest Europe between the late seventeenth century and the mid-nineteenth. Those with power did not find it in their self-interest to pay taxes to educate the children of others, nor would they have welcomed newly educated masses into the higher occupational circles. It is all too easy to quote the opposition of members of elites in Europe and America to tax-based mass education.[13]

Perhaps the most memorable listing of the specific arguments for blocking mass education was one given by Davies Giddy in Parliamentary debate on that same proposal by MP Samuel Whitbread for educating the poor, the bill backed by Malthus. On June 13, 1807 Giddy, later to become president of the Royal Society, made the reasoning quite clear:

> giving education to the labouring classes of the poor . . . would, in effect, be found to be prejudicial to their morals and happiness; it would teach them to despise their lot in life, instead of making them good servants in agriculture, and other laborious employments to which their rank in society had destined them; instead of teaching them subordination, it would render them factious and refractory, as was evident in the manufacturing counties; it would enable them to read seditious pamphlets, vicious books, and publications against Christianity; it would render them insolent to their superiors . . . Besides, if the bill were to pass into a law, it would go to burthen the country with a most enormous and

> incalculable expence, and to load the industrious orders of society with still heavier imposts.[14]

Three premises behind Giddy's classic statement were all correct. Yes, education would cause laborers to leave agriculture for better jobs. Yes, education was seditious, in the sense that it would raise public opposition to landed Tory supremacy. And yes, paying for mass education would have meant more taxes – even though the proposed tax rates that horrified Giddy would have looked negligible today. Speaking right after Giddy, a fellow opponent of the schooling bill claimed that it could add as much as 10 percent to the poor rates. The poor rates were in turn about 2 percent of national income, so the "most enormous and incalculable expence" of educating the poor could only have been as high as 0.2 percent of national income. The opponents carried the day, and Parliament voted down the bill to educate the poor.

WHO WERE THE EARLY LEADERS? It is not hard to show that the advance of mass schooling depended on the will of the politically powerful as well as on fiscal capacity and the demands of a modernizing economy. These political and economic forces stand out in any international comparison of schooling. Which countries led, which fell behind, and when?

To maximize the range of salient experiences being compared, we seek better coverage than was possible in Table 4.1's public-expenditure display. We seek abundant data on something close to the tax rate on behalf of primary schooling, the largest and most egalitarian part of the education budget. The desired share of public expenditures as a share of GDP can be proxied by the more abundant data on primary-school enrollment rates, thanks to this accounting identity for primary education:

(public expenditures / GDP) = (public expenditures as a share of total expenditures)
times (total expenditures per pupil)
times (the enrollment rate, pupils per school-age child)
times (school-age children as a share of total population
divided by (GDP per capita)

While the enrollment rate is not the only relevant component, its behavior drives much of any contrast between countries or between time periods. To see why, consider the lesser variation in the other terms on the right-hand side. The public sector dominates the total here, as it did in Table 4.1, so that the first term on the right-hand side hovers close to unity. The school-age population's share of the total population differed little, aside from its being lower in France. Finally, the ratio of (total expenditures per pupil) to (GDP per capita) also varied only moderately. That leaves the enrollment rate as a fair correlate of the fiscal commitment to primary schooling across historical contexts.[15]

Some leaders and followers in primary-school enrollments are revealed in Figures 4.1 through 4.3, where all countries are compared to data-abundant France.[16] Prussia had the lead in primary-school enrollments from 1830 or earlier until 1860, and continued to spend a greater share of GDP on public education until World War I. It was not a full democracy, even after manhood suffrage was supposedly legislated in 1848. Prussia's Imperial government continued to control the curriculum, and at times teachers' wage rates. Yet within these constraints from

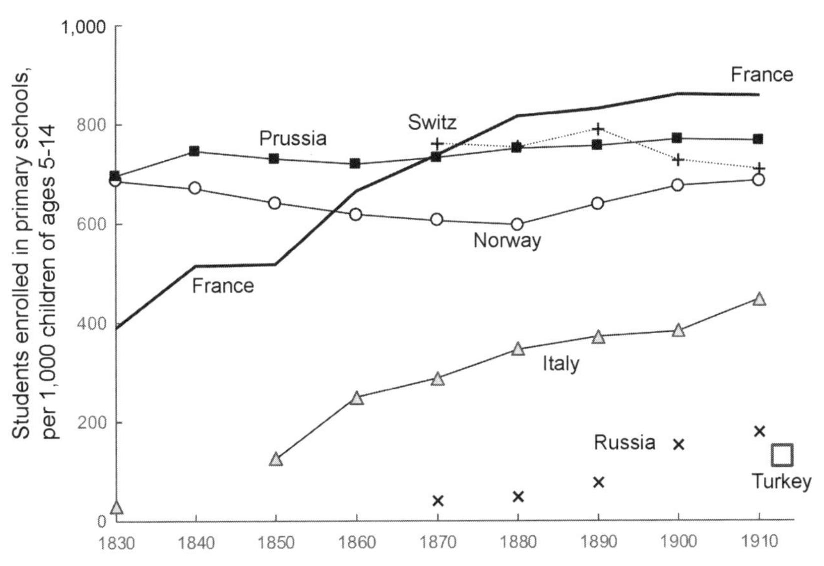

Figure 4.1. Primary-school enrollment rates, continental Europe, 1830–1913
Sources and notes: See Appendix A, www.cambridge.org/Lindert.

above, those localities that chose to raise more money for their public schools did so, hiring more teachers and raising enrollments for both genders and for all religious groups. The decentralized system facilitating such inclusive local schools was set in motion by the Stein–Hardenburg reforms, which immediately followed Prussia's humiliating defeat at the hands of Napoleon, whose troops were perceived to be better educated.[17]

By 1870, Prussia and the other German states had yielded primacy in primary-school enrollment rates. Within continental Europe, as Figure 4.1 suggests, France in particular had caught up, especially after a law of 1881 had abolished private tuition and fees for public schools, switching full funding to the taxpayers. The timing was governed by France's returning the Germans' historic compliment. Just as the defeated Prussians had learned a need for universal schooling from their reading of Napoleon's victory, so too France in the 1870s resolved to educate the masses more fully, as the victorious Germans had done:

> There was nearly universal belief among the French elite that Prussia had triumphed because of the superiority of its celebrated universities: a popular aphorism was that the University of Berlin was the revenge for the defeat at Jena. French praise for German education extended to all levels of the system. Journalists repeated the dicta that the Prussian elementary school teacher was the architect of [victory over the French at] Sedan and that the modern secondary education of the *Realschulen* had provided the scientific base for Prussian military efficiency.[18]

Although France had become a European leader in primary-school enrollments by the 1880s, as suggested by Figures 4.1 and 4.2, she was not a global leader. By 1860, that position was achieved by the four English-speaking offshoots in North America and Australasia, as shown in Figure 4.3. What advantages might these four emerging countries have shared? Three conspicuous possibilities are abundant resources, high incomes, and a high Protestant share. Each presumably played a part.

Another leading candidate would be egalitarian policy toward settlement, land ownership, and voting rights. Stanley Engerman, Elena Mariscal, and Kenneth Sokoloff have persuasively linked these factors in contrasting the development of the Americas. They show the likely

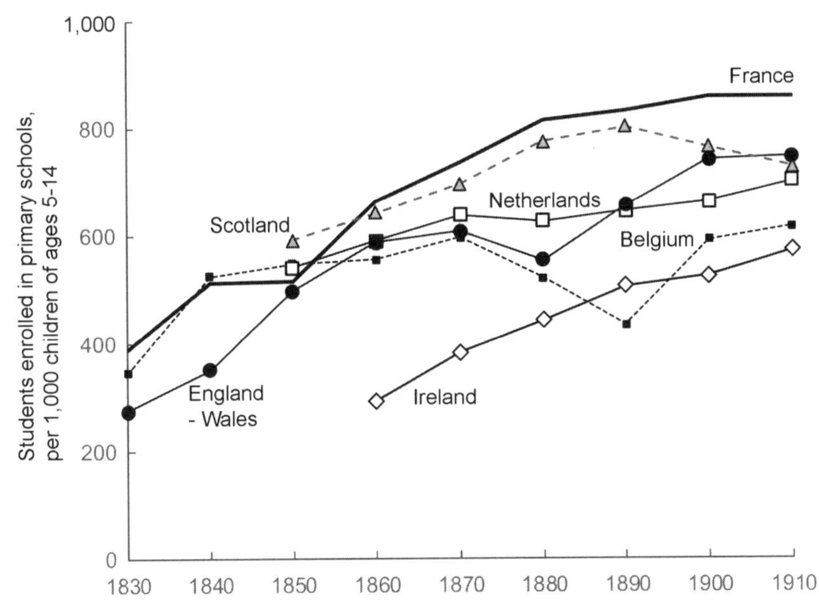

Figure 4.2. Primary-school enrollment rates, Northwest Europe, 1830–1910
Sources and notes: See Appendix A, www.cambridge.org/Lindert.

imprint of factor endowments and the inequality of political power on education, income inequality, and long-run growth. The endowments generated a more egalitarian result in upper Canada and the northern United States than in Latin America and the Caribbean. Those parts of Canada and the United States distributed settlement lands more equally, and political suffrage more equally, leading to more mass schooling as well as to income equalization and growth.[19]

What else might have promoted primary-school enrollments in parts of North America and in Australasia than in the rest of the Americas and in Europe, besides egalitarian land abundance, high incomes, and Protestantism? Some detailed research on American enrollments up to 1850 seems to underline three other forces.[20] One was greater affordability of the common schools. American teachers were supplied at wage rates that were lower in relation to non-teaching wages than they were in, say, the high-spending German states, partly because American society more readily welcomed females into the teaching profession, especially in the northern states.

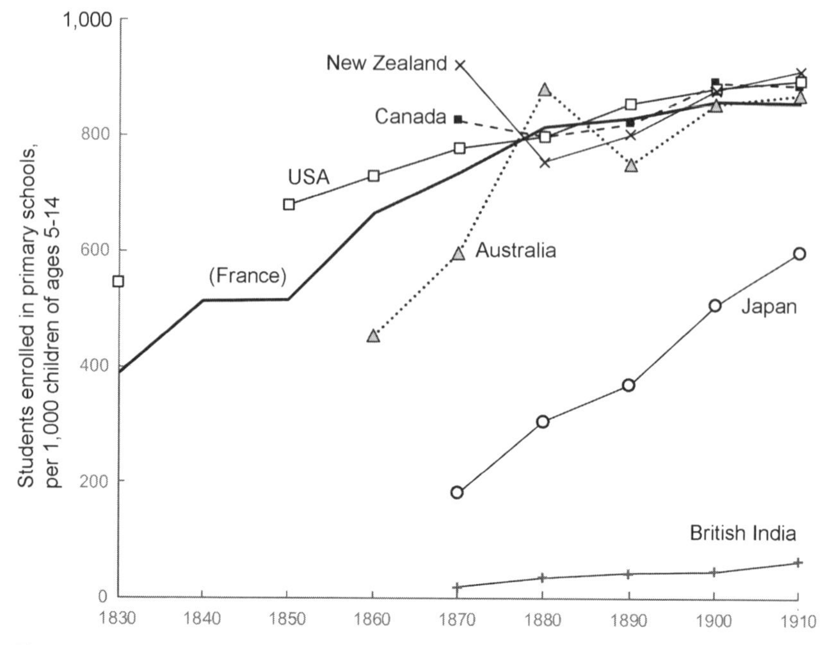

Figure 4.3. Primary-school enrollment rates, Pacific and Asia, 1830–1910
Sources and notes: See Appendix A, www.cambridge.org/Lindert.

A second force was the greater diffusion of voting power among the citizenry in much of the north, especially in rural communities. By contrast, in the southern United States, power was concentrated at the state level, where decisions about education were dominated by the top of society under unequal-representation rules. The distribution of local political voice appears to be a robust predictor of tax support and enrollments, both within and between regions. Extra local voice raised tax support without crowding out private support for education.

Finally, greater decentralization of government may have helped fund local mass education in the northern United States, in upper Canada, and in Australia. The link between decentralized government and better school funding will not seem obvious – and it should not, since the link is strong only in certain phases of development. The link can be strong and positive in some early stages of rising demand for education, while the link might be negative in some later stages.[21] Consider first an earlier stage in which most localities do not want tax funding for schools, and only a minority of localities want it. If the decision about school funding is to be made at the higher level, it will be voted down, meaning no school funding for anybody. Yet under decentralized institutions, with each locality making its own choices, localities in the progressive minority will go ahead with their schooling. Such a decentralized progressive outcome seems to have come about in the northern United States, upper Canada, and Australia.[22] There remains the unsolved task of weighing the roles played by these different factors – resources, average incomes, religion, egalitarian land policies, egalitarian voting rights, and decentralization in government – in the advance of mass education in the countries of recent settlement.

WHY DID VICTORIAN ENGLAND LAG BEHIND? School money and enrollments in the rest of the world lagged behind the leaders in varying degrees, as suggested by the other time-lines plotted in Figures 4.1–4.3. We return to most of their stories in the next three chapters.

The oddest of these lags are those displayed in Figure 4.2 by the countries in Northwest Europe that were world leaders in poor relief and in early modern literacy: England and Wales and the Low Countries. Narrative histories of these countries' debates over education policies reveal bitter disputes over the relationship of tax funding to the question of religion: Should taxpayers subsidize universal secular education, or should they pay for schooling run by religions? If religious schools deserved support, which religions? These countries were not unique in the heat generated over the issue of taxes, schools, and religion. Yet in France and the United States, at least, the disputes had been politically resolved by 1881, whereas the Dutch and Belgians did not resolve the issue until around World War I.[23]

The strange lag of England and Wales poses a worthy puzzle. The time span of the lag covered most of Victoria's reign, the very height of Britain's industrial primacy and Imperial globalization. If England was one of the leaders in world literacy before, say, 1830 and regained a superior ranking in the quantity and quality of public education later, after 1900, why the long lag in between?

The English lag and the subsequent catch-up seem to have been due in large part to two influences. First, the control over English schools remained centralized in the hands of Parliament. Municipalities and Poor Law Unions were not allowed to raise local taxes for primary education, and as long as a large share of those with political voice opposed tax funding, it did not happen. Thus, a progressive place with strong demand for a schooled labor force could not override Parliamentary opposition, like that voiced by Davies Giddy in the quotation above, as long as opponents prevailed in most other constituencies. As a result, tax funding was held back. Even such ostensibly progressive reforms as the Forster Act of 1870 did not unlock the cash box.

A second factor turned the tide in favor of tax-based universal schooling. The second force was that extension of suffrage, which finally enfranchised a clear majority of adult males in the Third Reform Act of 1883–1884, as we saw in the previous chapter.

By 1891, the expanded electorate seems to have secured passage of the Fees Act of 1891, after which England and Wales finally began catching up rapidly. As we are about to see when reviewing the more recent record of tax-funded education, both Britain and the Netherlands have returned to the upper ranks, having achieved high enrollment rates and relatively good scores on international tests of curriculum learning.

CHAPTER 5

Public Education since 1914

ONLY SINCE 1914 HAVE THE MORE DEVELOPED COUNTRIES pushed their governments to provide more than just basic primary schooling and minimal relief for paupers. At long last, the whole set of conditions needed for broad public spending of all sorts was finally achieved.

After 1914, the clearest social-spending success in promoting both economic growth and economic equality came on the educational front. This chapter maps and explains the achievements, and the limitations, of the spread of universal public education in the now-developed OECD countries. The rise of the other kinds of social spending in the same OECD countries, many of which developed true welfare states over the twentieth century, will be the focus of Chapter 6. Chapter 7 then explores how, when, and where the rest of the world followed suit.

Focusing on education alone, this chapter tests the strength of these historic links relating public education to human earning power:

Link (A)	fiscal capacity and political will	→	taxes spent on educating children
Link (B)	taxes spent on educating children	→	years of education per adult
Link (C)	taxes spent on educating children and years of education per adult	→	skills and knowledge
Link (D)	skills and knowledge	→	greater human earning power

For the now-developed OECD countries as a group, of course, the whole chain has proven to be a strong one. Yet which of these countries forged the strongest links, and when and how? This chapter probes the strengths and weaknesses of the individual links relating money to schooling to skills and earning power, Links (B) through (D). For the now-developed countries, the initial fiscal and political preconditions, and Link (A), were already tested in Chapter 3's coverage of their pre-1914 experience. Since 1914, prosperous nations have continued to gain the fiscal capacity for very large budgets, and the spread of voting rights, won in so few countries before 1914, finally enabled the masses to demand tax-based progressive social spending of all types.

The rest of the history of the preconditions for developing world-class education and human earning power, that Link (A) again, will return to center stage in Chapter 7, in a negative form. There, we will diagnose the failure to deliver that education and earning power in the countries still struggling with inferior education in the twenty-first century.

For the developed OECD countries, the rest of this chapter sketches why the gains have been widespread but not universal. In terms of the *quantities* of education delivered, I will argue that:

- Tax-based education expenditures rose massively in the OECD countries. Since 1910, their share of GDP has more than tripled in all cases except in Germany, and even for Germany that tax effort has more than doubled.
- Public education continues to overshadow private efforts in primary and secondary education, as it already did in the late nineteenth century. The growth in adults' years of educational attainment, private plus public, has been driven by government budgets.[1]
- In their average years of education attained by adults, the United States and other leaders pulled ahead of the rest of the world until roughly the 1970s. Since then, these average quantities have been converging internationally, both within the OECD and worldwide.
- Adults' years of schooling have also converged *within every country* since 1914, and even since 1870. Thus, with the years of adults' education converging both internationally and intra-nationally, the whole world is becoming more equal in adults' years of schooling.

- There has also been an impressive gender convergence in education in all regions of the world except the Middle East and South Asia. Among the most advanced countries, females were already matching males in the completion of basic education in the later nineteenth century, and since the 1970s females have also been receiving a slight majority of university degrees.

In terms of the *quality* of schooling, i.e. the delivery of learning per year, the progress has been less certain, and probably more uneven across countries. The paucity of pre-1960 data on children's achievements of learning still clouds our view of any country's progress, or lack of progress, over the long run. Nonetheless, a tentative world history of educational quality achievements is emerging, mainly for the OECD countries. We shall find that:

- Advances in human earning power are clearly linked to the accumulation of learning of new skills, which in turn is clearly dependent in part on the resources invested in education.
- The good or harm done by school-choice systems depends critically on their design. Regulating private-school pricing and admissions criteria seems necessary to limit the social inequities associated with school-choice schemes such as vouchers. Pressuring school systems, and students, with centralized graduation exams has promoted learning, contrary to the frequent attempts to denounce "merely teaching to the test." While the United States and many other countries continue to resist centralized exams, such exams appear to be Darwinian survivors in the global competition among institutions. In addition, imposing secularization from above has helped to resolve the social wars over schools and religion, with mutual disarmament.
- Among nations today, achievement tests for teenagers show patterns that do not match the patterns in the quantity (years) of adults' educational attainment. The United States, still a leader in terms of quantity, has a decidedly mediocre standing among rich countries when it comes to the learning achievements of 15-year-olds. East Asians, Finland, and Canada stand out in those 15-year-old test scores. Eastern Europeans also test consistently better than Latin American countries having the same average incomes.

- Circumstantial evidence says that America may have been mediocre in the quality of schooling initially, when it was emerging as a leader in enrollments back around 1850. There was probably a peak of American relative school quality, in the high-school graduating class of around 1966, after which rigidity in the school system caused a fallback relative to other countries, whose inputs were catching up.

Again, this chapter concentrates on the community of historically leading OECD countries, and Chapter 7 will explore how, and why, other regions' commitments to education departed from the paths of the forerunners.

THE LEADERS SPENT MORE, ATTAINING MORE

On the eve of World War I, Germany was still the world leader in devoting a share of national income to taxes that were spent on public education. So we saw in Chapter 4 (Table 4.1) when comparing those few countries that supplied the numbers needed, a group that probably included every country that spent substantial sums for this purpose. Germany then lost that leading position due to the two world wars and to Nazism. By 1960, when the shares of national income devoted to public education are finally revealed for virtually all of the developed countries, Germany had come to spend a lower share than the median OECD country. It remains in that below-median position today, as shown in Table 5.1.

Which countries have made the greatest tax efforts on behalf of public education since 1960? Table 5.1 gives this leadership distinction to the Nordic countries, the Low Countries, Canada, and New Zealand. Perhaps surprisingly, the United States has never been a leader in tax efforts on behalf of public education – even though children have always been a higher share of the whole population in America than in most other developed countries. This mediocre outcome in terms of paying taxes for education needs to be borne in mind when we turn to other ways of comparing educational quantity and quality across countries.[2]

How would such public expenditures have been transformed into educational outcomes and human productivity? We seek answers to this

TABLE 5.1. *Total public expenditures on education as a percentage of GDP, twenty-three countries, 1910–2015*

	1910	1930	1960	1970	1980	1990	2000	2010	2015
Argentina	0.1	1.8	1.9	2.8	3.0	3.5	4.6	5.0	5.8
Australia	1.0		2.8	4.2	5.8	4.7	4.9	5.6	5.3
Austria			2.0	2.7	3.8	5.0	5.6	5.7	5.5
Belgium			4.5	6.0	8.0	4.8	6.0	6.6	6.6
Canada	1.7		3.0	6.9	6.0	6.0	5.4	5.4	–
Chile	1.0	1.8	2.2	3.8	4.2	2.3	3.8	4.2	4.9
Denmark			3.8	7.1	8.0	6.7	8.1	8.6	7.6
Finland			6.6	6.3	6.2	5.3	5.7	6.5	7.1
France	1.0	1.6	3.4	5.0	5.7	4.5	5.6	5.7	5.5
Germany	2.3	3.3	2.4	4.0	5.1	4.4	4.5	4.9	4.8
Greece			1.6	1.9	2.4	2.0	3.2	4.0	..
Ireland			3.0	5.2	6.5	4.7	4.2	6.0	3.8
Italy	0.5		3.7	4.5	5.6	3.0	4.3	4.4	4.1
Japan	0.3		4.0	3.6	5.0	4.6	3.5	3.6	3.6
Netherlands	2.3		4.5	6.7	7.2	5.3	4.6	5.6	5.4
New Zealand	1.8		2.7	3.5	4.2	4.8	6.6	7.0	6.3
Norway	0.8		3.8	6.4	6.3	6.3	6.5	6.7	7.6
Portugal			1.4	1.7	3.1	3.6	5.2	5.4	4.9
Spain	0.4	0.7	0.9	2.0	2.6	3.6	4.2	4.8	4.3
Sweden	1.3		4.6	6.2	6.5	5.3	6.8	6.6	7.6
Switzerland			3.1	4.1	5.5	4.5	4.8	4.9	5.1
UK	0.7		3.6	5.3	5.6	4.7	4.5	5.8	5.6
US	1.4	2.7	3.6	5.3	5.7	5.0	5.4	5.4	5.0
Minimum	0.3	0.7	0.9	1.7	2.4	2.0	3.2	3.6	3.6
Median	1.0	1.8	3.1	4.5	5.6	4.7	4.9	5.6	5.4
Maximum	2.3	3.3	6.6	7.1	8.0	6.7	8.1	8.6	7.6
Std. dev.	0.7	0.9	1.3	1.7	1.6	1.2	1.2	1.1	1.2
(US-median) divided by std. dev.	0.6	1.0	0.4	0.5	0.0	0.3	0.4	−0.1	−0.3
The top four countries, by expenditure share:									
(1)	Germ		Finl	Dnk	Dnk	Dnk	Dnk	Dnk	Dnk
(2)	Neth		Swed	Can	Belg	Nor	Swed	NZ	Nor
(3)	NZ		Neth	Neth	Neth	Can	NZ	Nor	Swed
(4)	Can		Belg	Nor	Swed	Finl	Nor	Swed	Finl
The ranking of the United States:									
	5th-6th		10th	9th	11th	7th	10th	13th	13th

Sources and notes: The figures refer to government expenditures on all levels of education, starting with primary.

The main source for 1850–1910 is Lindert (2004, vol. II, Appendix Table C.3).

The main source for 1960–1981 is OECD (1985, Annex C).

The main source for 1990–2015 is http://data.uis.unesco.org/?ReportId=172#, accessed Oct. 24, 2018. In a few cases, values for 1990–2010 that were not reported there

TABLE 5.1 *(continued)*

were taken from UNESCO Institute of Statistics homepage: stats.uis.unesco.org/unesco/ReportFolders/ReportFolders.aspx. Particularly erratic was UNESCO's reporting of these shares for Belgium, Ireland, and the United States.

For "2015", each of the shares is from one of the years 2014–2017, mostly from 2015.

For Argentina in earlier years, see the sources cited in Arroyo Abad and Lindert (2017).

The Canadian figures for 1880–1900 refer to primary and secondary education only.

For Chile, Díaz, Lüders, and Wagner (2010).

For France in 1930: Carry (1999), mid-range estimates.

For Germany, the 1930 number is from Diebolt (1997); the 1990 number refers to unified Germany in 1993.

For Greece, the "2010" share is really for 2005.

For Portugal, Sergio Espuelas has kindly supplied the education spending shares for 1950–1979, from the data set underlying his (2012) article.

For Spain, the share for 1910 is from Diebolt (2000); those for 1930–1980 are from Espuelas (2013); and those for 1990–2016 are from UNESCO.

Sweden's numbers for 1880–1910 are for public primary schools only.

question for countries *all over the world* since the late nineteenth century, and not just for the countries and years for which we have the public-expenditure measures shown in Tables 4.1 and 5.1. We are in luck: Even without many reliable numbers on the expenditures themselves for most countries before the 1980s, we can infer how public expenditures impacted a nation's educational attainments from the history of a non-expenditure measure: The overall average years of attainments themselves, which are traced much more easily than the actual public expenditures.

The leap from *public* education *expenditures* to overall *national* education *attainments* may seem dangerous. Yet it can be made quite safely. Over time and across countries, the overall amount of schooling is tightly tied to government-funded schooling. By the 1860s and 1870s, it was already true that taxpayers paid for most of educational funding in the leading countries.[3] Today, the public sector has become even more dominant. Among thirty-five OECD countries in 2015, taxes paid for 90 percent of pre-tertiary education, for 66 percent of tertiary education, and for 83 percent overall. Within this grand average, the tax-based shares are even higher for the richest countries than for such still-developing OECD countries as Chile, Mexico, and Turkey.[4] For any broad comparison across decades, or between countries with very different average incomes, you can bet on a simple rule: the extra education achieved by adults in the richer setting was paid for mainly by taxpayers.

The global data show enormous gains in the years of education attained by the adult population over the last century and a half. Today, the world's average adult of working age (15–64) has over eight years of schooling, even though that average includes the poorest countries and continents. Virtually all of that achievement has come since 1914, marching in step with those public expenditures. Worldwide, the average adult had less than a half year of schooling back in 1870 and still only 1.4 years of it by 1910.[5]

The country with the greatest average years of schooling has been the United States for at least a century and a half, as shown in Figures 5.1–5.3. This contrasts sharply, of course, with that middling performance of the Americans in the share of income paid in taxes for schools, shown back in Table 5.1. Which leadership result tells the truer comparative history – is it this clear American leadership in years of enrollment per adult, or Table 5.1's finding that the leaders in the share of national income spent on taxes for education were always in Western Europe? I will come to argue for the latter leadership story, that tax-based expenditures lead us toward a more informative history, since they bundle together the effects of Links (B) and (C) above, leading to a net ("reduced-form") result that ties the skills acquired by the adult population to the national funding of education. Still, there is value in tracing, in Figures 5.1–5.3, who led and who lagged in the building of a longer-educated population of working age.

That American lead in average years of education was sustained impressively until some time around the middle of the twentieth century, by which time the Americans had seized a particularly wide lead in secondary education (Goldin 1998, 2001). Since then, other countries have been catching up, though none of them has yet clearly overtaken the United States in this respect. The adult populations of Sweden and the United Kingdom started their convergence up toward American schooling levels right after World War II, followed by France's acceleration from the 1960s on. The schooling of the German adult population seems to have failed to advance until around the time of unification, but has been rising rapidly ever since. Russia, Japan, and Korea have all been slowly converging toward the American schooling average for decades. India remains far behind, as does China. Within Latin America, Cuban education

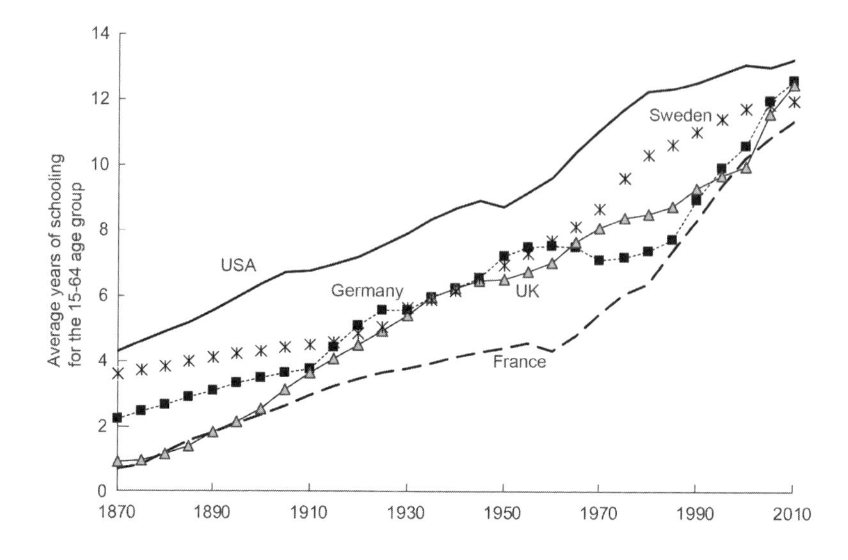

Figure 5.1. Average years of schooling attained by adults 15–64, in some leading countries, 1870–2010

Sources and notes: The main source is the major extension of the Barro-Lee database by Jong Wha Lee and Hanol Lee (2016), which built on Robert Barro and Jong Wha Lee (2013).

All series are averages of male and female rates, using the gender weights in the original.

For Figures 5.4–5.6, I calculated the gini coefficients for fifteen countries from the Lee and Lee divisions of levels of schooling into seven ranges (zero years, incomplete primary schooling, completed primary, incomplete secondary, completed secondary, incomplete tertiary, and completed tertiary), assigning average numbers of years to each range, and calculating the gini in the usual manner.

The Lee and Lee estimates omit post-baccalaureate years of schooling in graduate school and professional schools, coding just 16 years for anybody from the baccalaureate degree up. This top-coding problem is analogous to the top-coding problem in income distributions based on household surveys. Yet in the case of years of schooling, the top-coding has had little effect on averages or inequality up to 2010, unlike the omission of soaring top incomes in the case of top income-group coding.

Their detailed estimates made it possible to derive ("back out") the average numbers of years for the three incomplete levels (incomplete primary, incomplete secondary, and incomplete tertiary) for all of our fourteen countries. For some other countries, however, the derivation of average years without completion exceeded the boundaries of what was possible. This was true, for example, in Germany from 1990 on and in Italy from 1960 on.

has advanced rapidly since Castro's Revolution, albeit without remunerative opportunities in Cuba's dysfunctional economy. Brazil has expanded basic education very rapidly since the return to democracy in 1988, partly through implementing its conditional cash-transfer

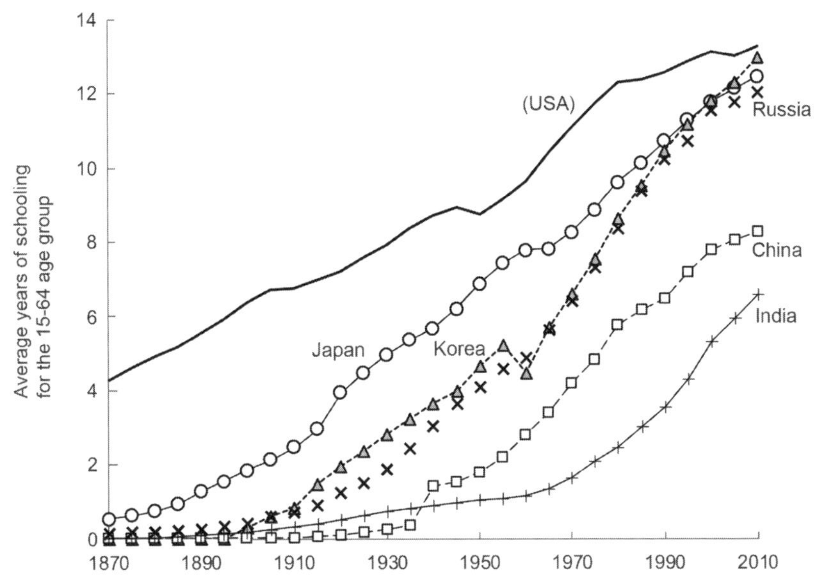

Figure 5.2. Average years of schooling attained by adults 15–64, in Russia and Asian countries, 1870–2010
Sources and notes: See Figure 5.1.

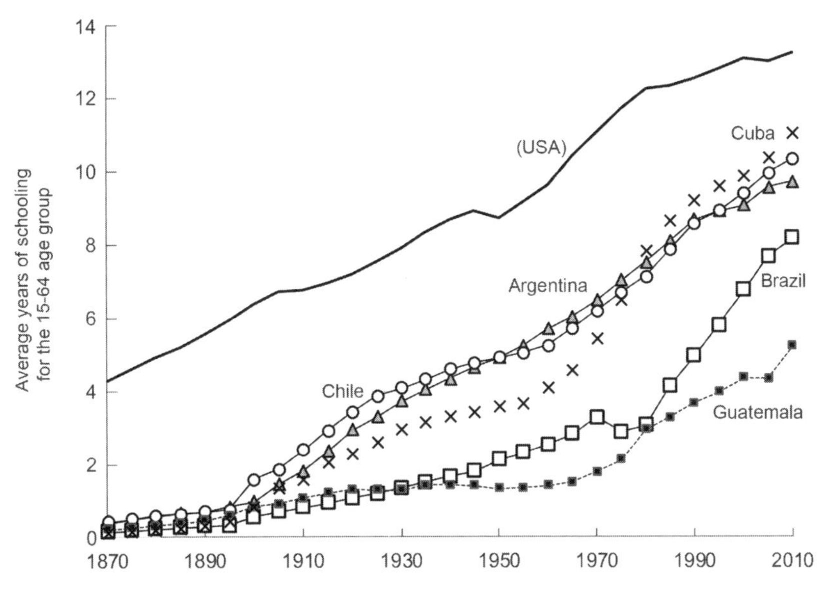

Figure 5.3. Average years of schooling attained by adults 15–64, in some Latin American countries, 1870–2010
Sources and notes: See Figure 5.1.

programs for the poor (*bolsa escola / bolsa familia*).[6] Most other Latin American countries have advanced their educational attainments more slowly.

EDUCATIONAL "CONVERGENCE BIG TIME" WITHIN EVERY COUNTRY

These signs of limited catch-up, or convergence, between countries in their schooling since the 1970s is augmented by, and even eclipsed by, the dramatic equalization of schooling *within* countries.[7] Indeed, schooling levels are equalizing within practically every country in the world.

A little reflection suggests that the attainments of years of education must become more equal when average education advances over time. To envision what history actually shows, imagine the inequality with which the process must have started. Say only one person is educated and literate, and is the tutor for His Majesty's son only. Everybody else starts with zero education. At this point, the inequality is clear enough: out of the whole population, the prince and his tutor alone have all the schooling. From that unequal starting point, the only way to keep the inequality is to keep the prince alone in school. As soon as education advances to include widespread primary education, there is no way that the elite with higher education can accumulate schooling as fast as the masses. There is an obvious upper limit on the number of years of schooling for the most educated. Years of schooling cannot be as concentrated as income or wealth. No top individual – Jeff Bezos of Amazon, or (Harvard dropout) Bill Gates of Microsoft, or any other – can have attained over a thousand times as many years of schooling as the average adult, as he or she could with income or wealth. Not as long as the least educated are rising from zero years to even, say, one year of schooling.

To summarize the history of inequality in schooling, Figures 5.4 through 5.6 use a customary gini coefficient, which we will introduce more fully in Chapter 10. Here, we need to know only that it is an inequality measure, capturing the extent to which something, in this case adults' schooling, is distributed mainly to a few instead of being equally spread over the whole population.

The history of any country's inequality of adults' schooling shows a striking pattern. Historically, every single country has expanded its schooling in an equalizing way. There was "convergence big time" within every country ever since 1870 (or earlier). The leaders in equalizing education were the same as the leaders in raising the average education. The laggards were also the same in both the equalization and the growth of schooling, and the timing was the same. Indeed, the comparative history of education inequality in Figures 5.4–5.6 looks like the comparative history of educational growth in Figures 5.1–5.3, turned upside down.

The trend toward more equal schooling has thus been global and rapid since the 1970s. The least schooled countries are catching up fast, gaining in average schooling faster than the leaders did in the nineteenth century. To be sure, in sub-Saharan Africa, the average adult's schooling is still only about one year, but the region's enrollment rates for children are accelerating, and this acceleration should be evident in the adult attainments by mid-century. We are marching toward more equal education of the whole world's population.

GENDER "CONVERGENCE, BIG TIME"

The same long sweep of history has also brought *gender convergence* in education in most countries. The unmistakable march toward gender parity in educational attainment was led by the advanced countries, as shown in Figure 5.7. Even as early as 1870, women were attending school longer in the United States and Canada, 4.2 years compared to 4.1 for men. And, since the 1980s, among the advanced countries as a whole, women have received the majority of university undergraduate degrees. In other regions, female were denied schooling, especially around 1910. The Middle East and the still-developing countries of South Asia are lagging behind the rest of the world by about a century, reaching advanced countries' female/male education ratios of 1910 only around the year 2010.

By contrast, the still-developing countries of Latin America and Eastern Europe have kept pace with the most economically advanced countries in terms of gender equity in education. Latin America is especially

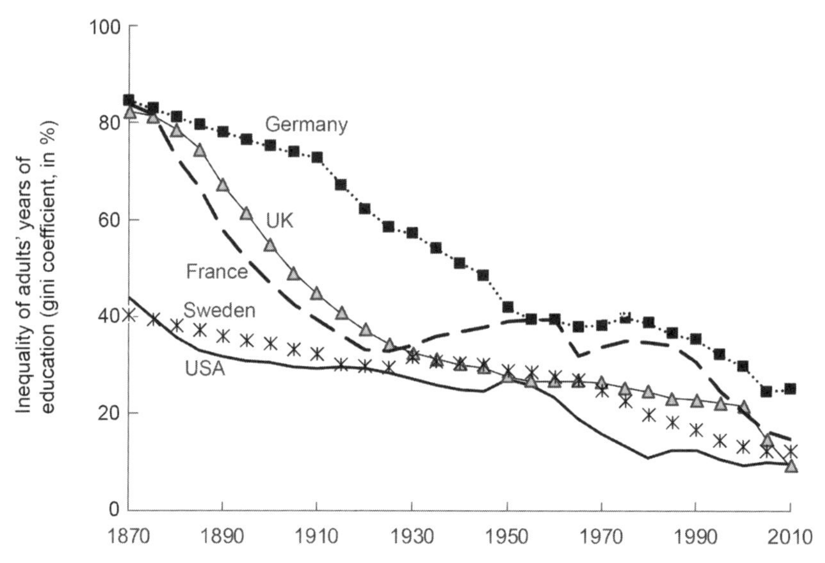

Figure 5.4. The inequality of years of schooling attained by adults 15–64, in some leading countries, 1870–2010
Sources and notes: See Figure 5.1.

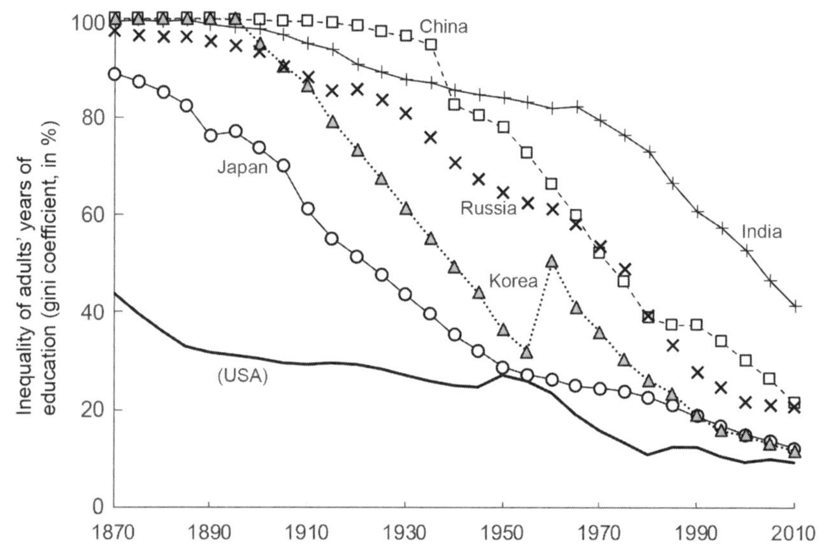

Figure 5.5. The inequality of years of schooling attained by adults 15–64, in Russia and Asian countries, 1870–2010
Sources and notes: See Figure 5.1.

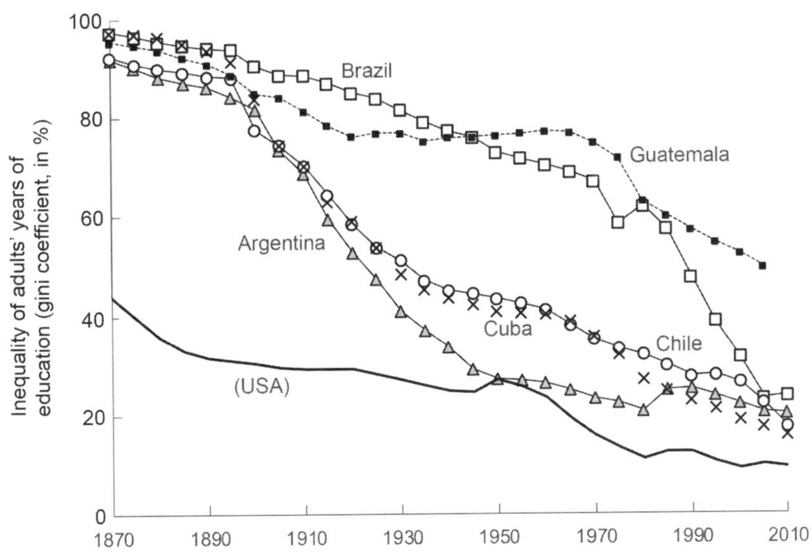

Figure 5.6. The inequality of years of schooling attained by adults 15–64, in Latin American countries, 1870–2010
Sources and notes: See Figure 5.1.

impressive. Even though it began the period with a female–male ratio under 0.4 in 1870, it rapidly expanded female education in the next few decades with the ratio exceeding 0.8 by 1910. South Asian countries like India continue to struggle with stubborn and persistent gender differences in education. Are economic or cultural factors responsible? Given the long history of such differences over changing economic times, culture is perhaps a bigger part of the South Asian story.

Educating females strongly promotes economic development, in ways that one would miss if one pursued only the direct effects of a female's education on her own wages. While it cannot explain all differences in economic growth, scholars agree that more schooling for a mother means fewer children and greater investments of time and money into the health and productive powers of each child. For a variety of familiar reasons, mothers have always delivered more inputs into child development than have fathers.[8]

The dependence of children's survival and earning power on mothers' education carries a clear implication for economic history: As emphasized earlier, the regions that gave a greater share of education to

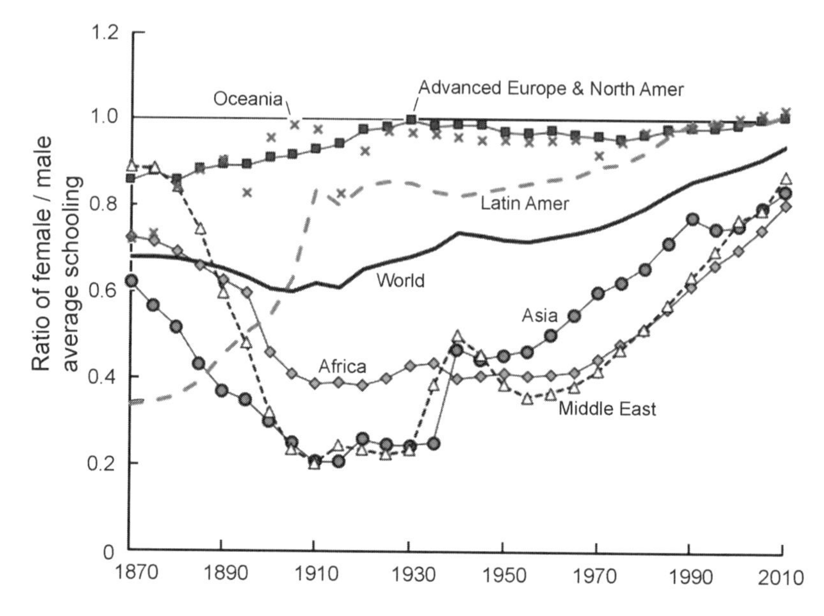

Figure 5.7. Female/male ratio in adults' schooling, by world region, 1870–2010
Sources and notes: The ratios were calculated by Latika Chaudhary from the data underlying Lee and Lee (2016). This diagram also appears in Chaudhary and Lindert (forthcoming).

For the Middle East, Africa, and Asia, their higher ratios before 1910 may be illusory, since very few of either sex were attending school in those countries in the late nineteenth century.

females in the past have, partly for this reason, achieved greater cumulative gains in life expectancy and GDP per capita. The pro-growth aspect of gender equity is something that the Eastern Europeans and Latin Americans have got right, and it is something that much of Asia, the Middle East, and Africa has got wrong in the past, though the education of women in those regions has been expanding rapidly since 1970.

WHERE AND HOW HAS THE "QUALITY" OF OUR LEARNING ADVANCED?

Aside from staying in school for more years, have people gained more knowledge for any given number of years in school? [9] Are today's eighth-graders, for example, smarter than eighth-graders were a hundred years ago? If so, does schooling itself deserve credit for the gain in learning efficiency? This is a tougher set of questions, for want of data, as I have already warned. Some rough clues can be followed over time, but cannot be compared across countries. Others give a clear international view today, but cannot be followed very far back into history.

Let us first look at the only kind of time-series information on nations' quality of learning that starts far enough back in the twentieth century to show how learning has changed over several decades. It is not the kind that one would think of as the most natural measure of what has been learned in school, and even less natural as a way to show the influence of tax-based school funding. But it is the best clue we have about learning that spans more than one generation, and psychologists tend to agree that it must have played a positive role.

WE ARE GETTING SMARTER AND MORE PRODUCTIVE: THE FLYNN EFFECT. A long-run clue that could conceivably relate to public money for schooling, and other factors, is the IQ test, or rather the whole set of varied IQ tests such as the Raven's progressive matrices, the Stanford Binet series, and the Wechsler series for children and adults.[10] The tests have changed over time, and different countries have applied different variants. The prolific research of James R. Flynn (1984, 1987, 2000, 2007, 2008, 2012) has carefully spliced together the different IQ tests over recent decades. Often, two vintages of the same test were given to the same, or similar, populations of students or of adults in the same year, allowing Flynn to convert old test scores into comparable new test scores. The richest IQ data bank is that for the United States, which allows one to follow trends in some tests over more than one hundred years (back to 1909), with separate trends for tests taken by children and tests taken by adults. Flynn and others have mapped out trends in the available IQ results for thirty-one countries, each over a different time span within the last hundred years.

We are indeed getting smarter. The global trend toward better IQ scores, the "Flynn effect," points to an average gain of 2.8 IQ points per decade, or seven points (almost half a standard deviation) per twenty-five-year generation. The improvement is common to peoples taking the IQ tests in all thirty-one countries. It has persisted over most of the studied sub-periods, between 1909 and 2013.[11] For the United States, the average IQ score in 2011 is 33 points, or more than two standard deviations, above the average in 1909. That is, the average American tests higher than did more than 95 percent of the 1909 ancestors who took comparable tests.

Which countries' populations are smarter, and which groups of people are smarter within each country? It would not be wise to use such IQ tests to compare different countries, due to international differences in the tests.[12] Within a country, however, the trends, combined with inter-group comparisons from the latest tests, can at least shed light on how we can compare the past and present for different groups. One glaring result illuminates the controversy over race and IQ. Flynn (2008, 2012, pp. 135–140) finds that blacks of a given age group in 2002 had IQs slightly higher than whites in 1947–1948, and far higher than whites in 1909. This result, like many others, implies that environmental factors account for IQ trends much more strongly than any possible factors inherited at birth. More generally, the IQ trend studies find that comparable long-run gains are experienced up and down the distribution by IQ, or the distribution by socio-economic status. All groups, thus defined, have advanced similarly across the generations.

WHICH SPECIFIC SKILLS ARE WE GAINING, AND WHICH ARE WE LOSING? Flynn and others have found that much of the gains have come from the subtests that focus on abstract thinking (such as the similarities test and Raven's progressive matrices). Only a small portion of the gains is due to improvements in knowledge of basic information, arithmetic and vocabulary, two skills that are no longer "frontier" skills for solving unforeseen problems.

The skills that IQ subtests show to be rising overlap with the skills being favored by trends in technology and the economy. They especially overlap with "general purpose technologies," such as electricity, communications technology, and information technology. Economic historian Rowena Gray has studied the types of skills favored by the electrification wave. She has found that it, like the more recent computerization wave, increased the demand for planning, clerical, numerical, and people skills relative to manual skills. This drift in skill demand has reduced the relative demand for dexterity-intensive jobs, which comprised the middle of the skill distribution. Claudia Goldin suggests that the same rise in demand for newer skills affected much of the economy, including many services.[13]

People have responded to such changes, of course. We invest more in our problem-solving and communications skills. At the same time, we are losing manual dexterity skills that are in declining economic demand, such as handwriting, sewing, or blacksmithing. Perhaps the only type of manual dexterity that is on the rise is the use of our thumbs for smartphones. Human minds are adapting to a more complex world, or, as Flynn summarized the shift in our skills, "the twentieth century saw people putting on scientific spectacles."[14]

DOES SCHOOLING DESERVE ANY CREDIT FOR MAKING US SMARTER? Credit for the IQ trends should be allocated among many environmental forces, including family environment (including family size), neighborhood environment, childhood disease environment, nutritional intake, the effectiveness of teaching, familiarity with the test itself, and education funding. All of these probably contributed to this upward march. We will never know exactly how much credit to give to each of these contributing forces, but we do have some indirect clues about the role of schooling effectiveness and funding. It is not just that the school enrollments and funding per student drifted up along with IQ scores. Rather, the IQ patterns are also consistent with a role for schooling: the upward drift is slightly greater for adults than for children in late primary school, and the IQ subtest scores have risen faster for the more complex problem-solving skills than for traditional skills that are taught in the home or in the earliest years of school. Psychologists Jakob Pietschnig and Martin Voracek summarize the likely partial role of education thus: "There is little doubt that education plays a role in explaining the Flynn effect. Nonetheless, schooling is unlikely to account for the full extent of the IQ gains, and in particular the large gains for fluid IQ cannot be attributed to better education."[15]

ACHIEVEMENT TEST COMPETITION IN THE TWENTY-FIRST CENTURY. A more direct reflection of how effectively the school environment has promoted true learning should show up in what are called "achievement test" scores, the kind that test whether you learned the basic curriculum material. By comparing IQ scores with the curriculum-learning achievement scores, we can at least see whether the two seem to go together. If so, the schooling process that teaches the curriculum material should probably deserve some of the credit for our getting "smarter" in the senses that show up on IQ exams.

Unlike the IQ scores, which are available for decades but are hard to compare across countries, achievement test scores can be compared directly across dozens of countries today – yet go back only one generation, for the most part. True, they might be extended back for two generations, if one accepts the estimates for 1964–2012 that Eric Hanushek and Ludger Woessmann have carefully assembled.[16] Yet up to 1994, the tests were still transitioning toward fairer and more complete coverage of the relevant student age group. The earliest waves of test results still came from the top academies in some countries, while covering nearly the full national population of students in fully schooled countries like the United States. We shall return to this issue of selectivity later in this chapter, while judging the history of American mediocrity in schooling.

For international comparisons, the best achievement tests are the waves of the Third International Mathematics and Science Study (TIMSS) since 1994–1995, and the math, science, and reading exams of the Programme in International Student Assessment (PISA) since 2000. TIMSS tests the math and science achievements of students of ages 9 and 13 every four years, whereas PISA tests the achievements of 15-year-old students in its three subject areas every three years.

The international PISA scorecard in the early twenty-first century is summarized in Table 5.2 and Figure 5.8. Before looking at such evidence, one would expect that the tested 15-year-olds would have higher achievement scores in richer countries, richer provinces, and richer cities. Indeed they did, in these 2006–2018 averages of the three subject matter scores (math, science, and reading). The lower scores of the poorer countries, to the lower left in Figure 5.8, may in fact overstate the

TABLE 5.2. *PISA achievement scores, 2006–2018, versus real income per capita, fifty-nine places in 2010*

	Income per capita, 2010	Average of 9 PISA scores, 2006-2018
Western Europe & offshoots		
Australia	37,381	510
Austria	36,474	496
Belgium	35,050	498
Canada	34,223	525
Denmark	35,608	501
Finland	32,684	529
France	31,065	500
Germany	33,613	506
Greece	25,430	466
Iceland	30,864	486
Ireland	35,704	509
Israel	24,391	463
Italy	29,195	481
Luxem. (b)	77,728	483
Netherlands	37,498	514
New Zealand	26,451	513
Norway	49,991	497
Portugal	22,886	488
Spain	28,923	485
Sweden	35,003	496
Switzerland	44,182	511
UK	32,284	502
USA	42,047	492
Latin America		
Argentina	14,085	392
Brazil	9,422	400
Chile	15,097	436
Colombia	8,293	402
Costa Rica	9,923	429
Mexico	12,348	415
Peru	8,632	385
Uruguay	12,621	423
Eastern Europe & former USSR		
Albania	7,234	404
Bulgaria	12,453	430
Croatia	17,015	480
Czech Rep.	23,047	497
Estonia	18,574	519
Hungary	18,654	487
Kazakhstan	14,461	406
Latvia	14,750	488
Lithuania	16,281	480
Montenegro	11,032	412
Poland	17,827	508
Romania	13,139	428
Russian Fed.	17,187	478
Serbia	9,340	439
Slovakia	20,905	475
Slovenia	24,709	503
Middle East and North Africa		
Jordan	6,111	404
Qatar (b)	111,074	381
Tunisia	8,922	384
Turkey	13,775	447
East Asia		
Hong Kong (a)	43,593	529
Indonesia	4,373	395
Japan	30,583	527
Korea, Rep.	27,079	533
Malaysia	16,576	419
Singapore (a)	58,268	552
Taipei (a)	32,889	516
Thailand	9,727	421

Source and notes to Table 5.2 and Figure 5.8: The source for the national average scores is OECD, PISA (2001–2019), at www.oecd.org/pisa/.
(a) Leading city only.
(b) Beyond the income range of Figure 5.8, which therefore shows only fifty-seven dots.
The real incomes per capita are the current price purchasing-power parity (PPP) values of gross domestic expenditures per person, from Penn World Table 8.1, as available on www.ggdc.net/pwt and www.internationaldata.org.

TABLE 5.2 *(continued)*

The PISA scores are national averages of the math, reading, and science literacy scores for 2006, 2009, 2012, 2015, and 2018, so an average of 3 tests times 5 testing years = 15 scores. In a few cases, however, a score was unavailable for one of the tests, or for all 3 tests, in a given year, so that some averages refer to fewer tests than 15.

knowledge acquired by their 15-year-olds. Their school enrollments up to age 15 were generally still incomplete, suggesting that the 15-year-old students taking the test may have been more learned than the national average of all 15-year-olds.

A remarkable regional pattern in the PISA results is that the formerly communist countries of Eastern Europe outperform countries with similar incomes per capita in Latin America. At the lower-income levels, the countries of the Balkans test higher than their Latin American counterparts, as in the contrast between Serbia and low-scoring Peru or Brazil or

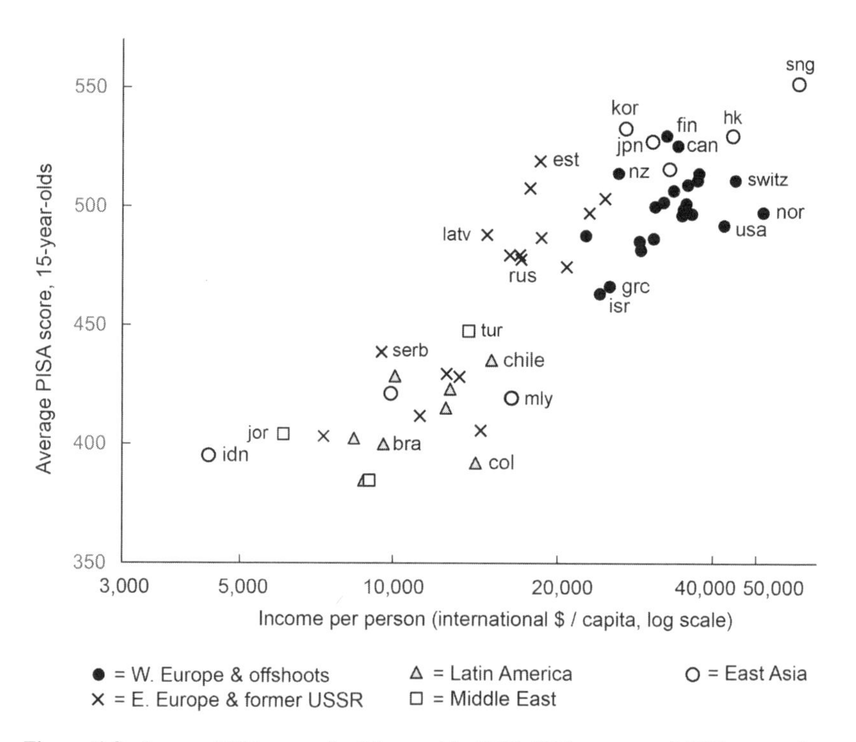

Figure 5.8. Average PISA scores for 15-year-olds, 2006–2018, versus real GDP per capita, fifty-seven places in 2010.

even (richer) Chile. Higher up the income ranks, and further to the north within Eastern Europe, the same superior results obtain. The region's top-scoring Estonia, and also Latvia, Lithuania, and Russia, came out consistently ahead of Chile or Colombia. Eastern European students also seem to come out ahead in comparison with regions other than Latin America: Estonia, Russia, and others have averages significantly higher than those of Malaysia, and Slovenia and the Czech Republic scored well above similar-income Greece and Israel. Chapter 7 will confirm that the formerly communist countries also spent more than Latin America on educating the average child of school age.

Among the highest-income populations, the top achievers have received a lot of praise in the media. These are the tested 15-year-olds of certain East Asian populations, plus Finland and Canada. Two of the top-scoring East Asian populations, South Korea and Japan, are whole nations, testing rural as well as urban students. Debate continues over just how South Korea and Japan seem to have posted the highest averages so consistently. The impressive averages from Chinese-majority populations, however, refer only to rich cities, including the city-state of Singapore, and the method of selection of sample districts for testing is not at all transparent.[17]

Among the countries of Western Europe and its English-speaking offshoots, some puzzles arise. Why should high-income Norway and the United States consistently test a bit lower than five other countries (Finland, Canada, Netherlands, New Zealand, and Australia) with lower income per capita? Part, though only a part, of these differences seem to relate to differences in the institutions that shape schooling (i.e. pre-tertiary education).

INSTITUTIONS THAT IMPROVE LEARNING: CHOICE, UNDER PRESSURE

Scholars have risen to the task of trying to infer statistically why some countries seem to deliver more learning of the core material than others. I shall concentrate here on recent contributions of Ludger Woessmann, working both separately and in conjunction with Eric Hanushek.[18] That research extracts some cautious but useful conclusions about what determined countries' average scores on the TIMSS and PISA tests since the

1990s. Two caveats need to precede their results here. First, it is hard to establish causation from the data given by a short history of a few dozen countries, as these authors clearly warn their readers. Second, this relatively short recent history conveniently fits the Hanushek–Woessmann emphasis on how money alone cannot provide school quality. As I shall argue when turning soon to the history of American schooling mediocrity, their de-emphasis on the relevance of school funding does not fit so well with the longer history of pre-university education, nor would it do justice to the role of inadequate funding in lowering student learning levels in, say, Indonesia or Brazil. These caveats notwithstanding, their interpretation of the institutional side of the international comparative results makes sense, and aligns well with other evidence.

For any given level of school resources per child, the institutional package that seems most effective is a universal schooling subsidy program combining at least these three features:

(1) public subsidies for approved private and public schools;
(2) enforcement of equal opportunities for parents to choose, independently of their income and ethnic or religious background;
(3) centralized controls on all schools' selection process, pricing, and curricula.

While the recent statistical work allows these three features to be separate and additive, the underlying national histories bring out the point that these features are necessarily complementary. That is, they have worked best in combination. To bring out this historical complementarity, let us turn to the drift toward (1) and (2), the contentious package described as "school choice" by its advocates and as "privatization" or "segregation" by its opponents. The unavoidable role of the centralized government-control feature, listed as (3) here, will quickly become evident.

Institutions that are aimed at leveling the playing field for parents, and at promoting efficiency through their right to choose, have been slowly spreading over the last hundred years, under the influence of three forces:

- political settlements of school-religion wars,
- Milton Friedman, and
- urbanization.

The pioneers in such national systems were the Netherlands and Belgium a hundred years ago, long before the modern debate among economists and politicians over school "choice" or "privatization." These countries had struggled mightily with political clashes over several redistributive issues, including who should pay for which schools, and whether to help or hobble religious schools. Both reached negotiated solutions around the time of World War I.

In the Netherlands, the nineteenth-century school expansion sparked a heated school struggle (*schoolstrijd*) between Catholics, orthodox Protestants, and secularists over school finance. Over the same decades, the left and right were fighting over extending the voting franchise. A compromise of 1917–1920 bundled generous subsidies to church schools with universal adult male suffrage. The school curriculum was centralized, and allowed little religious instruction, in exchange for decentralized ownership and management of schools. In the face of the new competition, the public-school enrollments dropped from 55 percent in 1920 to 30 percent by 1940, a share that has been pretty steady ever since. As of 2011, with around a third of Dutch students still enrolled in those strictly public schools, another third were in Catholic schools, a quarter in Protestant schools, and the remaining 8 percent in other schools, all of them funded on a fairly equal per-student formula.[19]

Dutch schools are currently subject to a lot of supervision and regulation. All school types (public, special, and private) are under the jurisdiction of a government body called Inspection of Education (*Inspectie van het Onderwijs*) that can demand that a school change its educational policy and quality, at the risk of closure. Publicly funded private schools are not allowed to charge private tuition fees, nor are they allowed to engage in selective admissions. While a school is allowed to design its own curriculum, and include religious doctrine, in practice the curricula tend to become secularized because all schools and all students must answer for their performance on the national exit exams at graduation, first from primary school and later from secondary school.

Belgium reached a similar settlement around World War I, again helped by a bundling of the school finance issue with the suffrage issue. In the conciliatory mood right after the war, the new majority of Liberals and Socialists were willing to trade support for Catholic schools for other concessions by the Catholic party.

France has some of the same subsidized private-school choice, but again the historical path has imposed constraints. By the start of World War II, a century of fights over this issue had left France in the secular mode of denying much aid to private schools. Then in November 1941, a decision was taken to allow subsidies to religious schools. Yet, because that solution was taken by the Petain government under Nazi domination, the subsidies were promptly removed immediately after liberation under communist pressure. The subsidies returned only after the 1959 *Loi Debré*, reinforced by the more permissive *Loi Guermeur* in 1977. Yet the aid to private schools, with its encouragement of school choice, is still not embedded in the Constitution and could still be withdrawn in a hostile political climate. Regulations tightly constrain private schools to be similar to public schools. All students in subsidized private schools take the national essay examinations on which public-school students have been outperforming students in private schools.[20]

Then came Milton Friedman's voucher vision. His thoughtful (1955) essay started with three key reasons why simple libertarian laissez-faire could fail to be optimal for education – market imperfections blocking competition, "neighborhood effects" (externalities), and our "paternalistic concern for children and other irresponsible individuals." While challenging the idea that government should actually run schools, he was clear that government should fund private and public schools at equal cost per student between the two school types: "parents who chose to send their children to other schools would be paid a sum equal to the estimated cost of educating a child in a government school, provided that at least this sum was spent on education in an approved school."[21]

Friedman's key emphasis was on the first two institutions listed above: (1) equal funding per student, and (2) free parental choice. That is, freedom on the demand side. Yet he was less specific about the freedoms of suppliers. While he referred to the need for regulations governing "an approved school," he wrestled with what freedoms the schools should have about pricing – note his phrase "at least this sum" – and about choosing whom to admit. He explicitly confronted the fact that something like a voucher system was already being proposed by segregationists in the

American South, who sought local support to keep blacks out of subsidized white schools. He grappled unpersuasively with this problem, and in the end retreated to the pious hope that free-market competition would somehow defeat racism.

Soon after Friedman's 1955 essay came another hopeful insight about free-choice thinking, one that applies best in densely urbanized areas, where people all live so close together that they can choose among many local schools. As Charles Tiebout (1956) theorized, people in major urban areas can choose their governments at the local level. Some prefer higher taxes that pay for better schools and other local public goods, while others do not. Thus, in a major metropolitan area, with many suburbs to choose from, people can vote with their feet – if the cost of moving or of commuting to a nearby school is zero. Those that highly value the extra tax-financed schools and other public goods can gravitate toward living in the higher-budget localities, while those who are more anti-tax move in the opposite direction.

Tiebout's story of local choice has a happy implication for efficient financing and operation of schools. Young couples who are going to move into their first house will sort themselves out among suburbs partly on the basis of their tastes for, or against, spending more tax money for schools. In the decentralized Tiebout urban world of shopping for the local government you like, a good local school system makes even childless oldsters willing to pay the extra taxes for schools, because they will be compensated through their property values.

Are the visions offered by Friedman and Tiebout too good to be true? Yes, unfortunately, the benefits of parental freedom to shop for the local school they like best are not delivered by the voucher plan alone, even in highly urbanized areas.[22] The devil is in the details, as Friedman himself seemed to anticipate. The history of school choice shows that the effectiveness of subsidized school choice in promoting efficiency and equity depends critically on certain institutional constraints on educators' freedoms. Even the Dutch, Belgians, and French – our pioneers in subsidized school choice from the early twentieth century – evolved a set of constraints on the process of matching schools with students. All three of them reinforced the effect of learning efficiency on parental choice by instituting high-stakes centralized exams. And typically, as we noted in connection with Dutch practice, publicly funded private schools cannot "top up" the cost of their schooling with extra fees, nor are they allowed to engage in selective admissions. These restrictions promoted equity by tilting parents' choices away from sorting by income or peer group.

We now can harvest the lessons of a richer international history, thanks to the spread of school-choice innovations since 1980. Let us start with historical experience under the famous Chilean school-voucher reform from 1980 to 2016, which defines a lower end of the spectrum of outcomes in terms of the efficiency and equity of subsidized school choice, and conclude with Swedish vouchers since 1992 at the higher end of the same spectrum.

CHILE 1980–2016. The school reform imposed by the Pinochet regime in 1980, and implemented in 1981, made fateful choices about the supply side, choices that seem to have heightened inequalities without raising true productivity in terms of average learning.

One key feature of the Chilean plan was indeed a step toward breaking up monopoly power in education, and pressuring educators to compete for the favor of parents: Upon seizing power, Pinochet promptly revoked teacher contracts and eliminated the teachers' union as a bargaining unit. Teachers were transferred from the public employee system to the private sector. By 1983, even public schools, meaning those run by municipalities, could hire and fire teachers without regard to tenure or a union contract, just like any un-unionized private company. By itself, the union-busting might have raised the efficiency of schooling. And to the extent that teachers had higher incomes than the families of their students, it might even have sounded egalitarian, at least to some.

Another feature of Chile's 1980s reform, however, worked against parental choice. The 1980s reform wave released all schools from the previously strictly defined structure of the national curriculum and from national standards. This destruction of that institution, (3), centralized controls, was fortunately reversed later. As early as 1988, the government introduced the SIMCE (*Sistema de Medicion de la Calidad de la Educacion*), the System for the Measurement of Educational Quality for fourth- and eighth-graders, a groundbreaking effort to provide student achievement data on a national scale. Until 1995, however, the absence of exam results kept depriving parents of one indicator of the quality of education in each school.[23]

A further inegalitarian feature of the 1980 reform involved private schools' freedom to cherry-pick the better students. While public schools were obligated to accept and accommodate all students, private schools could establish selective admission criteria, such as entrance exams and parental interviews. The vouchers were valued equally, regardless of the student's needs, and thus schools had an incentive to reject disadvantaged or disabled students, who were costlier to educate. This mechanism, plus the ability to charge topping-up tuitions and the visibility of peer effects, led to social-class sorting in Santiago and other major cities.[24]

A scholarly consensus now holds that Chile's 1980–1981 reform widened the inequalities of school quality, reinforcing the country's reputation for having one of the most unequal income distributions in the whole OECD community. The prevailing view also finds no gains in overall efficiency from the Pinochet voucher reform – as we might have guessed from the fact that Chile's student achievement test scores are lower than those of several other countries with similar income per capita.[25]

Chilean political discourse has shifted in favor of such criticism, and has passed laws transforming the voucher system into something more egalitarian, and possibly more efficient, during the two presidencies of Michelle Bachelet. First, in 2007, the government passed the Preferential School Subsidy Law (*Subvención Escolar Preferencial*, or SEP), effective in January 2008. This legislation added more means-testing to the educational voucher system. Under SEP, the voucher system gave "priority students," those whose family income was in the bottom 40 percent of the household population, vouchers worth 50 percent more than those given to the families of students in the upper 60 percent. Almost every public school chose to participate in SEP in 2008, as well as almost two-thirds of private subsidized elementary schools. The SEP legislation also tightened schools' accountability, and curbed private schools' ability to select students based on their academic skills. This presumably leveled the playing field.

How did SEP affect the efficiency with which the school imparted learning? As for the 2008 shift toward more progressive targeting,

Feigenberg, Rivkin, and Yan (2017) argue that the early results do not allow us to show any net effect of the pre- versus post-2008 institutions on efficiency in learning. The study by Murnane et al. (2017) disagrees, reporting that individual fourth-graders learned *less* under the voucher system in 2005–2007, just before the improvements experienced in 2008–2012 under the more progressive redistribution legislated by SEP in 2008. In either case, recent data fail to reveal any efficiency gains from the voucher system as practiced between 1981 and 2007.

Then, in 2016, the second Bachelet administration passed the School Inclusion Law (*Ley de Inclusión*), which further restricted the roles of families' ability to pay, student achievement, or other potentially discriminatory factors in the admissions process. If the School Inclusion Law remains in effect, and is not reversed by President Sebastian Piñera or his successors, it would appear that the era of the Pinochet voucher reform will have ended in 2016. The political outcome remains to be seen, of course, and we must also wait to see whether statistical studies will show continued gains in equity and/or efficiency from the legislation of 2008 and 2016.

WHAT ABOUT THE TOP-SCORING COUNTRIES? The countries that gain publicity for their perennially top PISA achievement scores vary greatly, and are sprinkled between East Asia, Canada, and Northern Europe. They nonetheless share some common features relevant to the achievement of student learning. They are all hard-wired with those three positive institutional features introduced earlier: (1) public subsidies for approved private and public schools; (2) enforcement of equal opportunities for parents to choose, independently of their income and ethnic or religious background; and (3) centralized controls on all schools' selection processes and pricing (though not so much control over curricula).

Yet there is little trace of a formal voucher system in Korea, Japan, Finland, the Chinese cities, Canada, or others in the top ranks of international achievement tests. In these countries *de facto* student choice has already been assured by urbanization and by national policies de-emphasizing "neighborhood" (catchment) schools. Formal voucher plans have not been implemented mainly because they do not seem to be needed.

In South Korea, for example, only metropolitan Seoul has experimented with vouchers, and only for the transition into secondary school since 2010. Two statistical studies report that this experiment has led to segregation by ability, but their results cover too few years of experience to be conclusive.[26]

Japan has no voucher system. Government support of private schools plays only a limited role. Only about one student in six is enrolled in a private school, and the private schools draw only about a third of their funding from government. Yet in Japan, as well as in Korea, accountability is enforced largely through their famously (or infamously) high-pressure graduation exams. Their national average PISA scores have probably been raised by the fact that the PISA achievement exams for 15-year-olds cover similar material to the national graduation exams.

Finland has also enjoyed global applause for the high scores of its 15-year-olds on international exams. What role have vouchers, or other subsidies to private schools, played in this achievement? Here again, as in Korea or Japan, there are no voucher-like institutions to appraise, largely because other forces have assured good performance. Fewer than 5 percent of 15-year-olds are enrolled in private schools, and those few private schools get almost all their money from the government (OECD 2017, Figures 2 and 6). Finland imposes clear accountability on students, teachers, and schools, driven largely by a demanding set of matriculation exams at the end of ninth grade. While teachers are well paid and given a good deal of autonomy in their teaching delivery, they lack job tenure, and can be dismissed.

Finland's high average performance, however, has recently been accompanied by a distinctive kind of segregation, at least in the big cities. A set of reforms in the mid-1990s introduced greater school choice by removing rules forcing students into neighborhood (catchment) schools. The reforms were not motivated by the classic vision of improving school quality through competition. Rather, the goal was to inspire children by enriching diversity in the curriculum, rather like America's experimentation with "magnet schools" in public-school systems, without the need for residential mobility within the same urban area. Results for 1996–2004 hint that the reforms, by introducing more variety for proactive shoppers, may have enhanced a bit of segregation by parental resources, but not conclusively so.[27]

AMERICA'S VERY LIMITED VOUCHERS. Ostensibly, school-voucher systems, as well as charter schools and tax credits for private schooling, seem to be spreading across the cities and states of the United States. By the end of 2016, fourteen states and the District of Columbia had classic voucher programs, and an additional thirteen states had scholarship tax credits and education savings accounts that were also usable in private schools.[28]

How would one reconcile this gradual spread of such school-choice systems with America's continuing mediocrity in international test scores, given that the global top performers have made little or no use of voucher-like mechanisms? One should not bother to search for any significant effects of American school-choice innovations on national results, either positive or negative, since the voucher-type programs have been so limited in scope. In every case, they have been targeted at low-income, or otherwise disadvantaged, households. That was true back in 1989, when the Wisconsin legislature passed the nation's first modern school-voucher program targeting students from low-income households in the Milwaukee School District. In 1996–1997, Cleveland, Ohio, followed suit with modest vouchers for students in fifty participating private schools. The results of such tiny pilot programs were apparently positive, largely because the participating students were being liberated from particularly disastrous city school systems in Milwaukee and Cleveland. The same limitation applies, so far, to all of the growing numbers of voucher-type programs in the United States: All are restricted to serving disadvantaged students, and only with schools that choose to participate.

The limitations on American vouchers are best illustrated by the largest of all the state-level programs, the Indiana Choice Scholarships program launched in 2011. As of the 2018–2019 school year, only 3.2 percent of K-12 students were in the "Choice" participating schools, and another 4.3 percent in other non-public schools, for a total of 7.5 percent in all non-public schools. The limitation was built into the original legislation: To qualify for a scholarship that could cover only up to 47 percent of average public-school costs per student, a student had to come from a family with an income less than 150 percent of the poverty line.

While some features of Indiana's Choice program, as signed by Governor Mike Pence, hinted at a victory for private religious schools, the fine print imposed strict boundaries. Yes, a private school can "top up," charging tuition on top of the Indiana Choice scholarship – but "a Choice school is not allowed to charge Choice Scholarship students additional fees and costs that are not routinely charged to non-Choice eligible students." Yes, a private religious school can keep its religion classes and/or its religious affiliation – but (1) "admission standards for Choice Scholarship students may not be different than the standards used for non-Choice eligible students," (2) "all participating schools are required to have a lottery policy [for admissions in the event of excess applications]," and (3) "Indiana statewide assessment tests must be administered as part of a school's participation in the Choice Scholarship Program."[29]

It seems likely that any major expansion of government subsidies to private schools in the United States, especially at the federal level, would be possible only with further tightening of government controls, requiring both achievement test accountability and restrictions on curriculum. That was already true in the nineteenth century's initial expansion of public schools. Most states of the United States passed secularizing Blaine Amendments in the later nineteenth century to placate the Protestant majority's fears about Catholic schools. Similarly, as in the Netherlands and elsewhere today, many American voters would resist turning taxpayers' money over to Islamic madrassas and cult schools, again leading to collective enforcement of relatively secular curriculum rules.

SWEDEN SINCE 1992. Thus far, the verdict on voucher systems seems a bit negative. The literature keeps finding cases in which such systems worsen social inequalities, yet cannot turn up evidence that they have improved learning on the average. We have also seen that the global top performers seem to have got their good results from other forces, not from vouchers. In particular, centralized institutions seem to deserve the most credit.

There is, however, a national school-choice experience that seems to have yielded statistical evidence of a positive effect on average learning, and the timing and nature of the positive effect also seem plausible.[30] As far back as 1992, Sweden set up a school-choice reform with those same institutional features that seem to have accompanied sustainable school-choice innovations over the last hundred years. Under Sweden's 1992 legislation, a participating student's home municipality had to provide the chosen publicly funded private school, or "independent school," with a grant, equivalent to most of the average per-student expenditure in the public-school system. The publicly funded private schools must follow the national curriculum. They are not allowed to charge extra "top-up" fees. Nor are they allowed to select students based on ability. Hence, we should expect less school segregation than what has been found from the establishment of the Chilean private-voucher schools. Under these rules, the market result is that 86 percent of Swedish pre-tertiary students attend public schools and 14 percent attend independent schools.

Enough time has passed for a solid statistical study of the results. Anders Böhlmark and Mikael Lindahl were able to analyze the school outcomes of all individuals finishing the ninth grade of compulsory school (normally at age 16) each year from 1988 through 2009 in Sweden. They were able to exploit the ways in which participation differed over time and place. As it turns out, the present independent schools improved individuals' average performance at the end of compulsory school. They further find that the positive effects primarily took the form of city-specific *external effects*, reflecting school competition. Having the results for all students, not just those choosing the private schools, they were also able to establish that independent-school students did not gain significantly more than public-school students. They did not find positive effects on school expenditures. Hence, the educational performance effects are interpretable as positive effects on school productivity. Strikingly, for most educational outcomes, Böhlmark and Lindahl did not detect positive and statistically significant effects until the 2000s, approximately a decade after the reform. This is notable, but not surprising, given that it took time for independent schools to become more than a marginal phenomenon in Sweden.

How school-choice reforms work out has thus clearly depended on how well the political process has shaped the whole institutional package that combines demand-side freedom for parents with careful controls on suppliers' behavior. Many countries, like Chile from 1980 to 2008, got the formula wrong, and ended up widening social gulfs without any clear efficiency gain. Sweden may have got school-choice reform right since 1992.[31]

THE DEBATE OVER MEDIOCRE AMERICAN SCHOOLING

How does one explain the fact that Americans seem to be receiving only a mediocre education by rich-country standards, until they enter tertiary education? This issue is highly politicized, of course. Progressives, backed by the teaching profession, keep insisting that more government funds need to be spent on education at all levels. Conservatives keep insisting that spending more would not help, warning that teachers would eat up the increases while blocking school choice and other market-oriented policies to improve teaching efficiency.

So far the evidence marshalled in this American debate has been geographically broad but historically shallow. Even within the empirical confines of this debate, restricted to the years since the 1960s, the data offer some help to both sides. The view that spending more tax money will not improve educational quality can draw on countless studies showing the absence of any clear positive schooling effects of larger budgets.[32] It could also note that countries like Korea and Japan now capture higher international test scores while spending less than their American counterparts, as we saw in Table 5.1. The opposing view, that more money would improve quality, can draw on the fact, also shown in Table 5.1, that the mediocre-looking American school system still spends a lower share of national income on pre-tertiary education than do the European leaders in tax effort for public schools, even though the Americans have more children per adult.

To come to a verdict on the sources of today's mediocre quality results, we need to add a deeper history to this debate, a history that reaches further back than just the 1960s. Fortunately, that longer history is coming into view.

WAS THERE EVER A DECLINE IN AMERICAN SCHOOLING-QUALITY TO EXPLAIN? Were Americans ever ahead in quality, measured as schools' contributions to human productivity and earning power *per year of enrollment*? Or were they always mediocre? As an initial warning sign, recall that even before 1914 America was not a leader in tax-based education expenditures as a share of income (Table 5.1), despite being a clear leader in enrollments and in adults' accumulated years of schooling. Such contrasts suggest that inputs per enrolled student must have been lower in the United States than in some other countries. The American shortfall in inputs could have produced a lower quality of schooling per year before 1914. Let us look more closely at this early evidence, and at the scraps of evidence we have about subsequent movements in the average quality of American education.

To offer a "spoiler," this section's tentative conclusion will be as follows: As of 1850, the quality of American education was already mediocre relative to that in Western Europe. The United States improved its quality of education, again relative to the also-improving Western Europe, up until the early baby-boom birth cohort of 1948, which passed through kindergarten and primary schooling in 1954–1962, through high school in 1962–1966, and through university in 1966–1970, having benefited from the higher-education boom of the post-Sputnik era. By that time, its curriculum learning was probably better than average among OECD advanced countries, though still not top. After that, its relative standing dipped until the high-school student body of around 1980, and has regained ground slightly since about 1990.

IN THE BEGINNING, QUALITY WAS NOT HIGH. Before 1914, and especially at the dawn of our national data in the 1850 census, American schooling exhibited what Carole Shammas (2015) has rightly called "educational sprawl," meaning fewer days of attendance per enrolled year, spread out over more years. America's high enrollment rates for school-age children, and its high adult years of schooling, tended to hide its low quality of education per year of enrollment, both relative to today's quality and relative to the quality in Western Europe back in, say, 1850 or 1914.

This was especially true in rural areas. Students moved in and out of school on an irregular basis, blending work experience with further installments of school learning. They went to school more regularly in the winter and summer than in fall or spring, and responded to daily changes in work and weather. Children might begin their studies at the age of 3 or 4, and might be resuming them past the age of 20, after long absences. Such student transience has probably inflated some of the enrollment and attendance rates for the United States before the late nineteenth century. There was probably some double counting of students who attended the separate summer and winter sessions, especially when they went to different schools.[33]

Another indirect clue about schooling quality, a negative one, is the pupil/teacher ratio, or school crowding, or average class size. On this measure, the United States compared well with Western Europe back in the mid-nineteenth century, where classes were more crowded on the average. However, given its rural setting, America's lower pupil/teacher ratio was not a clear sign of quality, since it often reflected one teacher's teaching different levels at once, whereas in the more urban setting typical of Western Europe, the then-higher pupil/teacher ratio might have included more separation by school grade.

Overall, American schools did not deliver such a high quality of learning before 1914, largely because they gave each student such low inputs per year of enrollment.

A LIKELY RISE IN QUALITY, UP TO THE MID-1960S. If there were signs of relative mediocrity in American schooling dating back to the earliest data, admittedly for different reasons from the mediocrity revealed in today's international tests, was it indeed the case, then, that the mediocrity has persisted throughout American history? Perhaps there was no peak of relative quality in between, as in the old person's T-shirt inscription "Over the hill? What hill? I don't remember any hill."

Yet some scraps of circumstantial evidence suggest that the quality of American schooling rose up to the mid-twentieth century, both absolutely and relative to other prospering countries. For one thing, we define learning achievement today in a way that would have translated the quantity of schooling attainment into learning levels. Today's TIMSS and PISA exam sweepstakes is designed to highlight the advanced countries in which children of a given age have learned the most. That's *children* of a given age, not *enrolled students* of a given age. The distinction matters little for 15-year-olds today, since all of the leading countries have fully enrolled their 15-year-olds. Yet in earlier times, merely getting more and more students into school, and for more days each year, must have meant a rise in learning by the time they had reached the age of 15. That is, raising the quantity of primary and secondary schooling raised the average quality for the population of children at age 15 or 16. As seen earlier in Figure 5.1, the rise toward full enrollment came earlier and faster in America, culminating in nearly full high-school participation by the early postwar era. Thus, for children of a given teen-age, learning advanced in America, even relative to other countries – until the 1970s, after which the other countries closed the enrollment gap.

A second bit of indirect evidence of rising quality relates to class size. By this yardstick, American quality has clearly risen ever since the earliest data, especially at the primary-school level. As we noted, the early schools crowded more children into each teacher's classroom, often forcing her to teach students at different grade levels each day. That translates into fewer effective teacher-days for every one hundred student-days. In 1909, after some initial improvement in adding grade levels, public primary schools still had 34.4 pupils per teacher, meaning fewer than three teachers per hundred students. By the year 2000, there were only about twenty pupils per teacher in public primary schools, or about five teachers per hundred students. So on this indicator, improvement was continuous, even up to the start of this century.[34]

A final indirect clue relates to population growth and suburbanization, culminating in the early postwar "baby-boom" era. The high water mark for residence-based freedom of school choice for white Americans might have been reached around 1950, when young couples chose among fast-growing suburbs in the early postwar housing boom. For African Americans, that freedom rose rapidly in their great northward migration in the 1940s, although much more slowly across the second half of the century.

NEW RIGIDITIES AND THE LIKELY DOWNSLOPE IN RELATIVE QUALITY SINCE THE EARLY 1960S. It now appears likely that the relative quality of American schooling declined after the mid-1960s. Some causes of this relative decline have also come into view.

At first glance, the trends in international test scores do not show any obvious decline in America's standing. Ever since the 1960s, the headlines seem to have announced that the United States has always been in the middle of the rich-country pack when it comes to tests of teenagers' knowledge of math, science, and interpretive reading. So say the best summaries of those test scores by those who published the results, and by Eric Hanushek and Ludger Woessmann, who ably wrestled with the difficult task of splicing together the averages scores from what are actually different tests since 1964.[35] Yet there are at least two reasons to doubt that America's international ranking remained frozen. One is that Hanushek and Woessmann, in grafting together the test results from different decades, had to make assumptions that practically guaranteed this no-trend result.[36] Another is the strong likelihood that other countries were highly selective in choosing whom to test in the 1960s, but not so selective in administering the PISA and TIMSS exams today. What may look like a constant mediocrity of American teenage performance since the earliest tests in 1964 should be viewed instead as a downward trend in American relative achievement 1964–1994, masked by the removal of a bias against the Americans in the early tests. The bias against America (and other fully schooled and fully sampled countries) is clear in the earliest tests. Those tests are taken only by students, not by the whole population in their age group. Back then, the tested students in other countries were still an academically select group, unlike the Americans. Among tested 17-year-olds in 1970, for example, fully 75 percent of them in America were finishing high school, versus only 45–47 percent in Belgium and Sweden, and below 30 percent in all other tested countries. Little wonder that American students failed to shine in those international comparisons back in 1970.[37] Yet by the time of the TIMSS in 1994, nearly all of the tested age groups, ages 9 to 17, were in school in all the tested countries, making the comparisons fair. Thus, there was probably a decline in the relative performance of American students sometime between 1964 and 1994, if one could hold constant the degree of selectivity.

Movements in average test scores *within* the United States since the mid-twentieth century support the same suspicion that the relative mediocrity of American teenagers' learning of school material is a recent development. Elsewhere, I have collated other studies of the movements in several kinds of American test scores since the 1950s. Specifically, these were the Iowa Test of Educational Development, taken by all 17-year-old students in Iowa, and the larger test samples of math, science, and reading of 17-year-old students in the National Assessment of Educational Progress (NAEP).[38] As long as the other developed countries did not share these same swings in test scores, but instead kept slowly improving, then the evidence from within the United States again says that this country's performance slumped after the mid-1960s.

These tests show that average test performance of 17-year-olds, which was rising earlier, dipped from about 1967 until around 1980, and has regained ground since about 1990.[39] When the decline in test scores was most visible between the mid-1960s and the early 1980s, there was no end to the list of culprits suspected by Americans concerned about the quality of their children's primary and secondary schools. As I summarized elsewhere, the suspects included:

> Too much TV. Too much extra-curricular activities. Bad diets and not enough exercise. Grade inflation. Fuzzy-headed liberal dilution of the curriculum with courses that do not teach the basics. Fluffy teacher-education courses. The rise of public-school bureaucracies. The rise of teacher unions and collective bargaining. Too many ill-prepared immigrant students. Urban decay. The breakdown of the traditional family. Stingy taxpayers.[40]

Most of the accusations failed to identify culprits that prowled only in the United States and only in that 1967–1980 era of sagging scores. One pattern points us toward culprits that struck only when the victims were enrolled in school, and only beyond fourth grade. Tests of younger children, those under the age of 10, did not yield declining scores in any documented period, either in the Iowa tests or in the NAEP tests. The

1967–1980 test-score decline was apparently caused by something that happened to American children *after fourth grade*.

With the benefit of two more decades of historical experience and scholarship, we can single out three of the most likely culprits. The first is the sudden consolidation of America's school districts, which seriously restricted parents' school choice. Between 1940 and 1970, the number of separate public-school districts plunged about 85 percent, while the number of students soared. There has been no rebound, no proliferation of new districts since 1970. The giants, led by the City School District of the City of New York (over a million students) and the Los Angeles Unified School District, set up more rigid rules blocking parents' choices. The fact that it was harder and harder for a family to escape a school district would not have brought much harm as long as school quality were upheld in the increasingly large districts. Yet more concentrated school districts may have combined with a second force to restrict students' school choices and dampen the productivity of educational inputs.

That second force is the spread of state legislation facilitating the rise of teachers' unions. The period from 1960 to 1974 saw a jump in the share of states where laws facilitated collective bargaining and permitted teachers' unions to strike under certain conditions. By 1988, when only 19 percent of the US labor force was unionized, fully 75 percent of public-school teachers belonged to unions. It is possible that the centralization of districts contributed to the mobilization of unions, as in Kenneth Galbraith's "bigness begets bigness" explanation of the rise of unions more generally. Standard economic reasoning would expect that the combination of local producer monopolies and union strength could raise costs to captive student consumers.

Did the consolidation of districts and the rise of the power of teachers' unions damage the quality of American schooling since the 1960s? So far, the evidence sides with the critics in pointing to the combination of these forces as a major erosive force in the quality of American schooling.[41]

A third force that seems to have weakened the delivery of quality learning in American schools also took the form of a restriction on choice. A few states passed laws imposing funding-equalization formulas, in response to various complaints about unequal school funding. The idea of making schools more equal could be defended on its own grounds, that is on equity grounds. Yet in certain states, the restriction of parents' ability to shop for better schools seems to have worsened average student outcomes. In other words, the effect was to "equalize downward" in school quality. The three state-level changes where the downward effect on quality appears most clearly are New Mexico 1974, California's famous Proposition 13 in 1978, and Oklahoma in 1987.[42]

Unless similar things silently happened in other OECD countries, with similar timing – as seems unlikely – it would appear that these three choice-restricting developments in the United States since the 1960s have lowered its average learning relative to other countries.

THE STRONGEST LINK

The start of the chapter offered a sketch of the causal linkages being explored here. Here is that sketch again:

Reprise –

Link (A)	fiscal capacity and political will	→	taxes spent on educating children
Link (B)	taxes spent on educating children	→	years of education per adult
Link (C)	taxes spent on educating children and years of education per adult	→	skills and knowledge
Link (D)	skills and knowledge	→	greater human earning power

Link (A), the influence of fiscal capacity, and of political will, to fund universal schooling, is explored in Chapters 4 and 7. So far, this chapter has reported on the more complex and controversial Links (B) and (C), surveying how public inputs seem to have raised skills and knowledge.

The remaining link, from skills and knowledge to greater human productivity and earning power, is the strongest – a "slam dunk," in the basketball metaphor. So we learn not only from common intuition but also from economic studies using the economists' productive-function approach. The same strong effect of better schooling on earnings is confirmed by the rates of return on public education expenditures.[43] As long as government funding remains a positive determinant of the quantity and quality of education, public education undeniably promotes economic growth.

CHAPTER 6

More, but Different, Social Spending in Rich Countries since 1914

WHILE GOVERNMENT EDUCATION EXPENDITURES WERE clearly productive, more controversy has surrounded the other forms of public social spending, such as health, public pensions, anti-poverty spending ("welfare"), and public housing. When, where, and why did these more controversial forms of social spending grow? This chapter traces and explains their growth, concentrating on the OECD countries where they grew most.

Just as striking as the postwar emergence of high social budgets has been the century-long "mission shift," a major shift in what the government social budget is spent on. More and more, the growing social budgets drifted away from education and from helping the poor, toward insuring the powerful and elderly against outliving their retirement nest eggs. For the rich countries as a whole, an apt summary of this mission shift would be Price Fishback's (2020) summary of the evolution of social spending within the United States: "Social insurance has increased far more than public assistance, so 'rise in the social insurance state' is a far better description of the century than 'rise in the welfare state.'" After mapping the rise in social spending and the shift in what it was spent on, this chapter offers preliminary explanations of both the rise and the shift. Behind the rise lie such forces as fiscal capacity and democratization. Behind the move toward health spending lie both the medical revolution and women's votes. Behind the drift toward public pensions lies the rising political power of the elderly, but especially the elderly in occupations that have political clout. Using the core OECD trends as a standard for comparison, Chapter 7 will then explore other regions of the world, asking how they departed from that standard.

THE GREAT RISE OF SOCIAL SPENDING

SOME EVEN BECAME WELFARE STATES. For all the speed with which governments have expanded their education budgets over the last hundred years, the other kinds of social spending have grown even faster. Figure 6.1 traces this growth, as a share of national income.[1] If we arbitrarily define the arrival of the "welfare state" as the date at which the country began to spend more than 20 percent of its national income on these kinds of social spending, then the welfare state had arrived sometime around 1970. Figure 6.1 shows that the Netherlands had

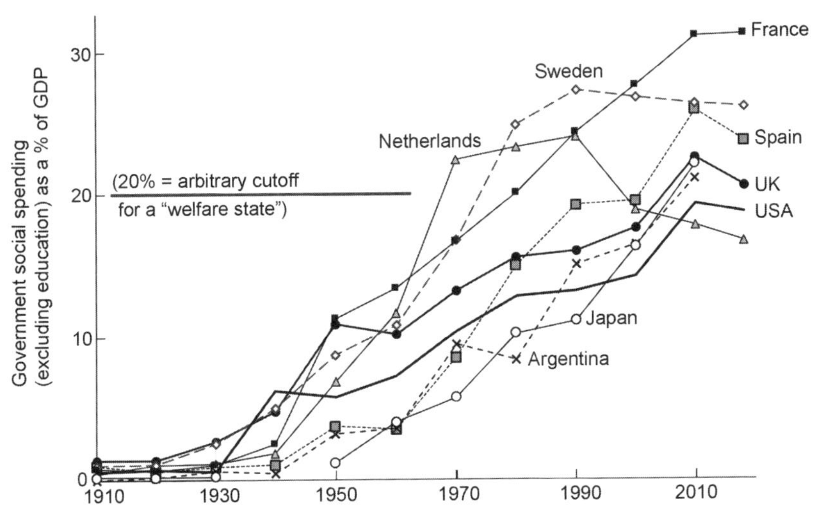

Figure 6.1. The share of GDP spent on social programs, selected countries for 1910–2018 (excluding public education expenditures)
Sources and notes: For 1910–1930 except Argentina and Spain, Lindert (1994).
For Argentina in 2009, see Lustig (2018). For Argentina 1910–2010, see the development of the time-series in Arroyo Abad and Lindert (2017).
For Spain 1910–1980, Espuelas (2013).
For the other six countries 1940 and 1950, see Hedberg, Karlsson, and Häggqvist (2018). For 1960 and 1970, see OECD (1985). This older OECD compilation, however, seems to exclude any government spending on housing. That exclusion can be sizeable, as it was for New Zealand 1951–1971 and Britain 1950–1970, at least (see Thomson 1996, pp. 45, 50). For Britain 1950–1970, I have replaced the older OECD estimates with those of Thomson (1996, p. 50), now including housing. I have not spliced the OECD's older 1960–1981 series to its newer series from 1980 on.
For 1980 on, except for Argentina: www.oecd-ilibrary.org/social-issues-migration-health/data/social-expenditure/aggregated-data_data-00166-en, accessed Dec. 19, 2019. Available annually, with the latest few years being preliminary estimates.

reached this social-spending commitment by 1970. The underlying annual numbers give these years for graduating into the welfare state: West Germany 1967; Netherlands 1968; Denmark 1971; Belgium 1972; Austria 1975; France, Norway, and Sweden 1976; Finland 1977; and Italy 1978. Spain and Portugal graduated later, partly because they did not achieve full democracies until the mid-1970s. The Netherlands is the clearest case of a country that has exited from the welfare-state ranks, perhaps permanently: After bobbing above and below the bar between 1990 and 2005, it has remained below the bar ever since.

Some other core OECD countries may be thought of as clearing the 20 percent bar only backwards, as if they were high-jumping by using the famous "Fosbury Flop." That is, they backed up over the bar only when recessions cut their GDP while their social-spending commitments were rightly maintained in such a slump. So it was for Britain, Ireland, Japan, and New Zealand during most of the Great Recession era, from 2008 to 2014. Greece's Fosbury Flop started sooner, in 2006, and has still not been reversed. Then in 2020, as already hinted, the coronavirus made a whole host of rich nations do the Fosbury Flop. Even the United States with its outpouring of emergency aid, suddenly crossed over the bar into what might be considered welfare-state status.

Somewhat unfairly, my holding the bar at 20 percent of national income denies welfare-state status to the United Kingdom until the recession year 2008, even though the term "welfare state" was earlier attached to the pioneering and durable British social programs instituted soon after the Beveridge Report back in the 1940s.[2] With this glaring exception, however, the 20 percent bar (still excluding public education) serves fairly well to divide the settings most usually described as "welfare states" from other settings.

Is the commitment to social spending still marching upward, or has it been reversed recently? A closer look at recent year-to-year movements since 1980, in Figure 6.2, summarizes the OECD's answer for thirty-six countries. The simple average seems to have a slight upward trend, one that combines upward ratcheting in the recessions of the early 1990s and 2008–2010 with stable shares in other years. The maximum shares show the same tendency even more dramatically. There was a conspicuous 1991–1995 jump and drop in the social-spending share in that maximum

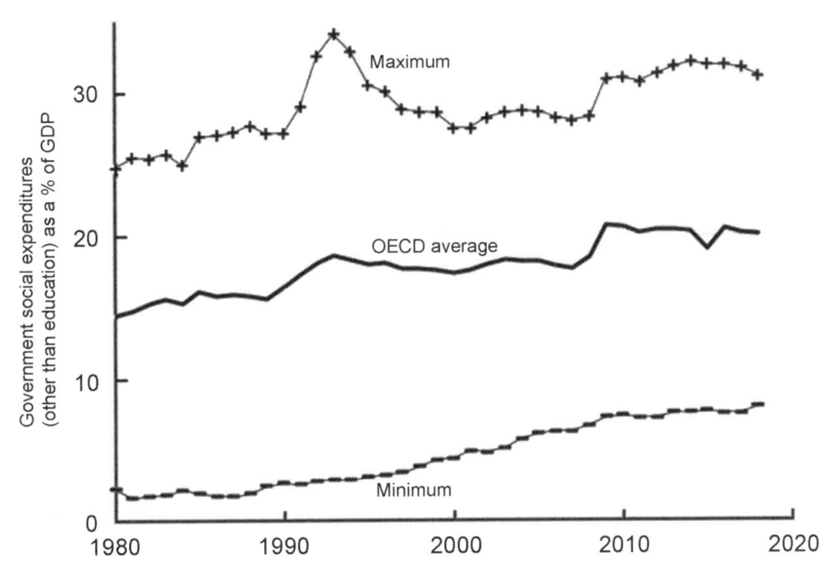

Figure 6.2. The share of GDP spent on social programs, thirty-six OECD countries, 1980–2018
Source: The OECD's series SOCEXP, available through OECD iLibrary.

country, which was Sweden until 1998. Then France took the lead, and showed a jump in the Great Recession of 2008. To judge trends correctly, one must factor out the business cycle, taking care to avoid comparing high social-spending shares during slumps with low shares at other times. Combining the long 1910–2018 view of Figure 6.1 with the close-up view since 1980 in Figure 6.2, we can see that social spending still claims a growing share of the world's product, but more slowly than it did before 1980.

DEMOCRATIZATION, WOMEN'S VOTES, AND OTHER CAUSES. What explains the upward march over more than a century, and why did different countries become welfare states while others did not? Recent research has made great strides toward explaining this increasingly global rise, despite a familiar statistical handicap. The handicap is that the unit of observation we are trying to explain is too big to fit into a statistical laboratory. We cannot explore and explain the behavior of whole governments by generating thousands of treatment cases and control cases, as is done in today's best experiments on large data sets.

There is no choice but to accept the few dozens of political units and several years of data that history has dealt us. As statisticians have repeatedly warned, causation cannot be inferred as reliably in this non-experimental real world.[3] That said, recent scholars have been able to extract what look like the most likely causal influences on social spending, both for public education and for the other types of social spending that are the main focus of this chapter.

The force that drove social spending more than any other is what some have called "democratization," though it could also be labeled "the spread of political voice" or "the spread of politically inclusive institutions" to fit some broader truths. Let us accept the shorter label "democratization" here. Its positive influence on the size of the social-spending budget seems well established in historical settings ranging from the mid-nineteenth century to the early twenty-first.[4] The democratization effect first emerged in samples restricted to the main developed OECD countries. It was upheld, however, even in global samples that included the few communist non-democracies that had large social budgets, such as Cuba or Poland. The implication for the great rise of social spending is clear enough: That rise is explained in large parts by the democratization of more and more countries.

Democratization did not just spread political voice down the socio-occupational ranks, from the elite to the masses. It also took the form of votes for women, legislated before 1920 in frontier lands of North America and Australasia, and arriving in all OECD democracies (except Switzerland) before World War II. Scholars have found that both the initial victory of female suffrage and the subsequent rise of women's share of active votes raised the share of national income devoted to tax-based social spending. The positive impact of women's voting power was especially evident in the public expenditures on education and health.[5]

Reinforcing the link between democratization and the rise in social spending was that frightening set of macro-shocks of the early twentieth century, in the form of world wars, revolutions, hyperinflation, and the Great Depression. Such shocks made more and more middle-income people look at those in need and think "that could be me." The effect has endured long after the shocks have passed.

When one seeks to explain why countries differed so greatly in the heights to which their social budgets rose, other forces besides democratization and macro-shocks need to be given their due. For example, social spending has remained lower in some of the world's most durable democracies, such as the United States, Canada, Australia, New Zealand, and postwar Japan.[6] Fortunately, recent research has spotlighted a few additional forces that seem capable of explaining the international differences as well as the trends over time.

Nations and localities differ in their willingness to spend taxes on social programs largely because some have greater ethnic fractionalization than others. Taxpayers tend to reject spending "our" tax money on safety nets and schooling for "them." Several writings have persuasively shown this negative effect, even though it is usually a "fixed-place effect," meaning that its statistical power could be due to something else that varies only by place. Despite the statistical drawback, it is hard to miss the fact that voters are less willing to pay taxes for social assistance and social insurance if their tax money is perceived as going to foreigners or persons of different race. Thus, whites in the southern United States have often avoided paying taxes for services benefiting blacks, Central American governments have spent less for large indigenous populations, and Imperial governments have denied spending tax revenues on services for their colonial populations. On the other side of the same coin, scholars have long noted that ethnic homogeneity helps to explain why smaller, more homogeneous countries, such as the Nordic countries, have less problem with paying taxes for education and other collective social spending.[7]

The aging of the population also helps to account for some of the growth of total social spending's share of GDP and for the international differences in that share. This would seem like simple common sense if all social spending were directed to the benefit of the elderly, in public pensions and long-term health care – at least up to a point. When the elderly were still a small share of the adult population, as in the international experience of 1880–1930, having an older population not only raised the share of pension spending in GDP but also raised the share taken by total social spending. However, by the 1962–1995 era, with older populations, the social-spending budgets of OECD countries showed signs of responding less positively to further population aging. While having an older population could still evoke a greater share of public pensions spending in overall GDP, the result was typically a lower pension spending per elderly person. That makes sense, since at some point, having still more elderly makes it harder to fit expansions of public pension spending into the national budget.[8]

THE SHIFTING MIX

Thus social spending accelerated after 1914, especially after 1945, largely in response to democratization.

Yet the money was increasingly targeted at different groups across the twentieth century. Social spending shifted away from public schools and from anti-poverty "welfare." Public schooling, despite rising support, received a declining share of what the taxpayers were asked to pay for. Both were eclipsed by the steady upward march of tax-based health care, and by a jump of government pension subsidies between 1910 and 1960. The classic anti-poverty "welfare" spending, on which so much attention has focused, remains a small share of social spending in all developed countries, despite the intensity of assertions about "soaring welfare costs" since the 1970s. These shifts in the mix of rising social expenditures since 1910 for thirteen OECD countries are revealed by Figure 6.3. Education's share dropped from 62 percent in 1910 to 27 percent by 1960. It stopped declining to 1970, at a baby-boom peak in schooling, and then declined very slightly, falling to 25 percent of all social spending by 2010. The share of anti-poverty programs, or "welfare," either stayed steady at 21 percent or declined from that, depending on how we handle the change in the data series at 1980. What increased are the expenditure shares of public pensions, between 1910 and 1960, and of public health spending over the whole hundred years.

One might look at Figure 6.3 and think of a simple explanation: "Well, of course, we would naturally expect that schooling's share would fall, and that pensions and health care would take a rising share, just because people have fewer children and we are living more of our lives in retirement and in declining health."

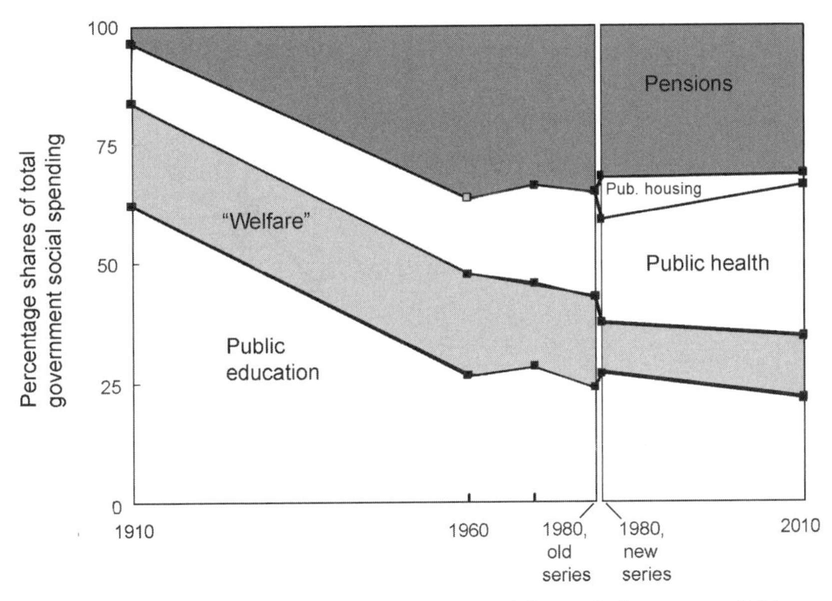

Figure 6.3. Types of social expenditures as shares of the total, the average of thirteen OECD countries, 1910–2010

Sources and notes to Figure 6.3 and Figure 6.4: The sources are the same as those to Figure 6.1, except that the age-group shares in Figure 6.4 come from Mitchell (1998a, 1998b, 1998c) for 1910, and from United Nations (2015) for later years.

The thirteen countries are Australia, Canada, France, Germany, Italy, Japan, Netherlands, New Zealand, Norway, Spain, Sweden, United Kingdom, and USA.

The weight given to each country is its real gross national expenditures at international prices (rgdpe in the Penn World Tables) for the year 1960.

The numbers for public housing before the 1980 new series were too close to zero to show up on the graph.

"Welfare" is the sum of family assistance and labour-market assistance. In the new OECD series for 1980–2010, pensions are the sum of all "elderly" benefits plus survivor benefits.

For the latest shares of GDP spent by general government or central government on the three categories public health, social security, and public education, see http://data.imf.org/, expenditure by function of government (COFOG series).

Yet something else has also happened in these thirteen leading countries, as revealed by Figure 6.4 and Table 6.1. Their taxpayers are paying a higher share of income per capita on public pensions *per elderly person* – and this support ratio for the elderly rose even faster than the support for public education per child of school age all the way from 1910 to at least 1980. It is as though societies had come to the conclusion that the kind of insurance they needed most was not

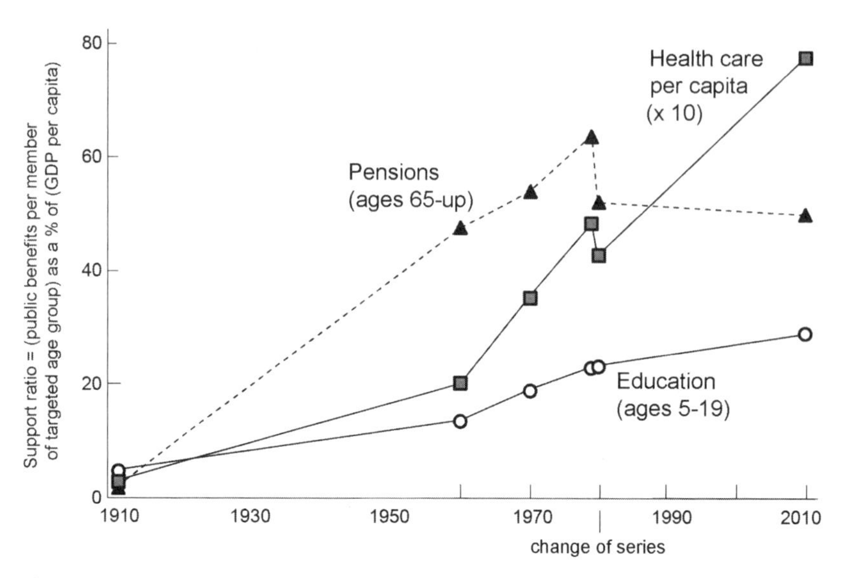

Figure 6.4. Support ratios for target groups, by type of social expenditures, the average of thirteen OECD countries, 1910–2010

insurance against children's having low earning power in later life, or anti-poverty insurance, but rather insurance that the elderly would not run out of money in their retirement years. A tilt toward the elderly might also underlie the upward march of support for public health, given that medical expenses are greatest, and may have risen fastest, for the elderly. We will see in Chapter 12 that these countries' generosity of support for public pensions peaked a little later than 1980, though in all cases it peaked before the year 2000.

Why the big shifts in social mission? Let us start with health, for which the upward march has persisted even to this day.

THE LONG MARCH TOWARD PUBLIC HEALTH INSURANCE

Government health insurance, and often government health-care provision, arrived only in the twentieth and twenty-first centuries mainly because this is when dramatic medical advances occurred, bringing what Angus Deaton (2015) has called *The Great Escape* from morbidity and mortality.

TABLE 6.1. *Public education support versus public pension support, thirteen countries in 1910 and in 2010*

Support ratios = (expenditures for this age group, per person in the age group) (GDP per capita, total population)

	In the year 1910		In the year 2010	
	For school age 5–19	For the over-65s	For school age 5–19	For the over-65s
Australia	0.03	0.14	0.30	0.33
Canada	0.06	0	0.31	0.30
France	0.04	0.03	0.32	0.80
Germany	0.07	0.02	0.35	0.51
Italy	0.02	0	0.32	0.75
Japan	0.01	0	0.28	0.51
Netherlands	0.06	0	0.33	0.38
New Zealand	0.07	0	0.35	0.35
Norway	0.02	0.01	0.38	0.75
Spain	0.01	0.004	0.36	0.61
Sweden	0.07	0	0.54	0.52
United Kingdom	0.04	0.07	0.35	0.40
USA	0.05	0	0.27	0.51

Sources and notes: For 1910, the public old-age expenditure shares of GDP come from Lindert (1994) and most of the education expenditure shares are from Lindert (2004, vol. II, Appendix C). An exception is Japan's public education share for 1910, kindly supplied by Yuzuru Kumon.

The old-age and survivor spending shares in 2010 are from the OECD's current SOCEXP series at the OECD iLibrary, and the public education expenditure shares are from UNESCO.

The age-group shares used here and in Figure 6.4 come from Mitchell (1998a, 1998b, 1998c) for 1910, and from United Nations (2015) for later years.

Starting back in the mid-nineteenth century, gains in health were the result of public investments in sanitation and vaccination, not the usual social spending related to physician services and hospital care today. An understanding that cholera and typhoid spread through polluted water came in the 1850s. Shortly afterwards, scientists confirmed that bacterial and viral pathogens caused diseases. Vaccines to prevent infectious diseases arrived in the 1890s. Then, public health campaigns became commonplace in the United Kingdom and United States, where people were taught the importance of washing hands and disinfecting water, among other lifestyle changes, to prevent the spread of disease. State and local governments played a critical role by promoting health campaigns, cleaning the water supply, and building sewage facilities.[9]

Then in the twentieth century, personal medical care became something worth buying – and something very expensive – and the pressure to tap taxes for public health has mounted. It might seem paradoxical that improvements on the supply side should raise expenditures: Shouldn't supply improvements lower price, and thus lower expenditures if the demand is inelastic? The answer is that improvements in quality, plus rising incomes, raised the average quality of medical care more than the quantity. It is not that people go to the doctor or the hospital so many more times a year than people did a hundred years ago. Rather, high-quality and high-price health services are much more available, and people demand them more.

Three other forces also played major roles in the rise of public health spending. One was, again, that frightening set of macro-shocks of the early twentieth century, in the form of world wars, revolutions, hyperinflation, and the Great Depression. A second force was longer life for seniors, the part of the population having the greatest annual health-care expenditures. The third force was that women gained the right to vote, which quickly raised pressure on local governments to fund health-care services. This has been demonstrated persuasively for the United States, where women got the vote in many states between 1869 and 1920, before getting it nationwide (Miller 2008; Kose, Kuka, and Shenhav 2018). Female suffrage thus shifted legislators' votes toward funding public health, raised investments in sanitary infrastructure, and saved children's lives.

Probably many of those states turned to greater spending on health care for the political reason made explicit at the federal level by members of Congress right after the Nineteenth Amendment to the Constitution was passed in 1920. Congress promptly appropriated new health-care funds in the Promotion of the Welfare and Hygiene of Maternity and Infancy Act (Sheppard–Towner Act) of 1921, out of a (temporary) "fear of being punished at the polls by American women, not conviction of the bill's necessity." As Senator Kenyon (R-IA) admitted to a reporter from the *Ladies Home Journal*, "if the members of Congress could have voted on the measure in their cloak rooms, it would have been killed as emphatically as it was finally passed out in the open under the pressure of the Joint Congressional Committee of Women."[10]

Note that this listing of forces promoting public health-care spending excludes overall "democratization," the most powerful force in raising the total social-spending budget over time – even though female suffrage had a strong effect on health-care spending. Ben Ansell and David Samuels (2014, pp. 157–164) have looked inside the effect on social spending to explore which kinds of (non-education) social spending were promoted by democratization between 1880 and 1930, and Ansell (2010, pp. 45–59) ran similar tests for the determinants of public education spending for 110 countries between 1960 and 2000. Their tests show that health-care spending was not significantly enhanced by democratization, whereas the categories most promoted by democratization were education and anti-poverty "welfare" spending (family assistance and unemployment compensation). The effects of democratization on public pensions and public housing fell in between – positive, yet not as strong as the effects on education and welfare. Regarding health care, one should conclude that their results seem plausible enough for the effects of the overall extension of voting rights to lower social classes, yet lacked the right samples for revealing the positive effects of votes for women on health care.

MISSION SHIFT TOWARD PUBLIC SUPPORT FOR THE ELDERLY

Why have public pensions also marched upward, by every measure, over the last hundred years, and is there any prospect that the march will stop?

THE PRIME SUSPECT: GRAY POWER. We can begin with the likely leading role of two forces that delivered "gray-power," forces that also raised the demand for tax-based health care and health insurance in the twentieth century. One was that improvement in life expectancy, which allowed for longer life past work, thus increasing the risk of longer income dependency. The other was, again, that votes were given to women, who were both the majority of the elderly population and the majority of its caregivers.

The rise of gray power probably goes a long way toward explaining the great 1910–1980 rise in generosity of public support for the elderly. That makes sense. As the share of the elderly in the population keeps rising, so does the share having a direct self-interest in fiscal favors for the elderly. Improved survival also raises the awareness of middle-aged voters that they too will soon face a longer stretch of old age and retirement, raising their sympathy for support from younger taxpayers. International data for 1950–1999 confirm a positive influence of a higher elderly share of the population on total social spending other than education (Ansell and Samuels 2014, pp. 164–169).

The positive effect of aging on the public pension budget has its limits, however. Logically, the greater the share of elderly in the adult population, the costlier it is to raise their pension benefits by any given percentage – and the more thinly their pension benefits must be spread across the elderly population. Predicted result: Beyond some point, a greater elderly share of the population means stronger opposition to raising benefits, and weaker support for it. So at some point, the upward curve relating the rising elderly share to generous pension support has to turn back downward. Past political behavior seems to show these limits at least to some extent in the already-aged OECD countries since the 1990s.[11] When has, or will, that turning point come for the leading economies? Again, there seems to have been such a turning point between 1980 and 2000, and Chapter 12 will divide countries greatly threatened by further aging from those hardly threatened.

ALSO AT WORK: THE DECLINE OF FAMILY SUPPORT FOR THE ELDERLY. Beyond gray-power politics, however, another basic economic trend has been at work since the early twentieth century, possibly raising the demand for government pensions. There has been a quiet global decline in intra-family, or intra-household, transfers to the elderly. This could have made the political process turn toward subsidizing the elderly – and/or the causation could have run in the other direction: Independent political shifts toward generous public pensions could have freed up younger adults from the burden of supporting oldsters. The greatest likelihood is that the political and home-economic developments promoted each other.

From the household side, we can now see at least three home-economic changes that would have reduced the support for the elderly from younger adults within the same family or household as the economy develops. First, to keep something obvious in view: Improved survival means that the *elderly population grows as a share of all adults.* Thus there are more over-65s, more retirees, per adult under 65, and their consumption needs to be supported one way or another.

Second, *co-residence has declined* over the last hundred years. Elderly persons no longer live in the same households as their young children nearly as much as their counterparts did a hundred years ago. While this trend has continued longest in the most developed countries, it has in fact occurred globally, even in societies where official pronouncements kept stressing the obligation of younger adults to care for their parents. This long trend is conveniently illustrated in Figure 6.5's mapping of the history of the kinds of living arrangements for the elderly in the United States since 1850. Back in 1910, over a third of those over 65 lived with their

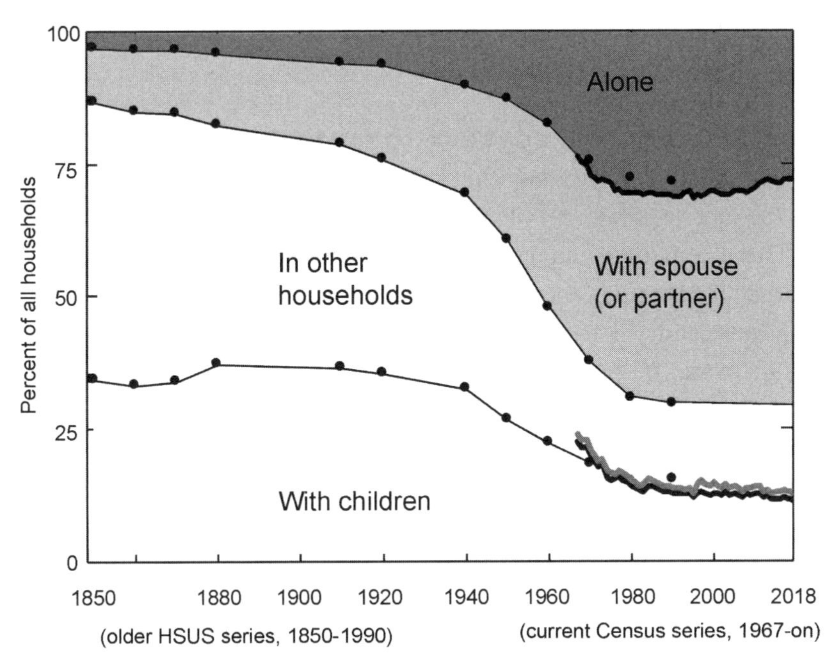

Figure 6.5. Where elderly Americans have lived since 1850
Sources and notes: Carter et al. (2006, vol. I), series Ae245–319; and US Census Bureau, Current Population Survey, Annual Social and Economic Supplement, 1967 to present, www.census.gov/data/tables/time-series/demo/families/adults.html.

For the Census series since 1967, the lowest line refers to those living with children, and the slightly higher line refers to those living in arrangements "beyond spouse."

children. By 2008–2018, this share has come to rest below one eighth. Most of this drop occurred between 1940 and 1980. Given that the adult generations are living separately, there is less likelihood that the older generation is being cared for, or paid for, by their adult children.

The third relevant trend is that *younger adult women are working* outside the home, especially since the early 1960s. This trend continues: Among the forty-two countries for which the OECD has reliable numbers, the labor-force participation of women in the 15–64 age range rose from 55 percent in the year 2000 to 60 percent in 2017.[12] The new career demands on their time undermined their ability, and their traditional willingness, to care for elderly parents. In this respect, the economics of caring for elderly dependents is analogous to the economics of having children: For the young adult, it is time-intensive, not commodity-intensive, and its relative cost rises with real wage rates. Meanwhile, males' labor-force participation has not changed much, nor have young adult males shifted toward caring for the elderly.

WHO PAYS FOR THE ELDERLY TODAY? With these trends having occurred in recent decades, where do we stand in terms of who is paying for the elderly today, and whether somebody will abandon them?

There are three main resources that support the elderly, or the retired: Their own accumulated resources, benefits paid by the general taxpayers, and aid from younger adults in the same household. The resources can be commodities (purchased goods and services), or they can be hours of time given. And the resources can flow in either direction between the generations. While we immediately think of purchases on behalf of the elderly and hours of care given to the elderly, the elderly can be net givers of money and time to the younger generations within the same household, such as free housing or grandparents' child care.

How do the net flows between the elderly and others look in today's world? For the flows of commodities, though not yet including care-time flows, the National Transfer Accounts (NTA) Project, led by Ronald D. Lee and Andrew Mason, has estimated the net flows for over twenty populations around the start of the twenty-first century.[13] Today's trading of money between adult generations can be summarized with the help of

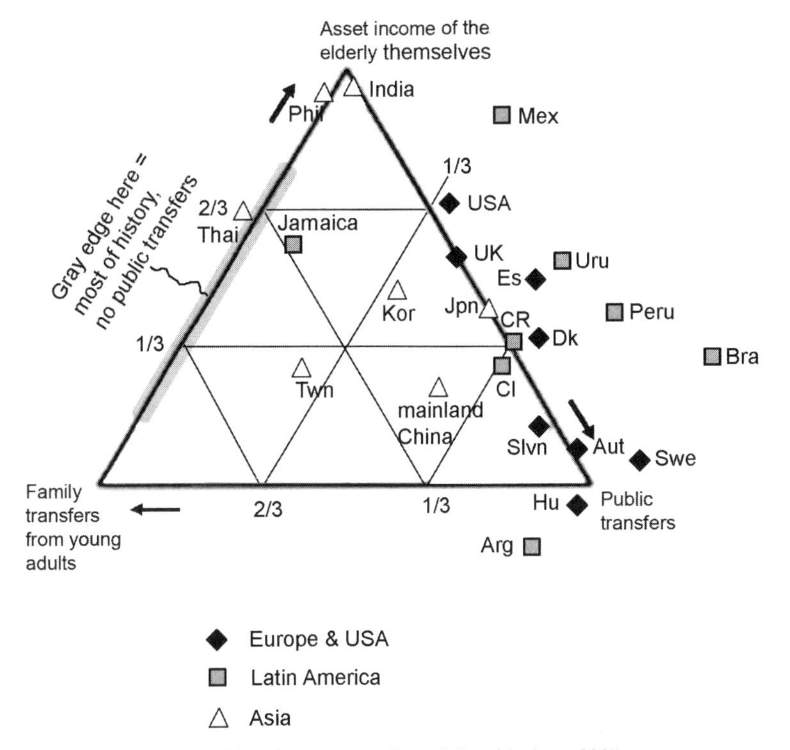

Figure 6.6. Who paid for the consumption of the elderly, c. 2005
Source and notes: The source is Ronald D. Lee (2016), reporting results from the National Transfer Accounts project.

As noted in the text, these estimates account for the consumption of goods and services purchased by the elderly, but not for the inter-generational flow of time services within the household.

the NTA team's triangle diagram in Figure 6.6 for the geometrically inclined – and, for the rest of us, summarized in words.

To put today's three-way choices in perspective, let us begin by recalling that until one hundred years ago, the elderly and retired received only meager resources from government. What they could consume had to come either from their own assets or from the younger adults in the same household. In Figure 6.6, the situation for millennia was in the gray area along the upper-left side of the triangle, i.e. where government support was zero.

The historic trends toward having the elderly live by themselves and having younger adults increasingly involved in their paid work have pulled these twenty-plus populations away from reliance of older adults on their children or other young adults within the same households – that is, away from the lower left corner, at which the elderly would have been taken care of within the home. In the early twenty-first century, in every population, less than half of the commodity value transferred to the elderly comes from the rest of the family or household. In fact, for most populations, the net intra-family transfer to the elderly is near zero or even negative. The only populations (other than Jamaica) for which it is still noticeably positive are those in East Asia, represented in the NTA study by mainland China, Taiwan, Thailand, and Korea.

Even in these East Asian settings, the net amount of help from the younger adult generation is likely to shrink toward zero, just as it already has done in Japan and in other regions. Why? Again, because of those long and steady trends that have accompanied economic development in the West. Consider what is already happening to the rate of co-residency between the two adult generations in China. In China's living arrangements for the elderly, something has to give, and soon. The official UN (2015) median forecasts say that over the thirty years between 2020 and 2050, China's population over the age of 65 will grow by more than 119 percent, i.e. *more than double*, while its population in the labor-force age range of 18–64 will *shrink* by 20 percent. China's inter-generational living arrangements cannot stay the same. The elderly will probably have to gravitate toward group facilities, to take advantages of economies of scale, in the face of a dwindling labor force of caregivers. At the same time, there will be abundant cases in which a grandmother takes care of a grandchild in their shared lodging, while the young adult couple live separately near their workplaces.[14]

So the developmental tendency in home economics has already pushed populations away from the lower left corner of the triangle, and the trend is likely to continue. Figure 6.6 also shows today's strong reliance of the elderly on government in the developed countries and in Latin America. For those Latin American countries, it also shows something that clashes with our usual intuition: The elderly are actually paying for some consumption by the younger members of the same households. Since they are receiving net transfers from government, it would appear that the elderly of Mexico, Uruguay, Peru, and Brazil are intermediaries, recycling money from taxpayers back to the taxpayers within their own households. Indeed, as we shall see again in Chapters 7 and 12, the Latin American recycling is concentrated in the upper-income ranks. Those who had careers in government and the higher-paid private formal sectors are so well paid in pensions that their incomes imply, in the NTA framework, that they are sharing these generous pensions with the younger members of their own households.

Thus, it is time to revise the traditional story of how younger adults within a family have accepted the responsibility for taking care of their aging parents. If that had remained the main source of support for the elderly, delivering, say, 80 percent of the consumption of the elderly, then taxpayers would never have shouldered more than 20 percent of the burden of elderly people's consumption. And yet much more than 20 percent of the burden was typically shifted to government. Later chapters will dig into country experiences with public pension spending, and its global future prospects.

An important feature of this set of home-economics forces in the rise of public spending on health and pensions is its broad geographic reach. Taxpayers were not called upon to pay more just because of idiosyncratic national political histories. The demand-side sources of the rise in public health and pension spending, like that rise itself, were felt by all of the two dozen richer countries. It was on the supply side of the political market for social spending that these countries differed, mainly because they differed in those two forces we encountered in Chapter 4's discussion of education: fiscal capacity plus political voice from below. These same two forces remain central to any explanation of today's wide gaps in social spending.

CHAPTER 7

Is the Rest of the World Following a Different Path?

IS THERE GOOD REASON TO BELIEVE THAT FIFTY YEARS FROM now the rest of the world will have as many welfare states as Western Europe has had these last fifty years? Perhaps the growth of social-spending budgets will spread around the world through some imitative learning about best practices.[1] Perhaps large social budgets will be delivered around the world by the spread of the same causal forces we noted in earlier chapters, such as democratization and prosperity. Or perhaps, on the contrary, we should take historians' warning that every region follows its own permanently unique path. Maybe we should recognize that Western Europe's history will never be replicated, and no other region is every likely to tax and spend so heavily for social programs. Which is it?

DEVELOPING COUNTRIES VERSUS THE LEADERS' HISTORY

Any guesses about future social spending outside of the North Atlantic and Australasia can be well educated by comparing the path that these leaders followed in the deeper past with the more recent social spending in the rest of the world. One mechanism for comparing today's social-spending behavior in, say, East Asia or Latin America with the leaders' more distant past is to hold constant a variable that is likely to shape social spending in the future. The best candidate for such a shaping variable is real GDP per capita, since we know that its many correlates (including democracy) should help to raise social spending.

So insights can be gained by asking: Is social spending in East Asia or Latin America lower, or the same, or higher than what the Swedes or

French or Americans were spending back when they had the same real GDP per capita? Granted, there are serious problems of comparing apples with oranges when comparing real purchasing powers over long reaches of time and space. Still, the comparison reveals contrasts that are striking enough to withstand a lot of error – say, even an error of 30 percent in either direction – in matching a long-past GDP per capita with today's GDP per capita. Figures 7.1 and 7.2 deliver the contrasts, first for the non-education part of public social spending and then, drawing on different sources, for public education.

The shares of GDP that governments around the globe devoted to non-education social spending in 2010 do not look lower than the share of GDP that the United States or Japan spent at similar levels in the past. Of the seventy countries shown in Figure 7.1's snapshot of non-education social spending for 2010, only five Asian countries (Azerbaijan, Thailand, Malaysia, Korea, and Singapore) are spending a lower share of GDP on non-education social programs than the United States or Japan spent at the same levels of real average income. The remaining countries in 2010 gave out greater social transfers than the Americans or Japanese had done earlier, at the same income levels. Far from showing that Western Europe was a uniquely high spender, Figure 7.1 reveals that many countries around the world seem to be following a path like that followed by Sweden at comparable income levels in earlier times, before Sweden emerged as a leading welfare state. And a few, such as South Africa, Brazil, and Hungary, are well above Sweden's historical spending on such social transfers, for given income levels. Even allowing for a wide margin of error in how past levels of GDP per person compare with those of today, it is clearly *not* the case that the rest of the world is reluctant to pay for as much social spending as were the leading countries back in the day.

Similarly striking contrasts will emerge when we combine a 2010 snapshot of public education spending with the video showing the past movements of the same kind of spending in leading countries in the past. To get the contrast right, though, we must first choose a measure featuring education spending per child of school age. Had we just compared the present and past shares of GDP spent on public education, the picture would have been badly distorted by countries' differing demography.

Had we missed this point, we might have announced that in 2010 much higher shares of GDP were spent on public education in Bolivia under Morales (7.6 percent), in Venezuela under Hugo Chavez (6.9 percent), and in Tunisia (6.2 percent) than in stingy Britain (5.6 percent). The trap here was set by the fact that the first three countries had much

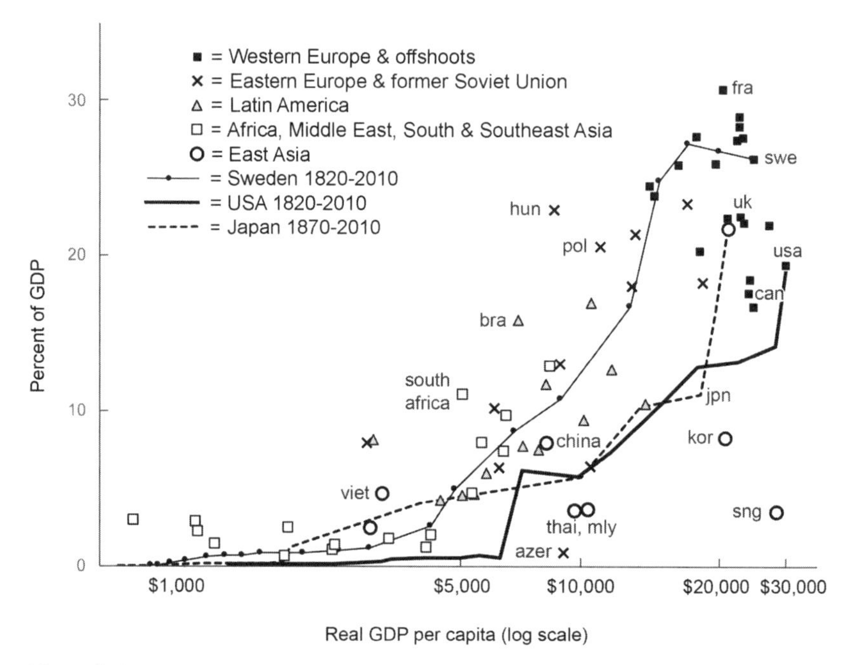

Figure 7.1. Public social spending c. 2010 in seventy countries, compared with its earlier movements in three leading countries (excluding public education expenditures)

Sources and notes to Figures 7.1 and 7.2: In Figure 7.2, the overlapping dots K, J = Korea, Japan.

For public social spending (other than public education spending) as a share of GDP, see the sources to Appendix A.

Real GDP per capita is measured in 1990 international dollars, as presented at the Clio-Infra internet site.

For public education spending as a share of GDP in 2010, all countries, see UNESCO (http://stats.uis.unesco.org/unesco/ReportFolders/ReportFolders.aspx.)

For public education as a share of GDP in France, 1820–1960, see Carry (1999); then the 1970–2010 numbers for France are from UNESCO.

For public education as a share of GDP in the United States, 1880, 1900, 1910, and 1930, see Lindert (2004, vol. II, Appendix C); for 1960-on, see UNESCO.

In Figure 7.2, the shares of total population that are in the 5–19 school-age range are based on the Brian Mitchell *International Historical Statistics* volumes for years before 1950, and on United Nations (2015) for 1950 and later. The age shares for prewar France actually refer to 1851, 1861, 1872, 1881, . . ., 1911.

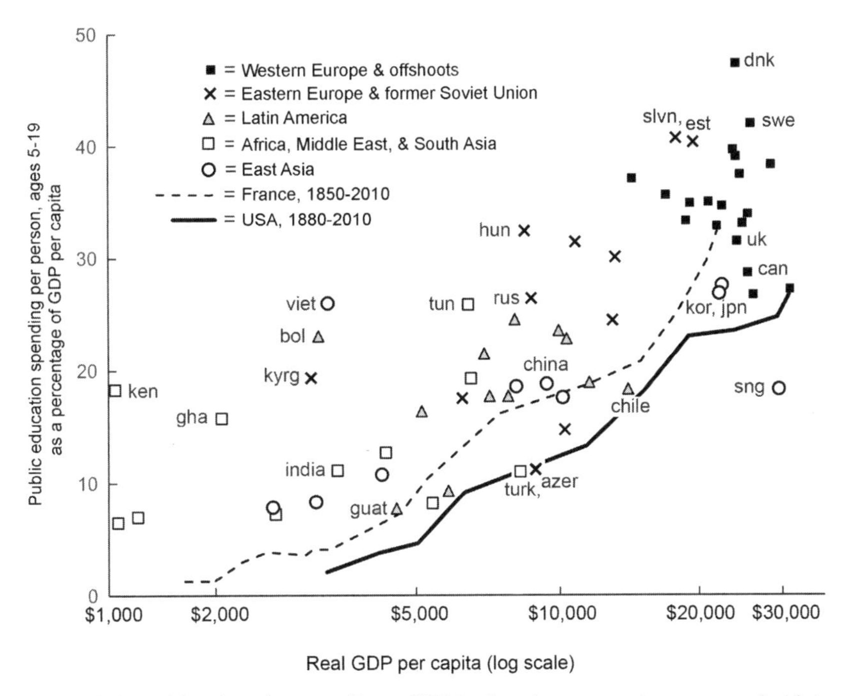

Figure 7.2. Public education spending c. 2010 in sixty-three countries, compared with its earlier movements in two leading countries

younger populations, with much greater shares in the 5- to 19-year-old school-age range: 33 percent in Bolivia, 29 percent in Venezuela, and 24 percent in Tunisia, versus only 18 percent in Britain. The measure we should prefer is a support ratio: (public education spending per child of ages 5–19) divided by (GDP per capita) in the same year. Figure 7.2 shows the global differences that emerge when we measure countries' commitments to public education in this way.

Contrasting public education support diagonally across time and space yields an even more striking result than what Figure 7.1 revealed for other social expenditures. Out of sixty-three countries, only one seems to have supported education less in 2010 than did the United States at a similar income level. That country is Singapore, and its accounting procedures may have misstated the government's contributions, for reasons we will note in Chapter 13. Aside from Singapore, only two other countries – Azerbaijan and Turkey, both on the border of Asia and Europe – spent as small a share of GDP on the average school-age child as did America at the same income level in earlier years. All other countries spent more in 2010 than American governments did in earlier history, and most spent more than even France, according to Figure 7.2. The suggested contrast is strong, even if it requires holding constant some GDP measures from very different settings: *In the early twenty-first century, countries all over the world committed more resources to educating the average school-age child than did the world's education leaders in the late nineteenth century, at similar income levels.* This finding, based on expenditures, reinforces an impression that one would have gathered from Chapter 5's mapping of the convergence in education attainments since about the 1960s. All over the world, the commitment of taxpayer support to education is accelerating much faster than it did in the earlier history of the leading countries.[2] Even throughout low-spending Africa, the Middle East, and Asia – aside from Singapore, that is – the levels of education support in 2010 were up to the standards set by history's leaders in earlier times. It is as though the whole world had learned a history lesson summarized in Chapters 4 and 5: Tax-based public support is a key to the advancement in education and earning power.

TOP-HEAVY PENSIONS FOR THE WELL-OFF

If today's social expenditures look at least as high as those of the historical leaders, both for public education (Figure 7.2) and for other social expenditures (Figure 7.1), one might gather that the whole world is heading toward high social-spending budgets, possibly exceeding 20 percent of GDP in the near future, along with income growth. High budgets, yes, but not always progressive welfare states of the sort that would promote both equality and economic growth. [3]

THE GLOBAL SNAPSHOT ALBUM, C. 2010. Social priorities come into focus when we contrast 106 countries' support ratios for different age groups, again around the year 2010, in Table 7.1 and Figure 7.3. To spot and judge their priorities in Figure 7.3, let us apply this very crude two-step visual guide: (1) Up is good for growth and equality, given the positive externalities from subsidizing education; and (2) the further

TABLE 7.1. *Public pensions versus public education spending, 106 countries, c. 2010*

	Public spending as a percentage of GDP		Support ratios	
	Education	Pensions	Educ. Spending per person 5-19 / GDP per 18-64	Pension spending per person 65-up, / GDP per 18-64
Argentina	5.0	7.4	11.6	41.7
Armenia ('11)	3.1	4.2	9.8	26.1
Australia	5.6	4.5	18.4	21.0
Austria	5.7	13.6	22.7	49.1
Azerbaijan ('07)	2.5	3.8	5.6	37.5
Bangladesh ('06)	2.1	0.3	3.5	3.8
Belarus ('08)	4.8	10.2	19.7	46.2
Belgium	6.4	9.9	27.2	47.7
Belize ('09)	6.1	0.9	9.3	13.1
Bhutan ('08)	4.8	0.0	8.5	0.0
Bolivia ('09)	8.1	1.5	12.9	13.6
Botswana ('09)	9.6	1.3	16.6	21.7
Brazil	5.6	6.2	13.6	58.4
Bulgaria ('08)	4.2	8.5	18.8	31.0
Burkina Faso ('09)	3.9	1.3	4.5	23.3
Burundi ('06)	3.6	0.7	4.0	11.6
Cameroon ('05)	2.9	0.4	3.4	5.5
Canada	5.4	4.3	20.1	19.9
Cent Afric Rep ('04)	1.6	0.8	2.1	9.7
Chile	4.2	3.4	11.5	22.5
China ('06)	2.9	2.5	8.3	22.0
Colombia	4.8	3.1	11.1	33.3
Costa Rica ('09)	6.0	2.8	14.3	24.1
Côte d'Ivoire ('06)	4.0	0.7	5.0	11.3
Croatia ('09)	4.4	10.0	17.2	36.6
Czechia	4.1	9.0	18.6	39.1
Denmark	8.6	9.5	28.6	35.0
Dom Rep ('09)	2.0	0.7	3.6	6.6
Ecuador	4.5	1.8	8.6	16.9
Egypt ('04)	4.7	4.1	7.6	44.0
El Salvador	3.5	1.7	7.0	12.9
Estonia	5.5	8.1	23.3	29.6
Ethiopia	5.5	0.5	5.1	6.5
Finland	6.5	10.9	23.8	39.9
France	5.7	13.6	19.0	48.7
Gambia ('03)	1.4	0.1	1.7	1.7
Georgia ('04)	2.9	3.0	7.9	12.8
Germany	4.9	10.6	21.1	32.4
Ghana	7.9	1.3	11.7	19.5
Greece	4.0	11.6	16.0	39.6

TABLE 7.1. *(continued)*

	Public spending as a percentage of GDP		Support ratios	
	Education	Pensions	Educ. Spending per person 5–19 / GDP per 18–64	Pension spending per person 65-up, / GDP per 18–64
Guatemala ('11)	2.9	0.3	4.0	3.3
Guyana	3.6	0.1	5.7	1.3
Hungary	4.8	10.2	19.7	39.7
India	3.3	0.2	6.2	2.6
Indonesia	2.8	1.0	6.1	12.3
Iran	3.5	2.2	9.8	29.1
Ireland	6.0	5.5	20.7	31.6
Israel	5.5	3.8	12.8	20.9
Italy	4.4	15.4	19.3	47.3
Jamaica ('04)	3.9	0.7	7.0	4.8
Japan	3.6	10.0	16.1	26.5
Jordan	3.2	4.0	5.1	57.1
Kazakhstan ('09)	3.1	2.7	8.1	24.5
Kenya ('03)	6.5	1.1	7.8	18.3
Korea, Rep.	4.8	2.1	17.4	13.3
Kuwait ('07)	3.8	2.7	10.9	88.0
Kyrgyzstan	5.8	2.7	11.5	35.4
Latvia	5.1	9.4	21.5	32.8
Lithuania	5.3	7.9	19.4	28.5
Malaysia ('09)	6.0	2.0	12.4	25.3
Maldives ('06)	4.6	0.2	7.2	2.4
Mali	3.3	1.6	3.8	25.7
Malta	6.5	9.0	22.5	35.7
Mauritania ('03)	3.1	0.6	4.1	9.2
Mauritius ('07)	3.2	2.9	8.4	27.0
Mexico	5.2	1.8	19.4	28.5
Mongolia ('09)	5.1	4.4	11.6	72.2
Mozambique ('06)	4.3	0.7	5.1	9.8
Namibia ('04)	6.3	1.3	8.5	19.5
Nepal ('06)	3.6	0.2	4.9	2.2
Netherlands	5.5	5.9	19.5	24.1
New Zealand	7.0	4.6	21.0	21.9
Niger ('06)	3.3	0.7	3.7	12.0
Norway	6.7	7.1	21.9	29.6
Pakistan ('09)	2.6	1.0	3.9	12.1
Paraguay ('14)	3.6	1.7	6.6	16.2
Peru	2.9	2.5	5.6	23.9
Philippines ('09)	2.7	1.1	4.4	14.8
Poland	5.1	10.0	21.8	50.2
Portugal	5.4	12.1	21.7	40.7
Romania ('09)	4.0	8.3	15.8	34.4

TABLE 7.1. *(continued)*

	Public spending as a percentage of GDP		Support ratios	
	Education	Pensions	Educ. Spending per person 5-19 / GDP per 18-64	Pension spending per person 65-up, / GDP per 18-64
Russia	3.9	8.2	17.4	43.1
Senegal ('06)	3.8	1.4	4.5	20.4
Serbia	4.3	14.0	15.0	59.1
Seychelles ('06)	4.8	2.9	12.5	26.0
Singapore ('09)	3.5	1.2	12.5	9.6
Slovakia	4.1	7.3	16.8	40.4
Slovenia	5.6	11.2	26.3	44.6
South Africa	5.7	1.0	8.9	11.6
Spain	4.8	10.5	22.4	40.0
Sri Lanka ('09)	2.1	1.9	5.2	16.9
Sweden	6.6	9.5	23.2	32.0
Switzerland	4.9	6.4	19.9	24.4
Syria ('04)	5.4	1.3	7.4	19.4
Tanzania ('11)	4.6	2.3	5.5	33.6
Thailand	3.9	1.5	12.5	11.9
Togo ('03)	3.3	0.8	4.1	13.3
Tunisia	6.3	8.7	16.6	74.4
Turkey ('12)	4.4	8.1	10.3	68.7
Uganda ('03)	5.0	0.3	5.1	4.7
UK	5.7	6.5	20.0	25.1
USA	5.4	6.7	16.8	32.2
Uruguay	4.0	8.8	10.1	37.1
Venezuela	6.3	5.0	12.9	53.7
Vietnam	5.1	2.7	12.2	26.0
Zambia ('08)	1.1	1.4	1.2	21.1

Sources and notes to Table 7.1, Figure 7.3, and Table 12.2: Unless otherwise noted, the countries' data refer to the year 2010.

The public spending on (all levels of) education as a percentage of GDP comes from UNESCO's uis internet database, latest data posted as of December 2019, except for China (2006), which was documented in OECD (2016). As far as can be discerned, UNESCO's sources are all reporting expenditures for general government, i.e. all levels, and not just central government. In all cases, the shares of total population in the school-age age group (ages 5–19), the adult working-age group (18–64), and the elderly (65 and up) are taken from United Nations (2015).

For countries covered in the OECD data set on social expenditures, the "pension" spending shares of GDP are the totals of the government's gross "old age" expenditures plus the smaller amount of its "survivor" expenditures. These are divided by the OECD's own estimates of GDP in current prices.

For countries not covered by the OECD, the pension expenditures as shares of GDP came from five other sources:

(1) The latest estimates from the Commitment to Equity Project's database, explained by Lustig (2018), were used in the following cases: Argentina (2012), Armenia (2011),

TABLE 7.1 *(continued)*

Colombia (2010, 2014), Costa Rica (2014), Dominican Republic (2013), Ecuador (2011), El Salvador (2011), Ethiopia (2010), Guatemala (2011), Iran (2011), Paraguay (2014), Russia (2010), Sri Lanka (2009), Tanzania (2011), Tunisia (2010), and Venezuela (2013).

(2) The Asian Development Bank (2013, and its linked technical reports) provided the shares of pension in GDP used for India (2009), Malaysia (2009), Pakistan (2009), Singapore (2009), Thailand (2009), and Vietnam (2009).

(3) Arroyo Abad and Lindert (2017) supplied the shares of pensions in GDP for Peru (2010).

(4) World Bank (2011, p. 10, Table 3) for Mongolia (2009).

(5) Pallares-Miralles, Romero, and Whitehouse (2012) are the providers of the pension shares of GDP for all other countries.

your country's dot lies down and to the right, the more it has traded away growth and equality to subsidize the current elderly generation. Up is good, in the rough sense that no leading country's young adults have clearly overinvested in children's education, so countries investing less would probably gain by emulating those higher up in Figure 7.3. The case against countries whose governments place them relatively to the southeast (down and the right) in Figure 7.3 is also useful, though crude. Money spent on supporting the elderly could have been invested in the young (moving up and to the left), with better implications for growth and equality in the future. We know of no "best" slope between support for the young and support for the elderly, even though slopes of 1.0 and 0.4 are drawn here to ease visual contrasts. For now, let the spotlight shine only on those with extreme tendencies, without any attempt to define a "best" practice.

Using the slope 0.4 cutoff here as the edge of the pension-oriented area spotlights low education support and high pensions in the broad global South: Latin American countries, the Middle East and Africa, and Asians from the former Soviet bloc, plus a few intriguing individual outliers.[4] These regions' social budgets show an aggregate bias toward the elderly, much like the OECD countries' own "mission shift" since 1910 that we discovered in Chapter 6. Why would they spend so much more on each person older than 65, relative to what they spend to educate each person in the 5–21 age group?

Their pensions are top-heavy, not universal. What sets the high-pension countries apart is not any generous coverage of the whole elderly

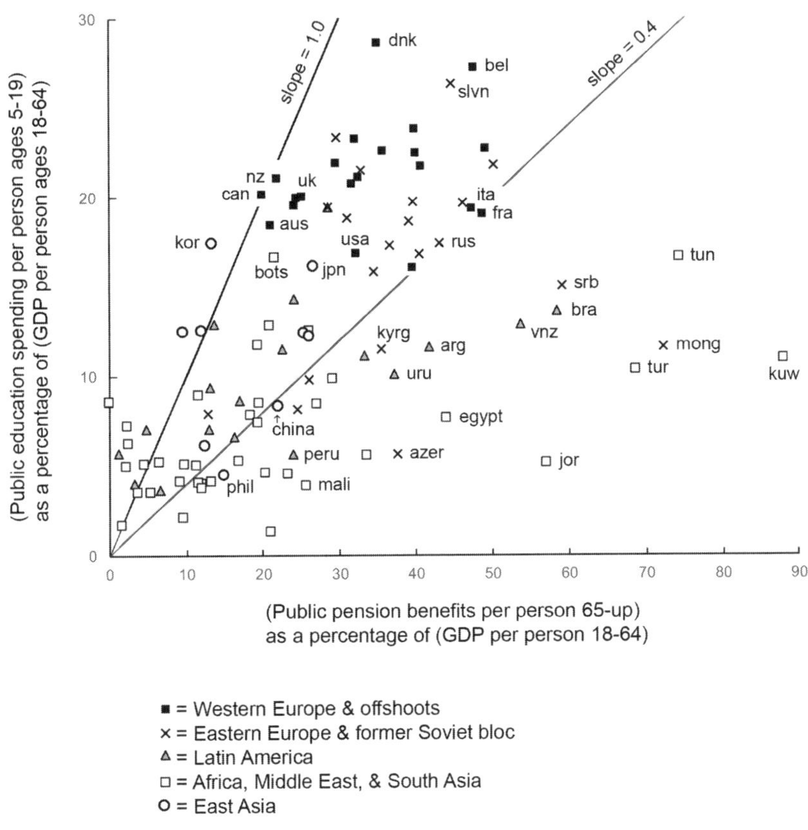

Figure 7.3. Public pensions versus public education spending, 106 countries, c. 2010

population. Rather, these countries' pensions stand out for being funneled toward those in the formal sectors who had high lifetime earnings, and especially toward those in the better-paid ranks of the public sector, such as top executives, military officers, judges, and teachers. The seeds for this biased pension growth were planted decades ago, when all public pensions were minimal and were restricted to those in the public sector. As time went by, these privileged sectors got pension increases that preceded and exceeded the late-arriving pensions for the poor.

TURKEY AND BRAZIL. Two countries in particular stand out as revealing troublesome preferences that may be applied to whole regions. Why do Turkey and Brazil have an average pension payout that is greater than half of GDP per person in the working-age group, ages 18 to 64?[5]

Turkey's worrying position in Figure 7.3 clearly reflects such elitist origins in public pension policy. Public pensions for old age date back to the creation of the Social Insurance Institution (SSK) of 1946, and the Retirement Fund (RF) of 1950 for civil servants. Both laws insured the favored civil servants against both good outcomes and bad – against outliving their savings, as well as against disabilities. Even though the SSK covered a wide range of formal-sector employees to some extent, its fragmented structure has subsidized pensions and health care much more generously for civil servants than for others, especially in the corrupt 1990s. As Chapter 12 will show more fully, Turkey's top-heavy pensions are still among the most problematic in all the (data-supplying) world, although Greece's are even more ominous because Greece has a much older population than Turkey.[6]

What is true of Turkey, and Greece, can also be seen elsewhere in southern Europe, that is along the northern shores of the Mediterranean, albeit only not as sharply. While their dots lie along the 0.4 slope in Figure 7.3, Italy, Spain, and Portugal tilt toward public pensions to a degree that deserves note. Do they also have top-heavy pensions favoring the well-off? Not so conspicuously as Turkey, but other evidence also suggests a problem with priorities. Social spending in these countries tilts not only away from education but also away from the poor, according to recent OECD comparisons.[7]

For Latin America as well, pension policy has favored the top formal-sector occupations ever since public pensions began in the nineteenth and early twentieth centuries.[8] Brazil may have the region's most inegalitarian and anti-growth pension regime. Regressive pensions are cemented into Brazilian law by the 1988 Constitution. Ostensibly a Constitution sealing the return of democracy after nearly a quarter century of military rule, this elaborate document should be thought of as the Brazilian Stakeholders' Constitution of 1988. Its legal language has built walls around vested interests, not least the public-sector pensions. Such protections can be removed only with difficulty, often requiring a federal supermajority and/or a favorable court ruling.[9]

Brazil's formula for setting the level of benefits is rigged in favor of civil servants. As Christian Aspalter has explained,

> The special social insurance system (the RPPS, *Regime Próprio de Previdência Social*) caters to civil servants. [Unlike] the general social insurance system, here the *last* salary of the civil servant is taken as the base for the pension formula, whereas it is the *average* salary for members of the general social insurance system, which then is also, since 1999, subject to a combined multiplier (called the "welfare factor") which is, as usual, designed to curb benefits.[10]

Another feature cemented into Brazil's constitutional walls is an indexation procedure that assures a budgetary breakdown as long as the population keeps getting older. The indexation mechanism for minimum pension benefits contributes substantially to the high level of pension benefits in Brazil. According to the Constitution, the minimum pension cannot be lower than the official minimum wage. Currently, the minimum benefit is thus equal to that minimum wage, and two-thirds of pensioners receive this benefit level. This has led to real increases in the minimum pension of almost 90 percent between 2002 and 2012. Given the strong political pressures for further minimum wage increases, keeping the minimum benefit indexed to the minimum wage is likely to result in rapid real pension increases. Even if the official minimum wage just matches the average market earnings of those of working age, the trend in pension costs is unsustainable, as will be emphasized in Chapter 12.

Yet another device making the system regressive relates to survivor benefits, which by 2011 took 2.8 percent of GDP, well above the 1.6 percent that was typical in Europe. The survivor benefit rules offer strong incentives for abuse. For example, a young person marrying a pensioner will be eligible to the spouse's pension for the rest of life, even if the marriage lasted only a few days and without any need to prove poverty.[11]

Then in October 2019, thirty-one years after the enactment of the problematic 1988 Constitution, both houses of Brazil's National Congress finally passed a potentially sizeable reform of federal pensions, after previous attempts had produced only minor tweaks in 1995, 2003, and 2013. They had little choice. Pensions were already taking 40 percent of the federal budget, and reliable projections predicted that legally mandated expenditures would consume the entire federal budget as early as 2022, leaving no room for any public investments or any other discretionary spending. Among other things, the reform raises the minimum age for retirement to 65 for men and to 62 for women in many job categories, and limits the end-of-career pension entitlement rates. The reform is complex, however, and pensions remain barely reformed for the military and the police, and for state and municipal civil servants.

Brazil and Turkey, while extreme, are not alone in revealing political preferences for the privileged elderly. Other studies have found the same tendency in other countries, especially other Latin American countries, Mediterranean countries, and India.[12]

Thus, nearly all the countries with relatively heavy public pension support and relatively low education support, showing up low and to the right in Figure 7.3's snapshot for 2010, are guilty of both favoring the well-off and missing the chance to promote economic growth just by reallocating the same amount of social funds. The missed growth opportunity seems clear enough. There are no known growth benefits to be had by taking money from the general taxpaying population and giving it to the current elderly, whereas if the same funding had been channeled into education, especially primary and secondary education, it would have reaped the high rates of return documented back in Chapter 5.

Of course, many countries are not guilty of such a misallocation of the aggregate social budget. As one can make out from Table 7.1 and Figure 7.3, countries further from the equator lean toward supporting the young, in this case by shifting tax money to education. Most, but not all, of these higher-latitude countries tend also to be rich democracies.

SAFETY NETS DURING AND AFTER COMMUNISM

Among the still-developing countries, the ones that seem most devoted toward aggregate social spending, and toward high levels of support for education, include the majority of the Eastern European countries for which we have the necessary data. The Czech Republic (or Czechia), Estonia, Hungary, Latvia, Lithuania, Russia, and Slovenia all appear to behave in a normal or average way in the global 2010 snapshots of Figures

7.1 through 7.3. So do Poland and Slovakia in terms of their high levels of social spending, even though Figure 7.3 found their mix tilting a bit toward the elderly. Why do these countries seem to favor more social spending than other developing countries, and also more than the leading countries spent out of similar average incomes in the past? Does this relate to their having been communist governments before 1990? One might expect so, given that communist regimes have proclaimed their egalitarianism more loudly than governments in any other region.

To understand the social-spending patterns of the formerly communist nations, and how it relates to their communist past, we must first take on the daunting task of documenting how their social assistance and social insurance worked in practice back in the communist era. There are no comprehensive data on government social spending as measured Western-style. Help for the neediest was delivered largely in kind, by state employers and work teams, as if they were following a job-related "second-pillar" approach in the jargon of Western pension policy.

While the communist-era institutions were very different from those in other countries, one can, on reflection, see that the complexity of the differences will not greatly affect our choice of social-spending measures. Consider, for example, a case in which the government confiscated a private house, and then let a government loyalist occupy it rent-free. This is a stark redistribution, one that does not easily fit the social insurance motive inspiring most social-spending programs. Redistributing that house also does not fit the notion of egalitarian social assistance, unless the recipient happens to be less able than the previous private owner. Yet on both sides of the institutional chasm, the logical choice of a measure of *social spending* is the same. The fact that the government is providing the home free of charge means that the rental value of that home contributes the same value to gross social spending as in a market economy. In both settings, the government's transfers in kind, like this house, or its transfers in cash, are gross flows of social spending as long as they are targeted at health, old age, disability, family needs, unemployment – or housing.

How large were those expenditures as shares of GDP before, during, and after communism? Table 7.2 gives a few gleanings for Russia/USSR and for China.

Soviet social spending has been partially illuminated by Gaston Rimlinger, by Soviet official data, and by Alisdair McAuley.[13] As of 1931, during Stalin's First Five-Year Plan, official figures say that the Soviet Union spent what amounted to 4.31 percent of estimated GDP on housing and other social programs, perhaps the second-highest share in the world, behind Weimar Germany's 4.96 percent. The Soviet figures do not, of course, reflect the unmeasured heavy taxation of the peasantry during Stalin's Collectivization campaign. By the 1960s and 1970s, under Khrushchev and Brezhnev, Soviet social spending had risen to 15–17 percent of GDP, roughly comparable to the Western European countries that were about to become welfare states on the 20 percent of GDP criterion. Its mix of non-education social expenditures was also similar to Western European practice. However, the Soviets spent a larger share of GDP on public education – 6.7 percent in 1960 and 7.7 percent in 1970 – than any OECD country other than the United States, Canada, and Sweden. The commitments to social spending and to education retreated somewhat, however, in the post-Soviet republics, including the Russian Federation. Broadly speaking, the shares of GDP they devoted to social spending as a whole, or to public education, settled back to the average practice of Western Europe.

For mainland China, we now have at least partial benchmarks before Mao, under Mao, and under state capitalism. As quantified in Table 7.2. China under Mao (1949–1976) lagged behind the Soviet Union in social spending. In 1960, during the heavily communal living of the Great Leap Forward, it still spent only 5.51 percent of a slumping GDP, only slightly above the 4.31 percent under Stalin during the First Soviet Five-Year Plan and well below the 1960 Soviet social expenditures (18.38 percent of GDP) under Khrushchev. During the post-Mao reforms, China has expanded its social spending to 6.8–8.5 percent of GDP, though these fluctuating shares are well below those of post-communist Russia and Eastern Europe.[14]

Looking at all post-communist or still officially communist Eurasian countries as a group since the 1990s, one can see a rough geographic pattern in their government commitments to social spending. Among these countries, the commitment tends to rise from east to west – just as it does in their never-communist near neighbours. In East Asia in 2009,

TABLE 7.2. *Social spending in Russia/USSR and in China before, during, and after communism (percentages of GDP, excluding public education spending)*

	Russia/USSR	China
1870	0.59	
1880	0.59	
1890	0.59	
1900	0.58	
1930	4.31	0.91
1940		
1950		2.94
1960	15.51	5.51
1970	16.81	
1980		7.84
1990		8.50
2000		6.77
2010	13.09	8.01

Sources and notes for Russia and the Soviet Union:
For 1870–1900, Steven Nafziger has kindly supplied budget numbers for the Imperial (central) government. Local governments probably allocated only negligible amounts on social spending, though possible noticeable amounts on local public education. The small amounts shown here were rather regressive expenditures on bits of health care for the army, navy, and a few other ministries with seemingly elite mandates. The nominal nations income denominator is available annually for 1885–1913 at http://gpih.ucdavis.edu/nominal GDP.

The Imperial government also spent a bit on education within the army, navy, and four other ministries. These amounted to 0.47 percent of GDP in 1890 and 0.42 percent in 1900. For 1900, Ansell and Samuels (2014, underlying data provided by David Samuels) came up with the same share by different means.

The 1930 numbers refer to the Soviet Union in 1931, and are derived from the 1936 *USSR Handbook* by David Samuels. Categorical percentage shares of GDP for 1931 were: welfare 1.19, pensions 1.56, health 1.03, and housing 0.53. The housing figure may be for expenditures to build housing for the future, and thus a capital-account entry, as opposed to an imputed rental value of housing provided or subsidized by government in 1931 itself. For 1960 and 1970, the numbers refer to social consumption expenditures (*obshchestvennye fondy potrebleniya*) of the entire Soviet Union, minus education and holiday pay, divided by McAuley's own estimate of Soviet GDP (McAuley 1979, p. 262). Dividing by the Mitchell volumes higher numbers on nominal Soviet GDP would have lowered these shares by about 30 percent.

For 2010, this table uses the CEQ Institute's "mid-range" measure, including half the benefits from partly contributory programs plus all the benefits from strictly non-contributory programs.

TABLE 7.2 *(continued)*

Sources and notes for China:
For 1933 (here "1930"), 1952 ("1950), and 1957 ("1960"), we have measures of "communal services" expenditure shares, plus the public share of estimated expenditures on housing services. The shares are those defined in current prices for 1933 and 1952, with indirect evidence on price changes between 1952 and 1957. The main sources are Liu and Yeh (1965, p. 68) and Liu (1968, p. 138). Indirect evidence suggests that the shares of all housing service expenditures that were paid by government were 1 percent for 1933, a very-rough 10 percent for 1952, and 61 percent for 1957. On these shares, see Wang and Murie (1999, pp. 46–99, esp. p. 81) and Zhang (1998, pp. 18–42). An in-depth study of how local social assistance and social insurance worked under Mao is Dixon (1981).

For 1980–1996 ("2000"), See Gu (2001, p. 94), which includes welfare spending and public housing for both *danwei* (workplace) and larger government units. The public housing expenditures for 1980 were extrapolated backward to 10 billion yuan from numbers given for 1981 and beyond.

For the year 2012 (here shown as "2010"), from OECD (2016, Table 5.9), citing "Asian Development Bank's Social Protection Index (SPI), World Health Organization (WHO)." Alternatively, the Asian Development Bank (2013, p. 14) gives a 2009 figure of 5.4 percent of GDP, for central government only.

Vietnam's central government spent less than 5 percent of GDP on social programs, slightly less than in China (5.4 percent for central government only). Among the central governments of formerly Soviet Central Asia and Transcaucasia, Tajikistan and Armenia spent less (1.2 and 2.2 percent), whereas the central governments of Kirghizia, Kazakhstan, Uzbekistan, Azerbaijan, and Georgia spent somewhat more (6.1–10.2 percent), still less than the Russian Federation. Moving further west, Russia's spending was exceeded by its nearest neighbours to the west, and the highest spending shares in the former Soviet bloc are those of its western-tier states of Poland, the Czech Republic, Hungary, and Slovenia, all of them around the arbitrary 20 percent threshold defining a welfare state.[15]

In other words, the policies in formerly centrally planned economies differ geographically in much the same way that their non-communist neighbors' policies do. The highest social spenders are Central-East European democracies that border on Western Europe's renowned welfare states followed by the Baltic Republics. In East Asia, Vietnam and China spend little, much like their Asian free-market counterparts (aside from high-spending Japan). Social support is also meager in some of the "-stans" and Armenia, resembling their South Asian counterparts. The main reason for the east–west pattern seems to be the age distribution. The higher social spending to the west (i.e. in Europe rather than in Asia) is not a reflection of greater concern for the poor.[16] Rather, it consists mainly of greater benefits for the elderly, who have been a higher share of the adult population, and of voters, in Europe than in Asia.

Mongolia, the only exception to the rule that Asians spend less among post-communist countries is also an exception to the rule that pensions tend to be top-heavy in developing countries. Post-communist Mongolia spent heavily, and disastrously, on pensions, designing them badly more than once. Soon after the conversion to a market economy, the government instituted pensions for the elderly generation that had lived through years of household-sector privation. Laudable and egalitarian as the objective was, the pension amounts offered were unsustainably generous in a rapidly aging economy. A reform in 1999 squeezed pension prospects for anyone born after January 1, 1960, while continuing the generous support for those born earlier. Younger adults protested the prospect of so much austerity down the road. To placate them, a 2015 law gave anyone born between 1960 and 1979 a choice between the austere new system and the generous old one. The entire 1960–1979 cohort, even remote herders, opted for the old system. Financial meltdown continued, though not solely due to the faulty pension system. Mongolia has received at least six IMF-led bailouts since 1990, and has gone through repeated rounds of rapid inflation. To relieve some of the austerity, Mongolia seized a silver mine from private Chinese investors in 2018, hoping to pay for some of the pensions. Negotiations are currently under way for another bailout.[17]

Setting unstable Mongolian policy aside, the broader pattern implies that decades of communism apparently had a lingering positive post-communist effect on education spending, and a hint of elevation in other social spending. The countries that have experienced the rise and fall of communism spend more than the leading countries had spent at similar income levels in the deeper past (Figure 7.1 again), although only slightly more than never-communist countries in the same regions today.

TOP-HEAVY PUBLIC EDUCATION SPENDING

Another top-heavy misallocation of social spending in some developing countries has occurred within the budget for public education. Why, despite their current efforts to catch up, have so many countries lagged behind in the development of a world-class education? This question has been before us for a long time. It was aptly posed by Richard Easterlin (1981) as "Why Isn't the Whole World Developed?" – by which he meant to ask why they failed to deliver universal primary education. Providing an answer to his question will also deliver a much-needed education-related supplement to the grand historical interpretation by Daron Acemoglu and James Robinson of *Why Nations Fail* (2012). Education policy failure plays a key behind-the-scenes role in all of history's contrasts between extractive and inclusive societies.

HIGHER-CLASS HIGHER EDUCATION. It is not just that many developing countries have missed the chance to invest in educating the young, without adding to their total social budget. Worse, when choosing *whose education* to subsidize, at which levels of education, many have also preferred the level of education that most exacerbates inequality and least promotes GDP growth. Countries where many adults never finish primary or secondary education tend to be countries that have previously discriminated in favor of subsidizing higher education available only to relatively few, at the expense of broad mass education.

Shifting extra government subsidies toward higher education at the expense of primary education lowers adult earnings and GDP, especially in the early stages of development. On this point, evidence contradicts a frequent view that development must trickle down from the top. Some have argued that still-developing countries need to stress excellence in higher education first, to get development well launched, training the teachers who will in turn train the masses in future generations. For example, a former minister of education of Venezuela argued in a publication of the National Education Council, an advisory board of the Ministry of Education: "Faced with the choice of providing a first rate education to one third of the population or a mediocre education for all, I would not vacillate. I would choose a first rate education for the third of the population, because that third would pull the country forward." Yet a mass of evidence, mainly from the late twentieth century, says that on average a developing nation gets a greater return on an extra peso, or rupee or other currency, on its primary education than on its tertiary education. Table 7.3 offers strong indirect evidence that poor societies systematically under-finance primary education. The evidence is indirect because it is confined to so-called "social rates of return" on the attainment of a higher level of schooling. These rates of return are as encompassing as they can be, but some of the returns to education are still left out. For one thing, such rates of return can only capture the returns and costs of extra school years, not the returns and costs of raising the quality of schooling at each level. That is, they can show only the damage done by rationing schooling, and not the damage from poor schooling. For another, they cannot measure the net external or inter-generational benefits of education, and are "social" only in that they include the public-budget effects of public financing and later tax collection from more educated adults.

For what they are worth, however, the studies summarized in Table 7.3 consistently show that the social rate of return on the extra (unattained) primary schooling is much higher in today's developing countries than either the marginal returns on higher education in the same countries or the rates of return measured for any level of schooling in high-income countries.

Which countries are most guilty of giving too little of their government subsidies to the masses, and too much to the heirs at the top of society? The fingerprints of elitist backwardness continue to be traced by comparative social scientists.[18] Table 7.4 spotlights a telling fingerprint of elitism in subsidizing education, namely the ratio of (public tertiary-education expenditures per pupil), divided by (public pre-primary + primary expenditure per child of primary-school age), a ratio that combines the disparity of subsidies with the incompleteness of mass enrollments at the primary level.[19] As can be seen, this ratio has remained at or below 2.0 for advanced OECD democracies, with an equalizing effect on adult schooling. While there is no way to calculate an optimal ratio, one can take the high productivity of aggregate human capital in the

TABLE 7.3. *Average social rates of return to investment in education 1970s–1990s, by level of education and by national income per capita*

Country group	Primary		Secondary		Higher
High income	13.4	>	10.3	>	9.5
Middle income	18.8	>	12.9	>	11.3
Low income	21.3	>	15.7	>	11.2
World	18.9	>	13.1	>	10.8

Source and notes: The source is Psacharapoulos and Patrinos (2004), Table A1. For updates, see Montenegro and Patrinos (2014).

A traditional economist's caveat applies here. In deciding about reallocating resources, we care about marginal rates, not average rates. In shifting money at the margin between tertiary and primary education, the net gains or losses will not necessarily equal the difference between the observed average rates.

A further caveat about primary education in high-income countries: Even then, enrollments were nearly complete, so that the group without any primary education was small and atypical.

advanced OECD democracies as a reasonable norm, say a desired range ranging near, or below, 2.0.

Developing countries have clearly differed in how they have chosen to allocate taxpayers' money between levels of education, especially before the turn of this century. Some developing countries and transition economies meet the advanced-democracy standard of holding subsidies for higher education per pupil at or below twice the subsidy per child of primary-school age. So it appears in Table 7.4 for Chile, Colombia, Iran, the Philippines, Thailand, and the post-communist countries of Eastern Europe. By contrast, the elitism support ratio has been well above 2.0 for many other countries, especially before the end of the twentieth century. These higher-ratio countries are ones in which the inequality of adult educational attainment has been greater than rates of return would seem to warrant. Comparing their ratios in Table 7.4 with their inequalities of educational attainment in Chapter 5, reveals the preferences for subsidizing elite education that persist today in India and mainland China. The same bias continues for sub-Saharan Africa.[20] For several other countries, the preference for subsidizing elite higher education at the expense of equality and productivity was still present in the late twentieth century, but has faded away in this century. In Asia, so it has been for Indonesia, Malaysia, Myanmar, Nepal, Pakistan, Singapore, and

TABLE 7.4. *An elitist indicator in public education expenditure, 1985–2017*
Each ratio = (public tertiary-education expenditures per pupil), divided by (public primary-school expenditure per child of primary-school age)

	1985	1995	1999	2008	c. 2017
OECD developed countries					
Australia	–	–	1.7	1.3	1.2
Austria	–	–	2.2	2.0	1.6
Belgium	–	–	–	1.8	–
Canada	1.5	1.6	–	–	2.1
Denmark	–	–	2.6	2.3	1.7
Finland	–	–	2.3	1.9	1.6
France	–	–	1.8	2.0	1.8
Germany	–	–	–	–	1.9
Greece	–	1.5	1.2	0.5	
Iceland	–	–	–	1.2	–
Ireland	–	–	2.5	1.8	1.5
Italy	–	–	1.2	1.0	1.1
Japan	–	0.9	–	–	–
Korea	0.9	0.4	0.3	0.5	0.5
Netherlands	–	–	–	–	1.9
New Zealand	–	–	2.3	1.7	1.4
Norway	–	–	–	2.8	1.7
Portugal	–	–	1.5	1.4	1.1
Spain	–	0.9	1.2	1.4	
Sweden	–	–		1.6	2.0
Switzerland	–	–	2.3	2.2	1.5
UK	–	–	–	1.3	1.4
USA	1.4	1.4	–	–	1.1
OECD 1988	2.0				
Europe & N. Amer.				1.2	1.3
Other East Asia					
China	27.6	11.4	11.2	–	–
Indonesia	6.7	–	–	–	1.6
Malaysia	10.5	9.4	–	4.2	1.6
Myanmar	–	5.1	–	–	2.1
Philippines	2.2	–	–	1.5	–
Singapore	7.7	–	–	2.6	3.2
Thailand	2.0	3.0	–	0.8	1.2
South Asia, Middle East, Africa					
India	8.4	9.1	–	6.8	5.7
Iran	–	–	–	1.9	2.3
Israel	–	–	1.8	1.3	0.9
Nepal	32.7	18.9	–	4.0	2.6
Pakistan	31.8	–	–	–	2.7
South Africa	–	–	–	–	2.6
Sri Lanka	7.1	8.3	–	–	2.6

TABLE 7.4. *(continued)*

	1985	1995	1999	2008	c. 2017
Turkey	–	–	–	–	2.3
Sub-Saharan Africa	–	–		10.4	7.0
Latin America and the Caribbean					
Argentina	–	–	1.6	1.3	1.3
Bolivia	–	–		4.5	–
Brazil	–	–	8.5	2.2	1.9
Chile	–	–	0.9	1.1	1.1
Colombia	–	–	–	1.3	0.9
Costa Rica	7.8	4.3	–	–	2.0
Domin. Rep.	4.4	1.6	–	–	–
Ecuador	–	–	–	–	5.8
El Salvador	–	2.7	–	2.0	0.7
Guatemala	–	7.9	–	1.9	1.6
Honduras	9.5	5.5	–	–	1.9
Jamaica	25.3	18.3	–	5.0	–
Mexico	–	4.7	–	3.1	2.5
Nicaragua	12.9	–	–	–	–
Panama	3.7	4.9	–	1.4	–
Peru	–	–	–	1.4	0.9
Trinidad & Tobago	–	18.4	13.7	–	–
Uruguay	–	–	3.0	–	–
Venezuela	–	–	–	2.2	–
Eastern Europe, Former USSR					
Armenia	–	–	–	–	0.9
Czech Republic	–		3.0	2.8	1.4
Estonia	–	–	–	1.0	1.9
Hungary	–	–	1.8	0.9	1.1
Latvia	–	–	–	–	0.9
Poland	–	–	–	0.7	1.2
Russian Fed.	–	–	–	–	–
Slovakia	–	–	3.1	1.2	1.3
Slovenia	–	–	–	–	0.9
Ukraine	–	–	–	–	1.5
World	–	–	–	2.1	2.0

Sources and notes: The main underlying sources are UNESCO, *Global Education Monitoring Report 2011, 2019*; and its World Education RepoRt, as later summarized in UNESCO's statistical site http://data.uis.unesco.org/. The OECD average for 1988 is from OECD, *Education at a Glance*, 1992, p. 63 (primary school only, assuming net enrollment ratio of 1.00). All numbers are combined averages for males and females.

Expenditures refer to current expenditures, excluding capital formation. In the case of the c. 2017 estimates, many of UNESCO's enrollment and population numbers refer to 2014, 2015, 2016, or 2018 rather than to 2017. The number for Singapore in 2017 is from data.imf.org, expenditures by function of government (COFOG).

Sri Lanka. In Latin America and the Caribbean, we see similar hints of improvement for Costa Rica, the Dominican Republic, Guatemala, Honduras, Jamaica, Mexico, Nicaragua, Panama, and Trinidad and Tobago. While these countries have restored a more egalitarian and productive educational structure in this century, their failure to do so in the twentieth century delayed the development of their human capital.[21]

Global studies of the elitist restrictions on public mass schooling tend to find it strongly correlated with the lack of mass democracy, that is restrictions on political voice. So say statistical tests by Ben Ansell (2010, pp. 68–71) covering fifty-two non-OECD countries in the 1990s. Confirmation comes from more detailed event studies of how school finance was impacted by democratic dawns or dictatorial crackdowns.[22] Generally, when democracies change from narrowly giving voice only to those with substantial power to granting universal suffrage, more is spent on basic education.

WHERE TEACHERS ACT LIKE ELITES. The fact that democratization and the rise of strong left-wing parties raise public spending on primary education does not always translate, however, into improved *quality* of education. Often, it can translate into greater power for teachers' unions, allowing them extra economic rents at the expense of educational quality.[23] In Chapter 5, we noted that in the United States, the surge in teachers' bargaining rights in the 1960s and 1970s was accompanied by a seeming slowdown in the delivery of learning, both absolutely and relative to education in other rich countries. The imprint of teacher power shows up much more clearly in certain developing countries, greatly raising teacher pay, cutting teacher effort, and checking the advance of learning.

One region and one country have stood out in the scholarly literature documenting the negative results of having teachers acquire the kind of political clout that usually accrues only to rich elites. The region is Latin America, where teachers' unions gained strength in the first half of the twentieth century and flexed their muscles until their suppression in Chile under Pinochet and their yielding to partial education reforms in several other countries in the 1990s. A highly publicized case in point is

Mexico, where in certain states the teachers remain solidly aligned with either the PRI or the PRD political parties even today. The partial reforms in the 1990s have required negotiating delicate agreements, delicately timed. Thus, in much of Latin America, even after the democratization of the 1990s, teachers have reaped economic and political rents at the expense of students and taxpayers.[24]

The country that has stood out most for its teachers' abuse of political power is India, where public-sector teachers have political connections and considerable monopoly power. Their monopoly power pays off in higher average pay, job security, and lower average burdens at the aggregate level. Given that power and security, teachers respond locally with simple unilateral absenteeism, paid yet unpredictable. India's lack of commitment to primary education manifests itself in huge class sizes, teacher absenteeism, and high drop-out rates. The problem is worst in India's "heartland" states, Bihar, Orissa, Uttar Pradesh, and (until the late 1990s) Madhya Pradesh. In the village of Palanpur in western Uttar Pradesh in 1983–1984, for example, a single teacher was responsible for carrying out the national mandate to educate all children of ages 6–10. There were 158 such children. The result in terms of educational quality was clear enough:

> [T]he most notable feature of the village school is that it has more or less ceased to function. The root of the problem is fairly obvious. The single teacher [upper-caste son of the village headman] has a "permanent" post, and his salary, which is quite high by local standards, is effectively unrelated to his performance ... [H]e has little incentive to exert himself.
>
> In 1983–4, the village teacher was taking full advantage of these circumstances. More often than not, he did not even take the trouble of coming to school at all. When he did, he would be accompanied by ten or twelve children at most, mainly sons and daughters of his own close relatives ... This did not prevent him from cheerfully entering 135 names in the school enrollment register.[25]

It is also in these poorer heartland states that secondary and higher education seems to have been supplied most abundantly in recent decades. In 1966, for example, the Lucknow *National Herald* voiced its suspicions by noting that India's poorer heartland states had a higher share of high-school students going on to university than Britain, France, Japan, or India's better-off southern states. One underlying factor seems to have been the entrepreneurial opportunity to create new high schools and colleges as a political base and cash cow for siphoning government grants at low cost. Running a primary school, which was handed down to village-level *panchayat* rule in the 1950s, is less lucrative, though it is still an opportunity to solidify a local partisan political base.

India's teacher absenteeism, while outstanding, is not unique to the country or to the teaching sector. According to a recent comparative study summarized in Table 7.5, random checks found double-digit percentages of absenteeism in six countries, both among primary-school teachers and among primary health-care workers at the start of this century.

Some modest reforms have been forthcoming, however, even in India. Recent studies have indicated that building incentive mechanisms into teacher salary structures can help improve student outcomes. For example, Muralidharan and Sundararaman's (2011) evidence from a randomized evaluation of a teacher incentive program in Andhra Pradesh, India, shows that implementing teacher performance pay in government-run schools led to significant improvements in student test scores, with no evidence of any adverse consequences from the program. Additional school inputs were also effective in raising test scores, but the teacher incentive program was three times as cost-effective. Duflo, Hanna, and Ryan (2012) also find that attendance-related bonuses to teachers would boost both teachers' school attendance rates and student learning outcomes in Rajasthan, India. For most of India and for many other countries, however, the abuse of teacher power remains significant, as a supplement to the larger abuse of elite power.

SUMMARY

To return to the question posed at the start of this chapter, the answer is yes, other regions are indeed following paths that diverge from the route taken by the industrialized leaders over the last two centuries.

TABLE 7.5. *Absenteeism among teachers and health workers, c. 2000*

	Provider absence rates (%) in	
	Primary schools	Primary health centers
Bangladesh	16	35
Ecuador	14	–
India	25	40
Indonesia	19	40
Peru	11	25
Uganda	27	37
Unweighted average	19	35

Source and notes: The source is Chaudhury et al. (2006, p. 92). Providers were counted as absent if they could not be found in the facility for any reason at the time of a random unannounced spot check. In Uganda, the sampled districts were divided into sub-counties, and schools in sub-counties with Level-III health centers comprise the school sampling frame. This sampling strategy may have had the effect of understating the national absence rate there, given that schools in rural areas appear to have had higher absence rates.

In terms of the overall effort to spend tax money on social programs, both for social insurance and for public education, while the later-developing regions have spent lower shares of GDP than do the leading rich countries today, they pay *higher* tax shares for social spending than did the leaders at the same levels of real income in the past. It appears as though lessons have been learned worldwide about the need to offer more taxpayer support on a broad social front, especially for education.

Since their social expenditures have risen to such above-history levels in the last half century, then yes, there is reason to believe that fifty years from now tax-based social expenditures will take more than 20 percent of GDP in several more countries worldwide, even without counting public education expenditures. If crossing the 20 percent threshold made a country either a "welfare state" or a "social insurance state," then yes, there should be several such high-budget states beyond Western Europe in the next fifty years. Japan has already risen above that bar with its long-run commitments to public education, health, and pensions. So have the westernmost countries of the former Soviet Bloc, namely Poland,

Czechia, Hungary, Slovenia, and Croatia. The three Baltic states spent slightly less on social insurance, but are near the 20 percent bar, and invest considerably in public education.

Yet other high social spenders of the next half century will probably not resemble welfare states, either in the sense of investing in public education or in the egalitarian sense of providing safety nets for the truly needy. Many countries in the still-developing regions of the global South have misdirected their expenditures, away from education and safety nets for the poor, primarily because political voice has been limited to those whose self-interest captured the social-spending agenda. Even the countries on the northern tier of the Mediterranean have tended to favor pensions for privileged groups over either mass education or anti-poverty programs. Among those for which we have sufficient data, the most conspicuous for misallocating social expenditures are India, Turkey, Greece, Latin America, and other nations within the global South. These same countries generally have lower PISA scores, lower GDP per person, and higher inequality to show for it.

PART III

WHAT EFFECTS?

CHAPTER 8

Effects on Growth, Jobs, and Life

HOW HAS SOCIAL SPENDING REALLY AFFECTED aggregate economic growth and wellbeing? Thanks to extensive scholarship in recent years, this chapter can say quite a bit about how the aggregate size of tax-financed social programs affects the economy. Given this new evidence, Chapter 9 will then explore why the tax-financed safety nets seem to have had the effects shown here, and Chapter 10 will show what we know about who paid for all this and who benefited from it.

COMPARING WHAT WITH WHAT?

How do governments that spend a bigger share of GDP on social programs compare with those that spend less? Note that the relevant comparison is between *real-world* practices, not between imagined hypothetical extremes. To understand how large social-spending shares of the national GDP relate to the level or growth of GDP per capita, one must first grasp the basic point that we are comparing the performances of real-world economies with greater and smaller shares of social spending. Any theory about a good or bad welfare state is just that: a theory. And theories often over-simplify. Real-world policies do not take the simple forms imagined in the classroom, or in ideological assertions, about what governments do with their taxes and spending.

In this chapter, we are asking about the effects of the size of total social budgets. We compare *whole national bundles* of social policies to see how they correlate with economic outcomes. There is wisdom in looking first at the whole forest, before approaching any trees.

THE EFFECTS ON GDP AND GROWTH

The first rule in real-world judgments about how the level and growth of GDP relate to government social spending is: *No cherry-picking allowed.* For example, it would not do for a critic of large government budgets to announce "the United States is richer than higher-spending Denmark, therefore Denmark's social spending is bad for GDP per person." Equally, it would not do for a defender of the welfare state to announce that "Denmark's income per capita grew faster since 1910 than that of the United States, therefore Denmark's social spending is good for growth." Also unfair would be the announcement that "Denmark is much richer than low-spending India, therefore Denmark's social spending is good for GDP per person." Such selectivity must be ruled out immediately. Any judgments based on contrasts between countries or contrast over time must start with the experiences of as many countries and as many decades of history as the data permit.[1]

SIMPLE CORRELATIONS. To sort out how social spending affects the economy first requires looking at how raising the total size of the budget seems to correlate with the level and growth of GDP per capita over as much experience as the data permit, before digging more deeply into causes.

Of course, as we are constantly reminded, correlation is not causation. It can only be a first clue about causation. This chapter can only whisper about the underlying causal suggestion that if a low-spending country were to behave like a higher-spending country, its economy might behave the way the higher-spending countries have behaved. The next chapter will explore what is now known about the likely causes of the patterns we are about to see in total social spending and the economy. Later chapters will dig into another kind of causal question, one already introduced briefly in Chapter 7, namely, how would economic performance be affected by shifting the same total amount of spending between different target groups, such as the elderly versus children?

The basic result seems clear enough. There has been no clearly negative correlation between social spending and GDP per capita any-time since the dawn of widespread social insurance in the 1880s. Nor do the statistical analyses of international experience reveal any GDP damage from social spending. The lack of a negative effect on GDP per capita holds whether one looks at its level or at its growth rate. It also holds despite a built-in cyclical bias toward negative correlation, caused by the fact that social programs are designed to spend more during slumps and to spend less during booms.

A first step toward establishing this non-negative result takes us to the recent history of how GDP per capita has correlated with total social spending when we take the "total" literally and include public education spending. Table 8.1 reveals the correlations for twenty-one countries supplying data to the OECD from 1960 to 2014. In most periods since 1960, the relationship between social spending and the *growth* of GDP per capita over the next seven to ten years looks slightly negative, as critics had warned they could be. Yet these negative relationships lack the strength to achieve conventional statistical significance.[2] If one asks how total social spending correlates with the achieved *levels* of GDP per capita, as opposed to its growth rate, the last two columns give a more positive answer. Greater social spending and greater GDP per capita have gone hand in hand, and significantly so throughout the late twentieth century.

Skeptics might try two rebuttals here. First, they could seize on the fact that the correlation with GDP per capita has weakened in the early twenty-first century. It has indeed, even though the correlations remain positive.

Second, skeptics can throw up the question asked in almost every economics seminar: "Have you considered reverse causation?" Surely, having a higher level of GDP per capita must make a country feel that it can bear greater tax rates to support social services.[3] Yet the likelihood that greater prosperity tends to raise tax-based social spending does not lend much support to the idea that social spending damages GDP. If that idea were correct, how could countries go on prospering decade after decade while also raising the share of their incomes spent on social programs that damage GDP? For the positive prosperity-to-spending effect to co-exist with a negative feedback from spending to prosperity (GDP), the correlations in Table 8.1 imply that prosperity must stimulate the political will to be taxed for social spending so strongly as to outweigh

TABLE 8.1. *How total social spending as a share of GDP correlates with growth and prosperity in twenty-one OECD countries, 1960–2014*

	The coefficient of correlation between the start-of-period share of total social expenditures in GDP and		
Time period	(a) the growth of GDP/capita	(b) the level of GDP/ capita, same year	(c) the level of GDP/capita, end of period
1960-1970	−0.21	0.57[a]	0.65[a]
1970-1980	0.05	0.61[a]	0.65[a]
1980-1990	0.18	0.61[a]	0.57[a]
1990-2000	−0.14	0.47[b]	0.56[a]
2000-2007	−0.40	0.38	0.34
2007-2014	−0.09	0.35	0.39
Simple average of these correlations	−0.10	0.50[b]	0.53[b]

[a] = significant at the 99% level; [b] = significant at the 95% level.

Sources and notes to Tables 8.1 and 8.2: Public education expenditures as a share of GDP are from the same sources as for Appendix A.

Non-education social expenditures/GDP for 1880–1930: Welfare, unemployment, pensions, health, and housing subsidies, as given in Lindert (1994, Table 1).

Non-education social expenditures/GDP for 1960–1980: OECD old series (OECD 1985); 1980–2007: OECD new series (as downloaded from the OECD iLibrary; for definitions, see OECD, *Education at a Glance*, 1998) and national sources; for 2014, OECD's SOCX database, as updated to 2016 at www.oecd.org/social/expenditure.htm, accessed through an institutional subscription to OECD iLibrary.

Real GDP per capita: 1880–1990 from the Maddison Project, via the Clio-Infra site; 1990–2014 from Penn World Tables.

The baseline twenty-one countries are Argentina, Australia, Austria, Belgium, Canada, Chile, Denmark, Finland, France, Germany, Greece (1960s on), Ireland (1960s on), Italy, Japan, Netherlands, New Zealand, Norway, Sweden, Switzerland, the United Kingdom, and the United States. That is, relative to the nineteen-country group used in uneven panels in Lindert (2004, vol. I, p. 17), the new core group of twenty-one drops Ireland and Switzerland (for want of sufficient pre-1914 data on social expenditures) and adds Argentina, Chile, Portugal, and Spain.

the alleged negative feedback from the spending. It seems implausible that prospering countries would keep demanding more of something that lowers their incomes. To put the point another way, if large social-spending budgets are nothing but a rich country's bad habit, like obesity or recreational drugs, why do we not see any easy evidence of its dragging down GDP per person?

To drive home this non-negative finding, let us now remove public education expenditures from total social spending, and re-run the

TABLE 8.2. *How non-education social spending as a share of GDP correlates with growth and prosperity in twenty-one OECD countries, 1880–2014*

	The coefficient of correlation between the start-of-period share of total social expenditures in GDP and		
Time period	(a) the growth of GDP/capita	(b) the level of GDP/capita, same year	(c) the level of GDP/capita, end of period
1880-1890	0.01	0.04	0.07
1890-1900	0.38	0.12	0.22
1900-1910	-0.13	0.32	0.26
1910-1920	0.11	0.44[a]	0.46[a]
1920-1930	-0.02	0.46[a]	0.50[a]
1930-1960	0.38	0.37	0.50[a]
1960-1970	-0.20	0.51[a]	0.57[b]
1970-1980	0.11	0.53[a]	0.58[b]
1980-1990	0.17	0.43	0.52[a]
1990-2000	-0.11	0.37	0.45[a]
2000-2007	-0.37	0.32	0.27
2007-2014	-0.14	0.28	0.30
Simple average of these correlations	0.02	0.35	0.39

[a] = significant at the 95% level; [b] = significant at the 99% level.

correlations. There are two reasons for dropping public education and retreating to less positive results. One strategic motivation is to avoid making it a slam dunk to show that social spending raises the growth and level of GDP per person. Including public education expenditures in the measure of social spending would have included all the pro-growth effects we documented in Chapters 4 and 5. Critics of social spending could object that their criticisms have never denied these positive effects, but have always concentrated on the more controversial social assistance and social insurance kinds of tax-based spending, such as "wasteful welfare spending."

The second reason for the strategic retreat is that only a few countries supply the data on public education expenditures for any year before 1960, as we saw in Table 5.1 above. To broaden the numerical test to include as much of the world's historical experience as possible, we set aside public education here.

Biasing the correlations away from the positive by excluding the clearly productive public education expenditures yields the results in

Table 8.2. As expected, removing public education from the social-spending measure makes the correlations less positive – but not by much. The negative correlation with growth of GDP still lacks statistical significance, and the positive associations with the level of GDP per capita are not much weaker than in the previous table. These positive associations appear to have been significant over most of the twentieth century. There is again a hint of less positivity after the year 2000, a point to which we return when discussing jobs.

The lack of any significant negative correlation between social spending's share of GDP and the level or growth of GDP is all the more remarkable since short-run gyrations in GDP should have caused a false bias toward a negative correlation. To see this bias, imagine a short-run slump in GDP, as in a recession or depression. The slump will cut the GDP denominator. At the same time, the slump should raise the social-spending numerator by raising such "automatic stabilizer" social spending as unemployment compensation and assistance to poor families. Result: A negative shock to GDP should show that the economy is doing worse at the same time that social spending is rising as a share of GDP. Having GDP shocks automatically trigger increases in the share of GDP devoted to social spending should show a negative correlation between social spending and the level (or growth) of GDP, inviting the false inference that the rise in the social-spending share lowered GDP. That negative bias was probably built into our results for 2010, a slump year. Yet despite this bias, Tables 8.1 and 8.2 do not yield negative correlations. Watch for that same deceiving negative bias in the data for the year 2020, when the coronavirus crisis slashed GDP and caused governments to hike social spending.

Within nations, as well as between them, we find no secure negative correlation between local governments' social transfers and either the level or the growth of their product per capita. For all the anecdotes about American companies fleeing high-tax states for low-tax states, there is no net result showing any damage to the higher-taxing and higher-welfare localities. The only time that the anti-government southern states in the United States rose toward the national average income per capita was in the period 1940–1973, when the south reaped disproportionate benefits from government military and aerospace spending.

Since the rise of welfare payments and other social spending in the 1960s and 1970s, there has been no erosion in the relative incomes or realty values of such larger-transfer states as Connecticut and California. There is no outward evidence that greater tax-based social spending has sparked any massive tax flight, causing a "race to the bottom" in tax rates and social spending.

What is true about social spending and GDP is just as true about total government budgets and GDP. Every kind of non-negative result shows up again in Jon Bakija's (2016) extensive tests relating total government taxes to GDP. No matter how he slices the international and long-run historical data, he gets the same result: No negative relationship, and arguably a positive relationship, between the size of overall government and either the level or the growth of GDP.

The overall message remains clear: The belief that greater social spending as practiced in documented real-world experience must somehow shrink the size of the economic pie is in trouble, and is forced to retreat.

Indeed, the rejection of social spending has already been routed from the battlefield by the coronavirus crisis of 2020. In that crisis, the United States hurriedly doled out more than 10 percent of a peak year's GDP in emergency aid, much of it in the form of unemployment compensation and other transfers to workers and the poor. Britain's Conservative government ramped up public spending on health care and other social services. The conservative Christian Democratic coalition of Germany and other European Union governments did likewise. They and the European Central Bank even exempted Greece, Italy, and other heavy EU debtors from the usual belt-tightening strictures.

Why was the response to the 2020 crisis so different from earlier refusals to help those in need? The 2020 crisis, like the Great Depression of the 1930s, convinced those with political voice that anybody could suffer in such times – "that could be me." It probably will, like the Great Depression of the 1930s, weaken the resistance to a more permanent and universal government social insurance. Even after the emergency has passed, continuing much of the new government aid may prove politically popular. It may prove impossible to squeeze the genie of larger social spending back into the bottle. Fortunately, the larger genie need not harm economic growth.

TOWARD CAUSATION, STATISTICALLY. To go beyond mere correlations, one seeks a statistical way to show the causal impact of exogenously greater social spending on GDP, holding other things equal and allowing for feedbacks in both directions. Scholars have done so, under a severe constraint that must be remembered in any discussion of what-causes-what at the national level. When the experiences of whole nations are being compared, there is no way to meet the highest statistical standard achieved by randomized control trials. History is not an experiment, and we must reason from the complicated clues it has left us.

Accepting this severe constraint, statistical studies have also produced non-negative results. Among the usual OECD countries' experiences, GDP has not been negatively affected by greater social spending, even when other things are held equal.[4] Another recent study has globalized this non-negative result. Fiseha Haile and Miguel Niño-Zarazúa (2018) have pooled the experiences of fifty-five low- and middle-income countries between 1990 and 2009, finding significantly positive effects of government spending on the social sectors (health, education, and social protection) on wellbeing. While their measures of wellbeing tend to help the case for positive effects by featuring education and health improvements, their results do seem to support the non-negativity results in Table 8.2 here. Finally, in a more global study, Daron Acemoglu et al. (2019, pp. 89–93), quantify the ways in which countries' shift toward democracy since 1960 has affected economic growth. They find positive impacts that are partly due to the fact that democratization ushers in greater public spending on health and education.

ON JOBS

Like average incomes and like social spending, job-holding has risen over time among the core OECD countries. Does the bundle of social-spending programs deserve any of the credit for the fact that a rising share of the working-age population actually has jobs? Or should it be blamed for holding back that rise of job-holding? Jobs should surely be the next target for international testing, since most of the fears about economic defects in social spending gather around the suspicion that more generous social spending kills jobs, either by giving people an incentive to avoid work or by giving prospective employers a disincentive to hire. Does it work that way?

WHERE THE JOBS ARE. A natural way to match the possible work effects with the possible GDP effects would be to replicate the correlations of Table 8.2 with a table relating social spending to the levels and changes in job-holding since 1880. Such a long-run replication is not yet possible, however, since national employment numbers are still not well aligned between countries until the end of the twentieth century, despite some valiant attempts by the International Labour Organisation and quantitative historians in academia and in private business. For the trends reaching back before the 1990s, we only have reliable time-lines on job-holding for fewer than a dozen countries. For the twenty-first century, however, we are in luck. The OECD has carefully aligned the recent employment rates for the working-age populations of more than forty countries, including all of the twenty-one countries whose histories of GDP and social spending we just examined. While we cannot test for effects on the level and growth of job-holding back to 1880, we can compare social-spending shares with employment rates in 2017, both for the same twenty-one countries, and for over forty countries.

To return to our finding that social spending seemed to lose some of its positive correlation with GDP among those twenty-one countries in the early twenty-first century, let us first ask whether the same recent weakness shows up when we relate social-spending shares to employment rates for the same twenty-one countries in the year 2017. It does indeed, as one can see from Figure 8.1's Panel (A). For jobs, just as for GDP per capita, the alignment of the twenty-one countries with social spending looks weakly negative. High-spending France, Belgium, Spain, Italy, and Greece have fewer than two-thirds of their working-age adults employed, whereas lower-spending New Zealand, Switzerland, the Netherlands, and Japan have all found jobs for over three-quarters of their working-age adults. So have the countries with larger social budgets at last begun paying a price in the form of lost jobs and output?

Using a wide-angle lens to capture a more global picture, however, erases the hint of lower job-holding among countries spending more in this century. The global cluster of nations in Table 8.3 and Panel (B) of

TABLE 8.3. *Jobs and social spending around the world in 2017 (social spending excludes public education spending, here as in Table 8.2)*

The core 21 countries	Public social spending as a % of GDP	Employment as a % of population ages 15–64	Other countries	Public social spending as a % of GDP	Employment as a % of population ages 15–64
Argentina	25.9	65.3	Brazil	15.9	67.0
Australia	17.8	72.9	China	8.0	69.3
Austria	27.1	73.0	Colombia	7.8	56.9
Belgium	29.2	62.4	Costa Rica	11.7	60.5
Canada	17.3	71.8	Czechia	19.0	73.5
Chile	10.9	60.6	Estonia	18.0	74.9
Denmark	28.1	74.9	Hungary	20.2	66.9
Finland	28.9	70.3	Iceland	15.9	83.8
France	31.8	64.6	India	10.9	45.8
Germany	25.1	76.7	Indonesia	10.7	63.3
Greece	24.8	53.0	Ireland	14.3	69.1
Italy	28.1	59.2	Israel	16.0	72.0
Japan	21.9	75.8	Korea	10.6	66.9
Netherlands	17.0	76.0	Latvia	15.8	68.0
New Zealand	18.6	81.0	Lithuania	15.8	69.6
Norway	25.3	73.6	Mexico	7.5	57.4
Portugal	23.7	67.9	Poland	21.0	61.1
Spain	23.9	61.3	Russia	13.1	72.5
Sweden	26.1	78.6	Slovak Rep.	17.3	65.9
UK	20.8	73.4	Slovenia	21.4	69.1
USA	18.9	67.2	South Africa	11.1	43.7
			Switzerland	16.1	79.0
			Turkey	12.5	50.8

Sources and notes to Table 8.3 and Figure 8.1: For the numbers of all persons 15–64 holding jobs, see https://stats.oecd.org/Index.aspx?DataSetCode=ALFS_SUMTAB#; accessed Dec. 19, 2019.

For the populations in the 15–64 age group, see United Nations (2015), including its median-variant projections to 2017.

Social Expenditure (SOCX), excluding public education expenditures, as a percentage of GDP are from www.oecd.org/social/expenditure.htm.

An exception: For Argentina, the employment is estimated by the International Labor Office (ILO) for 2017, and the social spending share for 2014 is from the sources cited in Arroyo Abad and Lindert (2017).

Figure 8.1 contrast with each other in a more positive way.[5] The additional twenty-three countries tend to have lower social spending and lower employment. Why do these low-spending countries from Asia and Latin America have much lower shares of their 15–64 populations at work than do the higher-spending countries of Northern Europe, New Zealand, and Japan?

The lower job-holding of the additional non-Europeans overstates an essential truth about differences in labor earnings. It overstates by letting you think that everybody not counted in their employment numbers is completely unemployed and earns zero. That is not true, of course. In these additional twenty-three countries, especially those in Latin America and South Asia, large shares of their adult populations find work in informal sectors that are not counted in the official employment numbers – such as the petty retailers peddling goods on street corners or by the roadside. Yet while one should not read the official numbers as if the informal-sector jobs were worth zero, the essential truth here is that the average person employed informally earns much less than the average person counted in the official formal-sector numbers. So the numbers in Table 8.3 and in either panel of Figure 8.1 give valid contrasts of different countries' labor earnings and labor productivity.

Had there been reliable numbers on job-holding in other countries beyond these forty-four countries, the overall associations would have been even more positive. Even without reliable numbers, it is clear that the countries failing to supply them tend to have low formal-sector employment, low GDP per person, and low social-spending shares of GDP. So the whole range of national experiences around the globe would show even greater positive correlations between any two of these three outcomes – job-holding, average incomes, and social spending. The more we know about economic behavior worldwide, the harder it is to believe that any of these outcomes negatively affects the others. In particular, the belief that a high social-spending share lowers jobs or outputs must retreat even further.

GENDER, AGE, AND JOBS. In the countries employing a lower share of their working-age adults, which adults are not finding as many jobs on the average? It cannot simply be that their governments supply less

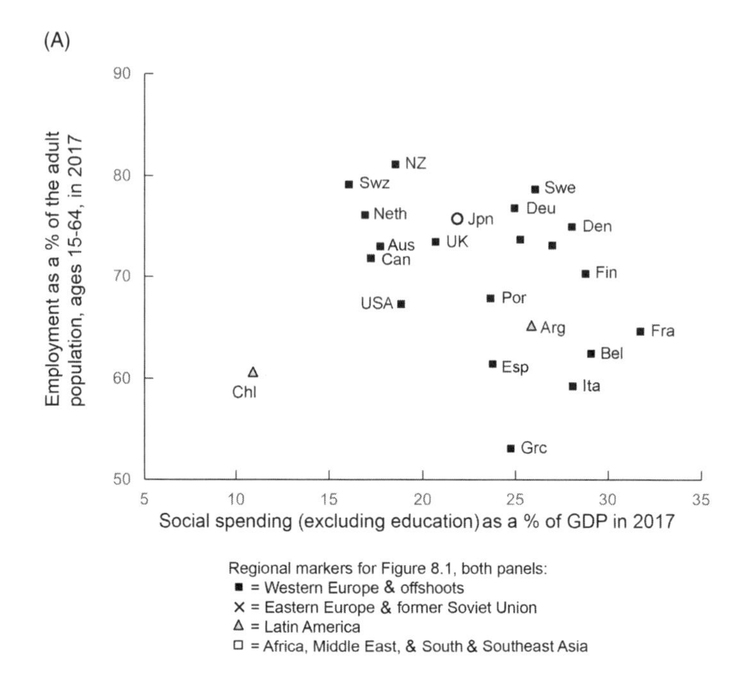

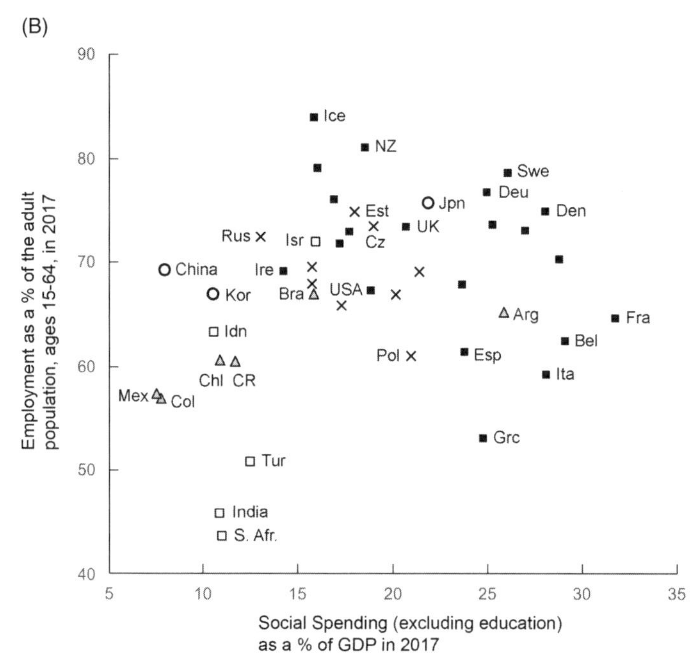

Figure 8.1. Employment of working-age adults versus social spending, 2017
Panel (A) For the same twenty-one core countries as in Table 8.2's view of GDP per person.
Panel (B) For forty-four countries.

support for job-holding. While such a failure to spend on job-creating programs might explain part of the greater job scarcity of Mexico, India, South Africa, or Turkey, that cannot be the story for high-spending Greece or Italy.

To explain the low work rates shared by all these countries, we need first to confront a pattern that they all share: they deliver fewer formal-sector jobs for females. The contrasts in the relationship of jobs to gender in the year 2017, shown in Figure 8.2, is one that has probably been true ever since economic development took off in the leading countries more than a hundred years ago. All over the world, females have lower employment rates than males, for a variety of reasons. Social suppression of

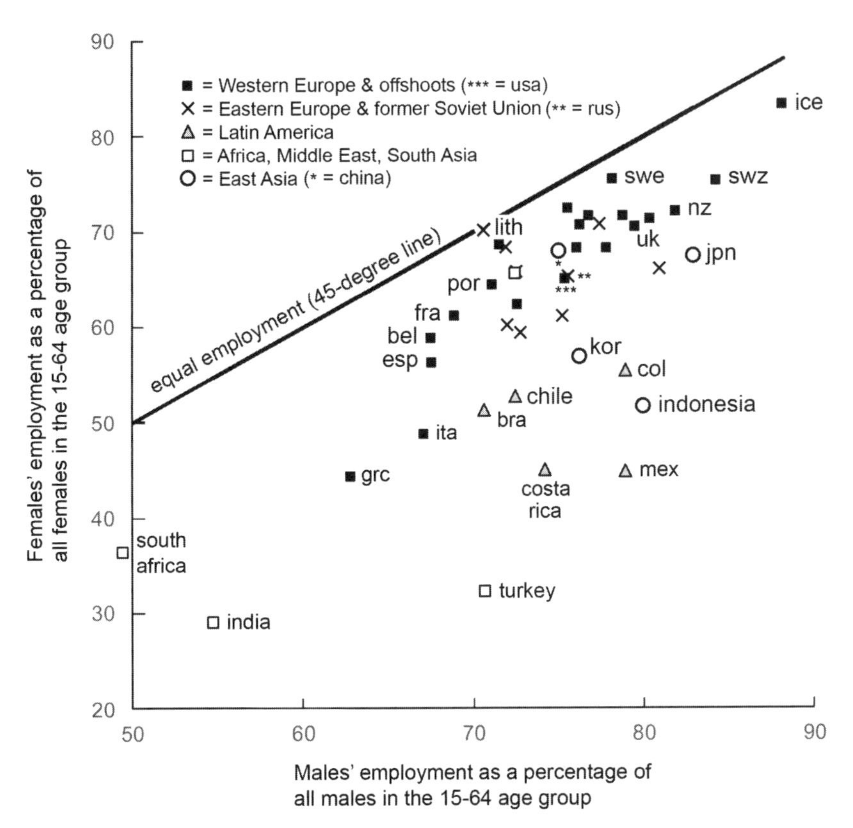

Figure 8.2. Gender and jobs in forty-three countries, 2017
Source: https://stats.oecd.org/Index.aspx?DataSetCode=ALFS_SUMTAB, accessed Aug. 19, 2018.

female work opportunities seems particularly likely in countries where their work rate is below that of males by, say, 15 percent of their working-age populations. The male–female job gap is wider to the south, far exceeding that 15 percent threshold in most countries of South Asia, Latin America, Mediterranean Europe, and Africa. Yet women also remain much less employed than men in Japan and Korea.

The social pressures holding down women's careers in these countries cannot be explained away as direct byproducts of lower education or of high fertility. True, in the Middle East and South Asia women's education is suppressed and fertility is high, as one would expect of countries where women have fewer jobs. Yet women's job-holding rates are also low in countries where they have nearly equal education and very few children, most strikingly in countries like Italy, Greece, Korea, and Japan, but also to some extent in Latin America. Why? Is it just that cultures differ "exogenously" for deep historical reasons, or do any recent economic institutions play a role?

It is not just females of working age that are employed much less than males. It is also true for either sex that both the young 15–24 adults and the older 55–64 adults hold jobs at lower rates than prime-age (25–54) males. A distinctive feature of all the countries with low overall employment rates (back in Table 8.3 and Figure 8.1) is that high shares of the jobs are held by males in that established-career age group 25–54. To identify which countries offer fewer employment opportunities for persons outside this advantaged male group, we can use a simple ratio of the employment rate for the whole 15–64 population to the employment rate for males in the prime 25–64 age group. This ratio can be thought of as a "job-equality" ratio. For the year 2017, this job-equality ratio varies anywhere from a low of 61 percent to a high of 93 percent across our forty-four data-supplying countries. The lowest rate (61 percent) is that for Turkey, followed by low rates for India, Costa Rica, South Africa, Mexico, Greece, Indonesia, and Italy, all of them having job rates for the whole 15–64 population that are below three-quarters of the rate for males 25–64. It is a southern group. At the top of the spectrum, Iceland has that 93 percent ratio, the most equal job-holding across males and females of working age, followed by Norway, Switzerland, Denmark, Sweden, Netherlands, Canada, and New Zealand, all of them having a ratio above 85 percent. It is a very northern group (if we allow New Zealand's high latitude to represent its being "northern"). In other words, the overall differences in job-holding, which were evident in Table 8.3 and Figure 8.1, take the form of differences in the dominance of job-holding by the advantaged group, namely males 25–64.[6]

It seems highly unlikely that the job concentrations in southern nations are explained by any low desire for work on the part of females and young adult males. Nor do the employers in these lower-work countries have peculiarly low demand for female or young adult labor. The explanation must lie to a large extent in institutional barriers that somehow deny these groups access to jobs for which they would be qualified.

While every country has its idiosyncratic labor-market institutions, there is one institution that helps to explain why the scarcity of job-holding outside of the advantaged male 25–54 group extends to many countries whose low fertility and high education should have fostered more careers. That institution consists of employee protection laws (EPLs) protecting established long-term employees against being fired. As several scholars have established, this protection creates a dual labor market consisting of insiders and outsiders, where the insiders tend to be males over the age of 25. Such EPLs seem to have had their greatest impact in Greece, Italy, Portugal, and Spain from the early 1970s on, and in Sweden between 1974 and 1991.

While EPLs may serve to protect jobs at low cost for a few years, the consensus is that sooner or later they act as a drag on both employment and productivity. As the years pass, employers' firing problem becomes a hiring problem. They are more reluctant to hire fresh employees of unknown productivity when faced with the EPL restrictions on their ability to dismiss those who do not work out. Largely for this reason, young workers on the outside tend to stay on the outside. To some extent, there could be productivity benefits from employers being pressured to develop the productivity of workers they cannot shed. Yet as time has passed since the early 1970s, such productivity benefits are outweighed by the fact that EPLs impede the rise of newer sectors who would otherwise have hired, and developed, fresh workers.[7]

Two key points emerge from the broad-brush evidence regarding the determinants of international differences in employment rates. First, their north–south geographic contrast must be due in large part to institutional barriers to long-term careers for young adults, and highly restrictive employee protection laws seem to be one main barrier. Second, the EPLs and other guilty institutions have no obvious relationship with the levels of social spending, since the barriers seem to be present in both low- and high-spending countries. Such restrictive labor laws are not an inherent part of the welfare state. Instead, they tend to be an institutional feature of only one type of welfare system, namely Gøsta Esping-Andersen's (1990) "corporatist" welfare state.

NO WORK DISINCENTIVES AT ALL FROM WELFARE SPENDING? REALLY? If the broad-brush international evidence cannot come up with any clearly negative net effect of larger social-spending budgets on growth or jobs, any reader could rightly demand a deeper reality test. What happened to those work shirkers and "welfare queens" imagined by critics back in Chapter 1? Would not a closer look reveal such anti-work behavior, with negative effects even on overall GDP?

Yes, economists have indeed found extensive evidence to support the critics' suspicions about work disincentives from specific kinds of policies. Statistical evidence shows that marginal taxation on workers' earnings can reduce labor supply. High-quality research since the 1960s has found statistically significant negative effects of some real-world payments of unemployment compensation and poor-family assistance ("welfare") on people's job-holding and their hours of work.[8] While some of the studies were a bit removed from observing the results of actual policy changes, others hit the mark by being based on actual policy experiments. The most famous of these policy experiments were the Negative Income Tax field studies conducted in selected urban and rural areas of the United States in the early 1970s. These studies found that poor households receiving subsidies without work requirements did indeed work less during the experiment. While primary breadwinners, usually male, did not work any less, many secondary earners did take advantage of the fact that staying home was temporarily more affordable, and worked less.[9]

These valid negative results are subject to two limitations, relating to size and relevance. As for size, they test something that is not large in its overall impact. "Statistically significant" does not mean large. It only means that the true effect is not likely to be zero or of the opposite sign, at least within the context of the model that was tested. That is, these studies have ended up with the kind of result most frequently published in highly scientific studies of micro-economic behavior: "small but statistically significant."[10] This literature has also focused disproportionately on classic means-tested welfare programs. These over-criticized programs keep applying to a smaller and smaller share of the population, as we saw in Chapter 6.

Even more important are the limitations on the relevance of the tests. Like the critics' theories they were designed to weigh, the statistical tests of labor supply address only some limited wrong-headed policies not typical of today's large real-world social programs. Governments all over the world have come up with design features that offset such work disincentives. They make sure that the programs reward good behavior, and avoid penalizing work.

Among developing countries, the best examples of social-expenditure programs rewarding good behavior are provided by today's "conditional cash transfers" (CCTs) to poor mothers.[11] CCTs arose from an innovation that we owe to policymakers in Brazil and Mexico. Back in the late 1990s, both countries introduced them virtually simultaneously, as Brazil's *bolsa escola* under President Cardoso (reorganized into *bolsa família* since Lula), and as Mexico's *progresa* under President Zedillo (later *oportunidades* under Fox, and then *prospera* under Peña Nieto). CCTs have since been implemented, with variations, by governments in over a dozen developing countries in Latin America, Africa, and Asia.

The core exchange in a CCT buys good behavior with cash to poor mothers. Receiving the cash payments is conditional on proving that each child has received the mandated health check-ups and inoculations, and that each school-age child is attending school. As for work incentives, the funds are not withdrawn if the adults in the household earn more, at least not until they have earned much more for a long period. Following what has become a global practice, the cash is given to the mother, not to any household male (unless he has sole custody), on the judgment that mothers will invest a greater share of household resources into child development. The cash is handed out directly from the federal social ministry, to avoid corruption under local community leaders. Note that the CCT programs tend to use carrots, rather than sticks – unlike the harsh "workhouse test" imposed on the poor in the mid-nineteenth century, that Dickensian world revisited in Chapter 3, and unlike some of today's harsher "workfare" mandates.

The more-developed countries have grappled with the issue of work incentives in their own ways, with mixed results. Ironically, the worst work disincentives have come from the stingiest programs. Consider a situation in which politicians demand that benefits for being unemployed, or for being poor, will be withdrawn just as soon as one earns anything. Such extreme "means-testing" has sometimes raised the marginal tax rate on labor earnings to 100 percent.

American history has yielded two such bad-practice cases, first in 1935–1967 and then in the 1980s. Federal assistance to poor single mothers was introduced with the Social Security Act of 1935. The then-small population of single mothers, mainly young widows who were expected to stay at home with the children, faced a 100 percent marginal tax rate on any earnings. Back then, in the 1930s, the defective policy applied only to a small share of the population. By the mid-1960s, however, opportunities for work outside the home began to attract more women, including a rising share of single mothers. In this setting, many economists, including Milton Friedman and James Tobin, ramped up their criticism of the 100 percent marginal tax rate on earnings. To allow the poor to keep much of their benefits while still earning modest amounts outside the home, federal reforms were enacted in 1967 to lower the marginal tax rate from 100 percent to 67 percent.

This reform was undone, however, in the early 1980s, when a conservative political reaction gave considerable publicity to any anecdotal discovery of a single perceived "welfare cheat" or "welfare queen." In this mood, the Reagan administration clamped down on any family assistance payments to households whose incomes were even a dollar above the poverty line, bringing the marginal tax rate on earnings back up to 100 percent, thereby discouraging work.

Fortunately, the disincentive to work was dialed back with tax credits for workers in the 1990s. In the United States, this tax credit is the Earned

Income Tax Credit (EITC), greatly expanded in 1993, from its modest introduction back in 1975. The British counterpart was the Working Tax Credit, which started as the Family Income Supplement in 1971, and is being merged into the Universal Credit since 2017. Similar employment-conditioned benefits for below-median earners now exist in Australia, Ireland, Canada, Finland, France, New Zealand, and Sweden. The marginal tax rates on extra earnings by low-income workers are now typically below 50 percent.

The earnings-subsidy idea is to get the poor launched into their careers by letting them keep most or all of what they earn. Eventually, in cases where the careers are so enhanced that their incomes approach the national median earnings, the subsidy must stop and the marginal tax rate rises again. Yet the statistical evidence finds that there is still a net gain in work and earnings, thanks to career attachment.[12] Support for such work subsidies has typically been bipartisan: progressives like the fact that it is a subsidy to workers, and conservatives like the fact that it reduces taxes rather than raising government expenditures. That said, the other side of the work-subsidy success in the United States is that it has made it easier for the political process to turn its back on the poverty population that has still not found work. As underlined by Hilary Hoynes and Diane Whitmore Schanzenbach (2018), the successful work subsidy of the EITC from 1993 was followed by the welfare-cutting "reform" of 1996.

The larger point is clear, then: that real-world welfare states do not design their overall bundles of social policies so wrong-headedly as to discourage work. They do not invite people to be lazy, contrary to a frequent fable.

ON THE LENGTH AND QUALITY OF LIFE

While not paying any clear net cost in terms of GDP, the large welfare states seem to have achieved many other things with their social transfers, as Lane Kenworthy (2019) has recently confirmed in some detail. Here is a quick list of major social goals they have served at least as well as other rich countries on the average.

(1) The welfare states tend to have *longer life expectancy* than other countries at similar income levels. Longer life tends to go hand in hand with spending more on public health, largely because both the extra public spending and the better health are both byproducts of the long-run development process. As countries prosper, infants have better chances of surviving to their first birthday, and even the elderly become healthier.[13] Each of the two probably promotes the other – spending more on public health lengthens life, but lengthening life can also cause more public spending on health, to care for an older population. A rough international correlation between the two shows up in Figure 8.3's contrasts of recent public health spending and the length of life in forty-one countries.

While we cannot quantify the causal effects, Figure 8.3 does help to give yet another soft hint of something positive about public social spending, in this case health spending. The most striking feature in Figure 8.3 is the failure of some countries spending over 4 percent of GDP on public health to live as long as 80 years from birth, at current period rates. The most conspicuous anomaly is, of course, the United States, with a life expectancy under 79 years, despite having a higher income than any other except Norway and Switzerland. Figure 8.3 also shows that the same shortfall in length of life is shared by the formerly communist countries of Eastern Europe and also in three Latin American countries. How these shortfalls might relate to the contrasting efficiencies in public health care will be explored in the next chapter.

(2) Their populations experience *less poverty* than people do in many lower-spending countries, such as the United States. That is, a lower share of the population falls below the poverty line, whether the poverty line is defined as a share of median income or as an absolute level of consumption per person.[14]

(3) They have consistently enjoyed a *more equal income distribution.* Updated estimates in Chapter 10 will show how much of this greater equality was due to fiscal redistribution from rich to poor.

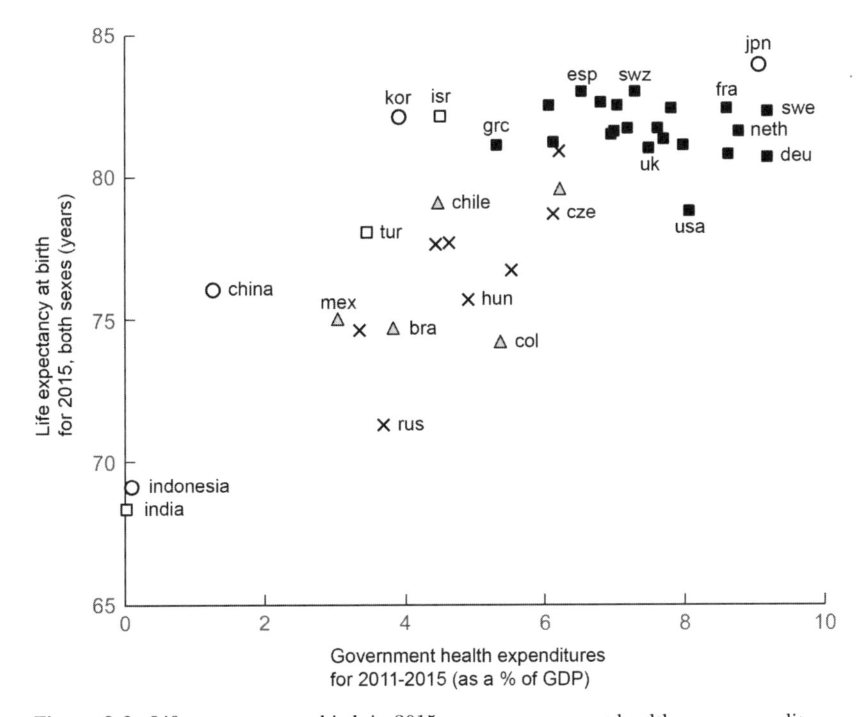

Figure 8.3. Life expectancy at birth in 2015 versus government health-care expenditures in 2011–2015 as a share of GDP

Sources and notes: The source for life expectancy is stats.oecd.org, via OECD iLibrary. The source for public health expenditure shares is the same, with the follow exceptions. China's number comes from the IMF's series on government (general) expenditure by function. The shares depart from the 2011–2015 average for Colombia (2014, from Lustig (2018)), Costa Rica (2010, Lustig (2018)), Russia (2010, Lustig (2018)), and India (2009, from Asian Development Bank (2013)).

(4) The high-spending welfare states are world leaders in having *clean governments*, despite what one might have predicted from the large amounts passing through government hands. The most widely used rating of government sleaze is Transparency International's annual Corruption Perceptions Index, which is based on surveys of international business people and on performance assessments from a group of international analysts. Contrary to its name, it is a rating of perceived government cleanliness, i.e. the absence of corruption. Out of the 180 governments being judged, which are viewed as the cleanest? The top dozen in the clean-government ranks for 2018, as for several years before that, consist of nine

Northern European countries with generally high social spending, plus three lower-spending non-European ones (New Zealand, Singapore, and Canada). Specifically, they were ranked thus in 2018: Denmark on top, followed by New Zealand, Finland, Singapore, Sweden, Switzerland, Norway, Netherlands, Canada, Luxembourg, Germany, and United Kingdom (with ratings from 88 down to 80). The lower-spending United States ranked only twenty-second in 2018, having dropped in the preceding years, both in absolute score (down to 71) and in international ranking (down from sixteenth to nineteenth in 2012–2018).[15] The governments looking cleanest in public eyes preside over societies in which people have a greater tendency to trust each other, to carry out collective solutions, and trust government to do its job honestly and effectively.

(5) Welfare states often run *smaller government budget deficits* – or, at least, there is no negative correlation between the GDP shares of social transfers and the net budget deficit.

(6) Finally, for what they are worth, international polls of public opinion find *higher expressions of personal happiness* in the high-spending welfare states, on the average.[16]

SUMMARY: THE "FREE LUNCH PUZZLE"

A great deal of circumstantial evidence on the relationships of social spending and economic performance has accumulated. While we cannot reliably measure the underlying causal influences, the circumstantial evidence does seem to acquit the high-spending welfare states from any net negative effect of their practices on incomes and work. At the same time, the extra social assistance, social insurance, and public education have been accompanied by longer and better lives. The recent verdict of Jeffrey Sachs is hard to overturn: "In strong and vibrant democracies, a generous social-welfare state is not a road to serfdom but rather to fairness, economic equality and international competitiveness."[17] Any objective reading of the mounting evidence should conclude that the countries with higher commitments to social assistance and social insurance – the welfare states, in conventional shorthand – have got all the social gains just listed without any net cost in terms of GDP. Elsewhere I have called this the "free lunch puzzle," where the lunch is free in this GDP sense.[18]

So far the welfare state appears to have been stirred, but not shaken. It looks like a Darwinian survivor.

CHAPTER 9

Why No Net Loss of GDP or Work?

HOW CAN THAT BE? HOW CAN SHIFTING A QUARTER OR MORE of national income from taxpayers to others do no net damage to national income?

It is time to follow through by exploring which parts of the policy bundle might be offsetting which other parts in their effects on GDP. To offset the widespread intuition that growth will be damaged by social supports and the taxes levied on their behalf, this chapter spotlights four positive features of the larger and more universal tax-based social programs that have been put into practice:

(1) The larger and more universal social programs tend to be financed by the kinds of taxes that conventional economists consider to be most efficient and GDP-enhancing.
(2) Contrary to common tales, the large-budget universal social programs are less bureaucratic and cheaper to administer.
(3) Countries with larger social budgets show a better understanding of the public economics of motherhood and early childhood development. Their greater commitments to tax-paid parental leave and to pre-primary education (e.g. for 4-year-olds) seem to contribute to growth and equality in the long run.
(4) Universal public health insurance is efficient, saving more years of life at lower cost.

A MORE PRO-GROWTH TAX MIX

WHAT THEORY SAYS ABOUT THE TAX MIX. Behind social spending lies a mixture of taxes that pay for them. Countries differ not only in the sizes of their social budgets, but also in the taxes they raise. To get a plausible rough idea of what kinds of taxes get channeled into the government's social budget, let us assume that the social budget absorbs different kinds of government tax revenues in the same proportions as do other kinds of government spending, such as national defense or road-building.

Conventional economic theory is certainly not neutral in the debates about which taxes a country should impose. It consistently predicts that some kinds of taxation do more damage to the level and growth of GDP than others, for any given way that the tax money is spent. "Direct" taxes on income and wealth are accused of doing the most direct damage to people's incentives, by threatening to grab a share of the gains in income and wealth one would get from being more productive. Many economists stress that directly taxing income and wealth is especially damaging when it is "progressive" taxation, taking greater and greater percentage shares out of higher and higher incomes, though the case against progressivity is not ironclad.

By contrast, "indirect" taxes, or taxes on consumption, are thought to be less harmful to GDP, for a couple of reasons. For one, they excuse from this year's taxes the part of income that is saved, and not consumed, this year. For another, they do not encourage leisure, because the taxed consumption is a complement to leisure. For example, if there is a tax on your consumption of drinks and entertainment and vacations, you might have more incentive to work more and save more for the future, in the hope that the pesky consumption taxes will go away.

Two kinds of indirect taxes are especially favored. One that gains loud applause among economists is the broadest kind, such as a flat percentage tax on all consumption. A value-added tax (VAT) in its purest form takes the same sales-tax percentage from everybody for everything. This is thought to do the least damage to people's willingness to work and take risks, because there is so little chance to evade it. In shorthand, broad is good. The other applause-winner is a sin tax, a tax on any activity that inflicts negative externalities on people other than the consumer of the sinful product.

Aside from direct and indirect taxes, history has produced a third major tax source, in the form of mandatory job-based contributions to social insurance. In common parlance, think of it as the "social security contributions" taken out of employees' paychecks, to fund future social expenditures on health care and pensions. This third type of tax gets low-to-middling marks from economic theory. On the one hand, it is a convenient revenue source. It might also have the advantage of being a broad and flat percentage tax for all employees. Yet it can have incentive effects that eliminate some jobs and output. Compulsory contributions from employee paychecks are a cost of employment, giving either the employer or the employee less reward from the job. Typically, the system of government-mandated paycheck contributions applies only to larger employers, e.g. those hiring more than fifty employees, and only to relatively full-time work, e.g. more than twenty hours a week. This generates the familiar negative press coverage about how firms will not hire the fiftieth worker or will not hire more full-time workers because of the cost of paying mandatory contributions to social funds. We will return to the case against job-based social insurance, the so-called "second pillar" of social insurance, when recounting the tragic history of American health care later in this chapter, and again in Chapters 12–14, when we confront the history of governments' involvement in occupation-based pensions around the world.

THE IRONIC GEOGRAPHY OF TODAY'S TAX MIXES. What the recent global history of the mixture of taxes reveals is not that the conventional theory is right or wrong about effects of GDP, but instead an ironic geography of where the conventional policies are followed. A right-or-wrong verdict on the GDP effects remains elusive. We lack robust statistical evidence that this kind of tax mix is really better for economic growth.[1] Rather, what we find is a striking disconnect between where the conventional economists tend to cluster and where their preferences about tax types are actually implemented.

The disconnect stands in the contrasts in tax style shown in Table 9.1 and Figure 9.1. Look first at the contrasting tax styles of the top two regions in Figure 9.1, namely the lower-tax, lower-social budget style of the four rich offshoots from the British Empire (Australia, Canada, New Zealand, and the United States) versus the higher-tax welfare-state homeland of Northern Europe. Many would expect the smaller government offshoots to have trimmed back the direct taxation of income and wealth, while the higher-budget welfare states soak the rich. Yet, ironically, the world's greatest reliance on direct income and wealth taxes occurs in those four lower-budget offshoot countries, which get 59 percent of their

TABLE 9.1. *Tax revenue shares, forty-one countries and six regions in 2016*

	Percentages of total tax revenue		
	Direct taxes (excl. SSC)	Indirect taxes	Social security contributions (SSC)
Argentina	14.5	48.9	36.6
Australia	68.0	32.0	0.0
Austria	28.5	36.8	34.7
Belgium	43.5	25.4	31.1
Brazil	25.8	40.9	33.3
Canada	58.7	26.4	14.9
Chile	34.8	58.1	7.2
China	28.4	51.1	20.6
Czechia	23.6	33.5	42.9
Denmark	63.3	36.5	0.1
Estonia	23.1	43.7	33.2
Finland	37.8	33.1	29.1
France	32.7	30.6	36.8
Germany	34.7	27.7	37.6
Greece	29.8	41.6	28.5
Hungary	22.2	44.6	33.2
Iceland	65.8	27.5	6.7
India	49.2	50.6	0.2
Indonesia	49.6	50.4	0.0
Ireland	49.2	34.1	16.8
Israel	40.0	43.4	16.6
Italy	37.4	32.5	30.1
Japan	38.9	20.7	40.4
Korea	42.8	31.1	26.2
Latvia	30.0	42.7	27.3
Lithuania	20.0	39.3	40.8
Mexico	43.3	43.7	13.0
Netherlands	31.2	30.6	38.2
New Zealand	58.4	41.6	0.0
Norway	41.2	31.4	27.4
Poland	24.1	37.8	38.1
Portugal	32.4	41.0	26.6
Russia	28.7	40.5	30.8
Slovak Republic	22.3	34.2	43.5
Slovenia	20.5	39.9	39.7
Spain	35.9	30.0	34.2
Sweden	38.4	39.0	22.6
Switzerland	49.6	26.1	24.3
Turkey	26.0	45.2	28.8
United Kingdom	48.3	32.8	18.9
United States	59.0	16.9	24.0
Regions shown in Figure 9.1[a]			
4 offshoots	59.6	18.9	21.5
9 North Europeans	38.2	30.1	31.7

TABLE 9.1. *(continued)*

	Percentages of total tax revenue		
	Direct taxes (excl. SSC)	Indirect taxes	Social security contributions (SSC)
3 Asian giants	38.0	58.5	3.5
5 Mediterraneans	34.6	31.7	33.7
4 Latin Americans	24.8	43.1	32.1
8 Eastern Europeans	23.4	38.0	38.6

[a] The regions are:
4 offshoots = Australia, Canada, New Zealand, and the United States.
9 North Europeans = Austria, Belgium, Denmark, Finland, Germany, Iceland, Netherlands, Norway, and Sweden.
3 Asian giants = China, India, and Indonesia.
5 Mediterraneans = France, Greece, Italy, Portugal, and Spain.
4 Latin Americans = Argentina, Brazil, Chile, and Mexico.
8 Eastern Europeans = Czech Republic, Estonia, Hungary, Latvia, Lithuania, Poland, Slovak Republic, and Slovenia.
Sources and notes to Table 9.1 and Figure 9.1: For Argentina (central government, including social security), China, India (budgetary central government), and Russia, the source is data.imf.org. For all other countries, the source is OECD (2018e).
Unless otherwise stated, the estimates refer to "general" government (the consolidation of central, regional, and local governments).
Government non-tax revenues (e.g. from government monopolies) are not included. In most cases, these were only small shares of total revenue. In the case of Russia, however, these non-tax revenues made up 51 percent of total revenue. The averages for regions were derived from the country data, using current-price GDP as weights for each tax type's share of GDP. The current-price GDPs for 2016 were derived from Penn World Tables 9.1, as the products of real GDP in 2011 international dollars and the 2016 price level relative to that 2011 base.

tax revenues from direct and progressive income taxation. By contrast, the nine Northern Europeans, most of them welfare states, collect only 37 percent of their taxes in this way. They take greater shares from the kinds of taxation preferred by conventional economics, especially such indirect taxes as the broad and flat VAT and sin taxes on such negative-externality products as alcohol, tobacco, and petroleum fuels – even though such indirect taxes are paid more heavily by the same working-class constituency that ushered in the arrival of the welfare state.[2]

While the Nordic countries, New Zealand, and Israel pioneered the flat value-added tax as far back as 1960, it has now been adopted, in varying degrees, at the national level in more than 160 countries. Why

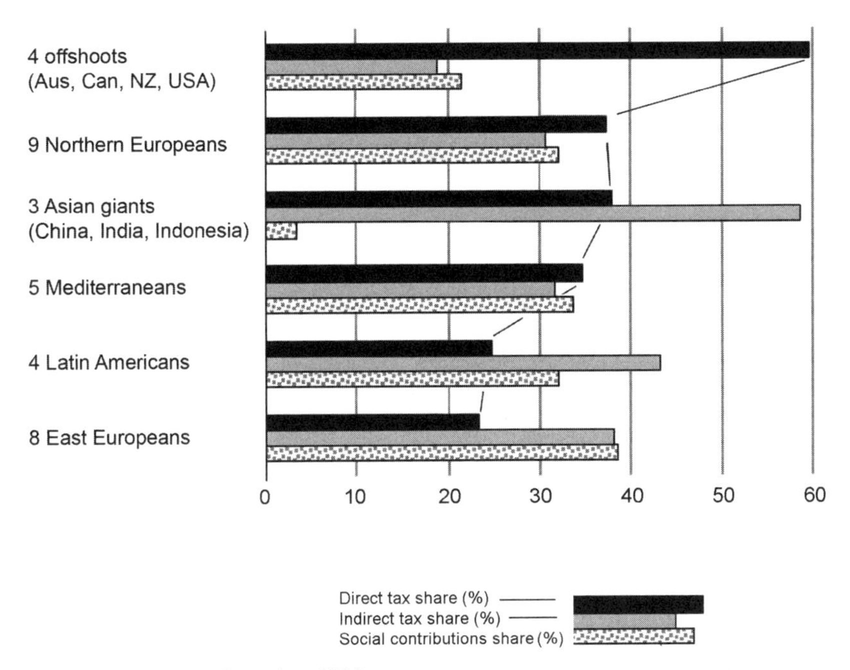

Figure 9.1. Tax mix by region, 2016

should the four low-budget free-market countries of North America and Australasia be the laggards in adopting the VAT and other indirect taxes, as shown in Table 9.1 and Figure 9.1? In particular, why should the United States have zero VAT at the federal level, and only about 8 percent of all tax revenue even if one included state sales taxes as if they were a VAT? After all, theory and history both say that the VAT is not progressive, low in disincentive costs, cheap to administer, and harder than other taxes to evade. It should be the kind of tax that is least abhorred by economic conservatives. As Murray Weidenbaum, a former chair of President Reagan's Council of Economic Advisers, said: "Many analysts believe that it is fairer to tax people on what they take from society, rather than on what they contribute by working and investing."[3] There have been several unsuccessful American attempts to introduce the value-added tax and similar broad consumption taxes into serious public debate. Broad consumption taxes were even proposed as a way to finance the union forces in the Civil War in 1862 and America's participation in

World War II in 1942, but were defeated. The VAT idea was floated again in the 1970s–1990s, but kept being dropped.[4]

So why was it adopted initially in all the welfare states, and then all over the world, but never in the United States? A quip by Lawrence Summers in 1988 explained why the United States had not yet adopted a value-added tax: "Liberals think it's regressive and conservatives think it's a money machine." Summers added that if the Republicans took more note of its being regressive, and the Democrats took more note of its being a money machine for big government, then America might someday adopt a VAT.[5] Of these two controversial features of the VAT – its alleged regressivity (taking more from the poor than from the rich), and the efficient money machine for big government – the latter is the truer sticking point. A uniform percentage tax on consumption is actually not regressive in practice, especially if it is permanent and is spent on delivering such universal benefits as basic health care. Appendix B explains what is wrong with the usual assumption that a flat consumption tax would be regressive, falling more heavily on the poor. The real sticking point is the money machine. America's economic and racial divisions have always created powerful antagonism to big government, and to big social spending, as noted in Chapter 6. Ironically, then, the kind of taxation used as a money machine for the large welfare states of Northern Europe gains strong support from conventional economics, but is successfully vetoed by American conservative politicians. This might have helped to make the GDP performance of the higher-budget European welfare states look more satisfactory, though we lack hard statistical proof of such a favorable effect.

Looking beyond the contrasts between just Northern Europe and its non-European offshoots, one finds other fresh geographic perspectives in Table 9.1 and Figure 9.1. It is in Asia that the style of taxation contrasts most glaringly with the tax mix of those offshoots in North America and Australasia. China, India, and Indonesia rely far more heavily on indirect taxes (consumption taxes), instead of taxing incomes as directly and progressively as the North Americans and Australasians. This contrast might be a byproduct of their having much lower average incomes. For at least a half century, economists have noted that tax styles evolve in a very predictable way over the course of economic development.[6] In the poorest initial phases, when the government is weak and the country lacks widespread information networks, the only way to muster revenue for the government is through indirect taxes, such as excise taxes on highly visible commodities and customs duties collected at border points. Direct taxes on income and wealth are harder to collect fairly and efficiently. Such were the hard realities for the newly independent United States in the 1780s, and so they remain for still-developing economies, like China, India, and Indonesia today, though these countries will soon have greater fiscal capacity to assess and collect such modern taxes as income tax and the value-add tax.

In between these two regional extremes, the collection of 58 percent of all taxes in indirect form in developing Asia and the collection of 59 percent of taxes in direct form in North America and Australasia, the other regions spread their collections more evenly across sources. In particular, they rely more on collecting mandatory social security contributions from paychecks, as shown in Table 9.1 and Figure 9.1. The reasons for this are not entirely clear. In the case of the eight formerly communist nations of Eastern Europe, the emphasis on payroll tax collections may be a holdover from the communist era, when central planning paid, and assisted, households through the workplace. Yet there is no obvious reason why Mediterranean Europe and Latin America make such large use of mandatory paycheck contributions, when they could have achieved the same revenues from extra value-added taxes. The VAT percentage rates could be lower than the rates taken from formal-sector payrolls, since the VAT burden could be shared with the large informal sectors in these regions.[7]

SIN TAX GEOGRAPHY. Aside from their use of the relatively growth-sparing VAT, the countries with higher social budgets tend to aim their other indirect taxes at targets that help fight bad behaviors while doing little harm to growth or to the rich. The bad behaviors that are best targeted are three kinds of addictive behavior that compromise human health: tobacco, alcohol, and fossil fuels. Which specific countries make the heaviest use of such growth-sparing sin taxes? Do welfare states still use it more, as they did in the late twentieth century? The current international contrasts can be captured by comparing countries' rates of taxation on cigarettes and gasoline (petrol).[8]

Cigarette taxes are high the world over, though least high in North America, as shown in Figure 9.2. In general, tobacco taxes tend to be highest in countries with two attributes. One attribute elevating tobacco tax rates is an inelastic demand for tobacco products. Where people will continue smoking heavily even when paying high taxes on their habit, governments naturally shift toward raising a lot of revenue by taxing that inelastic demand more heavily than other products, a strategy known as "Ramsey taxation" among economists.[9] The countries with the highest tax rates on cigarettes in Figure 9.2 have some of the world's highest

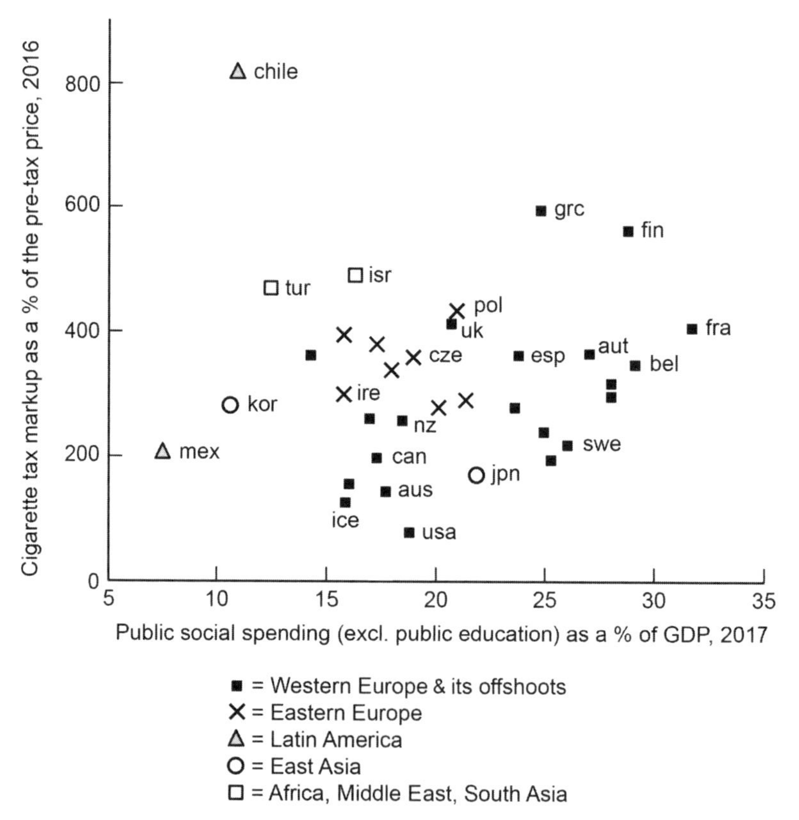

Figure 9.2. Cigarette tax rates, thirty-five countries in 2016 (rates as percentages of the pre-tax price)

Sources and notes: OECD (2018a, Annex Table 3.A.5) for the tax markups, and the OECD's social-expenditure database for the non-education social spending.

smoking rates despite facing the highest taxes. So it is for the chain smokers of Eastern Europe, Finland, Greece, and Chile.[10]

On the bottom side of Figure 9.2, one could reasonably suspect that the United States taxes cigarette consumption less heavily because it is such a larger tobacco producer. That may be a factor, but probably not the most important explanation. After all, tobacco-exporting Turkey taxes cigarette consumption more heavily. Rather, two other important factors are that America uses legal institutions to cut tobacco demand in non-tax ways, and that America has a perennial aversion to any kinds of taxes and to large government budgets.

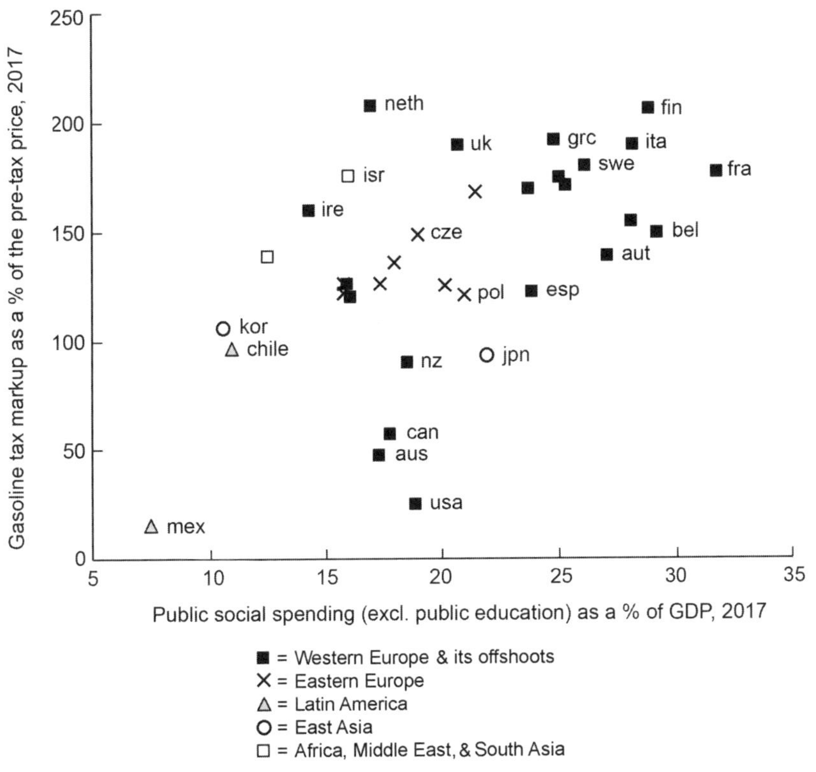

Figure 9.3. Gasoline (petrol) tax rates, thirty-five countries in 2017 (rates as percentages of the pre-tax price)
Sources and notes: OECD (2018a, Annex Table 3.A.6) for the tax markups, and the OECD's social-expenditure database for the non-education social spending.

America's smoking rate has been cut considerably through litigation in the courts. Forty state governments, led by Mississippi in 1994, have joined private citizen groups as successful plaintiffs winning huge court settlements against tobacco companies. In addition, legislators have responded to the health risks by passing some of the world's strictest anti-smoking laws. The American preference for law suits and prohibitions relates to that second factor, the same American aversion to the use of revenue-generating taxes that also limits their social spending. Hence America's odd combination of heavy government intervention and low taxes.

Among the rich countries that have formed the core of the OECD, the ones with higher taxes on tobacco tend to be those spending higher shares of GDP on social programs. One can see this in Figure 9.2 by looking only at the black squares, plus the dots for Japan and Korea, representing those core OECD countries that have been the focus of most research in the past. Among these, it is clear that high-social-budget countries tend to tax cigarettes more heavily. Again, that underlines that the welfare states make greater use of a kind of tax that look justifiable. Interestingly, the fuller global geography of cigarette taxes fails to show the same tendency, given the high tax rates in Chile, Israel, and Turkey in Figure 9.2. Still, above the main OECD countries, a positive relationship between the cigarette tax and overall social spending shows up in these data for 2016, just as it did in the late twentieth century.

The same relationship of sin taxes to the welfare state emerges in Figure 9.3's global geography of gasoline taxes in 2017. Again, it is the welfare states, those with social spending over 20 percent of GDP, that have shifted their tax mix toward the relatively justifiable tax types. Relative to the direct taxes used in greater proportion by the low-budget North Americans and Australasians, the taxes chosen by the countries with high social budgets do a better job of countering negative externalities.

DECLINING BUREAUCRATIC COSTS

The widespread fear of high bureaucratic costs of social programs, as in the phrase "bloated welfare bureaucracy," is unwarranted. Both on the expenditure-allocation side and on the tax-collection side, administrative costs become lower, the larger and more universal the population covered. In technology-sector jargon, social programs "scale" well. Universalist expenditure programs, to which everybody is entitled, are cheaper to administer because there is less bureaucratic need to investigate who should be excluded from the benefits. Similarly, on the tax side, broader taxes are also cheaper to administer.

On this, the historical evidence is even clearer than the evidence from cross-country contrasts.

DECLINING ADMINISTRATIVE COSTS ON THE SOCIAL-EXPENDITURE SIDE. Since the eighteenth century, administrative costs have declined as a share of the total amounts transferred to the poor, the sick, and the elderly. The reason: Stricter regimes are more bureaucratic and costlier, because of the cost of determining exactly who should be given carrots and who should be threatened with sticks. The expansion of social spending over the last hundred years has generally reduced strictness and replaced it with more universal entitlements, cutting the need for documentation and supervision.

This cost-saving was already described and documented for classic nineteenth-century poor relief in Chapter 3. Back in Charles Dickens' time, as noted in Chapter 3, societies intent on forcing all the able-bodied to work tried to emphasize "indoor relief," in which an Oliver Twist was kept in a poorhouse or workhouse. Officials never succeeded in getting such "indoor" relief to cover its own costs, or even just its administrative costs, by squeezing labor out of the inmates. The administrative costs of hiring the likes of Mister Bumble were a high share, often a quarter, of the total amount spent. By contrast, once democracy, prosperity, and other developments made society more willing to give aid to people in their own homes, with minimal supervision, the administrative costs fell as a share of the amount spent.

By the postwar era, administrative costs have fallen to almost-negligible levels in the high-income OECD countries. So say not only data on programs for the poor, but also data on pension programs. International data on pension programs show that administrative costs are less than 3 percent of the pension program budget in all high-income countries, and often below 1 percent.

Similarly, the administrative cost shares for health care are lower when health care is insured by government for the entire population. The main reason is that universal coverage, alias universal risk pooling, removes the need to screen people to see who is a greater risk than others. With such universal coverage, illustrative studies have shown, Germany achieved lower health-care administrative costs than the United States by 1990, and Canada achieved the same cost cutting relative to the United States by 2002.[11] In health insurance, as in welfare and pensions, bureaucratic costs are lower in the larger, more universal government-run forms.

DECLINING ADMINISTRATIVE COSTS ON THE TAX-COLLECTION SIDE. Similarly, the collection of taxes had historically declined as a share of the amounts raised, as taxes became more and more universal and easier to document. The earliest tax savings came when rulers' arbitrary exactions were replaced by relatively stable and honest customs and excise taxes, as described in Chapter 3. It was a transition that took centuries in Europe, and has still not taken place in many developing countries. Where rulers were finally forced to grant new freedoms and predictable taxes, cities, merchants, and industry flourished. While the customs and excise regimes had improved the overall efficiency of the tax system by the nineteenth century, bureaucratic costs were still substantial.

The hundred years from about 1870 to about 1970 then replaced the system of customs and excise taxation with lower-cost direct taxation, while at the same time improving the efficiency of tax collection within the expanding internal/inland government agencies. Figure 9.4 shows this decline in administrative cost shares from 1870 to 1970 in the United Kingdom and the United States. These cost savings further reduced the cost of any programs the tax revenues were spent on, such as the social programs that are our focus here. Since 1970, the rise of the value-added tax again made it cheaper and easier to collect revenues than under the older regimes of excise taxation.

INVESTING IN MOTHERS' CAREERS AND EARLY CHILD DEVELOPMENT

The third pro-growth feature of the welfare states' social spending has been their relatively generous investments in career continuity and skills

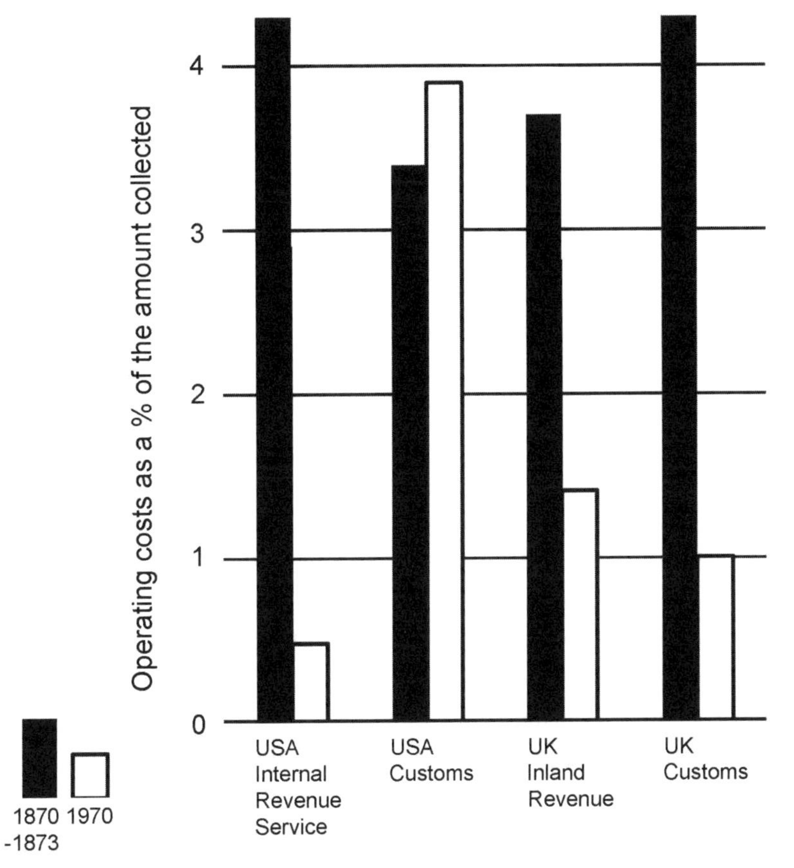

Figure 9.4. Tax-collection costs as a percentage of central government revenue, United Kingdom and United States, 1870 and 1970
Sources and notes: Sources for the administrative cost shares of tax collections are cited in Lindert (2004, vol. I, p. 304), and can now be updated to the present in the Internal Revenue Service (IRS) data book, www.irs.gov/statistics/irs-budget-and-workforce, accessed Jan. 5, 2020. I am indebted to Joel Slemrod for his directing me to the updated IRS series.

accumulation for mothers, indirectly also supporting their children's early development. Three "family-friendly" policy tools that are increasingly applied around the world are (1) government payments for job leaves by parents of newborns, (2) different forms of public day care, and (3) government subsidies for pre-primary education.[12] Their potential effects on the development skills matter more and more, as an increasing share of women's adulthood is career-oriented and children's futures are increasingly dependent on their skills rather than on their parents' property.

Who is applying these three kinds of government policies in the right amount? To set the stage for the emerging verdicts on the effects of these policy interventions, let us turn first to the task of identifying where they are implemented.

WHICH COUNTRIES HAVE MORE FAMILY-FRIENDLY GOVERNMENT EXPENDITURES. How are the large-budget welfare states linked with the practice of having government pay for parental job interruptions, for child care, and for pre-primary education in the first five years of life? In the long sweep of history, both the large social budgets and the family-friendly policies are youngsters. Among regions, it was the communist countries that took the lead in government-run child care and parental leave on a modest scale. Among democracies, substantial supports arose in the late 1960s and 1970s in response to the rise in women's labor-force participation, with Sweden leading the way. A pro-natal wave of supports has arrived since the 1990s, in response to concerns about low fertility rates.[13]

Today, over thirty countries report government supports related to the new children of working parents. Two kinds of support, namely paid parental leave and pre-primary education, are shown for the year 2016 in Table 9.2. The countries of Eastern and Northern Europe are still in the lead in providing both of these supports, and such family-friendly supports are indeed positively correlated with overall social spending.[14] Figure 9.5 illustrates some differences among selected countries. First, today's high levels of German and Swedish support still reflect the 1960s–1970s wave, generated by the rise in women's work and in the welfare state. The concern over low fertility since the 1990s is echoed in Japan's high allowance of paid weeks of parental leave, a remarkable contrast to Japan's longer-standing gender divisions. Today, even "salaryman" can take up to a year of paid parental leave (if he wishes, and if he dares), and mothers' careers receive some support. Japan's pro-natal support for paid parental leave has not carried over, however, into generous taxpayer support for pre-primary education.

TABLE 9.2. *Public investments in paid parental leave and in early education, thirty-five countries in 2016*

		Government expenditure measures:	
	Parental paid leave entitlements (FTE weeks)	Pre-primary education per child 0–4 as a % of GDP per person 18–64	Social spending as a % of GDP (excl. education)
Australia	7.6	2.3	17.8
Austria	51.2	6.7	27.8
Belgium	13.1	7.5	29.2
Canada	27.4	–	17.4
Chile	30.0	6.1	11.0
Czechia	53.1	6.4	19.1
Denmark	26.8	13.1	28.7
Estonia	85.0	4.2	18.3
Finland	40.6	8.3	29.8
France	18.8	6.7	32.0
Germany	42.6	6.8	25.1
Greece	23.3	3.4	25.7
Hungary	71.8	10.7	20.8
Iceland	15.5	7.7	15.1
Ireland	8.9	0.6	14.9
Israel	14.0	4.5	15.5
Italy	25.2	6.5	28.3
Japan	35.8	1.4	21.9
Korea	25.0	6.4	10.5
Latvia	53.3	11.0	16.1
Lithuania	62.0	7.4	16.0
Mexico	12.0	–	7.5
Netherlands	16.0	4.1	17.5
New Zealand	7.7	4.4	18.9
Norway	45.0	7.7	25.7
Poland	41.6	8.4	21.2
Portugal	20.4	5.9	23.7
Slovak Rep.	53.7	6.6	17.8
Slovenia	48.4	6.3	22.2
Spain	16.0	6.5	24.3
Sweden	34.7	12.8	26.4
Switzerland	7.9	5.1	15.9
Turkey	10.6	–	12.5
UK	12.1	2.0	21.2
USA	0.0	3.3	18.9

Sources and notes to Table 9.2 and Figure 9.5: The source for paid parental leave entitlements is the OECD's family database: http://www.oecd.org/els/family/database.htm#public_policy, Table PF2.1.A, accessed June 7, 2018, using an institutional subscription to iOECD Library.

Here the "parental leave entitlements" equals "paid maternity leave" plus "paid parental and home care leave."

For the United States, the paid parental leave here refers only to the (zero) federal provisions.

TABLE 9.2 *(continued)*

The data on government expenditures on pre-primary education as a share of GDP are those supplied annually by national governments to UNESCO: http://data.uis.unesco.org, accessed Jan. 3, 2020.
They refer to total general (central, regional, and local) expenditures.
The ratio of the population of ages 0–4 to the population ages 18–64 is derived from United Nations (2015), i.e. as forecast for 2016.
For Denmark and Estonia, the pre-primary education data refer to the year 2013.
The shares of government (non-education) social spending in GDP are those OECD social expenditures cited in Chapters 6 and 7.

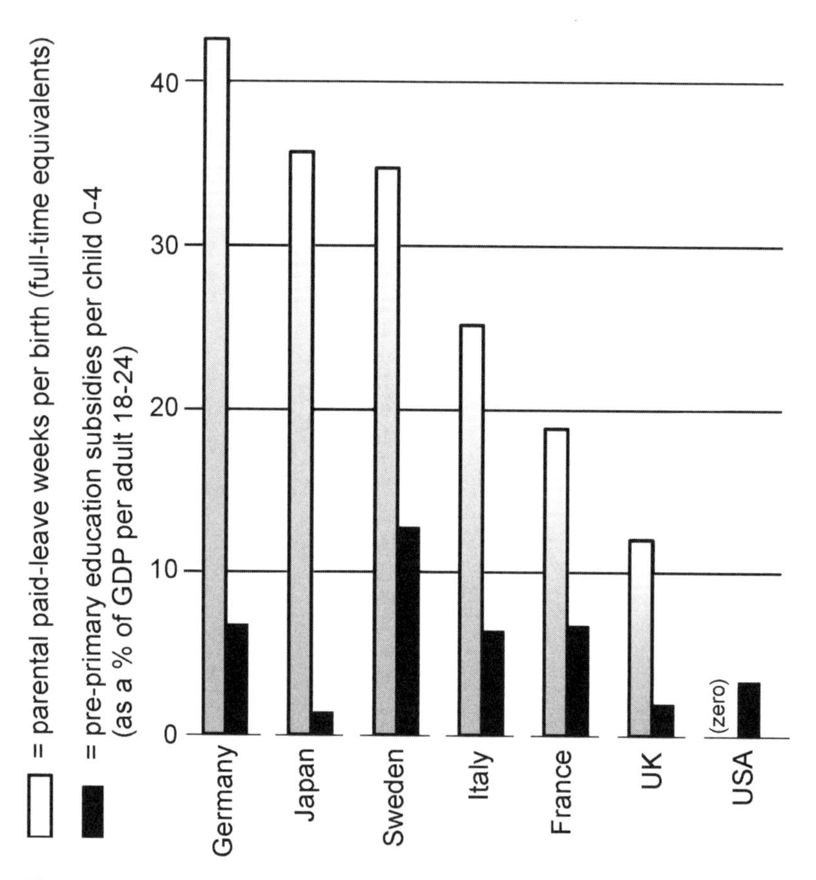

Figure 9.5. Public investments in paid parental leave and in early education, seven countries in 2016

The lowest levels of support are recorded in the English-speaking countries, especially the United States and Australia, with Japan again offering little in the case of pre-primary public education. At this bottom end of the spectrum, the United States has attained some notoriety for being the only country, other than Papua New Guinea, not to provide any national government payments for parental leave. Its 1993 Family Medical Leave Act does not pay government money for parental leave and does not require employers to pay for it either. Its provisions assuring re-hire rights and health insurance continuation do not apply to many parents in the private sector. In recent years, over two dozen states, led by California, have already provided more generous taxpayer support. With other states about to follow suit, the lack of any federal government support will decline in relevance. Yet two concerns will remain: The state levels of support are unequal, and even the most generous levels of state support are still well below the average for the other countries shown in Table 9.2.[15]

While paid parental leave can in principle be gender-neutral, it is rarely extended as generously to fathers as to mothers. Governments did not pay for fathers' leave before the 1990s, and most still paid for 0–2 days as of 2014. These policies are presumably based on general societal preferences, as filtered through the political process.

HOW DOES PAID LEAVE AFFECT PARENTS' WORK, AND THEIR EMPLOYERS? To be pro-GDP, a paid leave policy should raise women's employment, without damaging men's employment or employers' levels of output. The statistical literature reports that this policy goal has been met. Women have worked more in response to the paid leave policies, and employers and others have not yet been harmed significantly.[16]

It could have been otherwise, if paid leave had been overdone, or if employers' rights had been curtailed unduly. The danger of overdoing it is clear enough. Like most good things, subsidizing parental leave can be expanded only up to a point. Too long, or too generous, a paid leave might induce somebody to stay out of the labor force too long to get back on their most productive career track.

The other danger, the risk of unduly limiting employers' rights, also needs to be recognized. To avoid damaging economic growth, and to protect employers' incentives to go on hiring young women, there should be limits to the mandated infringements on their freedom. In principle, if somebody is to be compelled to pay for parental leave, it should be the parties who would benefit most from it. Would the firms themselves benefit directly from paying for parental leave? If so, they should have been in the best position to see that, and should have initiated paid parental leave on their own. Indeed, many private employers have voluntarily paid for employees' family leaves to some extent, and increasingly so in the twenty-first century. In a study of 1,135 private firms in 2017–2018, Claudia Goldin, Sari Pekkala Kerr, and Claudia Olivetti (2020) found a large share of firms offering their own nearly universal full-pay parental leave insurance, especially to higher-skilled employees with long-term employment bonds to their firm. Still, even the most generous American firms, like the most generous American state governments, provide fewer fully paid parental weeks than does the median OECD nation.

The instinct that taxpayers, through government, need to supplement such private parental leave coverage starts from a valid premise. A core reason is that private capital markets will not lend money on good terms to the parent of a newborn to tide them over an interruption in paid work. Lenders do not see any secure collateral, even if the parental leave greatly enhances the mother's near-future earnings and the child's eventual earnings. This market defect regarding parental leave is similar to the incompleteness of private lending for education in general.

This insight is borne out by recent estimates of how governments' paid parental leave affects mothers' employment, using international panels of experiences with different paid leave policies. They tend to show a modest, statistically significant rise in women's employment as long as the paid leave entitlement is shorter than fifty weeks. And, as one can sense from Table 9.2, most governments provide fewer than fifty weeks' paid leave.[17] The recent studies even seem to show a gender symmetry: the same damaging effect on pay prospects has been shown for stay-at-home fathers in cases where the mother retains a breadwinning career. The statistical literature has wavered on the question of whether the career losses are greater for the most-skilled or the least-skilled mothers. Recent results, based on American data, have shifted toward the conclusion that the white women with the highest-paying careers suffer the greatest setbacks to salary progress, due to losing so much experience time in a fast-track occupation. A governmental paid leave program improves employers' willingness to retain the same female employees and to hire women who might become pregnant later, since the government support lowers the cost of retaining the same employee relative to the cost of finding, screening, and hiring a new one.[18]

In other words, while theories could predict either more or fewer jobs as a result of government paid leave programs, the more generous family leave programs of the higher-budget welfare states have in fact raised female employment. In this policy realm, as in others, the real-world welfare states seem to have had the wisdom to provide something needed, without over-providing it.

WHAT EFFECTS ON CHILD DEVELOPMENT? All three family-friendly expenditure policies – paid parental leave, subsidized day care, and pre-primary education – are aimed at the child as well as the parents. All are embodied in greater expenditures in the welfare states than elsewhere. And for each policy, economists can easily imagine how its design might be botched, leading to poor returns in terms of child development. Yet for two of the three, the empirical evidence about effects on the child has come out strongly positive.

To start on a downbeat, careful studies warn that some public day care designs have had negative effects on child development. Michael Baker, Jonathan Gruber, and Kevin Milligan (2019) have studied how Quebec's introduction of cheap formal (non-family) day care for all children ages 0–4 in September of 1997 has affected those children up through their teen years. The day care centers met the usual standard among rich OECD countries, though their care was probably lower in quality than in such model programs as the Perry Project. Children placed under Quebec's formal day care had much the same cognitive development as others, but on the average they (especially boys) suffered from such "non-cognitive" outcomes as worse health, lower life satisfaction, and higher crime rates up through their teen years. It appears that parents choosing such care for their pre-school children, to free up their time for work or other things, paid a price in terms of the child's emotional development.

The cost was borne more by children of better-off parents than by disadvantaged children.

Similarly, another study of a day care system for infants of ages 0–2 in Bologna, Italy, in 2001–2005 has found that children of better-off parents suffered negative effects both cognitively (IQ-like tests) and emotionally by ages 8–14.[19] Like the Quebec result, this serves as a warning about formal day care as an alternative to parental care at home. It should be noted, however, that the admissions procedures of Bologna's day care system discriminated against children whose parents were affluent, forcing them to take facilities that were not their top choice.

Such negative results for formal (non-family) day care can also be read as positive results for subsidizing parental leave, at least for the job-holding subset of mothers. That seems to follow, because the baseline, or control group, for formal day care is care at home by a parent (usually the mother), and there is no reason to believe that parenting aided by a paid leave policy should be different from a random draw out of the larger population of stay-at-home new parents.

In contrast to the cautionary results about formal day care, the empirical literature is generally upbeat about the impact of public pre-primary schooling. Studies based on international comparisons suggest that the rate of return on pre-primary education, mainly for 4-year-olds, is even higher than the average return for primary and secondary education. Numerous studies based on a variety of micro-level interventions, mostly those in the United States, share the optimism. James Heckman and other researchers have formed an evidence-based advocacy website, www.heckmanequation.org, filled with research citations and policy punch lines.

Both the potential returns on public schooling for 4-year-olds and some lingering cautions have been well illustrated by a study of two US state programs offering public education funding for all 4-year-olds. Georgia since 1995 and Oklahoma since 1998 have stood out as two states with high-quality early schooling, offered universally.[20] As of 2011–2012, an estimated 59 percent of 4-year-olds were enrolled in Georgia, and 74 percent in Oklahoma. A Brookings study by Elizabeth Cascio and Diane Schanzenbach (2013) explored the early effects on family wellbeing and on test scores up through eighth grade, comparing these two states with other states, and with other birth cohorts in the same two states. They found significantly positive effects for children in lower-status families, defining status by mother's education or by the family's being poor enough to qualify for school lunch aid. For higher-status families, no significant positive cognitive effects showed up, apparently because the public school merely saved them a bit of money by crowding out their good private-school options. The study was as statistically sound as the data would permit.

How would such early returns translate into gains for the same children as grown-ups, and net gains for society as a whole? In any such study, the cost-benefit analysis has to be rough and somewhat conjectural, of course. Nonetheless, Cascio and Schanzenbach note that their respectable rates of return are likely to understate the true social gains from the extra early education. The calculations miss some non-cognitive gains in the form of communication skills and reduced criminal behavior. The calculations also omit some of the gains relative to no 4-year-old schooling at all, since the study compared Georgia and Oklahoma with other states where 4-year-olds' schooling was also improving somewhat. The tentative result is again optimistic: the pre-primary schooling that is more prevalent in countries with higher social budgets does bring economic gains to society as a whole.

UN-AMERICAN UNIVERSAL HEALTH INSURANCE

As far back as 1917, economist Irving Fisher lamented that:

> At present the United States has the unenviable distinction of being the only great industrial nation without compulsory health insurance. For a generation the enlightened nations of Europe have one after another discussed the idea and followed discussion by adoption. It has constituted an important part of the policy and career of some of Europe's greatest statesmen . . . .
>
> Certain interests which would be, or think they would be, adversely affected by health insurance have made the specious plea that it is an un-American interference with liberty. They forget that compulsory education, though at first opposed on these very grounds, is highly American and highly liberative . . . The truth is that the opponents of compulsory health insurance are in every case, as far as I can discover, subject to some special bias. They grasp at the slogan of liberty as a subterfuge only.[21]

When it comes to health insurance, universal public coverage is practiced by nearly all rich industrialized countries, even those whose overall social budgets take less than 20 percent of GDP. For the health sectors, the superior efficiency of a dominant government role is almost universally recognized, as is the superiority of a heavily public approach to primary and secondary education.

It would fit the general argument of this chapter if the universality and efficiency of health care were neatly correlated with the share of total social spending in the economy. Well, the international correlation is indeed positive. The basis for this correlation, however, is not a tidy stair-step, in which every extra bit of social spending tends to be matched with better and more universal health care. Rather, the world's health-care systems divide themselves between a cluster of fairly satisfactory universal-insurance and price-controlled systems in all the rich countries but one, versus the cluster of less satisfactory systems in all developing countries plus that one rich outlier.

The rich outlier is, of course, the United States. How its health-care system differs from those of the other rich countries is not a story of America's relying on competitive free markets instead of government spending. Private health-care markets are not so competitive in any country, and the government of the United States spends roughly as great a share of GDP on tax-based health care as do other rich-country governments. Yet, on top of that public health spending, America has huge private costs of health care, and the world's greatest share of health-care costs in GDP. Perversely, America is also exceptional among rich countries in having poorer life expectancy, as noted in Chapter 8.

Why the perverse American exceptionalism? Some of the roots of this tragedy go back to the nineteenth century and the start of the twentieth, while the main root goes back to the 1940s–1950s. The historical diagnosis needs to be detailed here. The options for curing the ills of American health care will be explored in Chapter 14's American finale.

THE RURAL DEFICIT IN AMERICAN HEALTH CARE. The United States has had a spatial problem with health care reaching back to the nineteenth century. That century overturned a long-standing relationship of health and death to cities and the countryside. Before the mid-nineteenth century, cities were death traps, where infections spread rapidly. Their death rates often exceeded their birth rates, so that they grew only because people kept immigrating from the countryside in search of better incomes. The mid-nineteenth century brought a new understanding that cholera and typhoid spread through polluted water, and local governments responded with investments in sanitation and water quality. Shortly afterwards, scientists discovered that bacterial and viral pathogens caused diseases, and then vaccines became more common. Cities, and hospitals, became healthier places. The twentieth-century advances in medicine completed the revolution. The impressive rise in the life-saving productivity of sophisticated modern medicine meant that you wanted to live in close proximity to hospitals and doctors. The more complex and sophistical health care became, the more its economics called for agglomerations of doctors centered on large urban hospitals.[22]

In America, as in other countries of low-density settlement, the lure of abundant land meant living too far from hospitals. Even small-town clinics need whole teams of physicians, to take advantage of economies of scale. The endearing image of a single doctor serving a small community was no longer the best practice for saving lives.

At the start of the twentieth century, changes in American health institutions made that long-run problem even worse for this country's rural population. The American Medical Association's famous Flexner Report of 1910 delivered a scathing verdict on the quality of the country's medical schools across the land, and sparked a sudden closure of all but the most rigorously state-licensed medical schools. From the 160 MD-granting institutions in existence in 1904, only 85 remained by 1920. The half of medical schools that disappeared tended to be located in smaller cities. As one would fear, this cut the supply of new doctors in the hinterlands. Doctors coming from small towns and the countryside, who were more inclined to practice there after medical school, were largely dealt out, widening the gaps in who had access to doctors. As a study led by Flexner himself showed, in small towns (population 1,000–2,500) the number of people per doctor rose from 590 in 1906 to 910 in 1923, while in large cities (population over 100,000) it rose only from 492 to 536.[23] While there would have been an urbanization of access to doctors in any case, due to agglomeration in medical care supply into centers of sophisticated medicine, the Flexner Report only accelerated the problem for rural America.

The early deterioration of rural medicine, and its acceleration in the wake of the Flexner Report of 1910, can also be seen in the number of months' pay that a rural Vermont farm laborer would have to pay for seeing the doctor.[24] The relative costs of a unit of physicians' services had already been rising from 1805 to 1910, but grew faster in the three decades after the Flexner Report:

	Percentage growth per decade in costs of physician services			
	Birth delivery	Office visit	Day home call, no mileage	Day home call, 5 miles
1910/1805=	8.4	1.4	3.1	2.7
1940/1910=	23.8	14.1	10.5	6.5

The rural–urban disparity continues today, in the United States, as in the other spacious countries. To stem the deterioration in rural health care, countries like the United States and Australia have turned to stopgaps such as traveling health stations, bush doctor services, and emergency tele-medicine. As the *Washington Post* reported in 2019, the rural care deficit is not shrinking:

> The number of ER [emergency-room] patients in rural areas has surged by 60 percent in the past decade, even as the number of doctors and hospitals in those places has declined by up to 15 percent. Dozens of stand-alone ERs are fighting off bankruptcy. Hundreds of critical-access [rural] hospitals either can't find a doctor to hire or can't afford to keep one on site.[25]

AMERICA'S JOB-BASED HEALTH INSURANCE TRAP OF THE 1940S–1950S. The middle of the twentieth century brought more self-inflicted setbacks in America's health insurance. Elsewhere – especially in Western Europe, Canada, Australasia, and Japan – the aftermath of World War II brought expanded health insurance plans covering everybody. In most cases, the private sector continued to provide the services under government regulation, while the government collected the insurance contributions from workers and taxpayers and paid out the benefits. In the case of the United Kingdom, the government itself has been the provider, through the National Health Service.

The United States did not follow suit. At the center of America's health insurance problems is a pair of historical wrong turns that left the United States with too strong a reliance on voluntary employer-based health insurance. The first wrong turn came in World War II and the 1950s. Employer-based plans gained popularity in World War II, when wage controls prevented employers' competing for scarce workers by offering higher straight pay, but allowed them to offer attractive fringes. The new demand for employee health insurance was reinforced by the rise in unions' bargaining power. Paul Starr has remarked on the irony of the role of the newly powerful labor unions in locking the country into the questionable link between jobs and health insurance:

> Oddly enough, although labor favored a compulsory system, its success in pursuing health benefits through collective bargaining had undermined the movement for a government program ... The union shop, which in the early fifties made union membership mandatory for over two-thirds of the production work force, enabled the unions to establish a "private fiscal system" able to levy a "tax" for health insurance.[26]

The other force sealing American health insurance into a job trap was a tax policy, enacted in 1943 and solidified in a 1954 Supreme Court ruling, that exempts employer contributions to employee health plans from taxation, either as corporate income or as employee income. Thus was created a private job-based health insurance industry that still stands as a powerful lobby blocking any reforms that would universalize health insurance under government control.[27] As an example of that blocking power, one major reform left undone by the Congressional fight over the Affordable Care Act of 2010 was its attempt to remove the special tax subsidies on employer-based health coverage, and to push the industry toward offering plans that are more portable from job to job. Also jettisoned in the same fight was President Obama's "public option," which would have offered individuals the option to buy insurance from the government in competition with private insurance companies.

A second costly wrong turn was taken in 1965, when the passage of Medicare confined America's public (alias "socialized") health insurance to those over 65 (plus the military). This second wrong turn was caused in part by the first one, the anchoring of one's health insurance to one's current job. The passage of Medicare in 1965 was targeted at the elderly because they rightly feared facing costlier health care with no job to offer them coverage after retirement. Some have tried to reduce this elderly bias by extending Medicare to all age groups, with only partial success. Since the 1970s, Medicaid has given government health insurance to those near or below the poverty line. In 2010, the Affordable Care Act succeeded in extending insurance more toward the young and poor, with expansions of Medicaid and the State Children's Health Insurance Program. It thus made partial steps toward making coverage more universal, while proceeding slowly enough to honor (to "grandfather") existing insurance arrangements.

Yet an American's 65th birthday still brings a jump in health coverage and health expenditures. As Figure 9.6 shows, government spending on health per person over 65, relative to the generosity of the same spending per person under 65, jumped from 3.0 when Medicare was passed in 1965 to 5.4 in 1987. Thereafter, this emphasis in favor of spending on the elderly eased back down, because of the rise of Medicaid expenditures for those under 65. Yet the United States still stands out as one of the countries in which health expenditures, like social expenditures in general, are tilted toward elderly beneficiaries. Not surprisingly, this country's mortality rates also look worse, relative to other OECD countries, before the 65th birthday than they look after that birthday.[28] Again, this health insurance trap was specific to the United States, and not to all countries with smaller social budgets.

THE PUBLIC SEEMS TO UNDERSTAND THE PROBLEM. The resulting inefficiency of the American health-care sector, with its high expenditures and its low contributions to longer life, is reflected in opinion polls asking people how they like their country's health-care system. In a 2011 Gallup poll, for example, people in the United States, Canada, and the United Kingdom were asked what they thought about the availability and quality of their health care. On the "availability of

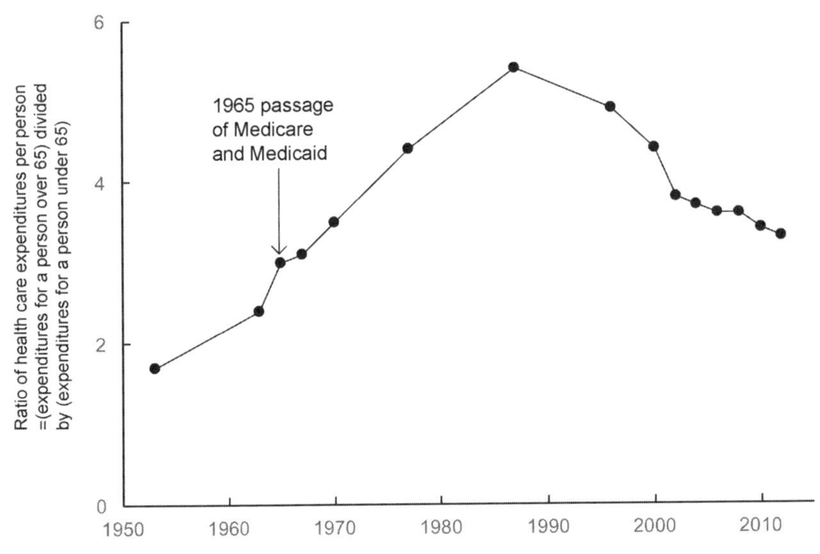

Figure 9.6. Health-care spending on the elderly, relative to those under 65, in the United States, 1953–2012
Source: Catillon, Cutler, and Getzen (2018, Table 4).

affordable health care," only 25 percent of American respondents said they were either "very" (6%) or "somewhat" satisfied (the other 19%). The other three-quarters were dissatisfied. By contrast, in Canada 57 percent were satisfied, and in Britain 43 percent were satisfied. On the question of the quality of the medical care actually delivered, however, the countries differed much less. The 48 percent share of Americans who were satisfied was close to Canada's 52 percent and Britain's 42 percent.

A more extensive poll of patients and doctors covering eleven countries in 2014–2016 offers more insight into what people liked and disliked about their health-care system. As Table 9.3 reports, the overall ratings again found the US health system least popular, though relative to the 2011 Gallup poll it rated Britain higher and Canada lower, ahead of only the United States. Looking at the more specific questions that produced the top row's overall rankings yields a plausible pattern, even though the rankings of countries in the middle have betrayed volatility since this series of studies began in 2004. American adults held the quality of delivered service ("care process quality") in average esteem, relative to the popularity of systems in the other ten countries. What dropped

TABLE 9.3. *Eleven countries' health-care rankings by patients and doctors, 2014–2016*

	Aus	Can	Fra	Ger	Neth	NZ	Nor	Swe	Switz	UK	USA
Overall ranking	2	9	10	8	3	4.5	4.5	6.5	6.5	1	11
Care process quality	2	6	9	8	4	3	10	11	7	1	5
Access	4	10	9	2	1	7	5	6	8	3	11
Affordability	8	9	1	2	10	5	3	6	4	7	11
Timeliness	11	4	8	10	5	1	2	6	7	3	9
Admin. efficiency	1	6.5	11	6.5	9	2	4	5	8	3	10
Equity	7	9	10	6	2	8	5	3	4	1	11
Care outcomes	1	9	5	8	6	7	3	2	4	10	11
Health expenditures per capita, 2011	3,800	4,522	4,118	4,495	5,099	3,182	5,669	3,925	5,643	3,405	8,508

Source and notes: The main source is Schneider et al. (2017), q.v. for definitions of the underlying measures.

The rankings are based on the survey responses from both patients and doctors.

Rankings ending in .5 refer to two-country ties. Thus, for example, 6.5 = tied for sixth and seventh ranks.

The expenditures per capita are measured in US purchasing-power-parity dollars, and reported in the 2011–2013 report in this same Commonwealth Fund series (Davis et al. 2014).

American health care to the bottom overall was that it was too high-priced ("affordability") and often not delivered effectively or fairly ("administrative efficiency" and "equity").

The polls thus reflect what the data show: Americans perceive, and actually have, poorer access to affordable health care, whereas the quality of health care seems similar for those who can get it. Translation: What the United States offers is health care of comparable quality, but at greater expense and with access tilted in favor of the well-off and the elderly.[29] We return to this concern in the final chapter.

ARE THE POOR, AND AMERICANS, INDIVIDUALLY TO BLAME FOR THEIR WORSE HEALTH? A defender of free-market health might seek to downplay the role of public health insurance in saving lives and productivity on the grounds that the poor die younger because they do not take care of themselves. Historical and analytical studies do allow a little retreat in this direction, but only a little.

It is true that for any given health system, even a free public system, the poor fail to consult physicians as pro-actively, and they indulge more in such unhealthy habits as smoking and alcohol. This self-care factor may partly answer a question posed by observers of British health history since the arrival of the universal National Health to ask: Why should an increasingly egalitarian health system encounter such persistent social gaps in life expectancy, with both the lowest occupational groups and their children dying sooner? Part of the answer seems to lie in those differences in protecting one's own health.

The same role of individual responsibility accounts for part, though again only part, of America's higher mortality since the mid-twentieth century. While the United States has made greater strides than most countries in curtailing smoking and limiting alcohol, it has been one of the world's leaders in sedentary lifestyle, unhealthy fast foods, sugared soft drinks, obesity, and – most recently – opioid overdoses (Case and Deaton 2020).

Yet studies acknowledging this role of individual responsibility also make it clear that a large part of the differences – between a country's rich and poor, or between America and other countries – lies in inequalities of access to health service. Health-care supply, rather than personal health-care demand, dominated mortality differences across the twentieth century from studies of regional inequality in health-care services and in mortality outcomes in America and Britain. America's supplies of physicians and of nurses, like its mortality rates, have been more unequal across regions than Britain's since 1890, largely due to the rural deficiency in access discussed earlier. Differences in personal habits of the poor could not have played as great a role as these clear differences in health-care delivery to different parts of the same country. That the supply of physicians and nurses did matter is also suggested by the downtrend in those regional inequalities of both the supply of doctors and nurses and the mortality outcomes between 1890 and 1970.[30]

The more general point behind such historical experiences seems clear enough. Whatever role might have been played by poor persons, or Americans, taking less care of themselves, their behavior was not an exogenous force that differed widely over time and space. Rather, their lower use of health care, like their earlier deaths, seems to have been due largely to the limitations on access to care that they have shared over so many decades – just as the people interviewed in the polls have said. Income inequality, combined with private and decentralized health insurance, has shortened life outside the welfare states.

A REALITY CHECK: HEALTH-CARE LIMITS. Even under universal coverage, people will not be covered for treatments deemed too expensive in relation to likely benefits. There have to be trade-offs, and hidden analysis of costs and benefits, regardless of the institutions. No health-care system can guarantee payment for "all the health care you need." Behind closed doors, priorities have to be set. No system can afford to guarantee you a free heart transplant. No system can work, financially, without limitations on access to specialists, devices, experimental drugs, and the like.

There seems to be a pattern in the ways that public and private systems ration life. The public systems provide less of the highest-budget life-extending services and more of the basic health services protecting mothers, children, and the poor. For example, experiences with inefficient overinvestment in CAT scanners and in (in-hospital) renal dialysis has forced American authorities to retreat toward rationing a lesser supply of the relevant equipment, much as the nationalized health systems of Britain, France, and Sweden have done. By contrast, the evidence on basic ground-level health care, featuring preventative medicine through public clinics, has continued to have such a high return as to suggest underinvestment in such care in the United States.

This pattern fits with the international contrasts in serving the elderly versus investing in the young, as noted in other chapters. In health care as in other social policies, Europe's welfare states have generally done a better job of investing in the young than have some more penurious countries, such as the United States and the countries of Latin America.

SUMMARY

So how much of Chapter 8's "free lunch" puzzle can be explained by evidence on positive aspects of more universal, and more generous, social spending? The Holy Grail of a systematic quantitative accounting, in a neat single table of results, still eludes us. The closest thing to such a systematic tabulation is the meta-analysis by Nathaniel Hendren and Ben Sprung-Keyser, which has impressively quantified the returns on recent American programs making incremental changes in all the categories of social spending. Their verdicts resemble those presented here. Yet their accounting applies only for the United States, and only to selected incremental policy changes at the margins of American practice.[31]

A more global judgment about the GDP effects of high social budgets in the real world must rest, for now, on the eclectic evidence on the four suggestions made in this chapter:

- The kinds of taxes used more heavily in the high-budget welfare states – broad consumption taxes like VAT, and sin taxes on products with negative externalities – are a closer match to what orthodox and conservative theories would prefer. The welfare states do not soak the rich so much. Rather, the not-so-rich workers who have tended to vote for the higher social expenditures are the strata of society that actually pay for most of those expenditures.
- Administrative costs actually claim lower shares of the value delivered in the broader and more universal welfare-state programs than are required in tougher, stingier programs. In shorthand, the welfare state is less bureaucratic than a small-government solution that tries to deny benefits to most of the population.
- A growing amount of evidence now favors such family-friendly policies as government-paid parental leave and pre-primary education. Such policies raise the human capital of the parents seeking long career paths and also of their children. Such subsidies could be overdone, but seem not to have been overdone in actual practice.
- Universal health insurance leads to longer lives and more affordable treatment.

There is at least a prima facie case that these four positive features of the welfare state have cancelled the GDP losses from any possible work disincentives of unemployment compensation and aid to poor families.

CHAPTER 10

Do the Rich Pay the Poor for All This?

POLICIES THAT BRING AGGREGATE GAINS FOR "THE nation as a whole" almost never benefit everybody. Anything that was clearly good for every single person would have been done already, without controversy. Anything big and controversial must hurt somebody. For example, spending on national defense eventually involves casualties, even if it brings military victory and saves lives overall. Building a new transport system across the nation kills small towns that are bypassed. A free-trade policy damages import-competing producers while it brings even bigger gains to others, resulting in net gains in GDP.

The same must be true for social spending, and indeed for any large expenditure or tax in the government budget. For all the net national benefits documented and explained in the last two chapters, somebody must be paying more for social spending than they get from it, and others must be pocketing more than the average gain – even if the social spending is a "free lunch" in the GDP sense used in Chapter 8. Who are the gainers and who pays the bill? Since social spending is often designed to level out people's consumption, between households as well as over time, a natural question is to ask about how it levels incomes between rich, middle, and poor. [1]

How has the distribution of taxes contrasted with the distribution of receipts of social spending, and of total government spending? Progressive (from-rich-to-poor) redistribution through social spending is still young, having turned upward just a couple of centuries ago – like other things in history, such as economic growth, the lengthening of life, and democracy.

After noting how little government budgets have redistributed over most of world history, this chapter and its online Appendices B and C introduce a new millennial collection of snapshots of fiscal distribution within each of fifty-three countries. Seeing today's patterns leads us into a fresh geography and history of fiscal redistribution, much of which was carried out through tax-based social-spending programs. Four findings will emerge:

(1) The twentieth century delivered a nearly global shift toward progressive (from-rich-to-poor) redistribution, even during the infamous rise in the inequality of market incomes since the 1970s. Seldom did any well-documented national experience show a slide back toward regressive (from-poor-to-rich) redistribution through government.[2]

(2) As a corollary, the rise in income inequality since the 1970s owes nothing to any widespread retreat from progressive government policies, because no such retreat happened. On the contrary, households' net incomes became increasingly unequal despite a tendency of government to equalize their resources.

(3) Today's progressivity seems to have been achieved more through egalitarian social spending than through more progressive taxation.

(4) The usual one-year measures of redistribution between richer and poorer groups do not capture the effects on *lifetime* income inequality, the inequality we really care about most. In particular, each generation's rising subsidies to children's education strongly reduced their later inequality of adult earning power, a global result previewed when Chapter 5 showed the equalization of adult education attainments. This adult-education effect reveals a still greater shift toward progressivity over the longer run, most notably in Japan, Korea, and Taiwan.

IMAGINING THE EXTREMES: ROBIN HOOD VERSUS DRACULA

To reveal when and where government budgets did the most, or did the least, to redistribute from richer toward poorer, we need a simple summary measure of inequalities before and after the effects of government taxing and spending. Economists commonly summarize income inequality with a "gini coefficient." This number between zero and one is based on a traditional Lorenz curve like that of Figure 10.1, which portrays the distribution of gross (pre-fisc) incomes in the United States in 2014. The curve captures the extent of inequality by ranking all households from poorest to richest. In this case, it shows that the poorest 50 percent got only 12.5 percent of all income, and the poorest 90 percent got only 53 percent. The gini coefficient measures inequality by adding all these

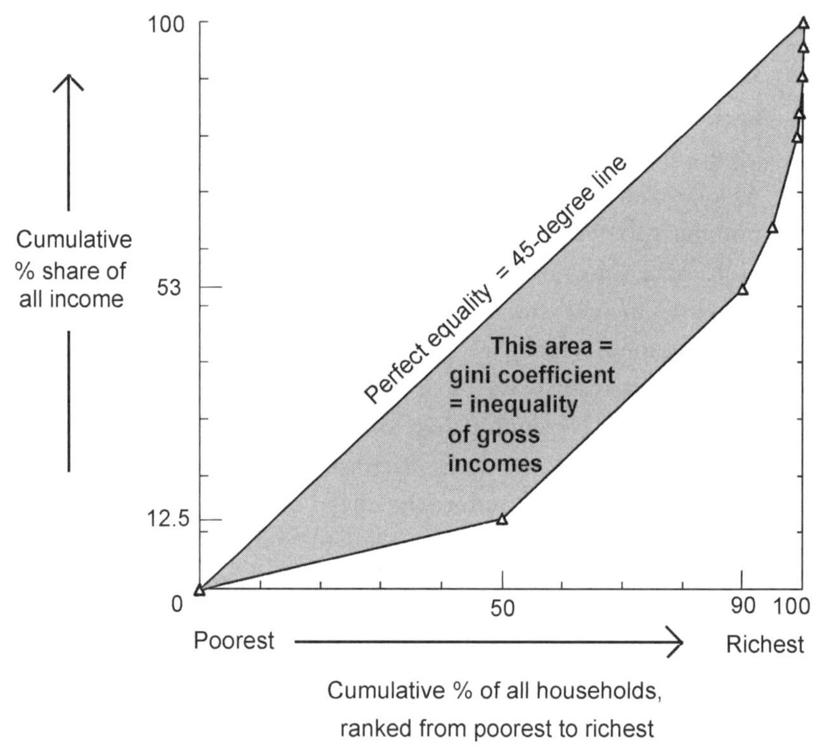

Figure 10.1. Summarizing the inequality of US market incomes in 2014: the gini coefficient

Source and notes: Figure 10.1 is based on Piketty, Saez, and Zucman (2016). Their study did not measure income inequality among households, as most studies have done, but rather among adults in the 20–64 age group, whether they were individually economically active or not. Figure 10.1's Lorenz curve has an artificial straightness between its turning points because the estimates aggregated the bottom 50 percent, the next 40 percent, and so forth. The true curve would have bowed downward more consistently, giving a slightly higher gini coefficient.

vertical gaps – the 50 percent minus 12.5 percent, 90 percent minus 53 percent, and so on, yielding the shaded area as a share of all incomes. For gross incomes in the United States in 2014, that gini coefficient was 0.542. An intuitive interpretation of the coefficient is that it (0.542) measures an imaginary Robin Hood extreme of egalitarian ("progressive") redistribution: the large share of all incomes that would have to be redistributed from richer to poorer to make all incomes equal.

If a government tried to achieve perfect equality with tax-based social spending alone, say transferring 23 percent of GDP, what is the imaginable maximum equalization that taxing and social spending could deliver? Well, it has to be less than the 23 percent share of income taken from some and handed to others, even in the extreme case of insistently soaking only the initially rich and giving only to the initially poor. Why less than the share taxed and transferred? If you take the whole tax bite from the initially rich and give it all to the initially poor, you will have changed people's rankings, and swapped one inequality for another, without achieving exact equality. It is not easy to drive inequality to zero. The actual handling of the transfers would have to be something subtler.

The problem of re-ranking was humorously illustrated by the trap that Dennis Moore fell into. Dennis Moore was a farcical Robin-Hood-wannabe of the eighteenth century, played by John Cleese of the Monty Python Flying Circus in the late 1960s (*vide* YouTube). Moore kept stealing from the rich at gunpoint and delivering to the poor. He kept this up until the once-rich were destitute and the once-poor became contemptuous of the shoddy goods he was bringing them from the rich-turned-poor. Inequality ended up the same, with the people having just traded ranks. Moore remained ignorant of the subtleties of re-ranking and the Lorenz curve until the final episode ("Blimey, this redistribution of wealth is trickier than I thought!").

Similarly, the inegalitarian ("regressive") extreme of having a Dracula-like dictator suck all resources from the rest of society and keep it to himself and his immediate henchmen has to be less extreme than Figure 10.1 might seem to allow. In the diagram, an imaginary outcome is portrayed by the whole area under the Lorenz curve (1 – 0.542 = 0.458), with the poorest 99.9999999 percent having nothing and the dictator sucking up everything. But our imagination should not run so wild. You cannot leave the rest of the population with nothing. They will die, and the economy will collapse. No parasite can survive without a living host to feed on. The only part of total income that could be redistributed from the poor and weak to the rich and powerful is that part left over after everybody gets at least enough to stay alive. As Branko Milanovic and his co-authors have pointed out, that potential maximum extraction from the poor can get bigger as average incomes grow, but it can never be as big as the share shown under the Lorenz curve.[3]

So real-world redistribution has to be somewhere in between, and removed from, these two hypothetical extremes. How much has redistribution through government budgets changed inequality, as measured by gini coefficients, and what role has social spending played in that redistribution?

To summarize as "progressive" or "regressive" the impact of government on inequality, we need to be clear about what we mean by redistributive neutrality. Where is the dividing line between progressive and regressive redistributions, that is, between those that are egalitarian and those that are inegalitarian? Progressive or regressive relative to what? In all that follows, we will use a handy borderline representing fiscal neutrality: It is the fiscal alternative policy that leaves the gini coefficient of inequality the same. An intuitive case that is sufficient for neutrality is one in which the net tax-minus-transfer gains are the same percentage of gross pre-fisc income up and down the income ranks. Everybody has their incomes changed by the same percentage, as they would be if all taxes and all benefits from the transfers were the same percentages of gross income no matter how poor or rich the group.

How far from fiscal neutrality, thus defined, has history pushed different countries, and in which direction – regressive or progressive? Were the movements caused mainly by changes in redistribution through taxes or by redistribution through expenditures?

TODAY'S PROGRESSIVITY AROUND THE WORLD

For the twenty-first century, fortunately, multiple studies have revealed how today's fiscal redistributions differ around the world, and have opened the door for writing new national histories. A wave of studies comparing income inequalities of dozens of countries has been led by the OECD, helped by data from the Luxembourg Income Study.[4] The redistributive experiences of Latin American countries have been compared in studies by the World Bank and the Inter-American Development Bank.[5] An even more global view of fiscal redistributions has been assembled in the current wave of developing-country studies and databases by the Commitment to Equity (CEQ) project, led by Nora Lustig.[6] These international studies launch our history of redistribution back over the last 200 years with their now-extensive set of snapshots from early in this century.

We can now compare inequalities in yearly incomes before and after taxes and transfer payments, and thus the net fiscal redistribution, for fifty-three countries around the world, in or near the year 2013 (Table 10.1 and Figures 10.2 and 10.3). Fortunately, our two main sources – the OECD and CEQ Institute – used broadly similar estimation procedures.[7] These two sets of studies somewhat understate the inequalities as measured either "pre-fisc" (incomes before taxes and transfers) or "post-fisc" (incomes after taxes and transfers). Both are based mainly on household surveys, which tend to understate the pre-fisc incomes of those in the top 5 percent of the household income ranks. And both also miss part of the top incomes hidden in corporate form or in tax havens abroad.[8] Yet since the post-fisc income distribution is derived by subtracting the better-seen taxes and transfers from the same biased pre-fisc distribution, there is only a limited bias in our measures of net fiscal distribution.

The clearest conclusion from the global album of snapshots taken around 2013 is that all of the data-supplying countries now practice progressivity in redistributing through government budgets. In all cases, incomes were made less unequal by taxes and transfers, as one would expect from social insurance programs. Figure 10.2 says so, by showing that every country's dot is below the 45 degree line where the inequalities before or after taxes and transfers would have been the same.[9]

Does this mean that governments all over the world practice progressive redistribution, transferring purchasing power from richer households to poorer ones? Generally, yes, but our fifty-three data-supplying countries are not the whole world. The fifty-three tend to have relatively transparent democratic governments. A national government not listed

TABLE 10.1. *Snapshots of fiscal redistribution in fifty-three countries, c. 2013*

		Gini coefficients of inequality (here expressed as %s)			
Country	Data years	Pre-fiscal market inc.	Post-fiscal final income	Implied progressivity of fiscal redistribut'n	Public social transfers as % of GDP
Argentina(a)	2012/2013	50.2	29.8	20.4	19.6
Armenia	2011	46.9	35.7	11.3	8.6
Australia	2013	42.4	32.1	10.3	18.7
Austria	2013	42.6	28.1	14.5	27.6
Belgium	2013	42.7	26.6	16.0	29.3
Bolivia	2009	50.3	44.6	5.6	10.0
Brazil	2008/2009	59.3	45.2	14.1	19.9
Canada	2013	41.1	32.5	8.6	16.8
Chile (d)	2013	50.3	41.9	8.3	10.2
Colombia	2010	57.2	50.6	6.6	9.3
Costa Rica	2010	51.2	40.0	11.2	14.1
Czech Rep	2013	38.7	25.9	12.8	20.3
Denmark	2013	40.1	25.5	14.7	29.0
Dom Rep	2006/2007	51.4	45.8	5.6	5.1
Ecuador	2011/2012	48.2	40.0	8.2	6.2
El Salvador	2011	43.7	39.4	4.3	7.4
Estonia	2013	45.0	35.7	9.3	15.9
Finland	2013	42.2	26.2	16.0	29.5
France	2013	44.5	29.4	15.1	31.5
Georgia	2013	50.7	38.3	12.4	9.3
Germany	2013	41.9	29.9	12.1	24.8
Greece	2013	51.2	35.3	15.9	28.0
Guatemala	2011	51.1	48.7	2.4	4.5
Honduras	2011	56.1	53.8	2.3	4.0
Hungary	2013	41.1	28.7	12.4	22.1
Iceland	2013	33.7	24.6	9.1	16.6
Iran (c.)	2011/2012	42.9	34.3	8.5	12.2
Ireland (b)	2013	53.3	31.6	21.6	20.2
Israel	2013	42.4	34.1	8.3	16.2
Italy	2013	44.5	32.9	11.6	28.6
Japan	2013	37.6	32.0	5.6	23.1
Korea	2013	30.5	28.0	2.5	9.7
Latvia	2013	43.3	34.5	8.8	14.4
Mexico (e)	2010	50.9	42.9	8.0	7.9
Netherlands	2013	39.6	28.4	11.2	22.9
New Zealand	2013	41.6	33.0	8.6	21.8
Nicaragua	2009	48.2	43.5	4.7	6.1
Norway	2013	37.7	26.2	11.5	19.4
Peru	2009	50.3	46.4	3.9	6.5
Poland	2013	42.3	30.4	11.9	19.0
Portugal	2013	49.6	34.5	15.2	25.5
Russia	2010	49.1	32.3	16.8	17.2

TABLE 10.1. *(continued)*

		Gini coefficients of inequality (here expressed as %s)			
Country	Data years	Pre-fiscal market inc.	Post-fiscal final income	Implied progressivity of fiscal redistribut'n	Public social transfers as % of GDP
Slovakia	2013	37.2	27.0	10.2	18.1
Slovenia	2013	41.7	25.5	16.2	24.0
S. Africa	2009/2010	77.1	59.5	17.6	10.6
Spain	2013	47.9	35.2	12.7	26.3
Sweden	2013	38.3	28.1	10.2	27.4
Switzerland	2013	34.0	28.7	5.3	19.2
Turkey	2013	40.3	38.2	2.1	13.4
UK	2013	47.1	35.3	11.8	21.9
Uruguay	2009	52.8	38.6	14.3	17.9
USA	2013	47.8	39.2	8.6	18.8
Venezuela	2012	41.1	34.1	7.0	15.7

Sources and notes: See Appendix C, www.cambridge.org/Lindert.

among Table 10.1's suppliers of usable income distributions is likely to be less democratic and less transparent.[10] We cannot rule out the possibility that such governments redistributed regressively, in favor of the rich and at the expense of the poor.

Among the fifty-three snapshots from data-supplying countries, today's fiscal redistribution has a distinct inter-regional geography. Three modern East Asian economies stand out for having achieved relatively equal incomes without same-year redistribution. These are Japan and Korea, as shown in Figures 10.2 and 10.3, plus Taiwan. Their distinctive pattern has drawn commentary for some time, and we return to it later when incorporating the longer-run effects of subsidies to mass education.[11] The United States, famously inegalitarian in comparison with most OECD countries, is shown to be closer to the center of the pack globally, once one includes the high income inequality and feeble social insurance in Latin American and African countries.

WHEN AND HOW DID PROGRESSIVITY RISE?

When did today's global tendency toward progressive use of government budgets first arise, and has it been retreating in recent years? Comparing

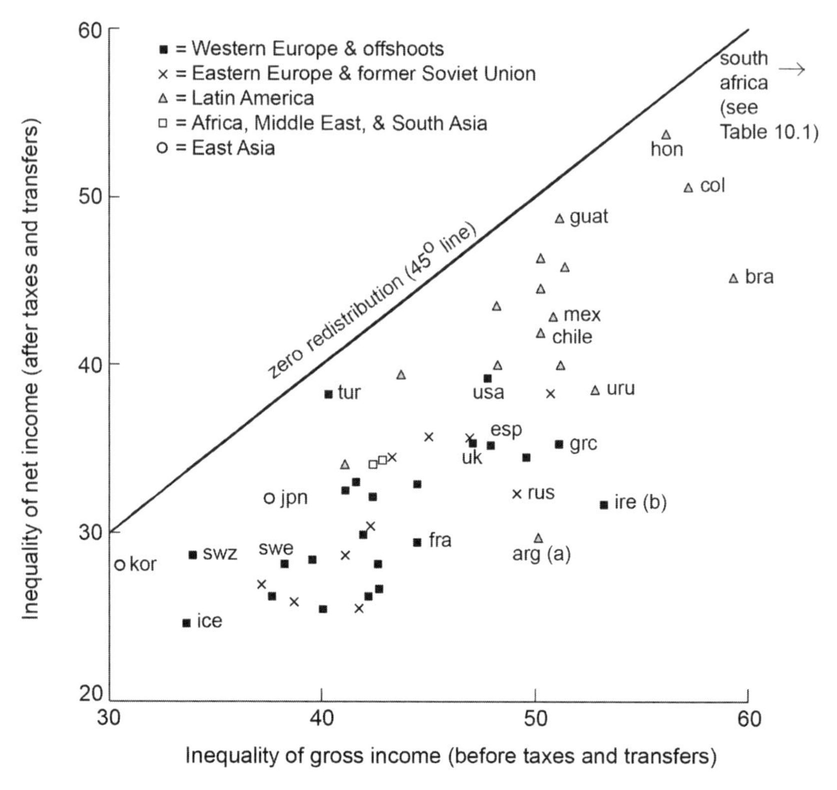

Figure 10.2. Recent snapshots of income distributions in fifty-three countries
Sources and notes: See Appendix C, www.cambridge.org/Lindert.

the mid-1980s, the mid-1990s, the mid-2000s, and 2013–2014, the OECD (2011 and 2018d) has generated measures of fiscal redistribution for many countries. While their measures could only cover direct taxes and cash transfers, owing to data limitations, they nonetheless represent the most complete multi-country view of how inequality has changed over these thirty years. Their estimates show a rise in progressivity, from the mid-1980s to the mid-1990s, with a roughly equal shift back toward regressivity since the mid-1990s. My interpretation of their results emphasizes the lack of a clear net change over the whole period, though the OECD authors choose to emphasize that progressivity since the mid-1990s failed to check the rise of overall inequality.[12]

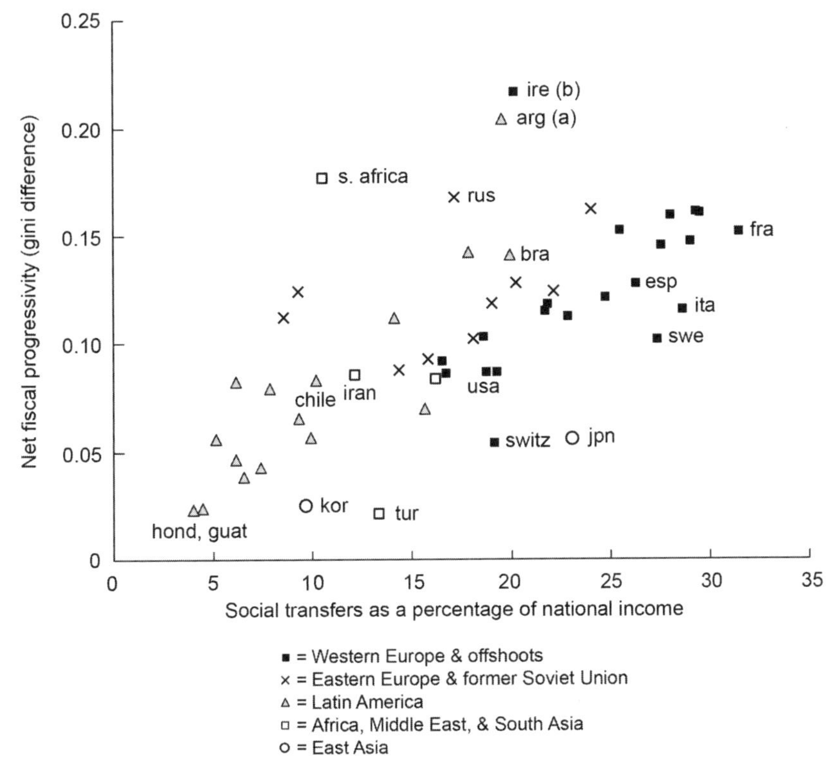

Figure 10.3. Social transfers help to deliver fiscal redistribution, fifty-three countries, c. 2013
Sources and notes: See Appendix C, www.cambridge.org/Lindert.

To reach further back than the 1980s, let us follow correlates that should have accompanied the yet-unmeasured earlier progressivity, based on what we see in the global album of recent snapshots. Table 10.1 and Figure 10.3 introduce a significant positive correlation between progressivity and the share of national income spent on social transfers.

It turns out that over history, as well as around the world in 2013, the size of the social-spending budget is the best indirect clue to a country's progressive rich-to-poor redistribution. Some might have nominated progressive taxation as a key to predicting progressive redistribution, using such measures as the top income tax rate or the share of taxes on income and wealth in GDP. Correlations between progressive taxation and the overall redistribution from rich to poor do appear in today's global cross-section, but are a bit weaker, a weakness we will soon rediscover when looking at individual country histories.[13] A surer guide for mapping the rise of progressive redistribution before the 1980s is to trace the share of social spending in incomes back over time.

As we look deeper into multi-national history, over the last 110 years, the same correlation between social budgets and redistribution from rich to poor seems to hold. Chapter 6 has traced the uneven rise of social spending for a wide range of countries. Two implications for the history of progressive redistribution seem to stand out. One is that back around 1910, before World War I, there were still no social insurance programs that channeled a large share of national product. By implication, prewar governments must have done little or nothing to help the lower-income groups by taxing the rich, and the whole history of rising progressivity must have unfolded over these last hundred years or so. Another feature from the history of social transfers is that it reveals no dramatic reversals. None of these last eleven decades experienced a major multi-country decline in social transfers. We pick up the rough and indirect hint that there was a rise in progressive redistribution, but never a major decline for any large subset of countries. Is the hint correct? We turn to some well-documented national histories.

THE UNITED STATES SINCE 1913

For the United States in the well-documented era of continuous income taxation back to 1913, we have the benefit of two studies that have set the world standard for consistency in redistribution measurement. These two studies deserve a quick introduction here, before we trace what they imply about American redistribution since 1913. Over forty years ago, Morgan Reynolds and Eugene Smolensky (1977) refined US data for 1950, 1961, and 1970 to yield complete income distributions before and after the effects of government budgets, based on consistent concepts of income and population. Looking through that twenty-year window of history, they saw remarkably less change in fiscal progressivity than the growth of government social budgets might have suggested. Yet despite their emphasis on null trends, their change-in-gini measures did show that redistribution down the income ranks advanced – and it accompanied a rise in social spending over those same twenty years.[14]

Now the team of Thomas Piketty, Emmanuel Saez, and Gabriel Zucman (2016) has introduced their own consistent system of "distributional national accounts" (DINA) for the United States all the way back to 1913. Their measures, like those of Reynolds and Smolensky, apply consistent income and population concepts. Here, as in their larger work with Tony Atkinson and others on the World Top Incomes Project, they also offer a solution to the problem of under-reporting top incomes that has plagued income distribution studies based on household surveys. For the years back to 1962, they deliver exactly what we seek here: measures of the effects of government budget redistribution on the whole distribution of income. Applying a few frugal assumptions, I have extended their coverage of the net effects of government budgets on income inequality back from 1962 to 1913.[15]

We start the new Piketty–Saez–Zucman (PSZ) redistribution history by focusing on the "Gini, overall redistribution" line shown in both halves of Figure 10.4. Its trend is unmistakably upward, toward progressivity, despite brief reversals under Ronald Reagan and George W. Bush. The overall net redistribution since 1913 has risen 9.51 percentage points, despite falling back by 1.37 points in 1980–1984, Reagan's first term, and by 1.00 points in 2000–2003 at the start of the George W. Bush presidency. From 1910, all the way until 1970, the trends in net progressivity closely matched those of the share of social transfers in GDP.

Since 1970, progressivity and transfers have continued to rise together, but the trend has been less steep for progressivity than for social transfers, which expanded faster in the broad forms of Medicare and Social Security than in the form of assistance targeted at the poor.[16] Overall, the redistribution helped the lower-income half of the population more and more, especially in the New Deal 1930s–1940s and the Great Society 1960s (Figure 10.4(B)). Conversely, the top income decile has continued to pay greater and greater net shares of national income in taxes. As for the *tax rates* paid by those at the top, these too have been creeping up for the top 10 percent of society – but

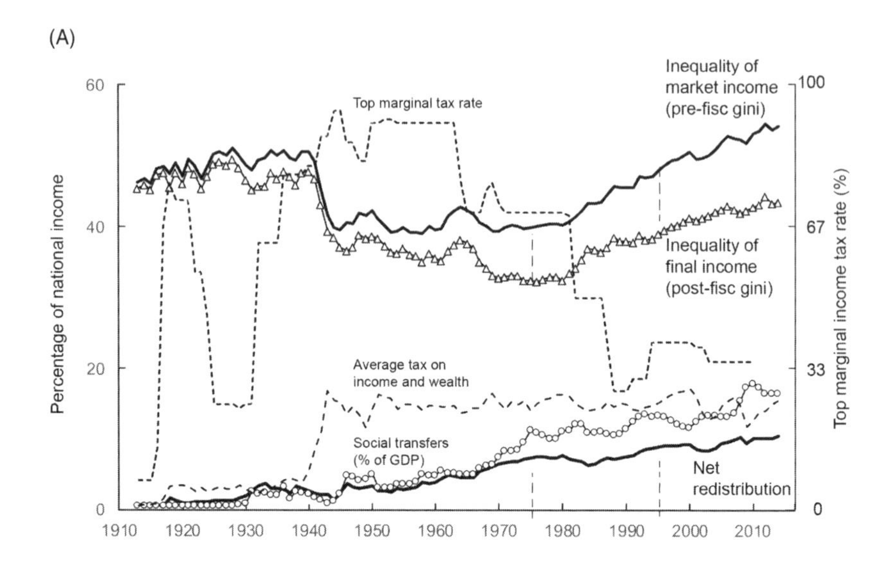

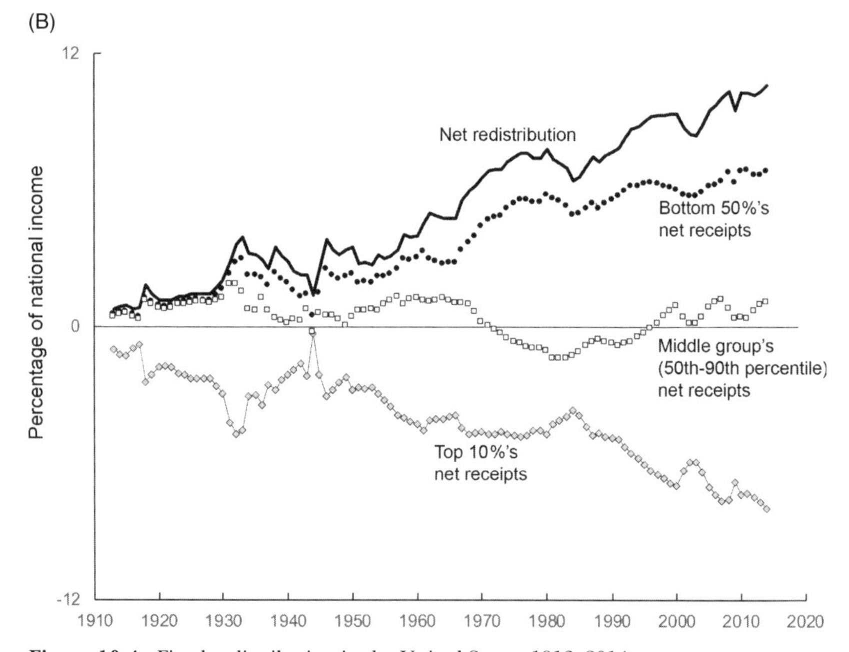

Figure 10.4. Fiscal redistribution in the United States, 1913–2014
(A) The basic gini coefficients, and how they follow social transfers better than tax rates.
(B) Net gains and losses for rich, middle, and poor Americans.
Sources and notes: See Appendix C, www.cambridge.org/Lindert.

have dropped for the very richest 0.1 percent since 1950, especially after the 2017 tax cuts for the very richest.[17] As for the 50–90 percentile group ("middle class," if you wish), the PSZ estimates find that it was disadvantaged between 1965 and 1983, but then favored from 1983 through 2000.

Note how American experience educates our choice of indirect fiscal clues about net redistribution when direct measures are lacking. The share of social transfers outperforms its tax-side rivals. As shown in Figure 10.4(A), the dramatic movements in the top marginal income tax rate are not mirrored in the PSZ measure of overall redistribution. Likewise, the average tax rate on income and wealth tells a very different story from the overall result in terms of redistribution between rich and poor. The one and only jump in that average tax rate occurred during World War II, when the sudden prosperity raised the share of households paying income tax from just the richest 4 percent to about 75 percent. The years since 1945 show no net gain in the average income and wealth tax rates. This result again suggests that the American history of fiscal redistribution is better followed, or predicted, by the movement of progressivity on the social-expenditure side, not the tax side.

WHEN WAS BRITISH POLICY NOT PROGRESSIVE?

British history will someday yield sufficient data for us to trace how government shifted resources between richer and poorer back to early modern times, supplementing the excellent telling of the larger fiscal history by other scholars.[18] While it is still early days for the writing of that long history of British redistribution, we have been given some clues, especially across the twentieth century, and even back to 1688.

For the twentieth century, Britain's numbers on who paid taxes and who got benefits were gathered frequently, but on an inconsistent basis. The official presentations have kept switching definitions. In addition, their income measures are largely based on household samples, subject to the usual problem of under-reporting top incomes, and their summary measures omit benefits delivered in kind rather than in cash.[19]

Nonetheless, we can start with fairly consistent measures offered by the Office of National Statistics since 1977, and then put boundaries on the possible progressivity or regressivity of taxes and benefits for earlier years back to 1911. For the years since 1977, the summary measures show no net change in fiscal progressivity, yet reveal some gyrations reflecting politics and the macro-economy. The famous regressivity of Margaret Thatcher shows up as a net drop of 4.2 gini percentage points in progressivity from her first year (1979) to her last (1990) as prime minister. In between, however, progressivity seems to have jumped to a peak in 1984, before plunging. The early peak progressivity, so contrary to what one would have expected under Thatcher, was an automatic byproduct of the combination of continuing unemployment compensation and high unemployment rates. The high unemployment was in turn triggered by the international slump and by Thatcher's disrupting labor markets and slashing subsidies to nationalized industries. The fact that social spending rose during the local progressivity peak of 1984, and also with the peaks of 1994 and 2009–2011, simply reflects the counter-cyclicality of social insurance.

To extend this history back in time from 1977 requires a retreat to identifying just a broad range of possible degrees of progressivity, rather than a single best-guess estimate, because Britain's earlier data are less complete and less consistent in their construction. I have been able to establish that more than half of the progressivity delivered by 1977, or today, must have been achieved after 1911.[20] That is, there cannot have been much progressive redistribution through government back in 1911, on the eve of World War I. Most of the rise of Britain's redistributing income from richer toward poorer happened between 1911 and mid-century, late in Clement Atlee's prime ministry. In other words, early in the century Britain still did relatively little for the poor, then helped them more and more at the expense of the rich up to mid-century, after which little advance or retreat in fiscal progressivity occurred, despite the heated debate ushered in with the election of Margaret Thatcher.

If Britain's governments transferred very little from richer toward poorer households under the Liberals around 1911, what stances had earlier British governments taken? The question here is more about the *direction* of redistribution between richer and poorer, and not so much about the magnitude. We have found that the poor neither received much nor paid much in taxes back then, so the net redistributions were not large. Was the direction of the flows toward or away from the poor? Early modern Britain offers evidence of some interesting fiscal shifts.

There are hints of occasional Robin Hood redistributions by earlier governments. From the 1780s on, as we saw in Chapter 3, local governments began to redistribute a noticeable share of their revenues to the poor. On the tax side, Joseph Massie (1761) in the mid-eighteenth century courageously guesstimated how much Britain's land taxes and its consumption taxes on luxuries tended to fall on the rich. So far, it might appear that Robin Hood, in the form of the British government, was finally coming out of hiding in the late eighteenth century, taking from the rich and giving to the poor.

Yet that same era in British fiscal history reveals a unique regressive twist, a twist that serves again to remind us to keep doing historical reality checks on the assumptions behind the usual ("flypaper") calculations. An episode in which the usual assumption does particular harm took place in Britain from the mid-eighteenth century to the mid-nineteenth. The mistaken assumption in this case is that the redistributive effects of a tax should show up in the distribution of who pays it to the treasury.

What little redistribution there was in Britain's budgetary flows of progressive taxation and poor relief was usually outweighed before 1846 by a regressive tax on the poor that hardly showed up in the budget at all, because it generated essentially zero revenue. That additional policy is England's infamous Corn Laws, which deliberately raised the cost of staple foods in the periods 1765–1793 and 1815–1846 – yet generated no budget revenue.

In fact, a closer look at the timing of the Corn Laws' impact on food costs helps us better understand when it was that Parliament actually redistributed income toward the poor before 1834, all policies taken together. Around 1765, England became a permanent net importer of grain, and the import duties stipulated by the Corn Laws began to become prohibitive – effectively stopping food exports, and thus collecting no duties.

To make wheat expensive was to make rural land expensive. Rents were probably bid up by the Corn Laws, to the advantage of landlords, who clustered near the top of the income ranks and who were less than a sixth of all household heads. To make wheat expensive was also to make bread expensive, raising the cost of living for the landless masses.[21] Any reckoning of how the poor were treated by the politically powerful in Georgian and Victorian England must give weight to the policy-induced increases in poor households' cost of living against the direct poor relief. In the 1770s–1780s and again between 1815 and the Corn Law Repeal of 1848, only those low-income households who received more in relief than they paid in higher prices and taxes were actually being subsidized.

Early modern Britain's only episode of significant net relief to the poor, and of significant direct taxation of the rich, was that French War period (1793–1815), with its fears of famine and insurrection. It was primarily then that the Corn Laws were suspended. Similarly, the income tax was paid by the top strata only in the 1799–1815 part of the wars. During peacetime, the rich paid few direct taxes, until a small income tax reappeared in 1842. The land taxes of 1688–1832 were fixed at levels low enough to be outweighed, for landlords, by the Corn Law aid to rents, at least in the periods 1765–1793 and 1816–1845.

Policy thus pushed the rest of the laboring classes, those not getting as much in poor relief as policy added to their cost of living, down toward the same level of subsistence to which those on relief were being raised. It is as if Parliament shared Mandeville's belief in the social utility of keeping the lower orders up to, but also down to, the subsistence level, since they "have nothing to stir them up to be serviceable but their wants, which it is Prudence to relieve but Folly to cure."[22] Perhaps England's policy combination of local poor relief and the Corn Laws helped to produce an "Iron Law of Wages" by policy design, not just from the workings of demography and the free market that Malthus and Ricardo believed in. While the labor-force effects of this mix were dynamic and complex, there is at least something classical in the look of a policy that pulled the most destitute up toward subsistence (mainly 1785–1834) and pushed other workers down toward it

(Corn Laws 1765–1793, 1815–1846). This suggestion accords with other scholars' finding strong circumstantial evidence of regressive fiscal policies in early modern Britain.[23]

How different was early modern Britain from continental Europe in having regressive policies at some times and progressive ones at others? For any period before the twentieth century, we are far from the good-data lamppost, and scholars have still ventured only a few guesses, bringing some small candles into the archives.

Some regressive tendencies, and signs of their early modern decline, have been described more fully for the Italian regional states and the Netherlands.[24] For the early modern Republic of Venice, Guido Alfani and Matteo Di Tullio used a mixture of data and assumptions to argue that government budgets were regressive, though decreasingly so between 1550 and 1750. For the Netherlands, the least regressive of these European states, the expenditure side of government may have remained regressive all the way from 1580 to 1910, due to the dominance of military expenditures, which were not less than all other expenses until the 1820s. Yet progressivity was seen as advancing on the revenue side. Regarding the composition of taxes in the Dutch Republic, increasing progressivity is suggested by De Vries and Van der Woude.[25] For these areas of Western Europe, at least, the direction was regressive in the sixteenth century, with slight hints of progressivity by the nineteenth. Thus for the continent, as well as for Britain, bringing more candles into the archives will shed more light on the extent to which intentionally regressive redistribution by early modern governments made households' income more unequal over successive generations, by concentrating property as well as power in the hands of those at the top.

EQUALIZING WITHOUT SEEMING TO REDISTRIBUTE MUCH: THREE LUCKY AND SMART EAST ASIANS

Thus far, this chapter has been charting, and has started to explain, the history and global geography of fiscal redistribution, as conventionally measured, and its correlation with the share of national income channeled into social spending. To broaden our understanding of how government shapes inequality over the generations, we need next to take two related steps: To explore how some populations have achieved greater equality even without seeming to redistribute much income each year, and to re-discover from their experience a strong influence of public social spending on inequality, an influence missed by the conventional measures of fiscal redistribution.

Have any countries equalized incomes without an annual political struggle over redistribution through taxes and transfers in the next government budget? Could a country pre-commit to equality by somehow making people more equal in their market incomes, with only modest anti-poverty transfers? This matters. Suppose that the answer is no. Suppose that no rich democracy has ever achieved "equal" incomes without devoting over 20 percent of GDP to social transfers. Such a history would speak volumes. It would lend support to the plea by Thomas Piketty, Emmanuel Saez, and Gabriel Zucman in favor of stiff taxation at the top and generous transfers to the poor.[26] Much of the global historical record supports this inference. There are instructive cases, however, in which incomes have been kept relatively equal without a welfare state.

Let us focus here on a group of three non-welfare states, a group that had less inequality of market incomes to begin with. Their governments have kept final incomes relatively equal by having people's incomes less unequal before taxes and transfers than the inequality of American incomes left over after taxes and transfers. Two of the three, Japan and Korea, stood out in the lower reaches of Figures 10.2 and 10.3.[27] Taiwan's egalitarian performance has been similar to that shown for Japan and Korea. As for Taiwan, since 1981 or earlier it has had low inequality both before and after taxes, along with low shares of its population living in poverty, and especially low child poverty relative to the poverty of the elderly. As of 1980, all three economies had relatively equal income distributions both before and after taxes, and these distributions have remained more equal than in the other rich democracies.[28] As Table 10.1 suggested, this relative equality still prevails both before and after taxes and transfers, despite some rise in inequality since the 1990s.

Postwar Japan, Korea, and Taiwan have an inequality history that contrasts not only with the usual Western economies, but also with the rest of East Asia. In mainland China, historic supports for equality were abandoned after 1978, replacing the strong equalization of the Mao "iron rice bowl" era with today's wide income gaps, matching or exceeding those of the United States.[29] Inequality is also high throughout Southeast Asia and in the tiny financial center city-states, Hong Kong and Singapore.[30]

How did this happen in Japan, Korea, and Taiwan? Four factors seem to explain most of the difference: (1) these economies' good luck in entering the postwar era with less unequal land ownership; (2) their postwar lucky timing in trade competition; (3) their blocking of immigration; and above all (4) their prior investments in primary and secondary education, which equalized incomes in a way overlooked by the conventional same-year measures of fiscal redistribution.

Our three East Asian populations all started the postwar era with land endowments that were less unequal than in other regions. Part of this egalitarian endowment was of long standing: The East Asian countryside has long been dominated by family farms with long-term control of the land that gave the farming families themselves a large share of *de facto* ownership and rents.[31] In Japan, this equalizing tendency was reinforced by two waves of egalitarian shocks. In the late nineteenth century, the Meiji Restoration took power and land-taxing wealth from the daimyo. Then, in 1937–1952, the wealthy Zaibatsu set up in the Meiji reign came under attack, first from the military government and then from the defeat and the American occupation. In Korea's case, the combination of colonization, World War II, and the Korean War meant that top accumulations of wealth had to start all over. Inequality in Taiwan was similarly restrained by Japanese occupation. To be sure, 1949 brought a new infusion of Kuomintang wealth, but with limits imposed by the confiscation of their holdings on the mainland. Equally important, the mainland influx brought a large number of small-business entrepreneurs. For all three populations, the postwar era started off with lower inequality than in other regions.

A second element of luck for the East Asian three, bringing prosperity with relative equality, was the international trade context they faced from the mid-1950s to the start of the 1980s. In that quarter century, they shared the good fortune of being the pioneers, along with Hong Kong, in opening up free trade with the huge OECD market at a time when their comparative advantage still lay in exporting manufactures that made extensive use of unskilled labor. Having this head start over other Asian competition allowed them an extra quarter century of relatively egalitarian labor demand patterns. The head start ended with China's opening to trade in the 1980s and India's shedding of its "licence raj" trade restrictions in the early 1990s. The rise of Chinese, Indian, and other Asian competition brought harder times for the less skilled in other developing countries after the late 1980s. A good illustration is the fate of Mexico after it unilaterally opened to trade under President Salinas (1988–1994). Instead of bringing an egalitarian gain to the unskilled, which is the theoretical (Stolper–Samuelson) result one might have expected from US–Mexican trade, the freer trade actually came with a widening of wage gaps within Mexico. It was the bad luck of Mexico's unskilled that their opening to trade came during the rise of lower-paid competition from Chinese and Indian manufacturers. That is, Mexico missed the egalitarian head start that Japan, Korea, and Taiwan had got between the mid-1950s and the mid-1980s.[32]

A third factor that has maintained relative equality in pay within Japan, Korea, and Taiwan has its sadder side. All three are gated communities, blocking large numbers of immigrants from gaining permanent residency. Restricting immigration of the less skilled has given these populations some domestic equality at the expense of global equality. By contrast, the countries of rising inequality since the 1970s, such as the United States and the United Kingdom, have absorbed above-average inflows of immigrants from lower-income countries, helping to maintain global equality while compromising domestic equality.[33] Here too, the East Asian approach follows a path taken by the United States in earlier times. As we shall note again in the next chapter, the Americans slammed the door on immigrants in 1921 and 1924, and did not re-open it widely until after 1965. Being a gated community for that half century reduced the share of American residents who were foreign-born. The immigration restrictions, combined with reductions in fertility, restricted the labor supply, raising unskilled wages faster than the incomes of the better off. This contributed to the Great Leveling of incomes between the 1910s and the 1970s – again gaining domestic equality at the expense of global equality.[34] The next chapter will globalize this same regrettable trade-off.

Finally, and most importantly for this study on how public social spending can promote equality, the three East Asian economies managed to maintain relatively equal earnings and incomes even after the low-skilled foreign competition had awakened on Asia's mainland in the 1980s and 1990s. In Japan, Korea, and Taiwan, labor had become sufficiently schooled and skilled that even the median earner was above the rising competition, and these countries' comparative advantage had shifted. Instead of trying to export apparel and cheap toys, they shifted toward importing them, with only a dwindling low-skilled share of the labor force suffering damage from the new competition.

As Chapter 5 already noted about Japan and Korea, these governments invested more in public primary and secondary education than others. Their adult populations have attained as many years of schooling, on the average, as have adults in the other world leaders – Canada, the United States, and the United Kingdom.[35] The emphasis on investing in basic education for all resembles the path taken before 1914 by North America. True, the Americans launched their famous land-grant universities with public money and public land grants as early as the Morrill Act of 1862. Yet as late as 1910, these subsidies remained much smaller than what American state and local governments were pouring into primary and secondary education, rather like the position of Japan, Korea, and Taiwan in the last sixty years.[36]

Thus Japan, Korea, and Taiwan have come up with a policy package that has kept household final incomes nearly as equal, after all taxes and transfers, as have the nine egalitarian welfare states – by making people more equal in their market incomes, even before taxes and transfers.

REDISTRIBUTION BEYOND THE SHORT RUN: PUBLIC MASS EDUCATION EQUALIZES ADULT INCOMES

These case histories illustrate a point that must be addressed by the emerging history of redistribution: Even if we restrict ourselves to fiscal redistributions, the effects of any one change in policy play out over many years, and cannot be captured by their seeming effects on rich and middle and poor within the same year. This year's social spending affects future pre-fisc inequality, i.e. the inequality of people's incomes before taxes and transfer payments. Conventional measures of fiscal redistribution all miss the effects that play out over many years.

The three natural channels through which this year's policies affect future inequality are government treatment of non-human capital, deferred payment obligations such as public pensions, and government treatment of human capital. The first of these three channels has been well introduced by Thomas Piketty (2014), by Emmanuel Saez and Gabriel Zucman (2019), and by the larger Piketty–Saez–Zucman research program on capital and inequality. They are filling in the intertemporal feedbacks whereby income and wealth taxation reduce this year's accumulation and future property incomes, especially for the very richest at the top of the distribution. The second of these three intertemporal channels, public pension obligations, will move to center stage in Chapters 12 and 13. Here, we turn to the third channel, the influences of public-schooling expenditures on future human capital.

A key implication of the mass-education effect will be that we have understated how much public education spending has cut income inequality over the last 150 years. The leveling of market incomes in the Great Leveling era from the 1910s to the 1970s was partly due to the hidden effect of rising public commitment to education, and the ominous rise of inequality since the 1970s would have been even worse without it. Far from explaining away part of the infamous rise of inequality since the 1970s, the fact that earlier outlays for public schooling must have leveled incomes, other things being equal, actually adds to the rise of inequality that still needs to be explained. After all, the continued convergence of adults' schooling should have left us with lower inequality, not higher.

The problem is that studies of fiscal redistribution typically count only the same-year effect of public subsidies to education. They have not treated the larger deferred effects. They include a same-year effect, as if the benefits of taxpayers' paying for your (say) fifth-grade education accrue to your parents this year and not to you, the student, any time in the future. Convention has thus equated public education with day care.

As convenient as this convention may be, it misses most of what public education spending does to the different income ranks.

Public spending on education affects the inequality of later market earnings and the progressivity of government's contribution to reducing that inequality, through two channels. One is that lowering the inequality of adults' accumulated schooling, that global "convergence, big time" revealed back in Chapter 5, should directly help to equalize their earnings for any given structure of pay rates. The other is that a rise in their average schooling should bid down skilled-wage premiums, further reducing the inequality of earnings and income. While it is not easy to trace these inequalities in education subsidies and in final earnings, this strong link should be pursued.

As Chapter 5's long history of educational attainment revealed, the "convergence big time" took place both within and between countries. In principle, it could have been otherwise: Countries that advanced most rapidly in their overall education could have been those who pushed higher education much harder than they pushed primary and secondary, making education more unequal while raising the average education. Yet it did not happen that way.

The inequality of schooling attainment bears the clear fingerprint of unequal government subsidies to education, as Chapter 7 dramatized for developing countries, especially India and Latin America. Countries where many adults never finish primary or secondary education tend to be countries that have previously discriminated in favor of subsidizing higher education available only to relatively few, at the expense of broad mass education.

PART IV

CONFRONTING THREATS

CHAPTER 11

Do Immigration Tensions Fray the Safety Nets?

TWO FUTURE THREATS ARE LIKELY TO JEOPARDIZE THE progress of social spending and its favorable economic and social effects. One has been developing for decades, and will continue to build slowly. The other will appear more dramatic in the short run. Both threats are demographic and political. The knowable trends in life expectancy, fertility, and migration may threaten the expansion and productivity of social spending through two politicized channels.

The longer-run channel, the one harder to block or modify, works through human aging. At we saw in Chapters 6 and 7, population aging has already shown signs of diverting social spending into less productive forms.

Fortunately, the longer-run threat from aging is more predictable than most future developments. We can more reliably forecast its implications for social spending and the welfare state in, say, the year 2050 than we can predict that year's technology, or its weather, or its World Cup winner. What makes the mid-century forecast clearer for the main threats to the welfare state is that it is driven by vital rates, that is by human survival, fertility, and migration. Demographers have been able to forecast survival, fertility, and migration well enough for generations ahead. Luckily for the purposes of this book, it just so happens that the future of social spending is one of those things depending more heavily on those predictable demographic vital rates than it will depend on the fuzzier future of standard economic variables. The population will continue to age, and Chapters 12 and 13 will concentrate on this slowly advancing threat.

This chapter addresses the other very real demographic threat – the shorter-run threat posed by the combination of rising immigration and the political backlash against it.

WAVES OF IMMIGRANTS – AND OF BACKLASH

Migration has come in waves. The wave-like feature is easily demonstrated by the history of the country that has absorbed the most immigrants. For the first century and a third of its independence, the United States was a country in which one out of every seven residents was born abroad (Figure 11.1). Yet anti-immigrant sentiments were evident as early as the 1880s. At the same time that the statue of "Liberty Enlightening the World" was being built as a French gift on Ellis Island, facing out to the Atlantic, the United States also banned immigrants from China with the Chinese Exclusion Act of 1882. Similarly, in 1907, in response to anti-Japanese nativism in California, the United States and Japan came to informal agreements that Japanese would be denied passports to the United States. Both restrictions were replaced in the early 1920s by the even tougher Emergency Quota Act of 1921 and the National Origins Act of 1924. These banned all immigration of Asians, while

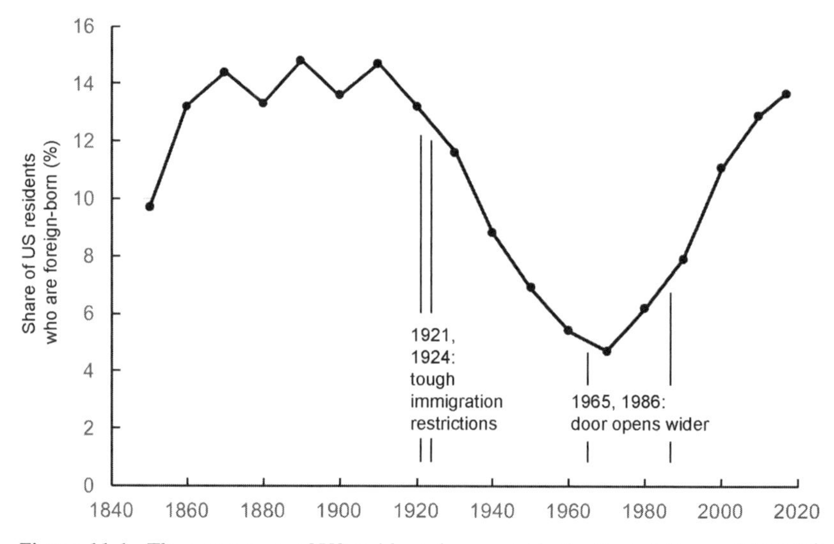

Figure 11.1. The percentage of US residents born outside the United States, 1850–2017
Source: United States Census Bureau.

benefiting those from Northern and Western Europe (whose migrations declined anyway), and shutting out many from Southern and Eastern Europe.

The anti-immigrant flames of the early 1920s were fanned by three historical forces. First, population growth had closed the open-land frontier, which had previously allowed separate ethnic groups based in Europe enough space to spread out and live separately. Second, the new immigrants of the 1900–1914 era were from Southern and Eastern Europe, perceived to be culturally distant from those that had arrived earlier. Finally, the victory of the Bolsheviks in the Russian Revolution of November 1917 sent a Red Scare across America. This new fear became associated with nationalities to the south and east, reinforcing the fear of immigrants.

For example, the *New York Times* of February 9, 1921 warned that immigration restrictions must be imposed because "American institutions are menaced" by "swarms of aliens whom we are importing as 'hands' for our industries . . . With the diseases of Bolshevism we are importing also the most loathsome diseases of the flesh." In the same year Vice-President Calvin Coolidge warned in an article in *Good Housekeeping* that "Biological laws tell us that certain divergent people will not mix or blend . . . The dead weight of alien accretion stifles national progress."[1] Such was the mood that passed the tough immigration bills of 1921 and 1924.

The effect on the foreign-born share was deep and lasting, as Figure 11.1 shows. By the 1960s, the share of all Americans born abroad had dropped from about 14 percent to about 5 percent. Yet after World War II, a more prosperous and self-confident America opened the doors again. The Immigration and Nationality Act of 1952 abolished direct racial barriers. In 1965, the Immigration and Naturalization Act, also known as the Hart–Celler Act, officially welcomed foreign-born refugees and relatives of Americans. Then in 1986, the Immigration Reform and Control Act granted amnesties to those who had entered the country without sufficient documentation, while threatening employers of undocumented workers with new fines. These liberalizations, plus postwar peace and prosperity, allowed the share of foreign-born Americans to return to its earlier heights by the early twenty-first century. Immigration has continued to rise, despite attempts to close the door again.

The recent rise of immigration has in fact been shared by all the richest democracies of Western Europe and North America. Over these years, the inflow of migrants has grown most clearly for Germany, which accepted a particularly large number of refugees in the 2015–2016 wave from Syria, Iraq, and Afghanistan. While this latest wave has been impeded by the migration barriers in response to the 2020 virus pandemic, Europe should expect further rises in the supply of migrants, both ordinary economic migrants and desperate refugees. The rich receiving countries all have poorer neighbors with dysfunctional governments. Economic breakdowns and humanitarian crises are likely. A horrific descent into civil war like that in Syria after 2012 could easily happen again in any of several large countries – say, in one of the large countries of Mediterranean North Africa and the Middle East. Such a civil war would send another wave of refugees to Europe. While some of the African and Middle Eastern refugees will also head to Australasia and North America, there will be an offsetting decline in migration from Latin America. That region has entered an era of low population growth, so there will be less demographic pressure to cross the Rio Grande, with or without a border wall (Hanson and McIntosh 2016).

The wave of refugees that crested in 2015–2016, like earlier high waves, raised nativist backlash against the arriving foreigners. Almost all European countries and the United States have seen anti-immigrant political parties capture a rising share of votes. Much of the accompanying rhetoric has been raw. Viktor Orbán, prime minister of Hungary, has repeated the phrase "the best migrant is the migrant who does not come."[2] In Denmark in 2005, Pia Kjaersgaard, then head of the nativist Danish People's Party, demonized Sweden's liberal welcoming of refugees thus: "If they [Swedes] want to turn Stockholm, Gothenburg or Malmoe into a Scandinavian Beirut, with clan wars, honour killings and gang rapes, let them do it. We can always put a barrier on the Oeresund Bridge [between Sweden and Denmark]."[3] In the American presidential election campaign of 2015–2016, candidate Donald Trump similarly demonized migrants, in this case from Mexico: "When Mexico sends its people, they're not sending their best ... They're sending people that have lots of problems, and they're bringing those problems with us.

They're bringing drugs. They're bringing crime. They're rapists. And some, I assume, are good people."[4]

Such raw xenophobia seems to be accompanied by many natives' genuine misperceptions about immigrants and their fiscal effects. To back up this point with objective measures of people's perceptions, Alberto Alesina, Armando Miano, and Stefanie Stantcheva of Harvard University (2018) surveyed people in six countries (USA, UK, France, Italy, Germany, and Sweden) in the winter of 2017–2018. People were asked about some magnitudes they perceived regarding immigration – how big is it, where do the immigrants come from, and what happens to them after they arrive? A virtue of this team's interview design is that people's answers can be compared directly with the actual numbers. Table 11.1 shows some of the results.

TABLE 11.1. *Perceptions versus reality about immigrants in six countries, November 2017 – February 2018*

		Native-born persons interviewed in					
		USA	UK	France	Italy	Germany	Sweden
What percentage of people in your country are foreign-born?	Actual	10.0	13.4	12.2	10.0	14.8	17.6
	Perceived	36.1	31.3	28.8	26.4	30.3	27.0
What percentage of your foreign-born are from North Africa and the Middle East?	Actual	4.4	6.0	38.9	13.1	18.8	25.0
	Perceived	20.6	20.9	28.2	33.9	32.9	37.2
What percentage of your foreign-born are Muslim?	Actual	10.0	23.0	48.0	33.0	30.0	27.0
	Perceived	22.7	33.9	50.2	47.0	43.9	44.8
What percentage of your foreign-Born have not finished high school?	Actual	22.0	16.6	39.1	49.1	35.1	33.7
	Perceived	29.0	25.6	51.6	43.6	37.2	40.9
What percentage of your foreign-born are unemployed?	Actual	5.5	5.7	16.6	14.7	6.9	16.1
	Perceived	26.4	27.0	38.8	41.8	39.2	37.2
Ratio of government transfers received by the average foreign-born, vs. the average native-born	Actual	1.23	1.42	1.39	1.29	0.72	1.44
	Perceived	1.17	1.02	1.77	1.34	1.13	1.28

Source and notes: Alesina, Miano, and Stantcheva (2018). The sample sizes are 4,500 native-born adult interviewees for the United States, 4,001 for the UK, 4,000 for France, 4,000 for Italy, 4,001 for Germany, and 2,004 for Sweden, for a total of 22,506 respondents.

First, as shown in the top row, people in all six countries greatly over-estimate the share of immigrants in their midst, imagining that about 30 percent of residents are foreign-born, when the true shares are only 10–18 percent. In five of the six countries, people also over-imagine the shares of immigrants that are Muslim or that come from North Africa and the Middle East. Strikingly, the only country that did not overestimate the Muslim share, or the share from North Africa and the Middle East, was France, the country where Muslims and trans-Mediterranean migrants was the greatest. People in all six countries made the further mistake of under-estimating the education of the immigrants; as shown in Table 11.1, they consistently overestimated the low-education share, the share of immigrants that had not yet finished high school.[5]

Regarding what happens to the immigrants after arrival, we often hear conflicting perceptions. Some nationals think that the immigrants are a fiscal burden because they work very little and get handouts, while others think they work too much, taking jobs away from the native-born. The team of Alesina, Miano, and Stantcheva came up with a clear result regarding work by immigrants of working age. In all six countries of Table 11.1, immigrants' unemployment rate has in fact been much lower than people tend to think, even in that winter of 2017–2018, when so many refugees still had not mastered the new native language or found jobs. Finally, people were asked whether the average adult immigrant received more transfer payments from government than the average native-born. The truth is that immigrants do receive more on average, because of their initial economic hardships. On this matter, the interview responses of the native-born were close to the truth, even though they had overestimated immigrants' unem-ployment and had underestimated their education.

HOW IMMIGRATION HAS AFFECTED GOVERNMENT BUDGETS

So have immigrants been a net burden or a net benefit to the native-born population? Economists have tried to add realism to popular perceptions, by studying the real-world effects of extra immigrants, or of measures to shut them out. Let us next survey how these effects have played out under the immigration policies practiced thus far, to sharpen our guesses about how different political outcomes and different policies might affect the tax burdens and social-spending behavior of the native-born populations in immigrant-receiving countries.

The results will depend, of course, on the type of immigration being restricted – which skill groups would be cut, which age groups, and what emphasis on refugees versus economic migrants, for example. To mobilize the existing empirical literature, let us begin with its tendency to summarize the effects of the observed recent mix of immigrants, without any detailed focus on a particular proposal for immigration restriction.[6]

IMMIGRANTS' EFFECTS ON GDP AND GOVERNMENT REVENUE PER CAPITA. The effects on government revenue, via effects on GDP, can conveniently draw on the literature estimating the effects of immigration on labor markets and productivity. That literature, while freely admitting the limitations of its evidence and its econometric estimation, generally concludes that the observed mix of immigration has probably raised GDP per capita a bit, especially in studies that try to guesstimate externalities.[7]

The slight extra GDP in turn translates into a slight addition to government revenue, slightly improving the affordability of social programs.[8] This bland and tentative positive result seems to enjoy a consensus, despite the heated controversy over whether natives' wage rates are lowered, or raised, or unaffected.

NET BUDGET EFFECTS IMPLIED BY EXISTING TAX RATES AND ENTITLEMENTS. Even if immigrants contribute slightly to GDP and government revenue, such slight positives could be swamped by the extra demands that immigrants place on social-expenditure programs. There is widespread fear that immigrants are a net fiscal burden, for which the already-arrived native population must pay. Opinion surveys have shown that people's fears of immigrants' negative fiscal effects loom even larger than their fears of effects on the labor market, such as their taking jobs away or lowering wages.[9]

The fiscal burden of an individual immigrant depends very much on the immigrant's age, since all countries tend to support children and the elderly, while taxing those of prime working age. The first-generation immigrants receive net benefits when they are still children of school age, and receive net benefits again in old age. In between, however, they are net taxpayers. The population of arriving immigrants is unevenly distributed, however. The first-generation immigrant population includes more adults per year of working age than children or elderly, so that the taxpaying of the middle age ranges is actually magnified relative to the expenditures on young and old.

How does it all net out fiscally, given the age distribution of arriving immigrants? The net fiscal effects of extra immigrants depend critically on one's time horizon. Instead of just asking "are immigrants a net fiscal benefit or burden?" we must ask "over what time span are they a net benefit or burden?" Table 11.2 summarizes this dependence conceptually, drawing on plausible longer-run simulations.[10]

TABLE 11.2. *The fiscal effects of extra immigrants depend on the question you ask about them*

The question you ask		Burden through public pensions?	Burden through public schooling, aid to young?
The "pay-as-you-go" question: Are today's immigrants a net burden on native taxpayers this year, "pay-as-you-go"?	→	**No**, immigrants pay for natives' public pensions.	**Yes**, immigrant children subsidized by native taxpayers.
The "one lifetime" question: Is one wave of immigrants a net burden on native taxpayers over the life span of the immigrants and their descendants?	→	**Yes**, if immigrants have lower lifetime earnings, they get an above-average rate of return on pensions, at expense of other taxpayers.	**No**, immigrants' childrenrepay the rest of society in productivity and taxes.
The "many generations" question: Are today's immigrants, + their children and grandchildren to 2100, a net fiscal burden?	→	**No**, they become heavy net taxpayers, like others.	**No**, they become heavy net taxpayers, like others.

Notes: If one could pay for pensions and other social transfers out of government debt, and out of the reserves of the pension system, then the left-hand side of the equation should be modified to include taxes paid in earlier and later years, not just in the current year. Yet they have to be paid sooner or later, and the problem remains essentially as stated in this pure same-year version of pay-as-you-go.

Note another simplification here: Taxation here refers only to those taxes that are spent on education, pensions, and other social benefits, and not the total of all tax revenues. This analysis ignores taxes channeled into non-transfer spending, such as national defense, highway construction, and basic government payrolls.

Suppose we take the usual short-run view, in the top row of Table 11.2, asking the pay-as-you-go question "Do today's extra immigrants cause a net drain on government budgets right now, in this same year?"[11] They often do so, since extra immigrants' families typically are a net drain through the host country's child-related social programs such as education. If this drain is greater than the tax revenues collected from adult immigrants, helping to pay for pensions and other public programs, then immigrants do cause a net fiscal drain this year. Fiscal-demographic simulations suggest that the net short-run fiscal effect is indeed negative. A typical mix of immigrant age groups is so tilted toward the young that the costs of child-centered social programs yield a negative net result for the first twelve to fifteen years after an immigrant arrival. This short-run negative effect would also show up in immigrants' use of non-contributory aid to those of working age. As OECD economists have rightly emphasized, the short-run fiscal impact depends above all on the host country's success or failure in helping the foreign-born find jobs.[12]

Next, suppose one takes a somewhat longer view, asking Table 11.2's second question about the net fiscal effects over the whole lifetimes of the first generation of new immigrants. Now the net effect is probably positive. True, the immigrants in old age probably get a net transfer from others, because public pension systems are typically designed to be progressive, giving a high rate of return to lower-income earners, such as first-generation immigrants. Yet while that first generation is aging, its children have already become productive adults, paying positive taxes instead of needing school money. These tax contributions should outweigh any intra-cohort redistributions toward foreign-born pensioners.

Finally, when we consider the whole lifetimes of not only the extra immigrants but also their children and grandchildren, the net fiscal effects become clearly positive, as again suggested in Table 11.2. We know that the eventual fiscal results are clearly positive, because in the long run the immigrants and their descendants pay more in taxes than they get in targeted transfers, just like the rest of society. So the answer to the net-burden question is clearly "no," not a net burden for any year beyond about the sixteenth year after arrival. The long-run fiscal effect of extra immigration is clearly positive.[13] That makes perfect sense: In the long run, we are all descendants of immigrants, and over our lifetimes we pay more in taxes than anybody receives in social spending – our remaining taxes cover such shared public goods as national defense and public transit.

WILL IMMIGRATION BACKLASH UNDERMINE SOCIAL SPENDING? FOUR OPTIONS

So under existing policies, extra immigrants will tend, on the average, to have slightly positive effects on GDP, and effects on the government budget balance will eventually be positive as well. These generally positive results suggest that immigration has not endangered social spending or the welfare state – at least not economically, and not with existing policies toward taxes and social spending. Yet recent political backlash against immigration threatens to cut immigration, one way or another. If it did, would the political reaction against immigrants also bring a reaction against social programs in general, even as they applied to those who are needy and native-born? The positive fiscal effects of immigrants and their descendants may be politically trumped by negative perceptions like those surveyed earlier in this chapter, especially in the wake of a large influx of refugees. Prevailing opinions can still be negative about the same fiscal effects, and about the negative effects on some native workers' earning power, not to mention cultural phobias and fears of terrorism.

There are four options, or four political scenarios, that could be followed in the near future. The first of the four is a baseline case in which the government resists all calls to restrict immigration – in other words, keeps the country's doors as wide open as before. Recent experience and recent surveys of public opinion tell us much about this baseline option.

OPTION 1: WELCOMING IMMIGRANTS WITHOUT DISCRIMINATION. As German Chancellor Angela bravely said in 2015, "*wir schaffen das*" (We can manage this).[14]

A country can welcome immigrants and, after paying extra for their initial training and language learning, give them the same kinds of need-based entitlements as are given to the native-born. Germany and Sweden led the world in choosing this option in 2014–2016. Germany accepted 890,000 permanent-type refugees from the Middle East in 2015 alone. Sweden accepted 163,000 that year, an even larger share of the national population than for Germany. A sustained use of this open-door policy would promote global growth and equality at the expense of domestic growth, equality – and harmony.

However, both countries soon hurried to close the gate, both at their own borders and at the Mediterranean borders of the European Union. By 2018, Germany had accepted only 185,000 refugee applications, a 79 percent drop from that 2015 peak of 890,000.

What kinds of countries would follow this first option, which implies a significant rise in social-spending obligations until the immigrants have learned the language and found jobs? The most likely candidates are indeed countries like Germany and Sweden, who welcomed so many refugees in the wave that peaked in 2015–2016. Initially at least, both countries have refused to discriminate against immigrants from distant cultures in their welfare-state system of entitlements, and have accepted the extra initial burdens that come with such arrivals.

Is Option 1 sustainable, either as an acceptance of more immigrants or as a commitment to universal social entitlements for all residents? As noted, both Germany and Sweden moved within a couple of years to restrict the acceptance of refugees for the foreseeable future. Will the other shoe drop – that is, will these countries cut social spending even for those that are native-born? This key question deserves careful reflection. No immediate answer has been given by the rising anti-immigration parties themselves. Germany's rising right-wing party Alternative für Deutschland (Alternative for Germany), while outspoken on many issues, has not come out against the welfare state. Nor have their counterparts in Sweden. Since 2011 or earlier, Sweden's right-wing "Sweden Democrats" Party (not to be confused with the Social Democratic Party, which has governed Sweden most of the time since 1932) has repeatedly denied that they seek to cut back the welfare state, knowing that the welfare state remains popular. Their leader, Jimmie Åkesson, was explicit about this – "We believe in the welfare state" – while also voicing suspicions about Sweden's mosques and Islamic community groups.[15]

The political climate can change, of course. For example, people can update their opinions about welfare programs, and change their votes, in response to new exposures to immigrants. We can gather two kinds of clues to upcoming trends: public opinions about the welfare state, and actual policy changes.

Public opinion surveys sometimes ask people whether they think that "social benefits" should be higher, and in a subset of those surveys one can exploit exogenous-looking variation in exposure to immigration to see if that exposure seems to reduce support for social spending. An early opportunity to conduct such a test occurred in Sweden in 1985–1994. At that time, the government's Refugee Placement Program assigned refugees to cities, with preference for secondary cities. That is, the refugees were not allowed to decide where they first lived. That suggests that which native-born Swedes came in contact with foreigners was initially exogenous, even though the refugees were soon able to change cities. Exploiting this geographic variation within Sweden, the research team of Matz Dahlberg, Karin Edmark, and Heléne Lundqvist (2012, 2013) estimated the effect of locals' exposure to immigrants on the locals' answer to the question "Are you in favor of decreasing the social benefits?" The authors found that there was indeed a tendency for Swedes more exposed to immigrants to favor cutting social benefits. And since the question about social benefits seemed to refer to universal benefits, the implication was that support for the welfare state was undercut by contact with newly arrived immigrants. If true, this would suggest something like the negative effect of ethnic fractionalization on the growth of social spending, as we described back in Chapter 6.

A more recent survey is that 2017–2018 survey conducted by Alberto Alesina, Armando Miano, and Stefanie Stantcheva, cited earlier in connection with Table 11.1. The authors found that people's support for generous redistribution is undermined by the perception that immigrants are more represented among the beneficiaries of redistribution. At first glance, this seems to reveal direct links between their fears of immigrants and their willingness to retreat from offering universal social benefits. However, the link is actually not so direct here. The fears about immigrants only take the indirect form of their being asked first about immigrants before being asked the payoff questions about social benefits.

Given this ordering of the questions, there is a strong chance that they interpreted the questions about social benefits as referring to immigrants as such, not to the more universal benefits of the welfare state.

A deeper test of the link between exogenous exposure to immigrants and support for income redistribution has now been carried out by the research team of Alberto Alesina, Elie Murard, and Hillel Rapoport (2019). Like the Dahlberg–Edmark–Lundqvist team, they exploited variation in actual exposure to immigrants among regions, in this case among 140 regions within sixteen Western European countries between 2002 and 2016. Controlling for many other things, they explored how regional exposure to immigrants made the interviewed individuals agree or disagree with the statement "The government should take measures to reduce differences in income levels." The effects were strongly negative, that is against progressive redistribution. Going beyond asking just about progressive redistribution, the authors also asked questions about social spending itself, such as whether one agrees that "social benefits place too great strain on economy," "social benefits cost businesses too much in taxes and charges," and "social benefits make people lazy." While social spending is indeed correlated with progressive redistribution, as shown in Chapter 10, the authors concentrated on the demand for redistribution, not on social spending itself. Still, their overall conclusion also strongly suggests a negative effect of exposure to immigrants on support for social spending. Importantly, and not surprisingly, they also found that cultural distance and low skills on the part of immigrants made the negative effect stronger. Implication: Welcoming low-skilled immigrants from very different cultures will weaken the universalist welfare state.

So far, all the studies are based on opinion surveys, and all suggest that an erosion of expressed support for social spending will result either from anti-immigrant prejudice or from actual contact with immigrants from distant cultures.

The second kind of relevant clue comes not from expressed opinions but from directly observed policy changes themselves. Have immigration shocks negatively affected actual safety-net policies? One econometric study has looked at the pool of twenty-five developed OECD countries for the period 1980–2008, testing for effects of changes in immigration on changes in aggregate social expenditures, controlling for time and country effects. The authors (Gaston and Rajaguru 2013) find no negative effects on social spending, either from aggregate immigrants, or from lower-educated immigrants, or from migrants from poorer countries. A similarly muted result comes from a study of the shifting generosity of social assistance payments among provinces in Canada between 1986 and 2001 (Green and Riddell 2019). Having a greater proportion of immigrants did not significantly reduce the generosity of social assistance to four kinds of household groups, with the slight exception of assistance to couples with children after a certain federal reform of 1996. Such studies have the virtue of testing for actual policy outcomes instead of accepting answers to opinion surveys. Their null results lose some value from the fact that they test only policy behaviors from before the slump of 2008–2009 and before the refugee shock of 2015–2016.[16] Perhaps the real policy backlash is yet to come?

There remains the threat of a policy backlash against the welfare states choosing the generous and even-handed Option 1, even though no reduction of universal benefits has yet occurred – neither in these statistical studies nor in the social-spending policies of Germany and Sweden since 2015.

OPTION 2: THE DOOR STAYS LOCKED. At the other extreme, consider the possibility of a country with a large social-spending share that simply blocks immigration. The main candidates are five Eastern European members of the European Union: the three Baltic republics, Slovakia, and Hungary. To think of a country that has clearly tried to shut the door recently, one can choose Hungary, the most outspoken in its opposition to immigrants.

In such a case, immigrants would cease to be a short-run budgetary burden, aside from the cost of enforcing the barriers at the border. Social spending for the native population could continue as before. Equality could also be promoted within the country, if the migrants being kept out would have competed mainly for lower-skilled jobs.

In the longer run, however, the restrictiveness of Option 2 would take a toll on the economy. As we have seen, after maybe twelve to fifteen years, the effects of a typical mix of immigrants on government revenues and net fiscal surplus would have turned positive, if the migrants had been allowed into the country. That is, the effect on government revenues and surplus of keeping them out would grow increasingly negative. So eventually, Option 2 comes with a growth cost relative to Option 1.[17]

OPTION 3: "WELFARE CHAUVINISM". A third possibility is that immigrants are still allowed to enter, but the government discriminates against them in its provision of social services. Practicing such discrimination, also known as "welfare chauvinism," should in principle make it easier to avoid dilution of benefits for natives. This strategy harkens back to the seventeenth century, when the European towns denied poor relief and other local services to immigrants, as noted in Chapter 3.

To what extent have immigrant-receiving countries practiced such discrimination recently? Thus far, countries accepting immigrants have been unwilling to saddle themselves with immigrants who are not entitled to basic social services. To date, the main case of discriminating against migrants in social program entitlements has been China's *hukou* system of internal passports, which blocked rural–to–urban domestic migrants from the better health, education, and other entitlements of the major eastern cities between the communal era of the Great Leap Forward and the partial relaxation of *hukou* in 1996. Again, there is a clear parallel to the settlements policies of seventeenth-century Europe.

In a federal system, discrimination in social services can gain advocates because a state or local population resists having to pay for immigrants' social services, yet is unable to block immigration, a policy reserved for the central government. Another near approach to welfare chauvinism, receiving immigrants while denying them basic services, threatened to arise when conservative Californians passed Proposition 187 in 1994. The proposition called for denying public K-12 education and other public services to the families of those non-US citizens who had entered the state without legal documentation. However, Proposition 187 was struck down by the state's Supreme Court, and has never been implemented. The political perils of welfare chauvinism were underlined in California's case: Republicans' support for Proposition 187 is believed to have doomed their party to long-run minority status in California.

The real test will be the policy reactions to Europe's heavy refugee inflow of 2015–2016. That test is currently in progress. Among the rising anti-immigrant political parties on the right, the support for welfare chauvinism has shown an interesting, but logical, pattern. Laurenz Ennser-Jedenastik (2018) has studied the policy pronouncements of right-wing anti-immigrant parties in the Netherlands, Sweden, Switzerland and the UK. These pronouncements have voiced strong opposition to social *assistance*, but not to social *insurance*. That is, they reject giving outright grants to the foreign-born on the basis of unemployment or poverty, but do not oppose contributory plans in which the foreign-born would pay into plans entitling them to later health care and pensions.[18] Thus, even the right-wing call for discrimination in social services has been only partial. Welfare chauvinism seems unlikely to be embodied in sustained policies.

OPTION 4: CHERRY-PICKING THE BEST EARNERS. A final option reacts to the anti-immigrant spirit with a combination of blocking boat people and over-border refugees, while admitting, or even actively recruiting, the highly educated and highly skilled. The usual formal name for cherry-picking of immigrants is a points-based immigration system that determines a non-citizen's eligibility to immigrate (partly or wholly) on the basis of that non-citizen's points in a scoring system including such factors as education, wealth, language fluency, or an existing job offer.

Here again, there is little threat to social programs for established citizens, since the skilled immigrants passing through the filter need little help and will quickly become net taxpayers.

This fourth option is now practiced widely among rich countries, with Canada in a leading position. Figure 11.2 shows some striking international patterns in the destinations reached by highly educated migrants. For one thing, they end up in countries where the native-born population is also highly educated. One reason for this is unrelated to immigration

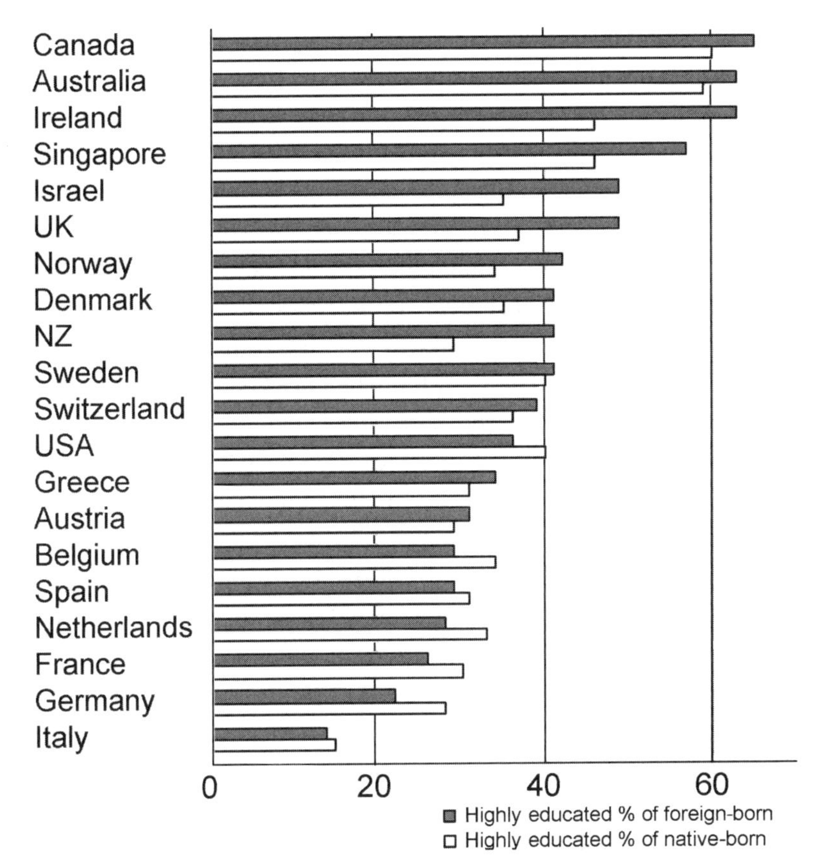

Figure 11.2. Percentage of foreign-born and native-born with post-secondary education, among the population 25 and older, twenty countries in 2015
Source: Connor and Ruiz (2019, Appendix B).

policy: Those with high skills tend to agglomerate in places where others have high skills, which in practice means major urban areas in the richest countries. Figure 11.2 shows this correlation of educated migrants with educated natives in the international snapshot taken in 2015.

The drift of the skilled toward high-education destination countries will continue in the future. Even if there were no shift in policy toward cherry-picking, the immigrant mix would contain more and more "cherries" in the future, for a simple reason unrelated to shifts in immigration policies.[19] As we noted back in Chapter 5, the rate of growth in educational attainment is much faster today than it was in the leading countries in the nineteenth and twentieth centuries.

While the tendency of highly educated countries like Canada to attract the highly educated is partly a byproduct of natural agglomeration tendencies, it is also a matter of explicit selectivity in immigration policy. The history of Canada and other countries makes this clear enough. Canada introduced a points-based immigration system back in 1967, replacing the older bias in favor of Europeans, and has refined the system ever since. Increasing emphasis has been given to job offers from Canadian employers and to fluency in English and/or French. Since 2006, and especially since the economic slump of 2008, Canada has generally tightened the skills restrictions even further, with the exception of its leading participation, along with Germany and Sweden, in the humanitarian acceptance of refugees from the Middle East in 2015–2016.[20]

Other countries have followed suit. In the 1970s and 1980s, Australia introduced a points system similar to Canada's, as did New Zealand in 1991. Between 2008 and 2010, the United Kingdom phased in a similar points system for immigrants from outside the European Union. The United States is drifting in the same direction. The appearance of an American lag in implementing skill-based immigration policies needs to be qualified in two respects, however. First, the United States already had such a skills-favoring policy between its restrictive laws of 1921–1924 and the Immigration and Nationality Act of 1952, before it shifted toward family reunion policies and widening the door for Latin Americans. Second, Figure 11.2's apparent skill deficit for US immigrants arises primarily from its being the immediate neighbor of Mexico and Central America. The United States receives a much larger share of immigrants from that region than do the other leading countries. If one excludes Mexican and Central American immigrants, the observable skills of America's immigrants are similar in those of Canada, Australia, and other top skill-importing countries.[21]

PROMOTING EQUALITY AND GROWTH: AT HOME OR WORLDWIDE?

So Option 4 looks better than Options 2 and 3 on domestic-efficiency and domestic-harmony grounds. Of course, a "cherry-picking" policy is no free lunch – with low-wage farm labor blocked from entering the country, who will pick the real cherries off the trees? Still, Option 4's cherry-picking would have three favorable economic effects, relative to a more balanced admission of immigrants. It would raise GDP per capita, generate more net revenue for government to spend, and avoid exacerbating visible domestic inequalities. It would also help to secure social insurance and social assistance within the country. Think of Option 4 as the national-level version of walling off gated communities, or to restrictive zoning laws designed to block the building of housing that the poor can afford.

Would it really placate the divisive anti-immigrant politics? Yes, it would help in this respect, according to a recent study by Simone Moriconi, Giovanni Peri, and Riccardo Turati (2018). Studying elections in twelve European countries, over the period 2007–2016, they find that preferences change more strongly in response to the low-skilled immigrant share among less-educated voters than for highly educated voters. Especially among less-educated and older native-born individuals, an increase in low-skilled immigrants makes their votes and attitudes more nativist, more anti-immigrant. Thus voting for nationalistic parties is more sensitive among lower-education native-born voters, and more sensitive in response to low-skilled immigration.

So the choice should boil down to Option 4 versus Option 1: Choose between promoting domestic goals and promoting world goals.

For now, the political pendulum on the migration issue is swinging toward Option 4's preserving productivity, equality, harmony – and social spending – within a country, at the expense of world productivity, equality, and humanitarian relief. The pendulum could swing back again in the future. Whichever way it swings, we face the same sad dilemma we saw in connection with Japan, Korea, and Taiwan in Chapter 10: There is an undeniable conflict between serving these objectives inside a country and serving them worldwide.

CHAPTER 12

Pensions and the Curse of Long Life

UNLIKE THE IMMIGRATION-CRISIS THREAT THAT COULD conceivably undermine public demand for social spending, another demographic and political trend threatens to over-supply it, perhaps triggering a fiscal crisis. This second threat is more certain, but slower acting, than the disenchantment with social spending that might accompany immigration backlash. The second threat relates to public spending that delivers greater benefits to the elderly than to younger adults or to children.[1]

We now know a great deal about the economics and politics of public pensions, thanks to global data from the international agencies, and especially from the OECD's staff. This chapter begins by identifying

- how an older population threatens public pensions,
- some popular counter-arguments that discount pension fears, and
- the budgetary logic that pension programs must respect.

It then provides a twenty-first-century global geography of which countries have been courting pension trouble and which have been insuring themselves against it. To these new perspectives, it will add predictions of which countries will have, and which will not have, budgetary leeway to improve the generosity of public pensions by 2050, without raising tax burdens and without forcing cuts elsewhere in the government budgets. A majority of countries has no such leeway, given the limits to economic growth and the speed of population aging.

Finally, I supplement these results about fiscal sustainability by naming some countries that are most guilty of short-changing human capital development for the young in favor of transfers to the current generation of elderly.

AGING AND THE PENSION SCARE

The secret is out. The world is getting older. Humans are surviving to later ages, and birth rates are dropping the world over, except where they have already stabilized below the population-replacing level. No longer are the improvements in survival concentrated among infants and the young, as was so impressively true in the first three-quarters of the twentieth century. In those days, improved survival meant more working adults per dependent. In recent decades, however, it is senior life expectancy and health that have improved dramatically.[2] In fact, the aging trend is accelerating right now: The number of elderly persons per hundred persons of working age will grow faster over the next thirty years than it has been growing since 1950, as shown in Figure 12.1. Demographers foresee a particularly strong acceleration in the aging trend for China, which is expected to pass the more developed countries in its elderly share. That trend is already in motion, with China's elderly population soaring while its working-age population has already begun to shrink in the last decade.

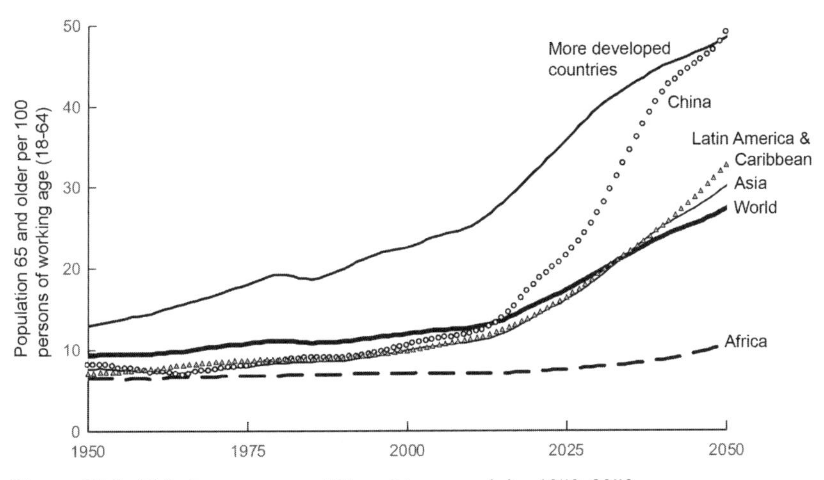

Figure 12.1. Elderly persons per 100 working-age adults, 1950–2050
Source and notes: The source is United Nations (2015). The levels from 1950 up to 2015 are based on estimates of actual age distributions, interpolating between census years. The levels from 2015 to 2050 are the UN's "mid-range" forecasts.

So the share of adult life that is spent at work is dropping. This is true, even though there has been no overall decline in employment ratios per year of prime working age, for example between ages 15 and 64, as we saw in Chapter 8. Despite that rise in employment for those 65 and younger, the share of adult life spent at work is still being pulled down by the rising share of those living past 65, who are still overwhelmingly retired.

Nobody can say that we have not been warned about dire consequences for public pensions. Every year, and almost every month, the press sounds an alarm about a future inability to pay for public pensions, citing the aging of our population as a prime mover. Two particularly prominent and authoritative alarmists were the World Bank's *Averting the Old Age Crisis* (1994, especially ch. 4) and *The Coming Generational Storm* by Laurence Kotlikoff and Scott Burns (2005).

Both writings do more than just sound an alarm about population aging. Both reveal a broader distrust of government spending, whatever it is spent on. *Averting the Old Age Crisis* is particularly extravagant in its condemnation of public pensions, with or without the worry of population aging. Two of its passages illustrate the dark mood of that "Washington consensus" heyday in the early 1990s. One dictum targeted the unfunded promises implied by defined-benefit pensions: "Hidden public debt – which needs to be paid off to reform pension schemes – often dwarfs the explicit national debt."[3] No reason is given why the government's social security promises to the current labor force need to be fully paid off in some "reform," or what the benefits of doing so would be. In another passage, after worrying that not enough reserves will be built up for funding public pension obligations, the World Bank authors warn of the danger that sufficient reserves *will* be built up: "The danger is that these reserves might make things worse, because they tempt governments to spend more – and to spend it on consumption rather than investment, while dissipating the reserves through negative real interest rates."[4] In this view, it appears, government spending is just plain bad. Yet no mention is made of the equally shaky mirror-image implication that not having enough reserves could be good because it would discourage government spending.[5] For their part, Kotlikoff and Burns simply went out of their way to grab scary headlines, by imagining worst-case scenarios about the breakdown of social security, complete with political instability, unemployment, and high crime rates, while avoiding any mention of growth benefits of government or of any dangers in the private financial sector.[6]

Nonetheless, let us extract their powerful signal from the ideological noise: Yes, there is good reason to worry about what aging may imply for the costs and benefits of public pension spending.

PUBLIC PENSIONS "ARE NO PROBLEM AT ALL": THREE WAYS TO THINK SO

Before exploring the basic budgetary logic of pensions and aging, and testing ideas against recent global history, let us address three frequent arguments inviting you to conclude that public pensions do not need to be reformed.

FUTURE GENERATIONS AS FAT CATS

(1) "The younger generations will be richer than we are, so public transfers to us, the elderly, are just a progressive redistribution toward those who have had lower lifetime resources."

On its own narrow terms, this *inter-generational progressivity* argument is probably valid. When pensions are paid out of general government revenues, the resulting transfers between generations are progressive in a steadily improving economy.[7] An extreme case is that of China. With average incomes doubling every few years, those whose adulthood reaches back into the impoverished twentieth century will have led a much poorer life than those Chinese who were lucky enough to be born in the twenty-first century.

Still, there are two rebuttals to this narrow argument. First, it is unlikely that transfers to your grandparents, progressive as they may be, are the most *productive* use of society's government revenues. If we broadly seek to increase the size of the pie for all generations taken together, pensions are less effective than investing in human health, knowledge, and skills, as is repeatedly noted in this book and elsewhere. Second, the current elderly generation is as wasteful of the environmental future as any generation in human history – surely as wasteful in absolute terms, and probably as wasteful per capita. They are already imposing serious environmental costs on younger generations, having enjoyed a better environment. Their wasteful consumption of environmental resources could be viewed as making them less poor and less deserving of a transfer from future generations.

PENSIONS ARE REALLY JUST COMPETITIVE WAGES, DEFERRED

> (2) "We have earned our pensions, because we have accepted generous-pension jobs where the regular straight pay is lower. It is just a way of deferring the pay we earned. Our pensions do not overpay us."

This assertion requires careful study, to be sure that the pay and benefit packages being compared would apply to persons with the same qualifications. One feasible test is to compare government and private workers, which are clearly distinguished in many data sets. The US Congressional Budget Office (2017) has carefully studied US federal versus private workers, 2005–2015. Its results show that only for the most educated groups of workers (Ph.D.s and professional degrees) did federal workers get paid less overall. For this top-education group, any extra old-age benefits were outweighed by a lower value of straight pay, canceling any gain in total compensation. In sharp contrast, federal workers with no college education got more than their qualifications would have been paid in the private sector, either in straight pay or (especially) in benefits, giving them more total compensation. The same appears to be true in many other countries. As we shall see for Latin America and Mediterranean Europe, public-sector workers got paid more in total compensation than their private counterparts. Justification (2) is generally false, at least in the public–private contrasts.[8]

HOW MUCH DID THE PENSIONERS THEMSELVES CONTRIBUTE?

> (3) "I earned my pension because I contributed to it while working. If you do not believe me, I can even show you the social security deductions on my pay stubs."

Of the three justifications, this one is the most complex.

Most of the world's government-managed pension systems take payroll contributions out of paychecks. Including at least some paycheck contributions in the system's design is politically astute. It enhances the support for continuing the public pension system, by giving those covered a sense of pride and ownership, leading to justifications like number (3) here. Given that covered employees do indeed contribute to some unknown extent, opponents of the system are forced to retreat somewhat. Their opposing arguments are weakened by their inability to measure the extent to which the pension system is underfunded, and the rest of society is being taxed, as they suspect.

So how do individuals' contributions to their own later retirement really stack up against the benefits they will receive later? What shares of public pensions are truly "funded" by the investment returns from the same individuals' contributions made during the earlier working years? Are these self-funding shares of government-managed pensions rising over time?[9]

Knotty problems entangle the actuarial accounting for contributions if they are not really individual and private. The mandatory government pension-contribution programs are in fact not private, even though they are often described as "privatized" pensions. The government has control over the magnitudes and the destinations of the invested contributions. One must first estimate rates of return that would have been earned on past payroll contributions to determine the accumulation of the reserve's asset value at the start of any period for paying out benefits. Aggregate studies are forced to multiply hypothetical accumulations of past contributions by equally hypothetical rates of return, such as the 4 percent rate used by the World Bank's *Averting the Old Age Crisis* (1994, ch. 4). Then one must determine what annuity values would be paid out, values that depends on the ages of the surviving elderly.[10]

To estimate the shares of today's public pensions that the beneficiaries could really be paying for their own retirement from their past contributions, it would help to base the calculation on real historical data as much as possible. Fortunately, for several OECD countries, we can draw on the OECD's history of actual contributions to "social security" since 1965, and on the market rates of return they could have earned on those contributions, thanks to the long-run Macrohistory Database developed by Oscar Jordà, Moritz Schularick, and Alan M. Taylor.[11] To use these real data, however, we must still make two hypothetical leaps. First, we must decide what market assets the reserves were implicitly invested in. Given most countries' social insurance institutions, a first reasonable choice would be the nominal rate of interest on long-run bonds (the Jordà–Schularick–Taylor "*ltrate*"). Second, we must guess at the share of the accumulated asset value that would have been paid out in annuities, instead of being plowed back. We assume that beneficiaries received each year's interest earnings as their annuity, while the same year's fresh contributions went into the pension reserve.

This combination of new facts (contributions and rates of return) and new assumptions (choice of asset and annuity factor) produces some suggestive measurements of how much of each year's old-age benefits are covered, or "funded," by payouts based on past contributions. Panel (A) of Table 12.1 reports some results from this exercise for sixteen OECD countries between 1984 and 2013, on the assumption that the contributions had been invested in lower-risk bonds. While the levels of their funding shares differ, they share a common trend over these three ten-year periods. For nearly all of these countries covered by the OECD, the funding share shows a down-trend since the early 1990s. A natural first suspicion is that the recent underfunding was due to a political lapse into greater pension deficits. A more likely cause, however, has been the decline in low-risk interest rates over the last quarter century – something that most writers could not have observed, because it has happened so

TABLE 12.1. *The estimated shares of pension benefits funded by interest on earlier payroll contributions, sixteen countries in 1984–2013*

	1984-1993	1994-2003	2004-2013
Belgium	1.42	1.35	1.14
Canada	0.98	0.92	0.70
Denmark	0.05	0.03	0.02
Finland	0.97	0.97	0.66
France	1.42	1.27	1.03
Germany	1.07	1.02	0.88
Italy	0.89	0.70	0.63
Japan	0.89	0.40	0.34
Netherlands	2.33	2.34	1.62
Norway	1.39	1.05	0.62
Portugal	1.01	0.54	0.60
Spain	1.25	0.89	0.74
Sweden	1.27	1.07	0.72
Switzerland	0.62	0.59	0.44
UK	0.91	0.78	0.62
USA	0.84	0.83	0.60

Sources and notes: Contributions from 1965 on, in local currencies, are from the OECD statistics https://www.oecd-ilibrary.org/taxation/data/revenue-statistics/financing-of-social-security-benefits_data-00259 en?parent=http%3A%2F%2Finstance.metastore.ingenta.com%2Fcontent%2Fcollection%2Ftax-data-en, using an institutional subscription to iOECD Library.

The nominal long-term interest rate ("*ltrate*") from 1965 on is from the Jordà–Schularick–Taylor Macrohistory Database, http://www.macrohistory.net/data/

The "pension" benefits equal "old-age" plus "survivor" benefits, from the OECD's Social Expenditure series.

The table omits Australia and New Zealand. Though they are data-rich countries, neither used a system of mandatory contributions to social security.

No backward extrapolation has been made to estimate payroll contributions before 1965. Adding such extrapolated values would have raised the earliest (1984–1993) payouts from contributions relative to those in later years.

The OECD definition of its "social security" contributions makes clear that they cover more entitlements than just elderly pension incomes.

"Contributions for the following types of social security benefits would, inter alia, be included: unemployment insurance benefits and supplements, accident, injury and sickness benefits, old-age, disability and survivors' pensions, family allowances, reimbursements for medical and hospital expenses or provision of hospital or medical services. Contributions may be levied on both employees and employers" (OECD 2018e, para. 40).

This may have raised the (contributions/benefits) ratios somewhat.

recently. So if we accept that contributions to public pensions would have been invested in bonds, as several countries' institutions require, then contributions will have funded less and less of the pension benefits, albeit for an innocent reason, and not because of any political shift toward deficit finance.[12]

Overall, if one were worried about trends toward more generous pensions, one should derive no fresh comfort from these adjustments for the degree of underfunding. It too was worsening, a point that will affect this chapter's conclusions about the overall threats to public pension viability.

So those three ways of defending greater transfers to today's elderly thus fail. First, while transferring taxpayer money to today's elderly is probably a progressive redistribution from richer to poorer generations, doing so does not help economic growth, so that the multiple generations have less total pie to divide. Second, it is not correct to argue that most who receive generous public pensions as part of their occupation are receiving it at the expense of their own initial straight pay. Finally, the assertion that people have paid for their own pensions with earlier payroll contributions is complex. A rough calculation for sixteen countries, however, found that the share of public pension benefits funded out of past contributions is below 100 percent, and has been retreating since the late twentieth century. The curse of old age is not going away. In fact, its economic logic is inescapable.

THE BUDGETARY LOGIC BEHIND THE CURSE

As each nation gets older, a budget problem looms. Something has to give. To summarize the choices that have to be made, we need to look at some simple but compelling accounting logic. The logic is stated without algebraic symbols here, and with algebraic symbols in Appendix D.

Sooner or later, the government pension budget must cover its net payout of pension benefits to the elderly with a net amount of taxes paid by the non-elderly, net of all government expenditures devoted to serving the non-elderly.[13] That is, the net tax revenues taken from those of working age each year on behalf of the elderly must eventually equal the benefits paid to them. These annual averages should balance:

net tax tax revenues	=	*benefits paid to elderly*, or
(percentage tax rate on incomes)		(benefits per elderly person)
times (income per young adult)		*times* (number of elderly persons).
times (number of young adults)		

Keeping these two sides in balance will be increasingly difficult as the number of elderly persons (on the right) keeps rising relative to the number of working-age young adults (on the left). As we have been well warned, there will be more and more elderly persons per young (working-age) adult, as every national population in the world gets older. How can we keep the budget in balance, with more and more elderly to support per person of working age?

In principle, there is a painless way to keep the account in balance without raising the implicit tax rate on the young, and without cutting the purchasing power of the average pension benefit. The painless solution is to outgrow the aging process. *If* the average income of the young can grow faster than the elderly-population ratio (the number of elderly to be supported by each, say, 1 million young adults), we can be in the happy position of raising the real pension per elderly person and/or cutting the tax rate.

What are the chances that average incomes per person of working age will grow faster than the elderly-population ratio? The odds are shifting right now, according to the UN population estimates. So far, population aging has advanced slowly enough to be easily outpaced by the growth of incomes per person. For the world as a whole, over the thirty-five-year period 1980–2015, this population ratio grew at the slow pace of 0.59 percent per year. *If* aging had continued at that snail's pace, the number of elderly persons per one hundred persons of working age would not double until 119 years from now. Most countries could easily have achieved that growth rate of 0.59 percent, since World Bank figures show that the world as a whole world has achieved per capita income growth of 1.87 percent a year between 1960 and 2016, which would make the average income double every thirty-seven years. So that happy scenario implies that annual public pensions per elderly person can go on rising in absolute real value. That is likely to be true.

But can the public pension benefits *keep pace with* the real average incomes of the young, or are those elderly who depend on public pensions destined to fall further and further behind the rest of society? Actually, *we should expect them to fall behind* relative to annual incomes, as the accounting makes clear.

The likelihood that annual retirement benefits cannot, and should not, keep up with the growth or average incomes does not spring from any government involvement in pensions. The underlying logic relates to the share of life spent in retirement, with or without a government role. To see how general this point is, suppose that adults continued to live longer in a world with no pensions whatsoever, either through government or through employers. Suppose that you had to pay for all of your elderly consumption out of your own savings from younger years. In such a private-individual world, the likelihood that you will live much longer than your ancestors lived means that you are likely to earn income for a smaller share of your expanding adult life. Even as an individual planner, you should reckon that your improved life expectancy will force you to consume less per year of longer life relative to what you earn in each year of your work life. In this private-individual world, with longer life and with economic growth, each generation's consumption standards per year of old age simply cannot keep up with the growth of average income per work-year. In terms of *relative annual* incomes and consumption, your annual consumption in old age cannot keep up with your average annual income when working. In this sense, the curse of long life is inescapable, and is not specific to government-run programs.

Naturally, many people will tend to resist having the elderly fall behind. They will think that the growth of resources spent annually on the average elderly person should keep up with the average annual incomes of adults below 65. Yet, in an aging world, that is impossible without taking an ever-bigger bite out of the rest of society. An aging nation has to choose among *three unpopular options*:

(1) the nation can keep raising the gross tax rate on current workers' earnings and property, just to cover pensions; or

(2) it can keep cutting non-pension transfers per young person, either by lowering the benefit payments for entitled recipients or by cutting the share of young persons who are entitled to any benefit; or
(3) it can cut pensions per elderly person relative to annual income of younger adults' average incomes, with or without absolute cuts in real pensions. It can either keep (3a) postponing benefits to older retirement ages or keep (3b) slashing pension rates across the board. In either case, Option (3) makes the elderly fall behind.

Faced with such alternatives, which countries have yielded and allowed rightly annual pensions to fall behind in their growth relative to average incomes, choice (3), and which have chosen to raise taxes or cut other forms of spending?

WHO HAS KEPT PENSION BENEFIT GROWTH SUSTAINABLE, AND WHO HAS NOT?

We now have multiple criteria for judging which countries, out of the many countries now supplying data, seem to have put public pensions on a sustainable path, and which countries are courting trouble by distorting the rest of the government budget and its relationship to economic growth. The first five criteria use those kinds of indicators used in "stress tests" for judging whether financial institutions have been keeping good control of their obligations, in this case pension obligations:

Criterion (A) = Have annual public pension benefits been stabilized or reduced since, say, 1990, and/or have they still been kept below 10 percent of GDP?

Criterion (B) = Has the elderly support ratio been reduced by at least 10 percent over this quarter century, and/or is the latest ratio below 40 percent?

Criterion (C) = Would the pension benefits have been fully funded from previous contributions recently, even if they had been invested in low-risk bonds?

Criterion (D) = Is government debt low as a percentage of annual GDP?

Criterion (E) = Has the country kept some leeway to raise average real pension benefits between 2015 and 2050, if its average incomes grow at the same rate as in 1994–2014?

A sixth criterion will address this book's larger concern for long-run growth:

Criterion (F) = Has the country avoided an anti-growth age bias, by holding down its generosity toward the elderly relative to investments in the human capital of the young, more than other countries?

The first two criteria, (A) and (B), conveniently examine countries' trends in pension expenditures on a pay-as-you-go (PAYG) basis, as if everybody's pension was being paid for by younger adults within the same year. In fact, the pay-as-you-go perspective is not just convenient – it is also the politically realistic way to look at pension finance. One might think that the share of public pension benefits in the same year's GDP would be relevant only for judging "defined-benefit" pensions, those that institutionally define pensions in terms of what is to be paid out this year, whereas a "defined-contribution" system would legally tie pension benefits to what has been accumulated from the same individuals' mandated past contributions. The political reality, however, is that budgetary precommitments are soft, whatever the current laws may say. The available reserves from past contributions are just a guideline, a talking point. This year's pension benefits can be whatever share of national income this year's political powers want them to be.

To see that the so-called reserve funds are only marginally relevant, consider what happens to the political debate when the benefit entitlements generated by reserves from past contributions either rise above, or fall below, what is currently being paid to the elderly. In the United States in the year 2000, the Social Security reserves were in surplus, as was the entire federal government budget. The Clinton administration wanted to lock the accumulating Social Security reserves into a "lock box" to be spent only on Social Security benefits and on paying down the federal debt obligations of future generations – that is, on priorities espoused by the Democratic Party. Republicans denounced the lock box idea as robbery. Of course, when the Republicans gained power the following year, they passed the kinds of tax cuts they preferred, without regard to any state of the Social Security reserves or the overall deficit. Again, each year's pension benefits are implicitly taken away from other things this same year, in amounts dictated by this year's balance of political power.

The first criterion for judging real-world public pension behavior, Criterion (A), is straightforward: When and where have countries stopped the upward march of the tax rate implicitly paid on behalf of seniors' pensions? As we saw earlier, that implicit tax rate is captured by a single statistic: the share of public pension expenditures in the nation's income, its GDP. By itself, however, this one number could fail to reveal policy changes if the extra expenditures, or expenditure cuts, were driven only by changes in the age distribution. Let us therefore explore not just Criterion (A), the expenditure share, the implicit-tax share, of national income, but the others as well, turning next to Criterion (B), the extent to which policy has altered the relative support for the elderly. As the elderly share of the population marches upward over time, this elderly support ratio, this generosity of annual pension support, should be allowed to drop.

In which countries have the budget shares of pensions, and the generosity of pension support per elderly person, been kept under control? The top part of Table 12.2 applies Criteria (A) and (B) to thirty-six data-supplying countries, ranked according to their cost and generosity of pensions for the elderly. In terms of the share of GDP given over in taxes to cover public pensions (Criterion (A)), the five countries that actually reduced that share from 1990 to 2013 are Chile, New Zealand, Latvia, Netherlands, and Peru (and Argentina and Lithuania held that share exactly steady over those two dozen years). On the other side of the ledger, public pension spending rose by at least 2 percent of GDP over the same time period in thirteen countries, as the table shows. For ten of these thirteen, the increase had already brought their public pension commitments above 10 percent of GDP, well above average among the thirty-six reporting countries and even further above the world average.

For the viewpoint of the elderly, which governments were cutting their yearly support per elderly person since 1990, relative to the economy's average incomes? Recall that since all countries' populations have been aging, budgetary sustainability requires that such yearly pension support would fail to keep up with the growth of average incomes, even though we hope it could improve in absolute terms. Five countries – Chile, New Zealand, Germany, Netherlands, and Latvia – not only met this Criterion (B) between 1990 and 2013, but even cut the support ratio by more than 10 percent.

Countries showing the opposite trend would appear to be jeopardizing their governments' financial standing, by combining a rise in the generosity of pension spending per old person per year with that well-known population aging. Many countries have been taking that risk since 1990. By 2013, the elderly support ratio rose by at least 2.5 percent of GDP in a dozen countries shown in Table 12.2. Of these dozen, seven had reached yearly pension levels that exceeded 40 percent of the economy's

TABLE 12.2. *Which countries are most "reforming" public pensions since the 1990s, and which are least "reforming"*

Within each category, countries are listed from most extreme to just marginal. The countries [boxed thus] are ones featured in the text, because they show either consistently favorable or consistently unfavorable magnitudes under multiple criteria.

Reforming most	Reforming least
Criterion (A.) = Public pension expenditures as a share of GDP	
down since 1990	**up at least 2.0% of GDP since 1990**
[Chile], [New Zealand], [Latvia], [Netherlands], Peru	Czechia, [Portugal], [Greece], [Turkey], [Japan], [Italy], [Brazil], Finland, [Spain], France, Austria, Hungary, Poland
	AND the latest share is above 10% of GDP c2013 for: [Greece], [Italy], France, [Portugal], Austria, Finland, [Spain], Hungary, Poland, [Japan]
Criterion (B.) = Elderly support ratio	
down ≥ 10% since 1990	**up at least 2.5 % since 1990**
[Chile], [New Zealand], Germany, [Netherlands], [Latvia]	[Turkey], [Brazil], [Portugal], Belgium, [Greece], [Spain], Hungary, United Kingdom, Korea, Norway, Slovakia, Czechia
	AND the latest ratio is above 40% c2013 for: Turkey, Brazil, Greece, Belgium, Portugal, Spain, Hungary

TABLE 12.2. *(continued)*

Reforming most	Reforming least
Criterion (C.) = Share of pension benefits funded from previous contributions, 2004–2013	
Full funding, even though invested in low-risk bonds	**Underfunded,** even if invested in high-return assets
Netherlands, Belg., France	Australia, New Zealand, Denmark, Japan, Italy, Spain
Criterion (D.) = Government debt as a percentage of annual GDP, 2012–2018	
Low debt/GDP ratio (bottom 10% of nations)	**High debt/GDP ratio** (highest 10% of nations)
Estonia, Azerbaijan, Chile, Paraguay, Russia, Peru	Japan, Greece, Portugal, Italy, Belgium, United States, Singapore, Spain
Criterion (E.) = Leeway for raising real annual pensions, from 2015 to 2050	
Positive leeway	**Negative leeway,** ≤ - 0.5% per annum
Ireland, Denmark, Hungary Argentina, Sweden, Poland, China, Finland, Croatia, Norway, Armenia, Azerbaijan, India, Egypt, Latvia, Estonia, Georgia, Lithuania	Mexico, Colombia, Thailand, Kenya, Costa Rica, Korea, Brazil, Bangladesh, Turkey, Iceland, South Africa, Italy, Iran, Greece, Canada, Malaysia, Philippines, Spain, Japan, Israel

Sources and notes: The sources for the (A) and (B) criteria are the same as for Table 7.1. For these two criteria, thirty-six countries supplied the necessary data. For Eastern Europe, the starting dates for "since 1990" were mid- or late 1990s.

The source for the (C) criterion is Table 12.1, covering sixteen countries.

The source for the (D) criterion is www.gfmag.com/global-data/economic-data/public-debt-percentage-gdp, accessed July 10, 2019. It gave debt-to-GDP ratios for 186 countries for 2012–2018. A top or bottom decile would therefore approximate nineteen countries. Yet of the top nineteen or the bottom nineteen, this table selected only countries yielding data on other criteria as well.

Criterion (E) reproduces the lists of positive leeway countries (0.4 percent per annum and above) and most-negative leeway countries from Appendix Table C.1.

output per person of working age. Those seven – Turkey, Brazil, Greece, Belgium, Portugal, Spain, and Hungary – include some that will keep returning to center stage as we proceed through the review of criteria in Table 12.2.

Since only a half-dozen countries, out of thirty-six reporting countries, have kept pensions from taking a greater share of the pie away from taxes or from social spending on the young since 1990, a natural question arises: How did they achieve that? Each of these countries has its own distinctive history and politics, of course. The two most striking cases are the two with the largest percentage cuts: Chile and New Zealand. Chile's famous pension reform calls for a whole separate treatment in Chapter 13. Let us turn to New Zealand's experience here, both because its politics has shown so many similarities to OECD democracies that somehow treated pensions differently, and because New Zealand's cuts occurred within a defined-benefit system of the sort that is not supposed to achieve reforms so easily.

NEW ZEALAND. Of all the core OECD countries, New Zealand since the early 1980s has had the most dramatic cut in the relative generosity of pensions – preceded by the most dramatic rise in generosity at the start of the 1970s.[14] During the 1970s interlude, New Zealand supported its elderly ratio almost as much as the world leaders, Austria, Germany and Greece. Figure 12.2 spotlights the rise and fall of New Zealand pensions in comparison with five other English-speaking countries, using both the cost measure (Panel (A)) and the relative generosity of yearly pensions (Panel (B)).

In the quarter century after 1991, New Zealand slashed the relative generosity of pensions back below its level of the 1960s. In the face of gradual population aging, the government also cut the pension share of GDP nearly in half, again returning to the level of the 1960s. The other five countries in Figure 12.2 – Australia, Canada, Ireland, the United Kingdom, and the United States – also showed signs of restraining the growth of transfers to the elderly since 1990, but with less consistency. New Zealand stood out.

New Zealand's exceptional rise and fall of support for the elderly was not the result of any distinctive demographic, economic, or cultural movements. New Zealanders drifted with the same political and cultural currents that affected others. It just happened that for its elderly, the political stars all came into line, and then all moved out of line, in an extreme fashion. The auspicious star alignment came with the Royal Commission of Inquiry into Social Security in 1972, the passage of the Superannuation Bill in 1974, and the repackaged National Superannuation of 1977. As in the other countries to which New Zealanders were always attuned, entitlements and participatory

(A)

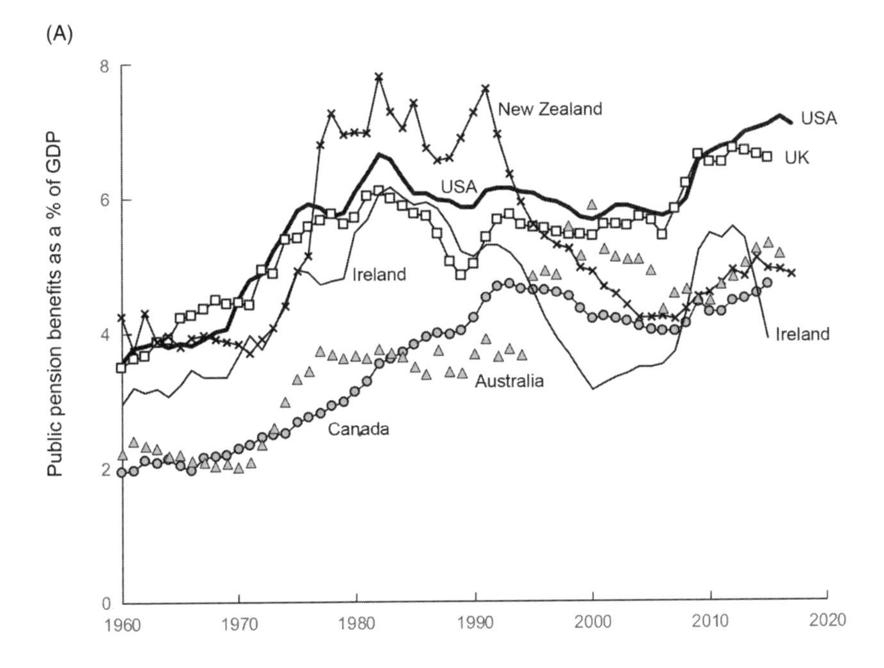

(B)

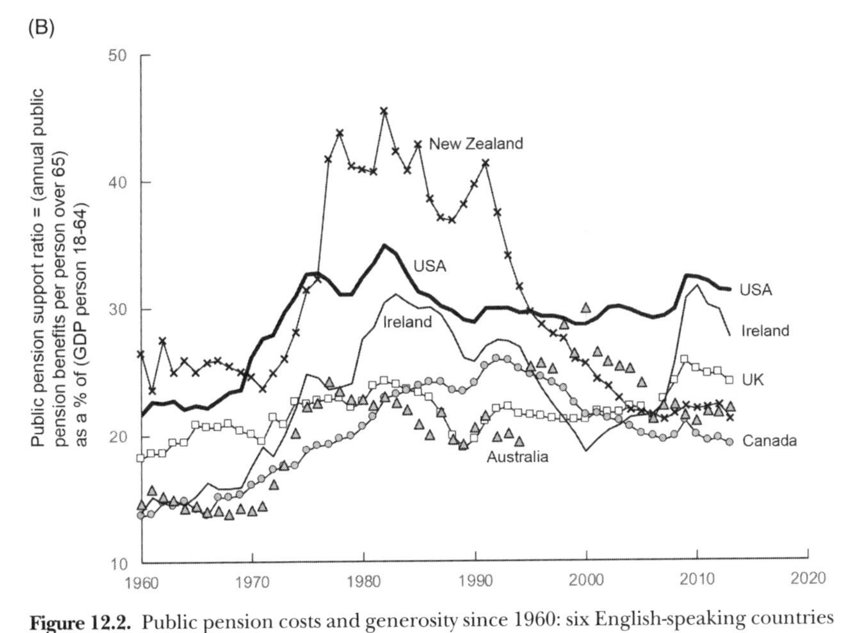

Figure 12.2. Public pension costs and generosity since 1960: six English-speaking countries
(A) Pension expenditures as a percentage of GDP (implicit tax cost).
(B) Public pensions per elderly person, relative to GDP per working-age adult.
Sources and notes: The numbers for 1980–2016 are derived from the OECD's SOCX database, as updated to 2016 at www.oecd.org/social/expenditure.htm, accessed through an institutional subscription to OECD iLibrary, and from the United Nations (2015) population data. Those for 1960–1979 are from OECD (1985), and are spliced onto the later series at the series-overlap year 1980.

citizenship blossomed in the 1970s. Even though the Royal Commission had raised difficult questions about switching to universalism instead of continuing to target the poor, both the National Party and the Labour Party decided that the moment had come for generous "superannuation." The National Party under Robert Muldoon danced artfully between dealing out generous superannuation payments and decrying the expense of it all. Yet throughout the 1980s, superannuation held its ground, with vocal gray-power support, continuing to take 40 percent of the entire social budget, even as deregulation and smaller government became as fashionable as in other countries.

Only with the 1991 budget did severe cuts actually arrive. The context was one of gaping government budget deficits and a bailout of the Bank of New Zealand, at a moment when the 1990 election had brought the more conservative National Party to power, displacing Labour. Pensions made an obvious target, given that New Zealand's generosity toward the elderly was still nearly as high as that of Austria, Germany, or Greece, just as it had been in the 1970s. That target, like other welfare programs, took a direct hit in "the mother of all budgets" in July of 1991.

New Zealand's steep cuts of the early 1990s, and Australia's cuts a decade later, were meted out in a noteworthy institutional context: Both countries had defined-benefit systems, not defined-contribution systems. Neither government collected payroll contributions that were earmarked for retirement, locked away in a separate reserve. Both left the level of pension support up to the general budget, on a year-to-year basis. While it is reasonable to fear that such an unbridled defined-benefit system could lead to underfunding and rising pension deficits, these two national experiences suggest that pension politics can swing in either direction, even without any pre-commitment to mandatory contributions. Even in the face of the usual outcries from the elderly, both countries did make cuts that lowered old-age support to levels that look modest in comparison with other rich countries.

One might suppose that having a defined-benefit pension arrangement could have made it easier to impose sharp cuts. In the absence of any presumptive actuarial link between past contributions and present benefits, all benefits were up for re-negotiation in the annual budget battle, and defined-benefit budgeting spotlighted them as an immediate redistribution between generations. The redistributive battle between young to old had already begun see-sawing across the 1970s and 1980s. In the budget crisis of 1990–1991, there was no effective answer to this rhetorical question put seven years earlier by Ann Hercus, the minister of social welfare: "Was it fair to pay all superannuitants 80 percent of the net average wage, when others were struggling? Was it fair to impose cuts in the standard of living of the working population – the sons and daughters of working superannuitants – in order to deal with the [overall budget] deficit and leave the better-off superannuitants alone?"[15] With redistribution placed so explicitly on the table in each year's budget, the defined-benefit system may not favor the subsidized elderly so securely as some political models imply.

The cohort of pensioners in that peculiarly generous 1972–1991 pension era were New Zealand's most fiscally advantaged, or "selfish," generation, especially those born around 1908–1913, just before World War I. Over their whole life cycle, however, their net fiscal gains were probably smaller, because earlier they had to pay taxes to support what David Thomson (1996) has called the early postwar "welfare state for the young," with its emphasis on young-family benefits. Had the pension generosity continued past 1991 to 2020, the ultimate selfish generation would have been those born around 1918–1933. But that cohort opportunity was erased, since New Zealand has tightened up on pensions ever since 1991.

TROUBLE IN MEDITERRANEAN EUROPE. More ominously, thirteen countries have let their public expenditures on behalf of the elderly rise by more than 2 percent of GDP over the period 1990–2013, in the face of that long-forecast population aging.[16] Six of these were in the Mediterranean region, including the two with the steepest rises – 9.2 percent of GDP in Portugal and 8.0 percent of GDP in Greece.[17] To prevent such increases, again, would require that yearly pension benefits advance more slowly than GDP per person of working age. No country in the Mediterranean region has achieved such a reduction. As Figure 12.3 makes clear, the only cases in which the generosity measure (that is, Criterion (B)'s support ratio) has even stopped advancing are Italy and France since the mid-1980s. In France's case, the specific design of pension reforms since 1995 has succeeded in raising senior employment,

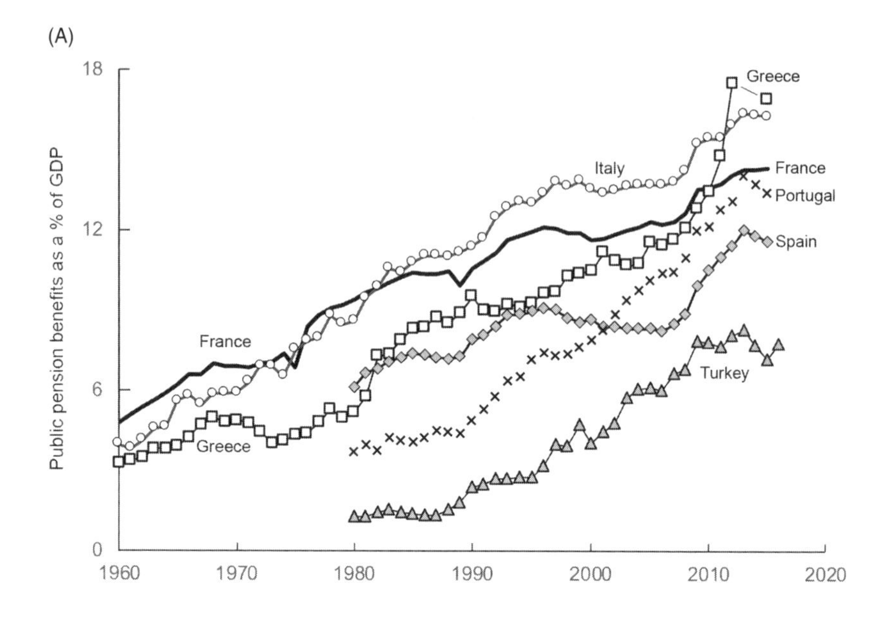

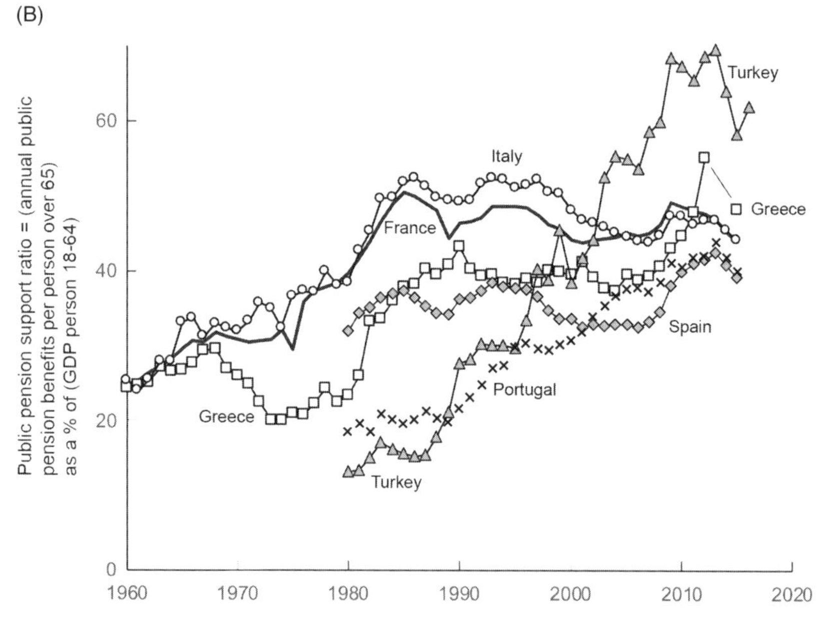

Figure 12.3. Public pension costs and generosity since 1960: six Mediterranean countries
(A) Pension expenditures as a percentage of GDP (implicit tax cost).
(B) Public pensions per elderly person, relative to GDP per working-age adult.
Sources and notes: See Figure 12.2.

thus cutting France's pension support ratio in Panel (B).[18] Even for these countries, however, population aging has continued to drive up the share of GDP spent on pensions since the earliest annual data in 1960 or 1980.

To give a sense of how that happened throughout the Mediterranean region, despite the global knowledge of the budgetary challenge that population aging implies, let us look briefly at three recent cases.

Greece. No developed country has a greater pension problem than does Greece. Its seriousness came as a shock starting in 2009, when the country's overall insolvency and its tax-collection inefficiency were revealed. Yet the public pension deficits were older. For more than a half century, Greece's public pensions have been claiming an ever higher share of GDP, rising from only 3.3 percent in 1960 to 17.5 percent in 2012, the highest rate among all developed countries. Even after a slight retreat to 16.9 percent in 2015, during the austerity imposed by Greece's creditors within the EU, the pension share was still the highest of any OECD country, followed by Italy's 16.2 percent.[19]

While Greece has historically given more generous average pensions at early retirement ages than the average European country, it has also historically suffered from an unequal distribution of pensions and social benefits, with already well-paid workers having a major advantage. As of 2010, Greece still stood out among OECD countries for having the same high replacement rate (benefits / salaries just before retirement) of 95.7 percent for high, middle, and low earners, whereas in OECD countries outside the Mediterranean region the system was progressive, i.e. the replacement rate for high earners was far lower than that for low earners (Symeonidis 2016, p. 19).

Greece's pensions were thus top-heavy as well as financially unsustainable in the aggregate. Those with political voice in Greece have been exploiting future generations.

Promises of reform have continued over the last decade, but not without reversals, and still without a resolution. Alexis Tsipras, the prime minister from 2015 to 2019, vacillated on the pension issue, just as he vacillated on repayments to foreign creditors. In 2015, he promised reforms cutting benefit generosity. Yet during the election campaign in the spring of 2019, Tsipras proposed to re-hike pensions in violation of the agreements with the Troika of creditor-country institutions. He and the Syriza party lost the May 26 election, however, to Kyriakos Mitsotakis and the conservative New Democracy party. Mitsotakis said before the election that he plans to "unblock privatizations, cut taxes and enact meaningful reforms to attract investment, increase state efficiency, and make the pension system viable." Financial details have not yet been provided.[20]

The jury is still out on Greek public pensions, after a decade of crisis unparalleled elsewhere in the OECD. Greece is extreme not only in its pension generosity and deficits, but also in its debts to foreign creditors, especially to other EU governments. It would seem politically obvious that the pensions could be slashed if and only if the country's aggregate external debt were also slashed at the same time. As Jeffrey Sachs urged back in 2015,

> Greece and [its creditors] need to come to a rapprochement . . . and agree to a package of economic reforms and debt relief. No country – including Greece – should expect to be offered debt relief on a silver platter; relief must be earned and justified by real reforms that restore growth, to the benefit of both debtor and creditor. And yet, a corpse cannot carry out reforms. That is why debt relief and reforms must be offered together, not reforms "first" with some vague promises that debt relief will come.[21]

Reforms are politically reversible, of course. One possible mechanism for tying the debt relief to the continuation of reform would be for creditors to take a year-by-year haircut, postponing Greece's repayment obligation schedule by one year for each year of reforms that suffice to meet the terms negotiated with the international institutions. A plan announced by the Euro-area finance ministers and Greece in June 2018 takes steps toward reducing pensions and raising taxes, but leaves all the basic issues the same. Some mixture of further pension cuts, tax increases, creditor forgiveness, and/or insolvency lies ahead.[22]

Italy. Ostensibly, Italy has enacted repeated pension reforms since 1990. In 1993, Italy cut the generosity of pension benefits, and in 1995 it launched a notional defined contribution (NDC) system to build in adjustments to changes in life expectancy and average incomes, while also raising the early retirement age for both men and women. And in 2011–2012, during a debt crisis, Italy's Fornero Reform raised the statutory age of retirement eligibility for women, the normal full-benefits retirement ages, and the minimum number of work years for early retirement. Yet in June 2018, the new coalition government of the anti-establishment Five Star Movement and the right-wing League promised to dismantle the 2011 pension reform "piece by piece."[23] By 2019, the 2011 reforms had been partly reversed, allowing many Italians with thirty-eight years of career service to retire with high benefit ratios at age 62. This history of modest reform and retreat has allowed Italian public pensions to continue their upward march, as Figure 12.3 confirms.

Turkey. Like Greece and Italy, Turkey has consistently ratcheted its public pensions upward, at least since the start of annual data in 1980. And even more than in Greece and Italy, the public pensions look so generous on the average because they are channeled in generous amounts toward public servants with high career earnings, ever since the Retirement Fund was set up for civil servants in 1950. Successive Turkish governments have devoted even less attention than Greece to solving the problems of the elderly poor – or the poor of any age group, for that matter. The only silver lining to Turkish pensions relates to their relative penury: The deficits on behalf of Turkey's privileged are still too small to jeopardize overall budget solvency.[24]

Note that the Mediterranean's heavy commitment to public pensions resembles some of the region's other policy attributes mentioned in Chapter 8, such as the rigid employee protection laws (EPLs), meager commitment to anti-poverty programs, high youth unemployment, and (until recently) low employment ratios for women. The common denominator in these policy dimensions is an unusually strong political dominance of senior males in the formal sectors, especially those in less innovative sectors of the economy.

PENSION FUNDING AND NATIONAL DEBT

The two criteria just presented, those relating to the same-year flows of pension benefits, implied taxes, and national income, are probably the most reliable in signaling which countries' public pension arrangements are healthiest or least in trouble. Yet a balanced judgment should rest on all six of the criteria introduced above.

Criteria (C) and (D) add additional insights about the financial stability of public pensions. In terms of the fullness of funding through past contributions, Criterion (C), we see a set of countries that are clearly underfunded, regardless of whether their past contributions were invested in low-risk low-return bonds or were invested, at high risk and return, in equities and real estate. Three countries were completely unfunded by contributions because they never tried funding: Australia, New Zealand, and Denmark. Three others – Japan, Italy, and Spain – had partially contributory systems, yet Table 12.1 showed that their contributions have clearly not achieved full funding, even if we suppose that past contributions fed into a high-return high-risk portfolio.[25] On the positive side, three other countries seem to have achieved full funding on the basis of past contributions: the Netherlands, Belgium, and France.

The most publicized criterion for judging overall budgetary soundness, and thus the possible perils of pension deficits, is the famous debt-to-GDP ratio, used as Criterion (D) here. Worldwide data on this ratio reveal that the most indebted 10 percent of nations include Japan, Greece, Portugal, Italy, Belgium, the United States, Singapore, and Spain. As of the end of 2018, Japan's public debt had reached 238 percent of a year's GDP and Greece's had reached 188 percent. Spain, the marginal case here, owed only about 100 percent of a year's GDP. While the debt-to-GDP ratio does not map directly into default risk, it is an important financial clue.

WHO HAS LEEWAY FOR MORE PENSION SPENDING UP TO 2050?

To see where the budgetary implications of pension spending are headed in the near future, and to apply Criterion (E), let us return to the basic accounting logic above.[26] Recall that for any given year,

net tax tax revenues	=	benefits paid to elderly, or
(percentage tax rate on incomes)		(benefits per elderly person)
times (income per young adult)		*times* (number of elderly persons).
times (number of young adults)		

To figure out who has the most leeway to let real benefits per elderly person, on the right-hand side, rise to the year 2050, we can start with this same logic about what it takes to keep pensions from taking an ever-rising share of income. To keep that from happening, the first term on the left-hand side, percentage tax rate on incomes, must stay the same from now to 2050. So any rise in those benefits per elderly depends on having the rise in income per young adult, or "economic growth" outrace "population aging," or the rise in the number of elderly persons per young adult.

To judge those chances, we need to have some idea of what will happen to those two key rates, the rate of economic growth and the rate of population aging up to the year 2050. The likely rate of population aging is estimated fairly well by those United Nations' "medium projections" of the population structure from 2015 up to 2050, the projections used in Figure 12.1.

How fast will average income grow between 2015 and 2050? We can only make rough guesses, of course. The best basis for guessing is to conjecture that the future growth of average real income might be the same as it has been in recent decades. To allow comparing the same "recent" time span for a wide range of countries, let us borrow the already-known growth rate for real gross domestic expenditures for 1994–2014 from the Penn World Tables. Choosing this twenty-year period allows us to start from a year for which the countries of the former Soviet sphere had at least partly recovered from its collapse. The choice may be on the optimistic side, by assuming that the economy will regain the trend line from 1994–2014 despite the 2020 crash.

The budget leeway for raising real pension benefits per year, at these rates of economic growth and population aging, is derived for each of fifty-eight countries in Appendix Table D.1. Its conditional forecasts are highly informative.

Some countries will be under strong pressure to cut their real pensions if they cannot improve their income growth rates above those they achieved recently in the recent period 1994–2014.[27] Most of the countries in this cautionary amber spotlight are developing countries. The choices before them can be illustrated with the cases of Mexico, Colombia, and Costa Rica.

Mexico is the country with the least room for raising average pensions, as the Appendix Table D.1 shows. It cannot avoid raising the share of pensions in GDP without cutting its average annual pension per elderly person by 2.7 percent a year, or by 60 percent over thirty-five years, if its elderly-population share grows at 3.1 percent a year, as forecast by the UN, and if its income growth remains as sluggish as its recent 0.3 percent a year. Avoiding higher taxes for pensions, or cutting other spending to make room for more pensions, seems highly unlikely. In other words, Mexico is probably destined to raise the share of GDP taxed to pay for pensions. Yet Mexico has leeway in another respect: As of 2011, its public pensions still took only 2.2 percent of GDP, so a given percentage rise in pension generosity would initially take a still-low extra share of GDP.

Colombia and Costa Rica will face similar pressures. They face greater pressure than Mexico inasmuch as they already spent more on public pensions in 2014: 3.6 percent of GDP in Colombia, and 4.4 percent of GDP in Costa Rica. The issue continues to generate a great deal of public debate in both countries, partly because the pension deficits favor some top occupational groups, particularly those employed in the public sector.[28] These developing countries are likely to violate the no-new-taxes-for-pensions constraint built into our accounting equations, just as the leading countries did in the twentieth century.

On the other side of the coin, several countries have considerable leeway to raise the real value of their annual pension benefits, because their incomes are growing rapidly and/or because they are aging more slowly. The geography of this lucky group is easily summarized: They are mostly a mixture of ex-communist countries, rich welfare states, and four developing countries with strong growth since 1994 (Argentina, China, Egypt, and India). A continuation of their recent strong growth would allow them to raise the real value of pension benefits until mid-century, although that pension growth still should not match the rate of average income growth, because their populations will continue to age. Particularly striking is that so many countries that were formerly in the Soviet Bloc have good leeway here, thanks to their mix of satisfactory recent growth and a predicted slowdown in their population aging.[29]

Thus far our first five criteria have applied "stress-test" indicators of overall budgetary pressure on public pension spending. They have implicitly asked: To what extent has each country succeeded or failed to hold down the aggregate cost of public pensions and to avoid imposing more taxes, or crowding out all other government expenditures, or raising the overall budget deficits and government debt? The underlying extreme fear here is that raising public pensions could push a government into insolvency and default. The validity of this fear is obvious enough in the case of Greece today, or of Argentina over the past quarter century.

This fear is legitimate for many countries, despite the paucity of documented examples of governments with heavy pension burdens that have gone insolvent. Both the paucity of clear past examples and the reason for greater pension-deficit fears in the future relate to the trend we have been documenting in this chapter and in Chapters 6 and 7 above: In the many countries we have just identified, pensions have risen above 10 percent of GDP, and above 20 percent of national government budgets. For these countries, pension deficits could play a significant role in future insolvencies.

THE FINAL FEAR: PRO-ELDERLY ANTI-YOUTH BIAS IN SEVERAL COUNTRIES

Yet there is another legitimate fear about public pension commitments: Even for a given size of the pension budget, might it be that some governments have incurred a high growth cost by favoring pensions over other kinds of government spending, or tax breaks, that may have higher rates of return? In particular, public education has the high social rates of return documented in Chapters 4 and 5.[30] By contrast, pension spending is close to a zero-net-return transfer for the nation as a whole. Not negative, but not very positive either.

Which countries have made this misallocation recently? Here is where we apply that Criterion (F): Has the country avoided an anti-growth bias, holding down pension generosity relative to investments in the human capital of the young, relative to other countries?

Three kinds of evidence are featured here, covering different countries and applying three different measures. First, Chapter 7 has already found

TABLE 12.3. *Which countries have the least, or the most, anti-growth age bias in their social-spending mix*

Least anti-growth bias	Most anti-growth bias
· Just contrasting pension support with education support, c. 2010	
Canada, New Zealand, Korea, Australia, Denmark	Jordan, Mali, Tanzania, Turkey, Mongolia, Peru, Uruguay, Argentina, Venezuela, Brazil, Colombia, Kyrgyzstan, Tunisia
· Adding estimates of health-care benefits specific to the elderly, 1985–2000	
Least anti-growth bias	**Most anti-growth bias**
Sweden, Australia, Den-Mark, New Zealand, Finland, Norway	Japan, United States, Italy, Greece
· Looking at how much social transfers reduced poverty among children and those of working age, as a measure of pro-growth policy, in 2005	
Reduced child poverty most	**Reduced child poverty least**
Denmark, Czechia, Sweden, Finland, Belgium, United Kingdom	Japan, Portugal, United States, Switzerland, Canada, Italy, Ireland

Sources and notes: The contrasts between pension support ratios and education support ratios are drawn from the results for 106 nations around 2010 (see Table 7.1 and Figure 7.3), updated to 2013.

The rankings changed little between 2010 and 2013.

The health-care benefits specific to the elderly are those estimated for twenty countries in 1985–2000 by Julia Lynch (2001, 2006).

The effects of government transfer payments on poverty rates by age group were estimated for twenty countries in 2005 by OECD (2008). Transfer payments in all countries succeeded in reducing the elderly poverty rate by 50 percent or more.

These lists are based on three different views of countries' performance according to Criterion (F), on anti-growth age bias. As in the previous table, countries are listed from most extreme to just marginal within each category.

which countries' governments favored pension benefits for the elderly instead of subsidizing education, around the year 2010. While there is no one ratio of pension generosity to schooling support that defines the optimum, it is safe to say that the more extreme cases favoring pensions lack justification for their being so extreme. Table 12.3 repeats a listing of pro-pension outliers spotlighted back in Figure 7.3, including Mongolia, several countries around the Mediterranean (Egypt, Jordan, Turkey, and Tunisia, and to a lesser extent Greece, Italy, and France) and several Latin

American countries (Brazil, Venezuela, Argentina, Uruguay, and Peru). The opposite tendency, of countries whose social spending was well tilted toward investing in public education and away from pensions, was most evident in Denmark, in three Anglo-offshoot countries (New Zealand, Canada, Australia), and in Korea.[31]

A second collection of evidence on pro-elderly bias covered fewer countries' behavior, but has the virtue of dividing health expenditures into patients' age groups. Julia Lynch (2001, 2006) calculated and analyzed such improved measures of age-subsidy bias among twenty-one OECD countries for the period 1985–2000. She established that a few countries stood out as subsidizing the elderly relative to children and those of working age. The gray-power outliers were Japan and the United States, followed by Greece, Italy, Spain, and Portugal. The least pro-elderly countries in terms of their social-spending mix were the four Nordics (Sweden, Denmark, Finland, and Norway) plus Australia and New Zealand.[32]

The third indicator, developed by the OECD (2008), also has the virtue of having calculated health-care benefits by age group. It answers the important question: Which countries' overall fiscal redistributions most effectively cut the poverty rates among children and those of prime working age, and not just among the elderly? Studying nineteen member countries' social spending around 1995 and again around 2005, the OECD team found a striking pattern by age group. All nineteen countries' transfers succeeded in cutting the elderly poverty population by half or better, and for both dates. By contrast, seven of them – Japan, Portugal, the United States, Switzerland, Canada, Italy, and Portugal –failed to reduce poverty among children by even half in 2005.[33]

SUMMARY: IT'S POLITICAL POWER, NOT THE POLICY DESIGN

Five criteria together have allowed us to identify which countries stand out most consistently as either clear reformers or clear risk-takers on the pension front, and a sixth criterion has asked which countries have succeeded or failed in tilting their social budgets toward investing in the young. Gathering the six together into a single behavioral ranking requires more than a little artistry. There is no reliable way to quantify the trade-offs between criteria, and for each criterion the set of data-supplying countries is different. Nonetheless, a few patterns stand out.

In terms of the sustainability of their pension finance, only four countries consistently receiving top grades since 1990: Chile, New Zealand, Latvia, and the Netherlands. These are the ones delineated in boxes, in the tabular summary of what the criteria tell us. The one important commonality to these four stable-finance cases is that none of them has had a very top-heavy pension system since 1990. These four have avoided the regressivity in favor of those having both top incomes and top power, which is a key threat to keeping a sound and pro-growth public pension system. Among the four, New Zealand in particular looks positively pro-youth, as Table 12.3 suggested.

The other point to note about these four stable-pension countries is a non-pattern: Their pension systems feature different institutions. New Zealand has a defined benefit (DB) system, as we have seen. The Netherlands mixes DB and funded defined contribution, with shifting wage-history bases for the DB. Latvia has an NDC system, one that uses formulas to generate pension entitlements in imitation of an individual's private savings system. Chile has a mandatory and centrally regulated system of forced savings. Given the sound state of pension finance in all four cases, their institutional diversity leaves a tentative suggestion, one that the next chapter will confirm: The institutional type may matter little in global perspective. Perhaps the balance of political power can achieve any financial balance or imbalance, and any bias in favor of either youth or the elderly, regardless of the formal institutions. It is as if they are not guided by any institutional rudder, but rather by the shifting winds of politics.

On the other side of the coin, Table 12.2's summary spotlighted seven other countries having the consistently worst pension finance since 1990, and dark prospects to 2050, given their outcomes as weighed by the first five criteria. The seven are *Greece, Turkey, Portugal, Brazil, Spain, Italy, and Japan.*[34] Ominously, their annual pensions per elderly person have been keeping pace with GDP per adult, and with wage rates.[35] This violates the basic accounting math, which has made it clear that their elderly support ratios should have retreated.

The behavior of these seven poor performers offers the same two tentative suggestions as for the four best performers, one suggestion based on a shared redistributive pattern and one based on their institutional diversity.

The seven non-reformers, in mirror image to the virtuous four reformers, tend to share a common trait about whom the pensions are favoring. With the exception of Japan, they tend to have top-heavy public pension systems that favor the well-off and politically connected. The other six countries, the five Mediterranean countries and Brazil, share that key defect: top-heavy pensions that threaten both the soundness of their pension system and their economic growth.

The non-reformers show no consistency in their pension institutions, again tentatively suggesting that the choice of system design is not binding. No institutional rudder by itself can keep pensions on course in the face of strong political winds. As we shall see in the next chapter's closer look at specific experiments with pension reform, how it works depends on who is working it.

CHAPTER 13

Approaches to Public Pension Reform

FEARS ABOUT THE SUSTAINABILITY AND FAIRNESS OF public pensions, such as those fears expressed in Chapter 12, have been building for nearly a half century. The threat of population aging is well known, and the fears have not been pushed aside. Global institutions have written prescriptions for better pension institutions, and many national governments have tried to swallow pension reforms.

Now that Chapter 12 has shown which countries seem to have the least sustainable pension symptoms and which seem healthiest, it is time for a global diagnosis of some of the institutional diseases, and a post-operative appraisal of three surgical procedures that have been tried.

THE CONVENTIONAL "THREE PILLARS" OF SOCIAL INSURANCE

The World Bank's 1994 book *Averting the Old Age Crisis* summarized its views of what kinds of pensions needed fixing by sketching three pillars for propping up a pension insurance system. Its diagram appears, with some simplifications, in Figure 13.1. The first pillar characterizes the public pensions paid out to retirees from taxpayers' pockets. It usually involves "pay-as-you-go" financing, with this year's working taxpayers paying for this year's elderly beneficiaries. The second pillar alternative is very different. Instead of paying taxes to the general government for this year's elderly beneficiaries, those of working age are compelled to save for their own retirement from their paychecks, with the government collecting their contributions and seeing that they are invested in government-approved ways. Such mandatory contributions might be specific to

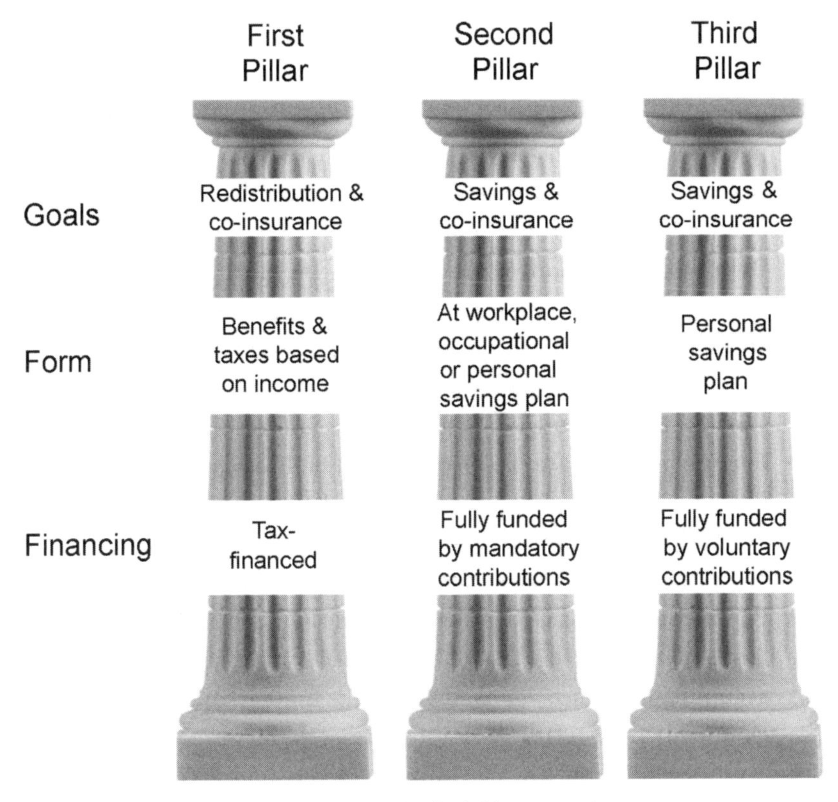

Figure 13.1. The conventional "three pillars" of old-age security
Source and notes: The source is World Bank (1994, p. 15). I have simplified their diagram, especially as regards the "Form" stratum.

the employees' occupations or might be universally collected from the whole workforce, using the formal workplace as a convenient collection point. The third pillar is the least controversial: Whatever voluntary savings you want to set aside for your old age are your own business.[1]

Glossary of some pension terms

- **Defined-benefit (DB)** pensions. In this arrangement, a person's pension is based on his or her wage history and years of service,

(cont.)

without earmarked individual contributions. Political commitment to such a pension system shifts the risk of varying rates of return to pension assets away from the worker/beneficiary to the employer or the government.

- **Defined-contribution (DC)** pensions. In this arrangement, a person's pension is determined only by the amount of assets accumulated toward his or her pension. Thus, a pure plan adjusts benefits to match available funds, and so the risk of varying rates of return to pension assets falls on the individual.
- **Funded** pensions are paid from a fund built up over a period of years out of contributions by, or on behalf of, its individual members. These are second- or third-pillar pensions, with **no "non-contributory" payments** from other taxpayers.
- **Pay-as-you-go (PAYG)** pensions are paid out of current revenue (usually by the state, from tax revenue) rather than out of an accumulated fund. Thus PAYG and funded are antonyms. Defined-benefit (DB) pensions are a type of pay-as-you-go arrangement, and the World Bank (1994) had PAYG in mind when describing the first pillar.
- **Notional defined contribution (NDC)** pensions. At their simplest, NDC pensions have two elements: their aggregate benefits are organized on a PAYG basis; but they mimic funded individual accounts in that a person's pension is strictly related to his or her lifetime pension contributions. Thus, a pure NDC system is pay-as-you-go, with the individual's level of benefits affected by national conditions. Systems can also incorporate redistribution, e.g. by offering credits for periods spent caring for children, and can be partially funded.

The pillars are meant to support any benefit entitlements for one's older years. In this chapter as in Chapter 12, however, we must focus almost entirely on pensions, setting aside health insurance, which also has the tendency to pay out its benefits largely to the elderly. The reason is, again, that it is too difficult to gather internationally comparable numbers on how medical benefits are distributed by age of patient.

Each pillar upholds principles, but without numbers. In urging reliance on one pillar or another, policymakers and economists never specify what is the "optimal" amount of that type of pension benefit. Even the prescription that pensions should be fully funded fails to tell us what dosage to use. A pension could be called "fully funded" by building on contributions of only 1 cent per year of one's career, delivering an annuity of, say, 4.5 cents a year in retirement. At the other implausible extreme, a fully funded pension might grab a third of one's paycheck and deliver an annual retirement benefit far greater than one's salary during each year of work – a violation of the underlying objective of smoothing one's annual consumption over all the stages of adult life. In between such extremes, the experts really cannot agree on an optimal amount of pension contributions, or even of overall savings. Yet even if the optimal amount is open to debate, historical experience can identify where some of the real-world policies have chosen the wrong pillars.

The conservative Washington consensus of the 1980s and early 1990s, and the World Bank's 1994 report, thought that the edifice of pension insurance was shaky because there were cracks in the first pillar, the one making taxpayers fund the needy. They argued that the first pillar, and its widespread "defined-benefit" programs in particular, tended to run deficits. The deficits would only get worse as their populations aged. That is, the World Bank was broadcasting the stern budgetary logic laid down in Chapter 12.

By contrast, it saw the second and third pillars as immune to deficits because they were fully funded by prior contributions. What you get in retirement depends strictly on what you were forced to save, or chose to save, when working, as amplified by the market rates of return that your savings earned in the interim. Do not expect to receive any "non-contributory" transfers from taxpayers. For sustainability, therefore, countries need to trim their use of the politically seductive tax-and-transfer first pillar, and lean instead on the fully funded second pillar, with its mandatory contributions supplemented by whatever third-pillar voluntary savings that individuals chose to accumulate.

The same World Bank report admitted that the first pillar had its merits, especially if it was a universal flat amount that guaranteed every elderly person against poverty. Such a universal flat pension would have the virtue of very low administrative costs: All the government needs to know about a person is their age, usually supplemented by knowing their citizenship and place of residence (World Bank 1994, p. 240). Yet the Bank's report kept downplaying this basic first pillar, with arguments about the evils of large government, as we noted in Chapter 12.

CRACKS IN THE SECOND PILLAR

SHOULD THE SECOND PILLAR EXIST? Contrary to the late twentieth-century orthodoxy, economic principles and recent experience now suggest that there are at least as many cracks in the second pillar, the one mandating contributions at one's place of work.

Only in narrow contexts does the use of workplace contributions toward pension insurance make sense, whereas the arguments against it draw on broader and more persuasive arguments. One small insurance sub-sector that might reasonably be thought of as requiring contributions from employers and employees is insurance covering accidents on the job (another is unemployment insurance). Pioneering examples were Bismarck's politically inspired social insurance laws insuring Prussian industrial workers in 1884 and 1891. At the time, his intervention solved a collective-action problem. Employers and organized labor could not agree on a system of workplace accident insurance even at the level of the firm, let alone industry-wide or nationally. Bismarck used autocratic power to dictate a workable solution to that particular insurance problem. Yet workplace accident insurance takes a small and declining share of all social insurance.

Another historical excuse, though not really a justification, for embedding social insurance in the workplace was that it has looked like a cost-saving place for collecting mandatory contributions to solve individual employees' myopic under-saving. It could indeed be an effective way to administer collections from formal-sector employees, leaving the government to find other ways to collect the corresponding contributions from the informally employed, the self-employed, and the unemployed.

Yet broad daylight reveals deep cracks in the second pillar, both in its basic blueprint and in its historical stress tests. The blueprint itself has been insightfully challenged by UN economist Larry Willmore, based on economic principles and his global experience with pension policy.[2] Willmore rightly criticized both the mandatory feature and the workplace locus.

As for the mandatory feature, one should immediately ask "Who is in charge here?" The paternalistic argument that workers might be myopic and not save enough for their own retirement implies that the government itself knows better. Should the same government officials that could not be trusted to keep the first pillar's tax-based pension benefits under control be entrusted with complete control of the mandatory pensions? As Peter Orszag and Joseph Stiglitz (2001, p. 37) put the same rhetorical point: "It is difficult to know why a government that is inefficient and corrupt in administering a public system [as claimed by those who are critical of such system] would be efficient and honest administering a private one.'' One should further ask, as Larry Willmore does: Do workers lose their myopia when they reach the age of full-benefit retirement, say on their 65th birthday? More broadly, why does the government not force others to lock up a fraction of their *property* income – such as interest, dividends, or profits – for their old age? Is it only workers who are short-sighted? By combining "government knows better than employees" with "employees under 65 are too young to know better," the second-pillar blueprint reveals a structural crack: The second pillar was apparently designed to support the interests of a wealthy male non-employee lobby seeking to appear pro-elderly.

The workplace-contributions feature reveals another flaw in the basic blueprint for the second pillar. Willmore points out the second pillar's glaring *lack of gender equity*. Using mandatory paycheck contributions as insurance against old-age poverty fails when it denies those who work in the home, or in informal sectors, any equivalent rights to anti-poverty support in old age. Of course, most people working in the home or as informal producers and vendors are females, and time-use studies show that they contribute as many hours of productive work as do breadwinner males. The workplace pension system short-changes them, raising the share of elderly females in poverty relative to that of elderly males.

In addition to the questionable welfare economics of its basic design, and its discrimination against those who work at home, the policy of relying on mandated paycheck contributions to insure old age has not played well in recent history. World Bank economists themselves have begun to retreat from the 1994 hard sell of mandated workplace contributions. A decade later, in 2004, a team of the Bank's specialists wrote in a more temperate style, seeing a more positive place for first-pillar public pensions within the three-pillar approach, in the context of Latin America. They called for more attention to the poverty-prevention pillar (first pillar), which should become increasingly affordable as average incomes rise. The mandatory savings schemes, previously emphasized as a crucial reform, "are not always necessary, but may be useful for transitioning from overly generous PAYG systems and in providing an initial boost to capital and insurance markets" (Gill et al. 2004, p. 4).

It is quite appropriate that the expert doubts about the second pillar were focused on Latin American experience. For that region in particular, historical stress tests also reveal multiple cracks. The telltale signs of cracks in Latin America's second pillar have shown up wherever the insurance was tied to specific occupations. Recall that throughout the region, as in the Mediterranean, the last hundred years brought occupational pensions and health insurance coverage from the top down, with subsidies flowing at first to the privileged occupations, especially those in the public sector, before any broad anti-poverty pensions. The result has been a system of "bloated and inequitable" redistributive pensions.[3]

CHILE'S FAMOUS PENSION REFORM: MISUNDERSTOOD AND EMULATED

Chile has become known as the successful pioneer in implementing a mandatory workplace pillar. Could that consensus be correct about Chile's solution to a policy flaw shared by most of Latin America and the Mediterranean? As five of our stress tests suggested in Chapter 12, Chile has indeed emerged as one of the countries with the best prospect for solvency of its pension system. The solution is long run in its effects, and does promise financial stability two generations later. It has never been overthrown by any of Chile's democratic governments since 1990. Yet history seldom delivers simple sermons. Chile's pension history is as fraught as any other country's history with nasty details – and it keeps being altered in response to perceived weaknesses.

Five common misperceptions about Chile's pension reform of 1980–1981 need at least partial correction. For one, it did not replace a universal social security system of the sort known in North America and Northern Europe. Chile never had such a universal social security system, not even under Frei or Allende.

Second, the old system was not exactly a defined-benefit or pay-as-you-go system of the sort usually pictured as the first pillar.

Third, it was not a privatization, even though many defenders to the political Right and many critics to the political Left agreed in calling it a "privatization." There was no privatization, because the central government in fact seized tighter control over people's paychecks and savings.

Fourth, the reform did not even fully replace the old occupational basis of the pension system. The Pinochet regime excused the military and the police from any such reform, and suppressed any discussion of the generosity of the pensions offered to these powerful interests, until democracy returned in 1990. The pensions of the military are substantially higher than those of the rest of Chileans, being most often similar to the income they have during active service. Their exemption from the reform continues even today.

Finally, for more than a generation the government has continued to run deficits on behalf of the pension system, to smooth out the generational impact of the reform. Part of the continuing deficit is projected to fade away, as the subsidized survivors from the old system die off. Part is called permanent, though permanency is always at the whim of politics.

THE UNDER-CONTRIBUTION CRISIS, BEFORE ALLENDE AND PINOCHET. Chile's older system was indeed occupation-based, complex, and out of control. It began in the 1920s as a very limited system for insuring civil servants, the military, and a few other favored occupational groups against income inadequacy due to old age, disability, and widowhood.[4] Yet starting in the late 1950s, under the presidencies of Jorge Alessandri Rodríguez (1958–1964) and Eduardo Frei Montalva (1964–1970), shifts in political currents transformed it into a sprawling non-system, consisting of over 150 different plans administered by thirty-five different national and local funds. Chile's non-system became a textbook example of how the lack of centralized controls can turn what were initially labeled as defined-contribution programs into pay-as-you-go money machines for taxing the rest of society. Social security contributions were tapped to finance other types of benefits; the insured found officially sanctioned ways to evade their contribution responsibilities; and new unfunded benefits were created, including earlier retirement. Between 1960 and 1970, the number of active contributors supporting each passive pensioner fell from 10.8 to 4.4, a result which cannot be explained by demographic trends, but rather is the consequence of political decisions to ramp up generosity (Cheyre Valenzuela 1988, pp. 69–70).

Experts did speak out as early as 1960, calling for serious reforms. The most useful overall scrutiny of the gathering storm was conducted by the Oficina de Planificación Nacional, or ODEPLAN, in 1971 (pp. 336–360). Weaving together the accounts of different pension funds, ODEPLAN produced a snapshot of the whole pension system as of 1965, which I have summarized and modified in Table 13.1. The ODEPLAN figures show the funding of the whole "social security" system, covering family assistance, unemployment compensation, and other social programs in addition to pensions. Still, well over half of these expenditures had already taken the form of pension payouts, and I emphasize pensions here.

By 1965, the system had clearly become underfunded. Even if people paid the "theoretical or legal" contributions to their own social insurance plans, they received more, thanks to the rest of society. The pure transfer from general taxpayers, that 983.4 million escudos in the first column, was already 5.1 percent of GDP, and by the time it got allocated to the different occupational sectors, the favored "contributory" classes were paying for only 38.2 percent of the benefits accruing to their social security accounts. Their accrued benefits took up 51.5 percent of the total social security budgets (1,350.6 million escudos out of 2,622.5 million), although they chipped in only 19.7 percent

TABLE 13.1. *Who contributed to Chile's social security, and to whose benefit, in 1965*

(A) Absolute amounts (millions of escudos = 1,000s of post-1975 pesos)

	"Theoretical, or legal" contributions paid by these	Actual contributions accruing to these	Percentage of accruals paid by own contributions	Benefits paid out to members
	The "contributory" groups insured through social security			
Wage laborers	133.8	535.2	25.0	724.6
Private salaried employees	163.6	348.5	46.9	347.5
Public salaried employees	219.2	466.9	46.9	751.2
Total contributions for the social security insured	516.6	1,350.6	38.2	1,823.3
	The rest of society			
Others (self-employed, private employers, &c.)	1,004.4	1,153.9	87.0	–
General taxpayers	983.4	0.0		
Investment incomes	118.0	118.0		
Total social security revenue	2,622.5	2,622.5		
Percentage contributed by/to the insured	19.7	51.5		

(B) Amounts per member of each covered group (escudos)

	"Theoretical, or legal" contributions paid by these	Actual contributions accruing to these	Percentage of accruals paid by own contributions	Benefits paid per passive members
	The "contributory" groups insured through social security			
Wage laborers	95.5	381.8	25.0	
Private salaried employees	609.0	1,297.3	46.9	
Public salaried employees	794.9	1,693.3	46.9	
Total contributions for the social security insured	265.5	694.0	38.2	4,133.5
	The rest of society			
Others (self-employed, private employers, &c.)	358.2	411.5	87.0	

Source and notes: The source is Chile, Oficina de Planificación Nacional (ODEPLAN) (1971, pp. 336–360).

The totals here refer to the entire bundle of social security insurance programs.

These include, in addition to old-age and survivorship pensions, entitlements for poor-family assistance, unemployment compensation, and insurance for workplace accidents.

Yet pensions accounted for a majority of the social security budget.

For comparison, Chile's GDP for 1965 = 19.11 million pesos = 19,110 million escudos (World Bank series available at gpih.ucdavis.edu/Nominal GDP). The total amount contributed and reallocated in 1965, or 2,622.5 million escudos, amounted to 13.7 percent of GDP.

of it themselves. The rest of society had to pay the other 48.5 percent of the favored groups' social security accruals, without substantial benefits.

Who were the general taxpayers paying for this through the general budget, and who were the favored classes? The tax burden was spread across all of society in a way that was probably slightly regressive. Indirect taxes on consumption, which fell largely on common folk, raised as much revenue as did direct taxes or taxes on copper.[5] The benefits, in the form of accrued social security entitlements, were tilted toward government, the military, and formal-sector workers, and away from others, meaning the self-employed, those in petty informal sectors, and private-sector employees. As the ODEPLAN report summarized the results, "Comparing the theoretical – or legal – supports by contributory sector, with the true ones, one observes ... that the insured absorb the greater translation of patronal and taxpayer supports. Their true support almost triples their theoretical support. In exchange, the sector '*otros*' ['others'] absorbs only a small part of the translation."[6] Table 13.1 underlines this discrimination by occupational class, showing that still-working members of the top three covered groups paid for only that 38.2 percent of their accrued entitlements, while the outside sectors had to cover 87.0 percent of theirs. In addition, the "passive" (retired or otherwise unemployed) members of the favored groups were paid even more (1,823.3 million escudos) than was being covered by paycheck contributions plus investment income (2,622.5 million minus the 983.4 million from general taxpayers). The occupational second-pillar selectivity of the system ended up shaping not so much a link to one's paychecks as a lobbying arrangement whereby favored groups organized to defeat parliamentary attempts at reform, and pocket net transfers from others.

The brief regime of Salvador Allende Gossens (1970–1973) tried to equalize social security, ramping up benefits and extending coverage to 90 percent of the economically active population by offering new coverage to merchants, small industrialists, and the miscellaneous self-employed of the informal sector. The minimum pensions for disability and old age were raised in 1972 to 100 percent of the minimum industrial wage. Yet with no insiders losing their previous privileges or bearing new taxes, heaping generosity on the outsiders meant financial ruin.

The chosen mechanism was the monetized hyperinflation of 1972–1973.

THE 1980–1981 PENSION REFORM. Almost immediately after the brutal coup of September 11, 1973, the military regime and its economic advisors began debating how to replace the crumbling second pillar with a mandatory system, making individuals of all classes pay for their own later retirement. So complex were the issues that the internal debates over designing the new system were not resolved, nor were the working arrangements implemented, until 1980–1981. To understand what happened back then, and the legacy that survives today, let us start with a description of the new pension system, following up with a description of how the old pension system was supposedly handled, and then with how the old pension system was *not* handled.

The new mandatory scheme imposed by the military government required all wage and salary earners in the formal employment sectors to pay 10 percent of their earnings (their defined contribution) into individual forced-savings accounts managed by private for-profit corporations that existed for this sole purpose – the AFPs (Administradoras de Fondo de Pensiones). As an individual, you could choose among these AFPs but only among the few that were government-approved. You had to pay a managerial fee on each deposit from your payroll, and got a market rate of return. Given the mandatory 10 percent deduction rate out of earnings, and the passage of time, the accumulated savings grew considerably. The market rates of return have been reasonably good for the AFPs, though for the individual account holders the rates were dampened by the payments of those fees on each forced deposit.

For people entering the labor force for the first time in 1983 or later, there has been no choice between new and old. You had to make mandatory contributions to an AFP and then choose among those government-approved AFPs. Earlier generations, however, were allowed to keep part or all of their pension accumulations in the old system, choosing between two variants. One variant would have them keep their old entitlements, under uncertain future rules. The other variant, favored by the regime, was to convert all their previous years of pension entitlements into government-guaranteed Recognition Bonds, which were annually adjusted to inflation and earned an interest rate. The bonds could only be cashed into the individual's pension fund at the time of retirement, disability, or death.

In describing the reformed system, most writers have presented only the steady-state version of how the reform was supposed to work in the long run, with little or no inspection of how some old rights were honored, while others were removed, in the great redistribution of 1980–1981. The reform's dramatic one-time combination of windfalls and confiscations is left hidden in the usual accounts of Chile's reform. Like those economic historians who struggle to decide what the French or American Revolutions did to people's livelihoods, we are typically shown the twilight of the old regime and the morning after, but not what happened in the revolutionary data darkness.

Those who had received defined-benefit subsidies, or had accumulated pension rights, under the old system could have been dealt with by the junta's reformers in any of at least these five ways, ranked from harshest to least harsh.

Option #1: The reformers could strip them of their previous public pension defined benefits subsidies, and force them to start anew with accumulating privately for old age. This would indeed have been a "privatization."

This was done, in effect, only to the previously uncovered population, who in 1965 were paying that 48.5 percent of all revenues for the social security system without receiving any pension benefits. The membership of this group consisted, again, of those left outside of government and the formal private sector – the self-employed, most women, farm workers, and informal-sector workers. The reform cut their defined benefits to a new, lower, minimum pension.

Option #2: The reformers could have demanded that the covered population, or the more than thirty social agencies managing their pensions, deliver evidence of the *contributions they had actually paid* in the past, adjusted for the brief hyperinflation and currency change that intervened in the early 1970s. That would have been consistent with the way that the new generations were to be treated under the mandatory-contributions system.

This was not done fully to anyone. The new regime counted their *years* of previous service, but *not the amounts* actually contributed from their paychecks. Instead, the government credited older workers at the higher entitlement rates implied by "actual" accruals like those in Table 13.1, when pricing Options #3 and #4:

Options #3 and #4: The reformers could give previous pension holders the choice of (Option #3) honoring all of their claims at a normal value in the form of Recognition Bonds, absolving them of any under-contributions before 1975, or (Option #4) letting them keep their old pension plans, soon to be merged into a centralized administration, under uncertain terms. As an incentive, the government allowed lower deduction rates from paychecks under the new Option #3 than it demanded for those sticking with the old (Option #4).

This was the main choice for those having old pension rights in the privileged civilian sectors. Given the choice, a majority of those with earlier pension rights chose to join the reformed system with its AFP management. By the end of 1983, 77 percent of the old-rights group had chosen the new Option (#3), enticed by government urging and by the lower payroll deduction rate of contributions to their new individual AFPs. Clearly, they were given a jump in wellbeing relative to the outsiders ("*otros*") who lost subsidies when subjected to reform option #1. The option of choosing between #3 and #4 was "grandfathered," i.e. denied to workers joining the formal labor force after the end of 1982, so that younger workers were either in the new AFP system or left to accept only the minimum pension later in life.

Option #5: The most generous option: The reformers could have honored all their previous pension rights *and* excused them from the reform, keeping their favorable treatment hidden from publicized accounts. The reformers did this for the armed forces and the police, and these groups remain exempt from the reforms even today. Apparently, what was good economic medicine for civilians was not administered to the military itself.[7]

HOW CHILEAN PENSIONS HAVE EVOLVED SINCE THE REFORM. As its institutional features should make clear, the 1980–1981 reform, far from eliminating the role of the state in the civilian pension system, expanded it in terms of regulation, supervision, guarantees, and financing.

Since 1980, the reform has been repeatedly fine-tuned, both by the military regime and by the democratically elected governments after 1990. The resulting pension system seems to be one of the world's most sustainable, as already noted.

The share of the working-age population covered has declined slightly since the initial sign-up wave of the 1980s. A majority of those formally employed still belong, yet participation remains only around 37 percent among those in the informal sector (Arenas de Mesa 2005). The inequality of pension coverage remains generally higher than it would have been under a more universal first-pillar scheme. One reason is the gender inequity built into that second pillar, which ties pension benefits strictly to the value of paycheck contributions (Arenas de Mesa and Mesa-Lago 2006). In addition, the fee structure for mandatory investments in AFPs tends to look more burdensome, the lower are one's earnings or one's employment rate.

A larger complaint centers on the AFP managerial fees. The mandatory contributions system has continued to exact disturbingly high administration costs of the funds with which workers are forced to place their contributions. Even after a generation of fine-tuning, Chile's administrative costs are eye-catching, either as a share of a workers' whole wage or as a share of the amount turned over to the approved investment managers, as shown in Table 13.2. The same high costs persist in Argentina, Colombia, El Salvador, Mexico, Peru, and Uruguay, which have emulated Chile's system. One might have hoped that the fund-management fees would decline as capital markets developed and became more competitive. That has not happened in these countries, leading to suspicions that the reforms were designed to favor an oligopolistic investment-fund sector.

Switching to a mandatory defined-contribution system should eventually shrink government pension deficits down to the first-pillar anti-poverty pensions alone. Everybody else should eventually be paying their own way, from paycheck contributions. Yet the Chilean reformers knew that an immediate switch to full funding would have had harsh effects on the generation reaching advanced age in the 1980s – the harsh effects described in the Options #1 and #2 above.

TABLE 13.2. *Fees and mandatory contributions in individual pension accounts, Latin American countries as of June 2007*

	Percentages of the average worker's salary		
Country	Administrative fees	Mandatory contribution	Fees as a percentage of mandatory contributions
Argentina	1.00	4.61	21.7
Bolivia	0.50	10.00	5.0
Chile	1.71	10.00	17.1
Colombia	1.58	11.00	14.4
Costa Rica	0.29	3.96	7.3
Dominican Rep.	0.60	7.40	8.1
El Salvador	1.40	10.00	14.0
México	1.02	7.48	13.6
Peru	1.81	10.00	18.1
Uruguay	1.79	12.22	14.6

Source and notes: The source is Kritzer (2008). Similar contrasts between countries were noted by Acuña and Iglesias (2001).

Instead, they spared them such a reckoning, passing on fiscal deficits to be paid after 1980.

The plans thus called for government deficits that would dwindle as the favored earlier generation died off. The next three decades have yielded the pension-deficit history shown in Figure 13.2. The two upper parts of the total pension deficit, namely the recognition-bond deficit on behalf of those who joined the new system and the operational deficit on behalf of those who stayed with the old, are the ones that were supposed to have shrunk. They did indeed shrink, both during the military regime (to an unknown extent) and since the arrival of democracy in 1990. Meanwhile, the two "permanent pension deficits," under the middle thick line, have not declined. The military has continued to receive the same pension subsidies since 1990, and the meager social assistance and minimum deficits have grown slightly. Overall, the government deficits have persisted for more than three decades, and even the transitory components, the operating deficit plus the recognition-bonds deficit, are not due to be phased out completely until 2045. Even this phase-out may not happen, as pressure for more universal anti-poverty pensions continues into the 2020s. Net

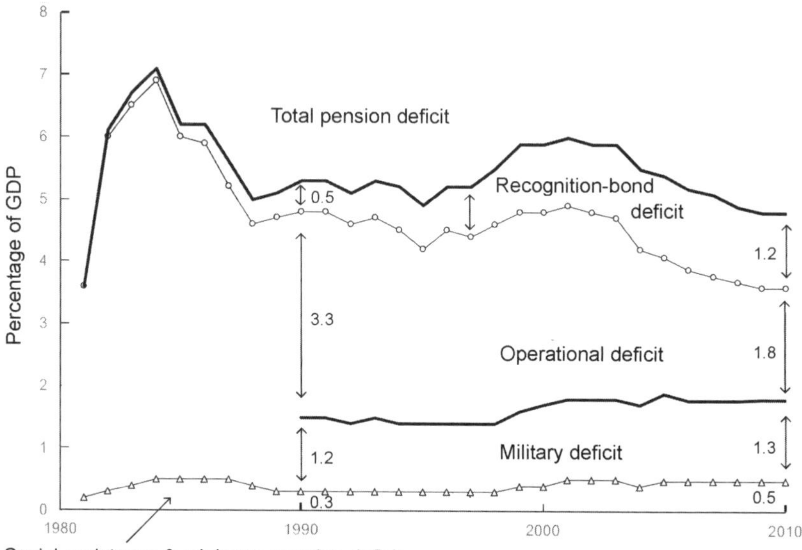

Figure 13.2. Chile's government pension deficits since the reform, 1981–2010
Source and notes: The source is Arenas de Mesa and Mesa-Lago (2006, p. 153). The figures for 2005–2010 are short-term projections.

Before 1990, the operational deficit and the military deficit were not separated out in the official data.

pension deficits also persist in other Latin American countries that emulated Chile's reform. The march toward eliminating deficits has thus been mercifully slow.[8] Indeed, the deficit has jumped in the short run. In the slump of 2020, Chile's government allowed citizens to make extra withdrawals of up to 10 percent of their AFP pension funds. Politically, it seems likely that these additional deficits will be covered by future increases in general taxes, contrary to the intent of the original 1980 reform.

EMULATION AND REVERSALS IN OTHER COUNTRIES. Chile's experiment became Exhibit A in the global policy push for state-mandated "privatization" of pensions in that heyday of "Washington consensus." Some twenty-one countries imitated Chile's "privatization" reform, as listed in Table 13.3. Starting with Britain's pension reform in 1988 under Margaret Thatcher, the international club expanded until 2005–2006, when nineteen of these follower countries had followed Chile's emphasis on forced saving, in whole or in part. Within the next ten years, half of them had reversed, and dropped the institution or modified it beyond recognition.

TABLE 13.3. *Countries that emulated Chile's mandatory defined-contribution reform*

(A) Those that have stuck with mandatory "privatization" so far

	Adopted privatization, in
Colombia	1993
Peru	1993
Costa Rica	1995
Uruguay	1996
Bolivia	1997
Mexico	1997
El Salvador	1998
Dominican Republic	2003
Panama	2008

(B) Those that tried mandatory "privatization" and then abandoned it

	Adopted privatization, in	Then reversed it, in
United Kingdom	1988	2013
Argentina	1994	2008
Hungary	1998	2010
Kazakhstan	1998	2013-2015
Poland	1999	2011, 2013
Latvia	2001	2009, 2010
Russia	2001	2012, 2013
Estonia	2002	2009, 2010
Lithuania	2002	2009, 2010
Romania	2004	2009
Slovakia	2005	2006, 2007
Czech Republic	2011	2014

Source and notes: The source is Sokhey (2017, Table 2.1). At times, Sokhey also lists Denmark, Netherlands, Sweden, and Switzerland as having partial "privatization" features, yet does not list their initial adoption dates or include them in her systematic analysis. Sweden's notional defined contribution, discussed later in this chapter, differs from the "privatization" reforms of the listed twenty-one countries. Singapore, whose experience we turn to next, was also rightly excluded.

The geographic contrast in stickers versus quitters is striking. Why has the switch to mandatory defined-contribution pensions stuck with the other

Latin American privatizing countries, other than perennially fickle Argentina? Why has it been reversed in all the European cases? One leading determinant of their divergent paths seems to be the origins of their second pillars, the institutions mandating individual savings under government supervision. The Latin American adopters were countries which, like, Chile, turned to imposing forced individual contributions on most of the workforce as a way of replacing a rotting older system that had originated as a top-down proliferation of special occupational schemes. Given those tainted origins of their unstable older pension systems, a broad state mandate made sense. In Europe, by contrast, the same sort of second-pillar "privatization" seemed only temporarily attractive without such a tainted history. Britain and the Eastern Europeans were revising a previously more universal pension system. Once the second-pillar fashion faded and the Great Recession spread in 2008, they found it easier to retreat from the idea in favor of first-pillar supports. True, the Eastern Europeans inherited an older system that was also workplace-related. Yet the system they inherited from the communist era lacked the discriminatory top-occupations feature that pervaded Latin American pension history. Given that the older system they inherited from the communist era tended to be universal and more even-handed, their political debates found it easier to abandon the Chilean model.

A LESSON LEARNED. Chilean pension history has thus delivered a stern lesson for other countries. The lesson, however, is not mainly about the pension reform imposed by the military regime in 1980. Rather, Chile's pre-1970 experience issues a stern warning about dividing social insurance into separate occupational entitlements for separate occupational or social groups. Such a discriminatory approach led to a lobbying disequilibrium. The insiders, the groups that were already powerful enough to get better separate insurance, gained extra resources, and extra incentive, to fight for further non-contributory subsidies from the rest of society. The outsiders were given less insurance and paid extra net taxes.

This unfair and unsustainable system forced first Allende, and then Pinochet, to come up with their harsh and radical solutions. Allende's 1972–1973 solution was itself unsustainable, because it required hyperinflation. The military regime's solution had three summary features. It imposed a basically sustainable system on all of civilian society – still exempting the military, of course; it gave a once-and-for-all reward to the privileged groups that had raided the treasury before 1970; and it smoothed out the costs of the needed repairs among subsequent generations, as shown by the tapering pension deficit.

Chilean pension history thus provides the starkest, most extreme, illustration of a global fact: *The first senior generation to receive benefits from an underfunded pension system was the biggest winner of all*, and some later generation(s) will have to suffer to pay the balance. The first generation gets benefits for which it paid little or nothing in its earlier working years. Some later generation(s) will have to undo the pension deficit by paying both for earlier generations' benefits and for their own later retirement. In Chile's case, the ultimate "selfish generation" was the generation of high-income employees in the formal sectors of the economy that entered the labor force between about 1960 and the end of 1982. Its privileged classes benefited from the underfunding and regressivity of the old pension system, and from the temporary regressivity of the reform that replaced it in 1980–1981. Far from investing in future generations, that selfish first generation taxed them, as is typical when a toxic dump must be cleaned up.

SINGAPORE: CENTRAL GOVERNMENT AS PENSION INVESTOR

Like Chile under Pinochet, the People's Action Party (PAP) in Singapore has been an autocracy. The similarities go further. Like Chile's "Chicago Boys" team, President Lee Kuan Yew and the PAP insisted on the superiority of individualism, private enterprise, and free markets, and rejected the welfare state. Like Pinochet's Chile, Singapore imposed a highly centralized system in which the government dictated what happened to people's payroll deductions. Like Chile, which hid the unreformed pension subsidies to the military from the budgetary accounts, Singapore has hidden large parts of the allocations of pension funds from public view. And like Chile's scheme, Singapore's has survived to this day.

Yet the result in terms of selfish generations is the opposite, because the two countries' schemes were born under opposing stars. Singapore's experience seems to predict that *the (future) first labor-force generation that is no longer overtaxed by an overfunded pension system* will be the biggest winner of all.

Extracting this history lesson requires starting once again, as with Chile, with seeing that the imposed system was quite different from what its proponents claimed.

THE CLAIMS. Singapore's government preaching about the virtues of individualism and private enterprise became loudest in the 1990s. The preaching has rested on contempt for the Western welfare state. Lee Kuan Yew, the country's first president and a force of nature, boasted in a 1994 interview with Fareed Zakaria: "We start with self-reliance. In the West today it is the opposite. The government says give me a popular mandate and I will solve all of society's problems." One of his successors, then-President Ong Teng Cheong, repeated the PAP sermon thus, when opening Singapore's Parliament in 1994:

> Developed countries in Europe, Australia, New Zealand, and Canada once proudly called themselves welfare states. Now they have to revamp their welfare systems in order to remedy the disastrous side effects of state welfare: weakened family bonds, diminished incentives to work, and impoverishment of the country's finances ... Their problems confirm that we have chosen the right path.[9]

At that same time, Singapore was building individual family responsibility into law. What soon became the Maintenance of Parents Act of 1996 obligated young adults to support their elderly if the elderly had insufficient pensions saved up. The act made it easier for parents to sue their adult children for insufficient support. No reliance on state handouts there, it would seem.

Singapore's chest-thumping false claims of system superiority, like those of mainland China today, are not without precedent. Britons believed in the superiority of their superpower status and of laissez economics throughout the century after Waterloo. Americans have claimed the same superiority ever since Teddy Roosevelt. After defeating Hitler in World War II and then launching Sputnik in 1957, the Soviet Union staked out equally strong claims of system superiority. For example, after the space flight of Nikolayev and Popovich in 1962, the Soviet press and loudspeakers repeated the refrain: "This feat convincingly proves the superiority of the Soviet system in all branches of science." In such company, Singapore and China may be allowed a bit of self-inflation, even though the claims are wrong.

THE REALITY OF SINGAPORE'S STATE-DRIVEN DEVELOPMENT. At this point, a reader might expect an attempt to disprove that Singapore's economic achievements are real, or that Singapore's pension system has anything to do with those achievements.

Quite the contrary. Singapore's achievements are real, and its pension-related Central Provident Fund (CPF) has played an important role in its national super-growth, as far as the limited data can reveal. What is most glaringly wrong in those claims of its past leaders is that Singapore's economic institutions, and its pension system, represent individualism and private enterprise. What Singapore practices is centralized state capitalism, or what Branko Milanovic (2019, pp. 67–128) has aptly called "political capitalism." The CPF is a successful government mechanism for taxing workers' payroll contributions to deliver more capital formation and faster growth than the country could have attained if the elderly population had been given a good return on its forced contributions to the state.

To underline the magnitude of Singapore's overall state involvement, in 2016 the share of operating revenues (mostly taxes) in GDP was 16.9 percent as conventionally calculated, plus 8.8 percent in forced payroll deductions, or 25.7 percent in all.[10] This was close to the government taxation shares for 2016 in the United States (25.9%), Ireland (23.3%), Turkey (25.3%), and Korea (26.2%).

Taxing workers to launch government-funded super-growth dates back to the Soviet Union under Stalin. The striking similarity between Singapore's development finance and that of Stalin was noted by Paul Krugman in his widely cited critique of the East Asian "miracle" (Krugman 1994, pp. 64, 70–71). Stalin himself acknowledged that his government-funded rapid growth under the First Five-Year Plan was paid for by a tax on peasants that was "something like a tribute (*nechto vrode dani*)," of the sort that the Mongols had earlier exacted from Russians.

Stalin's defense of the tax could fit Singapore's growth-financing strategy: "It is something like a tribute, something like a supertax, which we are forced to take temporarily in order to uphold and develop further the tempo of development of industry" (Daniels 1984).

In its colonial origins, Singapore's Central Provident Fund was far too modest, and too pension-targeted, to have been any such engine of super-growth. As set up by British colonial authorities in 1953, with a launching in 1955, it looked like a small defined-contribution plan to assure colonial government employees a positive return on their mandatory contributions, in the form of later pension benefits. Yet after Singapore's independence in 1965, once Lee Kuan Yew and the PAP had consolidated their power over trade unions, and had suppressed political opposition, both the CPF and other taxes diverted a large share of national income into government savings. Figure 13.3 shows the ascent of payroll taxation on behalf of the CPF. Before independence, employees and employers together contributed only 10 percent of the payroll in the covered sectors. By 1984–1985 this taxation had peaked at 50 percent of the paycheck of a middle-aged worker. It has since stabilized at about 38 percent of the paycheck for such a worker. On the average for 2012–2016, that level of deduction took in 8 percent of gross national income (GNI), and left a CPF surplus of 3.7 percent of GNI. Given that the overall government saving was 5.8 percent of GNI, the CPF surplus apparently accounted for a majority of what the government saved for investing in national development – an important contribution, even though total national savings, most of it private, amounted to nearly 48 percent of GNI.

The separate CPF accounts do not spell out the transfers of its surpluses to the rest of government, but they do tell us how individuals allocated the parts of it they were allowed to withdraw. The mandatory payroll contributions are divided into three accounts: an ordinary account usable for housing, capital investment, or higher education; a special account for old age and contingencies; and a Medisave account for health-care expenses. The government's cheery upbeat publications and websites advertise one's freedom of (constrained) choice among these different uses.

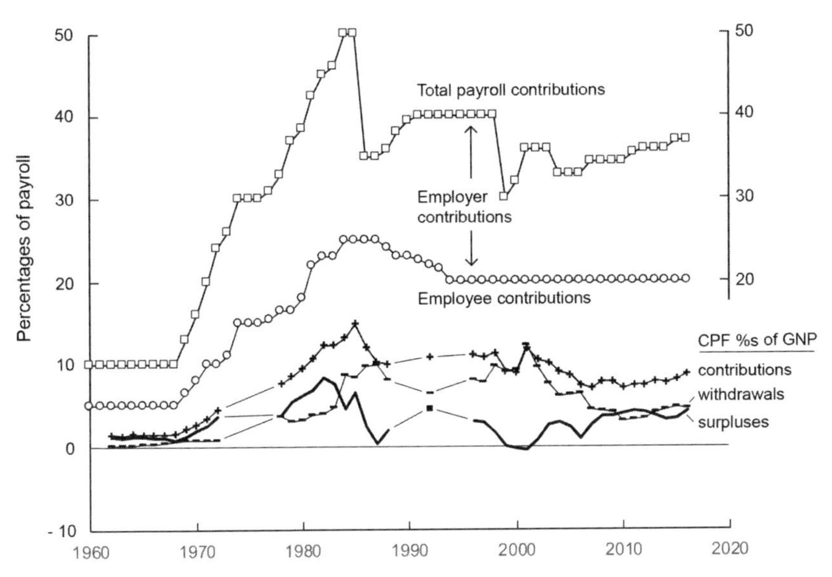

Figure 13.3. Singapore's payroll contribution rates, 1960–2016, and CPF shares of national income, 1978–2016

Sources and notes: The Central Providential Fund (CPF) rates of payroll contributions (deductions) are from https://data.gov.sg/dataset/contribution-rates-allocation-rates-and-applicable-wage-ceiling?resource_id=65db3d22-9b16-43a3-8d4b-a2133043a78b, accessed Mar. 8, 2020. The rates graphed here apply to employees at the age of 40, which were generally the same for all workers under 55.

The total payroll contributions to, withdrawals from, and surpluses in, the CPF are taken from Singapore's *Yearbook of Statistics*, various issues, as is the current-price gross national income denominator used in calculating the shares for 1978 and later years. For 1962–1972, the denominator for these three shares was GDP at factor prices.

How much has Singapore's government been devoting to social spending, either directly from the government budget or through individuals' withdrawals from CPF for social uses? Here the accounting data are not so clear. In the aggregate national income accounts, government spending on "social development" = 7.2 percent of GNI for 2012–2016, a very low share for so rich a country. It is not clear what "social development" includes, and which individual withdrawals from CPF this number has included or excluded. Very little of the tax goes into anti-poverty safety nets, at any rate. There are almost no universal benefits and the government's social assistance programs are means-tested with stringent qualifying requirements. The rates for public assistance schemes are deliberately set between 5 percent and 8 percent of per capita income.[11] Since per capita income is in turn only about 62 percent of average earnings per worker, the public assistance safety net lifts one only up to 3–5 percent of average income per employed person.

There are some oddities in the perennially high rates of payroll deduction and the perennial surpluses of the CPF. Why would a country as rich and educated as Singapore need to keep plowing so much into what was originally a compulsory pension fund? How and why does the CPF keep running surpluses despite the aging of the population? Would individual Singaporeans really save too little voluntarily? Was it really necessary to pass that 1996 Maintenance of Parents Act to keep elderly from being destitute in the face of such a flush Provident Fund and a fast-growing economy?

The answer to all these riddles seems to lie in government priorities about how to spend those payroll contributions. For all the show of providing for housing, medicine, and pensions, the CPF is so structured that those payroll deductions generate very little savings for the people who were forced to contribute throughout their careers. Here I follow some investigative leads offered by Mukul G. Asher and co-authors, who have warned that "The CPF balances are invested primarily by the Government of Singapore Investment Corporation, whose legal status is that of a private limited company – removing it from parliamentary or public scrutiny. This arrangement has not provided the members [individual households] with high enough real returns to capture the power of compound interest."[12] Table 13.4 shows a stark macro-economic contrast between the rates of return allowed on CPF contributions and the general rates of return in a booming economy. Since 1978, the interest rate that the CPF pays on the forced contributions has been a bit below zero, after adjustment for inflation. With GDP per worker growing at about 3 percent a year, the interest earned on one's forced savings is clearly falling behind. The shortfall looks even more dramatic relative to the internal rate of return on capital, again adjusted for inflation, which has exceeded 15 percent. While no official figures on this matter have been released, the secretive Government of Singapore Investment Corporation has probably earned similarly high returns with the money locked into the CPF.

The clouds surrounding the Central Provident Fund's poor returns do have some thin silver linings. A popular use of CPF balances is to take out subsidized low-interest housing loans. In addition, the government as landowner implicitly supplies free land sites under the real estate that households own. In this respect, Singaporean households benefit from rent-free land in the same way as public schools and public universities benefit from it in other countries.

Still, as Table 13.4 brings out, Singapore's households bear a special burden not borne by household investors in other countries, most of which have slower income growth rates than Singapore. In Japan and Sweden, as illustrated in Table 13.4, even a pension fund tied to the real rate of returns on long-term bonds would greatly

TABLE 13.4. *Singapore's real rates of return on forced savings, compared with other real rates in three countries, 1978–2016 (all rates are in percentages per year)*

	Interest rate	GDP growth per worker	Rate of return on "all" wealth	Internal rate of return on capital
Singapore	(CPF rate)			
1978-1990	- 0.4	3.6	–	16.1
1990-2000	- 0.2	2.7	–	15.9
2000-2016	0.4	2.5	–	15.4
Japan	(bonds)			
1978-1990	3.6	3.5	9.4	7.7
1990-2000	6.3	2.7	1.7	6.8
2000-2016	3.0	0.7	2.8	5.7
Sweden	(bonds)			
1978-1990	2.6	2.2	8.3	7.0
1990-2000	12.5	3.9	12.1	7.7
2000-2016	5.6	1.0	9.0	7.0

Sources and notes: The Central Provident Fund nominal interest rates are calculated as weighted averages of the 10-banks' deposit rates on fixed 12-month deposits and on savings deposits. Following official practice, the share weights are 80 percent for the fixed 12-month deposits and 20 percent for the savings deposits. To convert the nominal CPF interest rates into real rates, I subtracted the annual inflation rates, computed from the consumption price indices in Penn World Tables, version 9.1.

The growth rates in GDP per worker are the annual growth rates in real GDP per employed person, from Penn World Tables 9.1. More specifically, real GDP is measured from the output side of the national accounts, as converted into international purchasing-power-parity dollars of 2011.

The rates of interest on bonds and the return on "all" wealth (real estate, equities, bonds, and bills) for Japan and Sweden are from Jordà et al. (forthcoming). For these two measures, the final period ends with 2015, not 2016.

The internal rate of return on capital is from Penn World Tables version 9.1, and is defined in Inklaar, Woltjer, and Gallardo Albarrán (2019).

outperform the zero real rate delivered by the CPF. The bond rates in Japan and Sweden have even outperformed the growth of GDP per worker. Still higher are those countries' real rates of return on "all" wealth (a mixture of housing, equities, bonds, and bills) and their internal rates of return on capital.

Thus, relative to the negligible public pension provisions of the 1950s and 1960s, the CPF mechanism has brought only a limited gain. The two generations of those in the labor force since 1970 have been forced to pay it forward, to central government and to future generations. There are worse things than paying it forward, of course. As this book has emphasized, a large share of the world's governments has overpaid pensioners at the expense of the young and of national growth. Singapore's Central Provident Fund has at least delivered a kind of victory by subordinating pensions to investment benefits in owner-occupied housing, higher education, and in infrastructure.

That may not continue. The population's current high education, prosperity, and aging may force a change in policy. In at least one dimension, it clearly should be changed: The financial basis needs to be liberated from the job relationship, to stop handicapping labor relative to capital.

NOTIONAL DEFINED CONTRIBUTIONS: SWEDEN AND OTHERS SINCE THE 1990S

Like Chile in 1980–1981, Sweden in 1998 also enacted a major pension reform that has been emulated in other countries. It is not called "privatization," but an NDC system. If it works as intended, it will make public pensions sustainable indefinitely. In an ideal political world, an NDC system designed by experts could impose a fixed set of rules for adjusting pension levels to changing conditions. If one could enact a constitutional clause tying the country to that fixed formula, politicians could not violate the formula without being punished for unconstitutional behavior.

NOTIONAL DEFINED CONTRIBUTIONS PENSIONS, IN PRINCIPLE. The basic idea mimics a defined-contribution pension at the individual level with some wise indexing that proportions the total pension pie to each year's national movements in incomes, life expectancy, and the budget deficit. It only *mimics* defined contributions (DC), because it is still a year-to-year, pay-as-you-go, defined-benefit (DB) system, but one that keeps a link between your individual benefits and what you earned in the past. The defined-contributions label makes it look like a potentially regressive shift away from universal flat benefits and toward a share of what you earned, but that depends on politics.

Before sketching the wise indexing features, I start on the downbeat here, noting the key feature that the NDC design cannot dictate, and must inherit from the past.

It assumes a sustainable starting point. Before wise indexing can be set up, any NDC reform must start with a budget that has been brought near balance right now. This peaceful starting point more or less fit Sweden by 1998, after earlier deficits had been slashed in Sweden's wave of reforms starting in 1994. The same peaceful starting point fit Singapore's pension situation as of 1965, when pensions were miniscule and uncontroversial. But what if the system is out of whack in the first place, running unsustainable deficits and/or unfairly favoring one group over another, as in Chile in the 1960s and early 1970s, or in Greece and Turkey today, or when Mongolia botched its so-called "NDC" in 1999? Such differences in the starting point determine whether or not clever indexing can keep the pension system on course.

Four good indexing ideas. Starting from fairly balanced pension budgets, an NDC system should start with (1) a "balance ratio," defined as the ratio of the pension system's reserves over its obligations. This fail-safe balancing index says that if pension-system assets have gotten too low, dropping the ratio below one, annual pension benefits must be scaled back until the ratio returns to one. This first indexing ratio does not try to foresee what caused the imbalance.

Like most pension systems, NDC also includes (2) price indexing, to protect the real values against price inflation.

The two remaining good indexing ideas, (3) and (4), try to lessen the reliance on this balancing ratio by automatically adjusting pension levels to economic and demographic changes on a year-to-year basis. Recall from Chapter 12 that for a pension budget to stay in balance, any population aging must be met by some combination of changes in the net income tax rate devoted to pensions, in income growth, and/or in the ratio of elderly benefits to average incomes. By thinking about how the rates of change in Chapter 12's key equations must relate to each other, one can work out that, in terms of percentage growth rates,

(growth in average yearly benefit per elderly person)	=	(growth of the net tax rate) *plus* (growth in GDP per person of working age) *minus* (rise in the old-age population ratio).

Note that here, as in Chapter 12, the relevant groups are defined by age, not by employment or retirement status. Defining the formula in terms of age allows the aggregate indexing to use fairly incontrovertible and forecastable numbers in setting the aggregate, or "macro," index. How an individual's benefits relate to this macro index depend on the individual's work history, age, and household status.[13]

To be sustainable over the long run, any well-indexed system should keep the net tax rate from growing. That leaves the task of tying the average yearly pension benefit to the other two changes, one economic and one demographic.

So, next, an NDC system (3) indexes the growth of annual pension benefits to a measure of the trend in economic activity, such as the growth in full-employment GDP per employed person. Pensioners and workers automatically share in economic progress and share in economic losses from year to year. That offers a mechanism for relative political peace in changing times, if politics allows the indexing to be enforced.

Then comes the NDC system's answer to the curse of long life, which Chapter 12 represented with that rise in the old-age population ratio. An ideal NDC system (4) indexes annual pension funding to the projected aging of the population. Swedish practice starts a bit differently, with estimates of the number of years that a senior citizen is expected to live. Typically, this is set as the life expectancy at age 60, averaged over males and females. The logic is impeccable: The more years that your birth cohort is expecting to live in old age, the less you should receive in pensions *each year* from past savings or from taxpayers, to end up receiving the same total amount. On the average, people your age will be getting an amount of total pension that is independent of how long they live. By living longer, you get less per year, for any given age of retirement that you choose. Thus, for example, if you were born in 1980, and you worked from 2000 to 2045, your annual pension benefits would be tied to your earnings over those years divided by an index that is tied to the age-60 life expectancy calculated from survival outcomes around the year 2040. The longer your cohort of people is expected to live, the less your benefits each year, though of course your benefits are likely to continue for more years. This helps maintain aggregate balance in the pension budget.

Over time, the response to population aging must include not only lowering the average yearly benefits to offset the extra years of expected senior life span, but also a careful adjustment of individuals' retirement incentives. The longer they are expected to live, the later should be the age of qualifying for "full" retirement benefits. This task of fine-tuning the age schedule of retirement benefits faces the NDC system, just as it would face any other system, public or private. Working this way, an NDC system would achieve something that many other pension systems could also achieve, but only if the right parameters were built into their design and were adjusted over time. The NDC formulas can help to minimize the political negotiations over such adjustments.

The decision to name the new NDC pension system as a "defined-contribution" system seems to have reflected the policy fashions of the 1990s. Given that defined-contribution systems were then thought to be inherently more responsible, small changes got packaged as big shifts from defined benefits to defined contributions. For example, Ackerby (1998) described as Sweden's "shift from a benefit-defined system to an insurance-type contribution-defined system" a change that was in fact just a shift in the numerical formula through which individuals' career earnings were (already) reflected in their pension levels. Instead of basing the pension on the best fifteen years of earnings, as before, the new arrangements rightly based them on the earnings history over the entire working career. The same change could have been applied within a DB regime.

HOW IT HAS WORKED IN SWEDEN. Sweden's pension reforms seem particularly promising (in contrast to the government's mishandling of the covid-19 crisis in 2020). A necessary predecessor to the NDC reforms of 1998 was the crisis-driven overhaul of all economic policies culminating in the historical report of the Economics Commission (Ekonomikommissionen), headed by Assar Lindbeck of Stockholm University, on March 9, 1993. The coalition led by Carl Bildt and the Moderate Party swiftly enacted the report's main recommendations covering all sorts of macro- and micro-economic policies. On pensions and health insurance and unemployment insurance, the government cut the "replacement rates" to 70 percent of earned pay. With budgetary deficits thus brought under control, the well-publicized NDC system for adjusting pensions to changing conditions was launched in 1998.[14]

After 1998, each year the employee and employer have contributed 18.5 percent of the employee's gross pensionable income. Of the 18.5 percent, 16.0 percent is a pay-as-you-go contribution to this year's retirees, continuing the pay-as-you-go principle. The imputed nominal value of this large share of pensions rises with nominal national income, not with a price index. The remaining 2.5 percent goes into a mandatory retirement account, which the individual can privately allocate among securities. To this small extent, Sweden's pension system has been partly privatized.

Sweden's pension system applies all four of these indexing procedures.[15] Pre-commitment to such pre-determined formulas could remove the pension parameters from the political arena. Of course, social contracts can only make political pre-commitment easier. They cannot guarantee it.

Even Sweden softened its pre-set formula very slightly in response to the 2008–2009 slump. Under the original formula, the government was obligated to cut benefits for the two years 2010–2011. Afraid to follow through on the cuts in 2010, an election year for Parliament, officials changed the formula to stretch the reductions out over more years. This small retreat, plus non-pension tax breaks for the retired, yielded public acquiescence in retaining the NDC indexing system. The system remains intact, and it still works (so far).[16] Sweden has kept the pension support ratio, and the share of public pension spending in GDP, from rising since the mid-1990s. In addition, Sweden, along with Germany and Italy, has been able to induce a particularly large rise in the labor-force participation rate of both men and women in the 60–64 age group since around 1998.[17]

Sweden's recent small retreat from the strict index formula relating pensions to GDP suggests that the index should relate not just to the latest GDP but to a recent peak level of GDP. That would have allowed Sweden to index pensions to the peak year 2007 rather than to the slump year 2009. The same use of recent peak years would offer Swedish pensions even more cushioning to the coronavirus slump of 2020, which should not have been allowed to cut pensions.

OTHER COUNTRIES' EXPERIENCE. Just as some countries trying to emulate Chile's pension reform had to modify it, or abandon it, so too other countries have either modified the NDC design or retreated from it altogether. Several of them instituted their own versions of NDC even before Sweden: Italy launched an attempt in 1995, Latvia's sustained NDC system dates back to 1996. Others following suit included Kyrgyzstan (1997), Poland (1999), and Mongolia (2000), though not always with success.

While the literature typically lists *Italy* as a country with an NDC system since 1995, the resemblance has been questionable. The country's legislators must be credited with acknowledging the depth of the pension problem and for having tried to pass major reforms, not only in 1995, but also in 2004, 2005, 2006, and 2011, with the aim of pruning pension benefits. Yet the 1995 law itself was flawed by locking in pension differentials by occupational groups (i.e. by political lobbies), and by privileging "members with at least 18 years' contributions at 31 December 1995" – that is senior male workers. This resembles Chile's bad system of the 1960s more than it resembles an NDC. Of the series of reform attempts, the most durable has been the law of December 22, 2011, known as Decree Save Italy. Rather than indexing benefits ratios to life expectancy, as in an NDC system, Italy dictated an upward march of the full retirement age to 66 and, by 2021, to 67. Yet Italy's political paralysis remains, and the results we saw in Figure 12.3 show that the modest reforms could not keep pace with Italy's rapid aging. While the pension support ratio was reduced a bit from 1995 to 2013, the share of public old-age and survivor benefits in GDP kept marching upward, from 13 percent to over 16 percent.

After some initial trial and error, the newly independent *Latvia* launched its own, apparently successful, version of NDC in 1995. Like the Swedish system that soon followed, it indexed annual pension payments positively to national earnings and negatively to the share of elderly dependents in the adult population. It also includes that other essential feature: a first-pillar minimum pension as a safety net, below the pension entitlements that are scaled to one's career earnings. Latvia managed to cut its level of annual pension support between 1997 and 2007, with only a slight retreat toward higher replacement rates during the slump of 2008–2010. Overall, the pension support ratio has dropped enough, along with improving life expectancy, to keep the overall share of public pension benefits in GDP from rising.

Germany's pension reform, though not usually labelled as NDC, has imitated the aging-index part of Sweden's NDC system. In 2004, the federal German government introduced the so-called "sustainability factor" into its pension formula. This factor ties the current value of pensions to the ratio of pensioners to contributors in the system. The sustainability factor will eventually cut one's yearly pension payment by the same percentage as the rise in the ratio of pensioners to contributors. That is, it keeps population aging from changing the average pension payments one gets over all the years of retirement, much like Sweden's use of the life expectancy from age 60. The 2004 formula phases in the cuts gradually up to 2030, to spread the cost of the transition across two generations. And like Sweden, Germany softened its pre-commitment in the slump of 2008 by unplugging one of its index formulas temporarily, in order to prevent cuts in nominal pensions. Meanwhile, Germany's retirement age for receiving full benefits will creep slowly upward, in the same way as was legislated after America's 1983 Greenspan Commission on Social Security Reform.[18]

While the institutions called NDC were flexible, the idea retains traction because its indexing features make sense. They will presumably continue to diffuse.

WHAT WORKS: UNIVERSAL PENSIONS WITH OR WITHOUT THE SECOND PILLAR

Combining this chapter's post-operative appraisals of three countries' major pension surgeries with Chapter 12's reporting on symptoms around the world points to some clear lessons about what makes a pension system stable, fair, and efficient.

THE FIRST AND THIRD PILLARS SUFFICE, GIVEN POLITICAL CONSENSUS

As we saw for New Zealand and Australia in Chapter 12, so too for Chile and Sweden since the mid-1990s, a country can achieve sustainability plus insurance with DB and PAYG as easily as with the best compulsory-contribution plan. The key to successfully providing age-related insurance is political consensus. If a consistent political majority can agree broadly on how to mix progressive redistribution with a mechanism for national saving and incentives to work, that can be achieved by securing the first (state-financed) and third (voluntary) pillars alone. From a balanced starting point, the pension system can keep its stability by using indexing annual pension benefits to average incomes, life expectancy, prices, and the ratio of pension reserves to obligations, à la NDC. Faith in the indexing can be built up with experience, as it has more or less done in Sweden.

WHAT'S WRONG WITH THE SECOND PILLAR? Historical experience and economic principles have now combined to recommend that the employment relationship should be phased out as a basis for funding and controlling social spending. As Larry Willmore and others rightly argued, there is no need for the second pillar to support pensions.

Comprehensive mandatory contribution systems, like those in Chile and Singapore, are at least as sustainable as the autocratic regimes that impose them. And Chile's pension reform has survived democracy since 1990, though pressures continue to build for raising the basic-pension safety net. As a vehicle for ramping up savings and the growth rate at the expense of the current generations' consumption, the forced-individual-savings version of the second pillar has scored an obvious success in Singapore, and a partial success in Chile. Noting this in the case of Singapore, Milton Friedman once called Lee Kuan Yew "a benevolent dictator" and drew the lesson that "it is possible to combine a free private market system with a dictatorial political system."[19]

Possible, yes, if one is willing to give up on equality and the efficiency of curing externalities as goals. Yet even on these austere terms, mandatory payroll contributions are redundant. They are equivalent to a tax, which could be collected without payroll deductions, e.g. with a value-added tax on consumption. The payment of benefits could combine both a safety-net minimum and additional benefits proportioned to lifetime earnings. On the benefit side, pension payouts from accumulated payroll contributions can also be replicated with equivalent state-run formulas. In practice, the mandatory contributions have in given households a poor rate of return on their forced savings – by over-charging for portfolio management in Chile and some other countries, and in Singapore by paying a sub-market rate of interest.

Three other cracks have been exposed in the second pillar, as it has been erected historically. First, linking pensions to one's occupational group makes them less portable and creates divisions that can worsen future budgetary battles. Second, a system that is chained to payroll contributions cannot provide a basic anti-poverty safety net for those who work outside the formal labor market. Not surprisingly, this defect is clearest in countries that have placed a low priority on helping the poor, such as Chile and Singapore. Finally, the second pillar inescapably imposes a burden on the hiring of labor. No second pillar has ever mandated the same rates of deductions from property incomes. This inherent feature biases the economy against hiring labor, especially since part of the tax burden will fall on employers.

CHAPTER 14

Borrowing Social-Spending Lessons

We all know what to do, we just don't know how to get re-elected after we've done it.

Jean-Claude Juncker, then prime minister of Luxembourg[1]

LESSONS FROM GLOBAL HISTORY

CERTAIN SOCIAL POLICIES CAN BE CALLED DARWINIAN survivors in the sense that they have persisted and expanded, alongside satisfactory economic growth, in at least a dozen rich OECD countries over the last fifty years. Some of them, like relying on government to pay for most of education, have persisted even longer, without reversal. Handled carefully, the proven social policies can be prescribed to others. As already surveyed in Chapter 2 on "Findings and Lessons," earlier chapters have delivered the following "should do" list of three global lessons for government social policies:

- *Index annual pension benefits,* negatively to changing senior life expectancy as well as positively to peak GDP per adult. That will prevent any positive trend in the share of GDP that taxpayers spend on public pension benefits, without any absolute pension cuts.
- As much as possible, *uncouple the funding of social insurance from the workplace,* reducing reliance on the second pillar of social insurance. Prefer funding universal safety-net pensions and universal health care, with voluntary supplements.

– and, above all:

- *Invest in the young*, with a "cradle to career" strategy.[2]

Drawing on the lessons suggested by the global history of social spending, this final chapter illustrates how countries can adapt policies followed in their own past or in countries with similar histories. Our three illustrations depict policy options facing Japan, Venezuela, and the United States today. For Japan, only a nudge should be needed to make the needed repairs. For crisis-ridden Venezuela, a major overhaul is in order, though it would call only for policies already practiced either in Venezuela's past or in similar countries. For the United States to adapt policies from three near relatives – Canada, New Zealand, and Australia – simple nudging should do the job for anti-poverty "welfare," for pension policies, and for investments in early childhood, while more serious changes are called for in the case of American health care.

SHOULD VERSUS COULD VERSUS WOULD

There are reasons why policy opportunities promoting both equality and growth in average incomes are often still waiting there, unexploited. Political inertia leaves low-hanging fruit on the tree, and it rots. Obvious flaws in a country's social policies testify to the inertia that has been imposed either by dominant vested interests, or by political stalemates between competing interests. This pessimistic global fact stands out as clearly as does the optimism that countries could improve their lot with policy changes identified in the earlier chapters. Still, there could be a small intersection between the social policy changes that can be done and those that should be done, given a country's historical path and current political forces. Reformers must search carefully to find that small intersection.

Countries do not usually borrow policies from elsewhere except when first forming a state or when in the throes of a major crisis and regime change. For one of our three countries here, namely Venezuela, the opportunities are predicated on a major regime change. For the other two countries, finding a plausible counterfactual policy, at that intersection of the desirable and the feasible, probably requires borrowing from actual practices in institutionally and culturally similar democracies. There is no point in imagining an extreme counterfactual borrowing, such as "What if Japan became like Sweden?" or "What if the United States became like Singapore?" Our imagination should be limited to plausible possibilities, aided by history's having given similar conditions to national governments that just happen to have inherited different, but changeable, social policies.[3] Subject to this prudent constraint, the evidence suggests some limited borrowings that Japan and the United States should, could, and conceivably would adapt from international experience.

JAPANESE PENSION REFORM: SHOULD, COULD, AND MAYBE WOULD

Japan, more than most rich countries, must grapple with two glaring economic problems: gender inequality and population aging. And dealing with the latter must involve a significant change in social-spending policies.

Among the economically advanced countries, Japan is second only to Korea in short-changing women on jobs and pay. So say the data, year after year.[4] The imbalance has deep roots that progressive social-spending policies have not reached. Efforts have been made, of course. Equitable public education efforts have lifted Japan's women to gender equality in the years of education attained by women and men since the mid-1980s. Yet in all adult age ranges, Japanese women still do not hold formal jobs nearly as much as men, nor are their jobs nearly as high-paying. This imbalance cannot be solved within the confines of the social-spending policies addressed in this book. Even where Japan's social legislation seems to have lent a hand to women's careers better than in other countries, as in the parental leave policies noted in Chapter 9, little change seems to have resulted. This book's search for social-spending lessons must therefore leave this issue unresolved, and turn to the issue of financing the elderly, on which changes in social-spending policies could deliver more.

Japan has known about, and has debated, the financial implications of its extreme aging since the 1980s. The whole country understands that the working-age (18–64) population has been shrinking since the mid-1990s, and even the total population began declining around 2009. Meanwhile, the population keeps urbanizing, and rural towns are vanishing. The main crisis in social spending relates to support for the growing elderly share, not to insufficient investment in each young citizen.

The tyranny of demography partly explains why Japan is in such a precarious overall position. This tyranny has even been quantified. Noriyuki Takayama, Yokinobu Kitamura, and Hiroshi Yoshida (1999) have estimated Japan's generational accounts going forward from the year 1995. They find that *all* of the generational imbalance, i.e. the extent to which future generations of Japanese will face higher tax rates than those already born in 1995, would disappear if Japan did not continue to grow older. This implies that the upward pressure on pension budgets stems from the mere fact of aging, and not from any over-generosity in Japan's fiscal policy.

Japan's aggregate numbers amplify the same message: relative to other advanced countries, Japan has not been exceedingly generous to the average elderly person, nor has its relative generosity changed much since the 1980s. This point is driven home in Figure 14.1, which shows both the limits to support for the elderly and the cost implications driven by population again alone. Panel (A) of Figure 14.1 spotlights the level of relative pension generosity, again using the ratio of annual benefit payments per elderly person to annual GDP per person of prime working age (18–64). Between 1973 and 1986, during the oil shocks and Japan's speedy subsequent growth, the annual support per elderly person nearly tripled in generosity, reaching the levels paid out by America's Social Security system. Thereafter, pensions have stabilized in relation to the average national product per person of working age. Today, the level of annual support per elderly person shown by the latest figures for Japan is the highest in East Asia. The supports offered the elderly in Japan and the United States are also above those of other English-speaking OECD countries (Australia, Canada, Ireland, New Zealand, and the United Kingdom). Yet Japan and the English-speaking countries are much less generous toward the elderly than most countries of Mediterranean, Northern, and Eastern Europe.

While the stability and moderation of Japan's public support for the elderly may seem reassuring, that stable support level itself is a growing problem.[5] The budgetary logic of Chapter 12 returns to haunt Japan in a way dramatized by Panel (B) of the same Figure 14.1. The share of GDP claimed by public pension benefits continues to soar, having passed 11 percent. Once the pension share reaches 17 percent of GDP, Japan will have passed the shares achieved anywhere in the world by 2015. Future data releases will probably show that it has already done so in the coronavirus slump of 2020. Note the striking difference in the Japanese and American trends in this share of GDP, which represents an implicit rate of taxing the rest of society. While both countries seemed to share the same support levels for the elderly since the 1980s (in Panel (A)), their rates of implicit taxation are rising at very different rates (Panel (B)). The divergence is caused solely by the fact that Japan is aging so much faster than the United States, due to Japan's rock-bottom birth rates and immigration rates.

There must come a point at which Japanese politics comes to grips with the rising claims of elderly support on the rest of the budget, translating "should reform" and "could reform" into "will reform," since its population aging is not projected to stop until around 2055.

If one just reads the press accounts of how Parliament and the prime minister are dealing with the issue of paying for so many senior citizens in the future, one could gain a positive impression of dutiful reform, just as one gains from reading the legislative headlines from Italy. Japan's government has indeed been passing reforms. It has raised the mandatory retirement age to which people are entitled to keep their jobs, which in 2020 may be raised from 65 years to 70 years for both men and women. They also continue to debate raising the age at which people are entitled to draw the "full" benefits based on their previous work history, from 60 years to perhaps 70. This would be a major step. Yet, as of this writing, the legislation has not been passed, nor has a timetable been laid out for gradually raising the full-benefit age.

Japan's politics has delayed its ability to deliver anything more than modest responses when confronted with major difficulties. The emphasis is on consensus and lack of offense to others. And, like many other democracies, Japan has a distribution of elected representatives that is

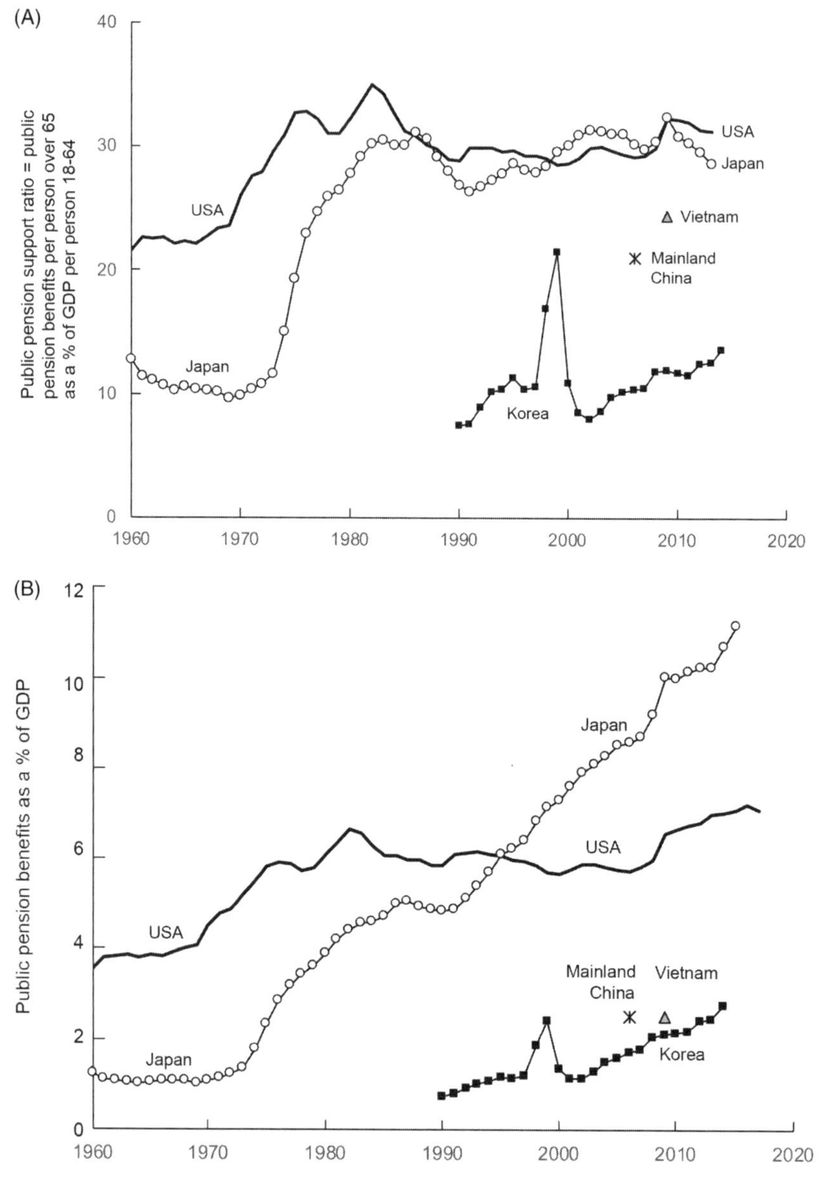

Figure 14.1. Public pension generosity and pension costs since 1960: Japan versus other countries
(A) Public pensions per elderly person, relative to GDP per working-age adult.
(B) Pension expenditures as a percentage of GDP.

distributed unfairly in favor of the conservative and elderly. This is because urbanization and rural de-population have given each 100,000 rural voters more representatives than each 100,000 urban voters in both houses of the Diet, or Parliament. While Japan has historically borrowed institutions from abroad, first in the wake of the 1868 Meiji Restoration and then in the wake of defeat in 1945, it has shown a built-in resistance to borrowing institutions without transforming them into something distinctly Japanese.

Japan could offer good excuses for clinging to the institutions that have delivered its highly civilized, clean, safe stagnation. The world's financial markets seem to agree that Japan's status quo is trustworthy. Its long-term bonds have one of the world's lowest interest rates, meaning that the market perceives almost no risk in its growing pension debt. The yen is a safe-haven currency, while the country maintains a current-account surplus in its international payments, thereby adding to its net creditor status. Still, the long-run mathematics of Figure 14.1 remains inescapable.

What steps should, and could, Japan take to check the rise of the taxation of the young for the elderly, and which of these are politically probable? The first step that one thinks of in comparative perspective is ruled out by Japanese social preferences and politics. As already noted, Japan will not import large numbers of young foreign workers, whose taxable earnings and care-giving could have bailed out the elderly. That has been tried on a modest scale, with continuing roadblocks in the path of accepting more permanent immigrants.

A second possible step would be to keep raising the age at which retirees can start drawing full benefits, while also changing the incentive structure to make them want to keep working that long. Japan has already made a bit of progress here. Back in the 1980s, the need for such reform was severe: Japan's various policies imposed one of the world's highest rates of implicit taxation on continuing to work if one were in, say, the 60–64 age bracket. The wisdom of reducing that tax rate has already won out, with a major drop in the taxation of earnings for 62-year-old men around 2006 and an even bigger cut on the implicit work tax for 62-year-old women five years later. Women in that age group now face only a 20 percent tax rate, quite low by international standards.[6] Japan has already taken advantage of some of the opportunities for improving senior work incentives, especially for women. With the help of such incentives, the Japanese already retire later than do workers in most countries.

Thus far, the debate has concentrated on the age of full retirement benefits, and the age to which workers are entitled to keep their jobs. Yet laws about *when* to retire do not specify *how much pension* one receives at retirement. What share of average earnings should the average retiree receive? This key parameter needs to be nailed down, to check any further rise in the share of taxpayers' incomes that is given over to public pensions.

The key extra step is to legislate a pre-commitment that checks any further rise in the share of GDP claimed by public pension budgets. For Japan, more than for any other OECD country, *annual pension benefits must rise more slowly than average pay and productivity* for decades to come, as explained in Chapter 12.[7]

The government and the Diet should agree to formulas for indexing annual benefits, as Chapter 13 has described for Sweden and other NDC countries. The crucial indexing link is the one that ties annual benefits, negatively, to the length of expected survival in retirement. This link means, again, that an age cohort's overall retirement benefits will be unaffected – but will be stretched more thinly over more years of retirement. The legislative pre-commitment to indexed pensions fits Japan's social preferences, in that the rules governing one's individual annual benefits are shared by everybody in one's age group. It is a shared social contract, of the sort that Japanese society honors so well.

A NEW VENEZUELA

Venezuela's case is completely different from those of most other countries. Its people seek not just better policies, but immediate life support. What necessary social-spending measures could be realistically implemented by a new government?

ROCK BOTTOM. We know from first-hand testimony that Venezuela had hit rock bottom by 2019–2020, even though the government stopped releasing statistics back in 2014. Everything had spiraled downward after 2013, when Nicolás Maduro took control after the death of Hugo Chávez. Oil output, the only number still publicized, began to plummet. Hyperinflation set in, shortages appeared, public service broke down, and crime rose. Maduro tried to use the court system and the police to suppress dissent. He also tried to stem the tide of his own monetized hyperinflation with price controls, in the King Canute tradition. In 2017, the United States, Canada, and other governments added to Venezuela's suffering and loss of life by imposing tough sanctions aimed at removing Maduro from office. As the economy continued to spiral downward, 5–7 percent of the population fled the country between 2015 and 2019, and the whole population dropped about 5 percent, according to rough United Nations estimates.[8]

In 2019–2020, Maduro tried to buy some short-run relief by making life easier for the country's well-off and internationally connected, most of them living in Caracas. One mechanism for achieving this elitist result was to allow dollarization, in a collapsing economy in which only those with government connections and overseas relatives could get dollars.[9] Of course, the Caracas high life could only last until the overseas assets were depleted.

A TRADITION OF EXTRACTIVE GOVERNMENTS. The mismanagement since 2014 can be viewed as a reversion to a long-standing tradition of Venezuelan governance. Any prescriptions about spreading safety nets over the rocks must be based on the sobering diagnosis of the country's many "pre-existing conditions," to use the medical euphemism for chronic bad health.

In the nineteenth and twentieth centuries, Venezuela's history was dominated by extractive governments. Many of them were outright dictators, or *caudillos.* Some were technically elected governments, though electoral voice was restricted to those at the top, due to wealth requirements, literacy requirements, and the lack of ballot secrecy. From the 1920s on, they controlled the country's new-found oil wealth, in league with foreign oil companies.

Today's policy options are best understood by starting the cameras rolling in 1958, when a national reform ostensibly banished dictatorship and opened a new democratic era. The promising fiscal reform options were analyzed in depth by the Shoup Mission (Shoup et al. 1959).

The results since 1958, however, have been sobering.[10] The Punto Fijo Pact of that year handed power to a coalition of entrenched politicians, dominated by the two parties AD and COPEI. This stakeholders' alliance between party leaders, the propertied, and labor unions shared power and oil revenues for the rest of the century, while also succumbing to the inefficient strategy of import-substituting industrialization. Puntofijismo never resembled "neo-liberalism," despite brief gestures in that direction in moments of austerity. Rather, it was closer to two other "-isms," to the "corporatism" in Gøsta Esping-Andersen's (1990, 1999) famous taxonomy, and to "Peronism." Its ability to control oil wealth was enhanced by partial-nationalization laws in 1971 and 1976, setting up Petroleum Venezuela (Petróleos de Venezuela S.A., or PDVSA) as a government money machine.

The rent-skimming alliance cemented by the Punto Fijo Pact thrived in the early 1960s and especially in the global oil boom of 1973–1980, which allowed the leadership to dole out riches instead of austerity. Then its performance began to deteriorate in the 1980s, as oil revenues took a sharp decline and external bank lending dried up. Public distrust of the legitimacy of the AD and COPEI led to protests and electoral instability.

Strong circumstantial evidence of dysfunctional governance can be seen in Figure 14.2's history of Venezuela's GDP per capita, projected against the steadier progress of its Colombian and Costa Rican neighbors. Consider what happened to GDP per capita over the whole Punto Fijo era from the signing of the Pact in 1958 up to 1996, on the eve of the electoral breakdown that led to Hugo Chavez's ascendency in 1999. In the background, over these thirty-eight years, Venezuela was blessed (or cursed, as many have said) with its oil riches. After the real price of crude oil held steady for fifteen years, it had jumped to four times its 1958 level by the peak in 1980. Even though oil then lost some of that purchasing power, as late as 1996 it still commanded about 25 percent greater real purchasing power than it had when the major political parties struck their deal back in 1958. Despite this golden opportunity for enrichment, Venezuela's real GDP per capita actually fell about 8 percent, and the country was overtaken by oil-deprived Costa Rica

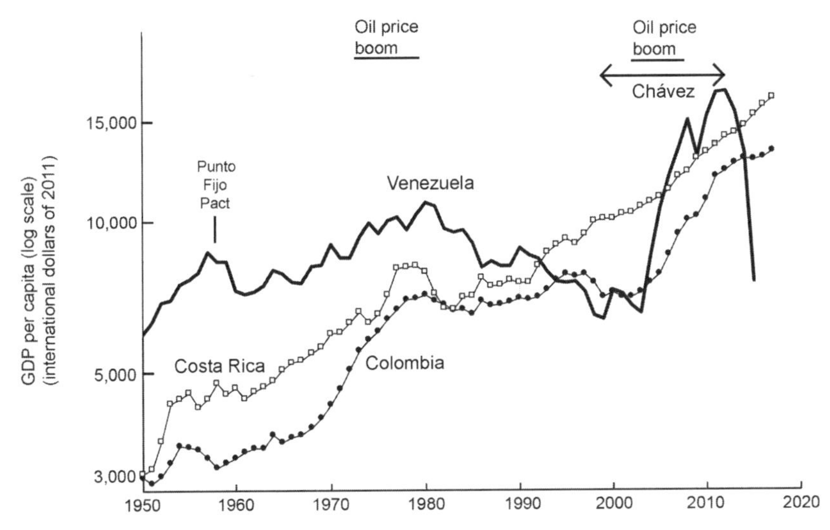

Figure 14.2. Venezuela's GDP per capita, versus that in Colombia and Costa Rica, 1950–2017

Source and notes: The source is Penn World Tables, version 9.1, https://www.rug.nl/ggdc/productivity/pwt.

I have omitted their estimates for Venezuela in 2016 and 2107, since official data were cut off by then, and the Penn World Tables are not accompanied by an explanation of how the 2016 and 2017 figures were derived.

and Colombia, as Figure 14.2 testifies. It would be very hard to account for this fallback without giving a central role to an extractive and dysfunctional government. By the mid-1990s, many Venezuelans had reached the same conclusion. Caracas had seen major protests and two coup attempts, one of them led by Lieutenant Colonel Hugo Chávez. The turmoil continued, stirred by a temporary dive in oil prices combined with President Caldera's inability to clean up corruption, as promised, and his unpopular refusal to pardon Chávez and other coup leaders. Democratic elections thus ended the Punto Fijo era, electing Chávez in 1999.

THE CHÁVEZ ERA (1999–2013) AND SOCIAL SPENDING. Chávez's turbulent time in office will always remain controversial. While his defenders will credit him with the strong growth shown in Figure 14.2, critics have plausibly dismissed this as good luck brought by the renewed jump in oil prices. Behind the GDP growth, lay shifts that have been used to support either side of the debate. Through it all, oil production remained basically unchanged, and the real growth was in other sectors, as Chávez defenders have noted. On the other hand, much of the non-oil real growth took the form of expansion of the government itself, with help from that jump in oil prices.[11]

All of government was transformed in this era, leaving a tangle of competing structures. To bypass opposition based in the existing agencies, Chávez repeatedly launched new campaigns organized by partisan community organizations, notably the many *misiones*, to build new infrastructures and meet basic needs of the poor. While much was built by this parallel state, much was left unbuilt. Quantity was stressed over quality. From 2007 until the death of Chávez, momentum slowed, while the rise in oil prices lost its steam. As Julia Buxton has summarized this phase in the context of health-care services, things began to unravel,

> given evidence of corruption, popular "fatigue with routine political engagement and increased partisan conflict at [the] local level driven by "hard core," ideologically committed *Chavistas* and their dominance of community level organization. The Community Councils, of which there were 23,000 by 2006, and linked organizations such as the Health Committees, reported problems of non-attendance by state and local officials who were meant to serve as the mechanism for articulating popular needs to ministries and channeling public spending.[12]

During this turmoil, however, social spending reached levels that are instructive for the future, both with their historic heights and with their relative limitations. In the context of Venezuela's own history, social spending grew as never before. Table 14.1 shows this. Twentieth-century Venezuela had failed to secure safety nets any higher than the levels shown for 1997–1999 here. By 2012, just before the death of Chávez, the share of national income taxed for public social spending was half again as great. It can be said the Bolivarian Revolution had delivered social protections unprecedented in the country's history. Like most countries devoting sizeable shares of national income to social spending, Venezuela shifted toward pension spending, compressing its shift into the Chávez years.

TABLE 14.1. *Social spending as a share of GDP, Venezuela, 1997–2014*

	Total social spending	Public education	Public health	Public housing	Social security	Other social spending
1997	9.7	3.6	1.5	1.4	2.9	0.2
1998	8.1	3.4	1.4	1.0	2.2	0.2
1999	9.3	4.1	1.5	0.8	2.9	0.1
2000	10.8	4.5	1.4	1.7	3.0	0.2
2001	11.9	4.8	1.5	1.0	4.3	0.2
2002	11.1	4.8	1.7	0.8	3.7	0.1
2003	12.0	4.6	1.5	1.1	4.5	0.3
2004	11.5	4.8	1.6	0.6	4.3	0.3
2005	11.2	4.1	1.6	1.3	3.9	0.3
2006	13.7	5.1	1.8	1.6	5.0	0.3
2007	12.8	4.8	2.0	0.6	5.1	0.3
2008	13.1	5.2	2.0	0.5	5.1	0.3
2009	13.0	5.3	2.1	0.2	5.0	0.3
2010	11.6	4.1	2.0	0.3	5.0	0.3
2011	13.4	4.3	2.4	0.3	6.2	0.3
2012	14.4	4.5	2.5	0.4	6.7	0.3
2013	16.1	4.7	2.8	0.9	7.2	0.4
2014	18.8	5.8	3.2	0.5	8.7	0.5
For comparison, in year 2012						
Colombia	18.4	4.5	4.6	0.6	8.2	0.5
Costa Rica	20.8	5.3	7.0	0.1	7.4	1.0

Sources and notes: For all three countries, CEPAL (Economic Commission for Latin America), social expenditures of central government, excluding environmental protection, https://observatoriosocial.cepal.org/inversion/en/countries, accessed Apr. 21–25, 2020.
For Costa Rica, central government only.

Yet the country's unprecedented social spending under a Left government was relatively modest in international perspective. As a share of national income, Venezuela spent far less than the United States or Canada, and less than the Southern Cone countries or Costa Rica or Colombia.[13] Similarly, Venezuela under Chávez redistributed much less from rich toward poor than in Argentina, Uruguay, Brazil, and Costa Rica, and even less than the United States or Canada. Its redistribution was about as progressive as that in Colombia, as best one can judge the rough estimates.[14]

The takeaway here is that by the end of the Chávez era, Venezuela's performance showed what was possible, and also what was not attained, in the way of social spending. A future Venezuela rising from the ashes should be able to replicate such social spending share of GDP once the economy has regained the heights reached at that 2012 peak. Doing so should have no worse incentive effects than similar spending rates have had in, say, North America. Before then, while the nation is still getting back on its feet, the social-spending share should be even higher at the lower initial levels of GDP.

What form should the social spending take when Venezuela recovers? It is actually possible to apply our three universal prescriptions to the case of a Venezuela that somehow emerges from the wreckage, even without daring to try to specify the future structure of the government itself. Modest doses of the social-spending part of the cure have already been delivered by Venezuela itself in the recent past, as we have just seen. And the information-technology revolution will ease the task of implementing and monitoring social programs, as it has already done for other developing countries.

BETTER INSTITUTIONS, AND RESOURCES, FROM WHERE?

The safety-net institutions that Venezuela might adapt to its current situation could draw strength from four sources.

(1) The country can select from the best of its own twenty-first-century social programs. Which institutions should survive from the Chávez era? Many should not, and should be pared or eliminated. Still, a cleaner and more efficient administrative structure could start with a national census plus repairs to Venezuela's existing health and education systems.

(2) Government revenues could still be tied largely to value-added tax and to oil taxes and rents through PDVSA for the foreseeable future, even though revenues will be initially very low, requiring emergency grants or loans from the international community.

(3) Institutional repairs can be designed with the help of multilateral institutions and global best practices. Neither the necessary foreign lending nor the social-program institutions need be

administered under bilateral agreements with any superpower – no lending or blueprints controlled by the United States, or by Russia, or by China. Fortunately, today's global and regional institutions offer not only funding but also a well-developed set of blueprints for administering the various social programs with a centralized information system.[15]

(4) There is a particular viable, and adjustable, institution for poverty relief invented in Latin America and exported from the region to the rest of the world. The institution of conditional cash transfers (CCTs) was independently innovated by Mexico and Brazil in the 1990s, and has since been transplanted, with modifications, to fifteen other developing countries on five continents. The core idea is to pay a household cash in exchange for proof that its members are engaging in specified positive-externality behaviors, such as health check-ups and school attendance.[16] Practicing "South to South" learning, Venezuela could adapt CCTs to its own conditions, and make them universal rather than means-tested.

FIRST STEP: A FLAT UNIVERSAL GRANT. The revival of social spending should start with a flat poverty-alleviating "demo-grant" denominated in hard-currency units, and based in a new national census. The grant should continue monthly, and can be permanent. More than most countries, Venezuela needs to ramp up its basic anti-poverty assistance. Yet for administrative convenience and political sustainability, the demo-grant should be universal, covering every individual, rather than being targeted only at the demonstrably poor (i.e. means-tested). The only data requirements should be clear proof of individual identification, length of residence in Venezuela, household membership, and age. The grant would deliver cash in proportion to the household's "consumer equivalents" based on the number and ages of its members. Even in a malnourished environment, experience suggests that a visible cash flow is likely to address basic needs better than any ill-focused agricultural plan for promoting food self-sufficiency and family farms.

When administrative capacities have been rebuilt, the demo-grant can become a CCT, setting aid conditions requiring proof of health check-ups, vaccinations, and (for school-age children) school attendance. The behavioral conditions may be waived, however, for the initial months of recovery from the emergency.

HEALTH CARE COMES NEXT. To deal with the health crisis that has worsened since 2015, Venezuela needs an immediate census-based update in registration with local health-care units, again for transparency and equity in the allocation of public services. Regular health registration updates are also needed for monitoring the CCT conditionality requirements (did they get their health check-ups, etc.). More generally, there is a case for integrating services within the benefits system, for efficient monitoring.[17]

Note that even at its peak, health care was not given the resources it received in neighboring countries, as Table 14.1 showed by comparing Venezuela with Colombia and Costa Rica in 2012. In this comparative perspective, health care was already underfunded even before becoming an emergency need since 2015.

IMPROVING EDUCATION. Throughout the twentieth century, as the government and/or petroleum multinationals prospered from Venezuela's oil riches, the country stood in bad light, even by Latin American standards, in its denial of tax-based education for the masses. As of 1958, basic education was so underfunded that investing more government money into it could have given a respectable rate of return, not only to the whole economy and society, but even to the government itself in extra future revenues. That is, succeeding governments were so opposed to taxes for mass education that they had left "money on the sidewalk" in the same way as did mid-Victorian England and Wales.[18] Thus, Venezuela as late as 1958 had less schooling than four poorer neighbors, namely Costa Rica, Cuba, Jamaica, and Trinidad–Tobago. That bias was spotlighted back in 1959, when the Shoup Mission published its task-force study of the whole fiscal structure of Venezuela: "Education has such a low priority in the national investment program that the level of education relative to income is one of the lowest in the world. Further progress in the non-petroleum sectors, particularly industry, agriculture, and government, will depend heavily on better education."[19]

Under the main-party political alliance of the next forty years, Venezuela did raise its average schooling levels to where they were no longer in the lower half of the Latin American ranks. That said, by 2000, the country still had lower adult education attainments than fourteen other Latin American countries, each of which had lower average incomes than Venezuela. However, in the Chávez decade 2000–2010, Venezuela's enrollments jumped, mainly by reducing the population share that had no education at all and by raising the share having completed secondary school (Barro and Lee 2013). Attempts to rebuild education in the 2020s can set the quantities of education finance, and education enrollments, that were delivered by 2010 as worthy and attainable targets.

REBUILDING PENSIONS. By 2018, many Venezuelan pensions had been made worthless by the breakdown of the fiscal system and the hyperinflation that had accelerated over the preceding five years. The lucky minority presumably consisted of those with the right connections to have stored up savings in hard currency.[20] How to rebuild the pension system after the currency and public finances have been stabilized?

Venezuela's pension plight is no worse than if the country had joined others in following Chile's example by placing its nest eggs into government-controlled individual accounts through mandatory payroll deductions. That possibility was debated in the 1990s, but "privatization" lost to intense opposition from unions and public-sector retirees.[21] Had Venezuelan workers been locked into a system patterned after that of Chile, their accumulated savings would have been wiped out in the hyperinflation after 2013. Instead, a new regime could build on an existing set of pension institutions and index it to GDP growth and to population aging. Venezuela's system, as updated in 2002, had a floor that could be firmed up in the absence of hyperinflation. The demogrant proposed here could be a foundation for restoring that basic universal pension.

Beyond that, Venezuela has been a traditional pay-as-you-go (PAYG) system, where working and contributing for 750 weeks qualifies an employee for a pension related to earnings history. A foundation of sorts is in place. For help on the knotty problems of design, the pension reconstruction team might seek the advice of Argentine experts familiar with how Argentina sheltered pensions against its hyperinflations of 1983–1984 and 1989–1990.

How would the new pension entitlements above the pension floor be structured? Like many other Latin American countries, Venezuela had given special pension treatment to its military and its public servants. Recall from Chapter 7 that as of 2010 Venezuela had one of the world's most serious biases toward public pension benefits and away from public education. The reforms could not revoke all such privileges, given individuals' past work histories, but would have to keep them under control. The formulas for re-calculating work-service entitlements would have to set them low enough so that they could be fully matched by current contributions, on a PAYG basis, when formal-sector earnings had recovered to levels of real purchasing power such as those attained in 2010. Beyond that, Venezuela should, as other countries should, index future annual old-age benefits positively to average earnings (or GDP) and negatively to life expectancy after retirement. Such are the suggestions that emerge from a combination of global experience and the country's own history.

THE UNITED STATES: SHOULD, COULD . . .

We close with a large country whose social-spending indicators are often middling in global perspective, yet below the performance of some comparable advanced countries in three key respects. Earlier chapters have revealed specific American deficits in the areas of pensions, health care, and supports for families with children under the age of six.

Which other countries' experience could be used to guide improvements in social policy in the United States today? The usual prescriptions have been based on some positive aspects of European welfare states. Yet the conservative half of America has long resisted the idea that we should learn anything positive from Europe. Typical was a US senator's recent response when asked "Aren't there lessons we could learn from welfare states like Denmark?" His politically savvy reply: "We need to work on what we know is right for America. We can't get involved in Europe's problems." If Americans have a problem, in other words, the solution should be invented in America, in isolation, without borrowing policies from Europeans. We do not borrow from Europeans.

All the same, the American debates over social policy could also be educated by better practices in non-European countries that resemble the United States. The more similar the country's history to that of the United States, the greater the chance that what should and could be changed actually *would* be changed with some course corrections in mid-flight. The three countries that offer the most promise for nudging American policy are Canada, New Zealand, and Australia. Consider the features they have shared with the United States: Settlement of frontiers, open spaces today, prosperity, democracy, dependence on immigration, and having served as allies in world wars fought mainly overseas. They also resemble the United States in social spending as a share of GDP – all four offer the poor and needy less than what the average OECD country offers, but more than China or Mexico. The shared history is strong enough that the nationalist press in the United States has not (yet) demonized the other three countries.

Let us consider four course corrections that might work, guided partly by how these other three countries' practices have evolved: a nudge toward their better public pension practices, a swerve toward their approach to health insurance, and nudges toward their handling of the poor and early childhood development.

AMERICA'S SOCIAL SECURITY IS FINANCIALLY SUSTAINABLE, BUT COULD USE BETTER INDEXING. The US pension system is not in serious financial trouble at the federal level. Nor are those run by national governments of Canada, New Zealand, and Australia. All four countries passed Chapter 12's five stress tests regarding financial sustainability. To be sure, there have been, and will be, pension-related financial crises in some cities and states within the United States. Cities filing for bankruptcy in 2010–2013, in the backwash of the Great Recession, included Stockton, San Bernardino, and Detroit. In all these cases, serious underfunding of the city's employee pension promises was a major force pushing the city over the edge. Some states are now in trouble, especially Illinois and New Jersey. Again, public-employee pensions have been a main source of their flirtation with bankruptcy. Yet at the federal level, Uncle Sam's ability and willingness to honor his pension obligations is not doubted by financial markets. Like Japan, the United States can borrow at some of the world's lowest interest rates.

More immediate than the dangers of distant pension costs to taxpayers is the fact that in the United States, more than in the other three countries, pensions continue to draw money away from other social spending, with negative implications for growth and equality. Even America's federal pension policy could use some nudging toward the pension restraints shown recently by Canada, Australia, and New Zealand.

All four countries have developed universal "social security" provisions for old age, with differences in timing. New Zealand was first, with a modest public pension bill in 1898, funded entirely out of general taxes. Its Social Security Act of 1938 added a universal "superannuation" to the lingering means-tested age benefits for the poor. The subsequent history featured a sharp rise in pension generosity in the early 1970s, and a sharp decline after the budget of 1991, as already sketched in Chapter 12.

Australia's Commonwealth Old-Age and Invalid Pensions became law in 1908 and took effect in 1909–1910. As in the New Zealand plan they were modeled after, the pensions were means-tested and non-contributory defined benefits (DB) funded by general taxes on a pay-as-you-go basis (PAYG). Over the next 110 years, Australia kept re-tweaking and re-targeting these public pensions, without any single landmark law. The system remains DB and PAYG today, now embellished with price indexing, graduated options for early retirement, and some means-testing.[22]

Social security did not arrive at the federal level in North America until the Great Depression of the 1930s (United States) and the aftermath of World War II (Canada). In the United States, the Social Security Act of 1935 set up a contributions pension for about half of the US workforce. More occupations came under the tent of coverage every few years. Then in 1972, a surge of generous new provisions tilted the long-run trend toward deficit, and slashed the share of the elderly who were below the poverty line. Led by the Greenspan Commission,

Congress and President Reagan in 1983 limited the rise of deficits by slowly advancing the age at which one could draw the full legal benefits.

Canada came last, partly because it needed a Constitutional Amendment, passed in 1951, in order to establish, in 1952, a federally funded pension for those over 70. Before that time, the only options were means-tested pensions in the spirit of the Old Poor Law. Another enabling constitutional amendment yielded the Canada Pension Plan and Quebec Pension Plan in 1966, followed a year later by a supplemental means-tested pension.

Thus did all four countries converge on a first-pillar system relying mainly on general taxes, with progressive favoring of the elderly poor, with cost-of-living indexing, and with graduated options for early retirement with partial benefits. Yet within this general convergence, the United States gradually emerged as the most generous country of the four, especially in the twenty-first century. This extra pension generosity is evident in Table 14.2.

How and when did the United States end up paying a higher share of GDP in public pensions than did Canada, New Zealand, or Australia?

TABLE 14.2. *Indicators of social-spending effort and related outcomes: comparing the United States to three commonwealth countries, 2010–2018*

	USA	Can	NZ	Aus	The USA level was
			The elderly		
Public old-age exp %, 2015	7.1	4.7	4.9	5.3	above the other 3
Public old-age support, 2013	31.2	19.1	21.2	22.0	above the other 3
			Health		
Total health exp, US$/cap, 2011	8,508	4,522	3,182	3,800	above the other 3
Total health exp % GDP, 2017	17.1	10.6	9.2	9.2	above the other 3
Public health exp % GDP, 2014	8.0	7.1	7.4	6.4	above the other 3
Health % paid by gov't, 2013	48	70	80	68	behind the other 3
Health performance rank, 2017	11th	9th	5th	2nd	behind the other 3 (out of 11)
Life expectancy, 2015	78.8	81.7	81.7	82.5	behind the other 3
			Anti-poverty safety nets		
Family & labor aids % GDP, 2010	1.9	2.4	4.2	3.4	behind the other 3

TABLE 14.2. *(continued)*

	USA	Can	NZ	Aus	The USA level was
			Early childhood and education		
Paid leave available to mothers, full-time-pay equiv. weeks, 2016	0.0	27.4	7.7	7.6	behind the other 3
Pub exp parent leave/birth, 2013	0.0	10.4	2.0	4.6	behind the other 3
Pub pre-primary educ supp, 2016	3.3	0.0	4.4	2.3	behind NZ, ahead of Can, Aus
Pub educ exp %, 2010	5.4	5.4	7.0	5.6	behind NZ, Aus
Pub educ support ratio, 2010	17.6	21.2	21.9	18.9	behind the other 3
PISA average score, 2006–2018	492	525	513	510	behind the other 3

Sources and notes: Public expenditures on pension (the OECD's "old-age" plus "survivor" categories) as a percentage of GDP in 2010 are from the sources used in Tables 5.1 and 7.1 and Figure 12.2.

Public old-age support ratio, defined as (public old-age benefits per person over 65) as a percentage of (GDP per person 18–64): The sources used for Tables 5.1 and 7.1, plus United Nations (2015).

Health expenditures, in US$ per capita, in 2011: Davis et al. (2014).

Public and private health expenditures as a percentage of GDP in 2017: the World Bank database, https://data.worldbank.org/indicator/SH.XPD.CHEX.GD.ZS, accessed Apr. 22, 2020.

Public health expenditures as a percentage of GDP in 2014: the OECD's social expenditures (SOCX) series. The percentage for the United States refers to the year 2013.

Percentage of health care financed by government and social security, 2013: OECD (2015, Table 9.8).

Health performance, overall rankings for 2014–2016: Schneider et al. (2017). See Table 7.3 for further detail.

Life expectancy from birth, as of 2015: stats.oecd.org, via OECD iLibrary.

Anti-poverty safety nets, 2010: The source is the OECD's SOCX database. Measured here are public social spending in the family and labor-market categories.

Paid leave available to mothers, measured in full-time-pay equivalent weeks, 2016: www.oecd.org/els/family/database.htm#public_policy, accessed June 7, 2018.

Publicly funded parental leave per child born in 2013, in thousands of PPP dollars. The given dollar figures were $10,397.60 for Canada, $1,969.37 for New Zealand, and $4,591.23 for Australia. The source is www.oecd.org/els/family/database.htm#public_policy, accessed June 7, 2018.

Publicly funded (pre-primary education support per pupil), as a percentage of (GDP per person 18–64), in 2016: UNESCO's uis database.

Public education expenditures as a percentage of GDP, 2010: The sources cited for Tables 5.1 and 7.1.

Public education (expenditures per child 5–19) as a percentage of (GDP per person 18–64), 2010: See the sources cited for Tables 5.1 and 7.1.

National average PISA score for reading, math, and science, 15-year-old test-takers 2006–2018: OECD, PISA, as cited in Table 5.2.

From 1960 through 1990, the United States and New Zealand advanced together, with more generous pensions than Australia and Canada, as was implied by the trends shown in Chapter 12 (Figure 12.2). In the 1990s, the ranks re-shuffled a bit, with New Zealand slashing its pension generosity after the 1991 budget, while Australia's many tweaks ended up delivering more to pensioners. In the early twenty-first century, or more precisely since 1998, American public pensions continued to creep up as a share of GDP, whereas Canada, New Zealand, and Australia held steady.[23] What happened was not any revolutionary legislation in favor of US pensioners. Instead, the usual political tug-of-war negotiated annual benefits that have kept pace with the advance of wages and salaries.[24] As emphasized in Chapter 12, merely letting annual pension benefits keep pace with average labor earnings, or with GDP per capita, asks for trouble as long as the elderly share of the population keeps rising. Keeping a stable pension support level in an aging population means allowing the share of GDP taken by pensions to continue rising.

What form should the adjustment of US pensions take to check the upward march in the share of GDP channeled into pension spending? The other three countries managed to use similar institutions – direct year-by-year negotiations in the legislature, with pay-as-you-go funding – to produce pension benefits that (rightly) rose more slowly than average pay. Yet the year-by-year approach would involve stirring more tensions in the divided American setting.

Another option would be a very slow and long-term commitment to a formula that holds down, without absolutely cutting, annual pension benefits. America already achieved that once, as we have seen: The 1983 agreement to raise the age requirement for full Social Security benefits until 2027, when it settles at 67 years for those born in 1960 or later. So one possibility is to do it again. Yet the pace would probably have to accelerate, given the forecasted rise in the ratio of (over-65 population)/(18–64 population) from 23.7 percent in 2015 all the way up to 39.7 percent in 2050. Trying to keep up with this rise by explicitly legislating that people must work much later to earn full benefits could be unpopular, with pushback in the form "they're at it again, messing with my retirement plans."

Less daunting would be the spirit of "everybody is adjusting slowly, fairly, and together" with formulaic NDC indexing. That requires politically selling a long-run pre-commitment to keep the amount of *total* pension benefits paid to each age cohort over all its years of old age in pace with the peak levels of GDP reached by the economy. Having the average individual's total pension payments fixed in proportion to GDP means, again, accepting a growth of *annual* pension benefits that is slower than the advance of average pay – a gentler outcome for the United States than for Japan, which is aging faster.

Here we should recall why the US Social Security system, like Japan's pension system, needs such indexing. It is not just for financial solvency. More importantly, the annual rate of old-age support needs to be held in check to allow better investment in the young, the American policy shortcoming with which we will conclude.

For their part, Canada, New Zealand, and Australia could also benefit from the same kind of indexing. Such a pre-commitment could relieve legislators of the task of sparring over each year's policies. Even if it is not raining in these three countries, while the rain falls a bit in the United States, they could benefit from fixing their roofs.

CATCHING UP IN HEALTH INSURANCE, AND HEALTH PRICE CONTROLS. The United States can learn health lessons from Canada, New Zealand, and Australia, and not just from Britain and Europe. The comparison with Canada, New Zealand, and Australia reveals something else that the comparisons with Europe alone cannot. Because our four countries are so similar in most respects, looking to Ottawa, Wellington, and Canberra from Washington shows the *more likely* shape that any health-care improvement in Washington would have to take.

What are those illuminating similarities? A key similarity is that none of the four countries relies on nationalized government-provided care, a "socialized" national health service. Among the world's non-communist countries, history has made that something very British. Having set off on that path in the 1940s, Britain will rightly stick with its workable and much-loved National Health Service, both in its English–Welsh version and its separate Scottish version. None of our four countries is likely to do so, however.

All of these four countries, and indeed all of the world's better-ranked systems, retain an option to "top up" one's public health insurance with supplementary private insurance. In response, a large share of health insurance is purchased privately in each country, albeit under legislated rules. Even in the United Kingdom, with its government-provided National Health, about 10 percent of health expenditures were covered by private health insurance as of 2013.

Two key features of successful public health insurance regimes are only recent, tentative, partial, and controversial, in America. Yet they are likely to become permanent, given that they have come to stay in each of the other three countries. The two keys are

- community rating, or its equivalent; and especially
- government control over health-care prices.

The four national insurance systems now share some form of *community rating*, which requires that health insurance providers must charge the same price (premium) to every covered person, regardless of their individual health status. Thus, in a community-rated insurance market, the insurer calculates its premiums by looking at the risk factors of the whole market population, and not those of any one individual. A closely related requirement is "guaranteed issue" meaning that all applicants must be accepted if they pay, regardless of their prior health condition, called "pre-existing conditions" in the American debate.[25]

The United States was the last of the four countries to climb aboard. Community rating and guaranteed issue did not arrive in Washington DC until the Affordable Care Act of 2010, passed when the Democrats held a majority in both houses of Congress. It remains a popular feature of that act, a point conceded by some Republicans.[26] Much earlier, Australia explicitly wrote community rating principles into its landmark health insurance legislation of 1875 and 1984. In a country where citizenship guarantees public health insurance, such as in New Zealand (more or less) since 1938 or in Canada since 1966, the issue does not loom so large, even though private companies still can, and do, use pre-existing conditions as a reason to deny somebody coverage for private supplemental insurance. Still, for coverage and premiums under the dominant public funding, Canada and New Zealand have implicitly leveled the playing field with community rating or its equivalent.

The second feature on which Washington still struggles to catch up with Ottawa, Wellington, and Canberra has been summarized bluntly: "It's the prices, stupid."[27]

To see that prices must play a central role in America's health-care deficiencies, let us contrast the health-related indicators in the middle of Table 14.2. The first indicator, total health expenditures per capita, quantifies what we have heard so often: Health care costs something like twice as much in the United States as in the other three countries, and the second indicator shows the same contrast in shares of GDP. The extra cost of American health care is paid for privately more than it is through taxation. American taxpayers pick up only about half the tab (48 percent), versus most of it in other advanced countries. If the Americans were paying so much more because they were getting more quality, that fact would have shown up in public appreciation and in health outcomes. Yet neither positive result has happened, as the last two health-related rows in Table 14.2 remind us. Public opinion, separately in each country, has rated the performance of the national health-care system (public plus private) lower in the United States than in any of the other eleven countries that are surveyed repeatedly over the years. The rankings of Australia (2nd) and New Zealand (5th) are much better, and Canada is rated only slightly better (9th). As we saw back in Chapter 9, the overall ratings differed for specific reasons. The quality of American health, as actually delivered, was rated about as highly as in the other three countries. Yet patients and doctors complain more about the affordability (price), efficiency, and equity of health care in North America than elsewhere. So the United States spends much more on its health care, and dislikes how it is allocated. The public's ratings are backed up, indirectly, by the well-known survival results: for all that extra health spending, Americans die younger.

Studies that directly compare the prices of health care across countries have also found that American care is higher-priced, and less efficient in the administrative sense. Pharmaceutical prices are the most famous example. For at least fifty years now, drug prices have been found to be much higher in the United States than elsewhere, even for the exact same product from the same US-based manufacturer.[28] While the task of summarizing price differences over the whole industry is complicated by the heterogeneity of pharmaceutical products and by authors' differing incentives to blame or defend the industry, the same finding consistently stands out above any methodological fog.

America's prices have also come out higher for other health-care sectors. So it was, for example, when scholars decomposed the differences between German and American per capita health-care spending back in 1990. Three-quarters of the (66 percent) excess in American costs were explained by input prices alone, and the remaining quarter was dominated by the higher administrative costs. In 2002, hospital and physician spending per capita was higher (by 84 percent) in the United States than in Canada mainly due to provider prices and administrative costs, and only slightly due to extra procedures in hospitals.[29]

Behind these higher prices lies the central fact that extraordinary market power pervades America's private health-care sector. Consumers are not sovereign, and sellers hide their high pricing by exploiting their informational advantages and their political lobbying power. While the whole sector can be called "transparency challenged," American hospitals are particularly opaque about prices. Paul Starr has underlined the point aptly with an analogy:

> Imagine if buying gas for your car worked like hospital care [in America]. If it did, when you pulled into a gas station, no prices would be posted. What you'd pay would depend on your car insurance, but no one could tell you what those prices or the total cost would be. It would depend on what several different mechanics – not all of whom would necessarily be "in-network" – determined your car needed. The bill would be incomprehensible, and most of it would be paid by your employer's plan. Eventually, the full cost would come out of the wages you and your fellow employees were paid, although you wouldn't be able to do anything about it. One thing we could say for sure: Gas prices would be very high under this system.[30]

The need for government regulation of health-sector pricing is globally recognized, although least so in the United States. Thus, our three comparison countries, like other advanced countries, have restrained prices more successfully, and this fact seems central to the American combination of high expenditure costs with poor results.

How do government controls come about? In all three of the federal countries – Australia, Canada, and even the United States – local governments moved first, before the national government. Price controls accompanied public financing of health insurance at the state/provincial level, before the national government set up its own system. (New Zealand went in the opposite direction, historically initiating national health care through social security in 1938, but later decentralizing partially in favor of district health boards.)

Yet the transmission from local initiatives to national policy did not proceed as far in the United States as it did in, say, Canada. The lead in Canada was taken back in 1945 by Tommy Douglas and Saskatchewan. Their hospital insurance plan covered every Saskatchewan resident. Other provinces sought the same protections. By 1961, with the federal government having agreed to share the insurance costs, all ten provinces had already provided hospital insurance. The system was increasingly federalized thereafter.

Similar sub-national leadership emerged in the United States, but later and without any graduation to the federal level thus far. Massachusetts took the lead, under prodding from Senator Ted Kennedy and with successful implementation under Governor Mitt Romney in 2006. The Massachusetts public health insurance system has succeeded and survived. Yet the lead was not so easily followed by others as it was in Canada. In 2011, Vermont tried to mount single-payer insurance system called Green Mountain Care, but it was defeated. Even California, a rich and often progressive state with recent budget surpluses and big-state clout in negotiating prices, has not taken up the public insurance baton. Rather, its Covered California merely facilitates exchanges of private insurance under the federal Affordable Care Act of 2010. At the federal level, the closest that Washington has come to emulating Canada's universal public health insurance was its passage of that Affordable Care Act itself, launched by the Obama Administration but subsequently sabotaged by the Trump Administration and conservative Justices on the Supreme Court. The Affordable Care Act has cut the share of uninsured American adults from about 20 percent to about 10 percent, and retains that popular ban on denial of insurance due to pre-existing conditions.

How could the United States emulate the successes of our three comparison countries in controlling prices while extending coverage? Its peculiarly troubled history suggests that any reform proposal must not only appeal to voters but also placate some of the following six lobbying powers in the halls of power: private health insurance companies, the nurses' associations, general physicians, specialist physicians, hospital associations, and the pharmaceutical industry. It would surely have to proceed step by step.

Two past victories of broadening federal health insurance and price controls have taken the form of packaging age-group-specific programs as good for everybody. The target-group coverage was accompanied by price controls, a coupling that could be extended. The first such success was the passage of Medicare for the elderly and Medicaid for the poor back in 1967. Both programs had broad enough appeal to gain majority votes, even though some conservatives states were particularly resistant to Medicaid. The second partial success came after the Clintons' overly ambitious and elaborate health plan was resoundingly defeated in 1994. In 1997, today's Children's Health Insurance Program (CHIP), then known as the State Children's Health Insurance Program (SCHIP), was passed into law as part of the Balanced Budget Act. It covers a broad range of families in the lower part of the income distribution. Every state participates. Of the fifty states, all but four cover families with incomes up to 200 percent of the federal poverty line. It was renewed to 2022 by the Bipartisan Budget Act of 2018. With CHIP, as with the larger Medicare, federal rules are in place that govern pricing.

These partial advances in group coverage have brought some limited success in controlling prices. The main price discipline in place is Medicare's control over the prices charged within its own program and its private top-up insurance program, Medicare Advantage (alias Medicare Part C). Is there an extension of coverage to another group that could further extend the government's ability to restrain prices?

One politically informed strategy is Paul Starr's (2018a, 2018b). The underlying idea here is to launch a voter-popular campaign, while placating part of the potential opposition through the prospect that the government's cost-controlling power will be enhanced. The vote winner, in his view, is the idea of extending Medicare's coverage to include the 50–64 age group. The plan could be packaged as delivering to the middle-age group some additional insurance that they have already been earning through their Medicare paycheck deductions. Granted, appealing to the 50–64 age group lacks the feature of investing in the young, a central prescription of this book. Still, the successful extension of CHIP for lower-income children would, for some time, keep some inter-generational balance even if Starr's plan were implemented. The expansion of Medicare would also be accompanied by an expansion of Medicare Advantage, that supplemental private-insurance partner program. For the private insurance industry, such an expansion could mean lower costs and more insurance business.

In terms of the lessons from the three other countries' experience, the Midlife Medicare expansion would emulate features they have put into practice: mixing a basic public insurance platform with private insurance top-ups, and cost-cutting power wielded by government.

ENDING AMERICA'S WAR ON THE POOR. America has withheld support from the poor much more insistently than have Canada, New Zealand, and Australia, three other countries that are less generous than the average high-income OECD country. So says the share of GDP spent on "welfare," or family assistance and such labor-market assistance as unemployment compensation. This share is another one of the indicators with which Table 14.2 compares recent snapshots of the United States and the corresponding pictures for the three comparison countries. Not only is less spent, but it is stretched across a poverty population that is a larger share of the total population in the United States than in any other rich OECD country.

The United States, in its anti-poverty spending and tax breaks since the mid-1990s, has further discriminated against the very poorest and in favor of the working slightly-poor and near-poor. Thus even though Canada, New Zealand, and Australia are also relatively low spenders by OECD standards, they deliver considerably more to the poorest than does the United States. Since the expansion of the Earned Income Tax Credit

(EITC) in 1993 and Clinton's "end of welfare as we know it" reform (PRWORA) of 1996, America has gone to one extreme in a centuries-old debate. The 1996 debate in America pushed us back to Europe's twelfth-century debate, as repeated in Britain's debate of the 1830s. Like many of those church scholastics in the twelfth century (Chapter 3), American policy has rejected giving aid to those "lusty," and "sturdy" young adults who should be told to support themselves. The classic "welfare" program giving cash aid on the basis of poverty and having children – called Aid for Dependent Children before 1996 and Temporary Assistance to Needy Families since then – has faded away. The main forms of aid to the poor are now the EITC work subsidy, Medicaid, and Food Stamps.[31]

Aside from its turning away from humanitarian concern for the poor, how has American policy toward them affected economic stability and economic growth?

First, the effect on economic stability. Safety-net spending is supposed to act as an "automatic stabilizer" of the economy, offsetting negative demand shocks with some positive extra spending, as we were reminded in Chapter 8. American welfare policy did offer some limited cushioning in the Great Recession of 2008–2009. The Great Recession of 2008–2009 would have been a bit deeper, had not the food stamp program (SNAP) automatically buoyed up food demand.[32]

In the collapse of 2020, however, America's federal safety nets were not at all automatic in their stabilizing effect. Even the food-stamp aid that had stabilized in 2008–2009 had been pulled back. In December 2019, the American president and some state governors unplugged part of this automatic stabilizer by denying even food stamps to impoverished childless adults. The loss of food stamp options left them totally exposed to the job-market collapse of 2020, without a reliable food source. Nor could those who had suddenly lost their jobs, or their small-business revenues, count on any other reliable aid, of the sort automatically supplied by government policies in Canada, New Zealand, or Australia. At first, aid was denied them when the economy shut down in March. Then, as we know, federal emergency aid gushed forth between April and July, in the Families First Coronavirus Act and the Coronavirus Aid, Relief, and Economic Security (CARES) Act. Yet even the relief paid out in those three months left many in need. The political over-emphasis on aiding only those who kept their jobs – those who satisfied "workfare" requirements and received Earned Income Tax Credits – was poorly suited to a crisis in which incomes dropped most for those who were either laid off or forced to quit in order to take care of children when schools closed. After late July, America's poor and its owners of small businesses were helped even less, for reasons unrelated to their own behavior. The White House and the Republican Senate majority declined to continue the levels of aid offered in April–July, again slowing down the recovery.[33] In the short run, then, US policy failed to stabilize because so few safety nets were kept firmly in place.

The effects of safety nets on long-run economic growth are controversial and hard to research. Still, long-run results are coming in, mainly for safety-net policies affecting children. What makes this possible are long-run data linkages for individuals. Such linkages have been especially available in countries with good perennial records on individuals, such as Sweden, Norway, and the Netherlands. Now, however, such linkages are allowing us to track distant adult outcomes for American children, some of whom were exposed to safety-net programs when growing up. Since children make up one third of the American poverty population, what happens to them should loom large in any debate over safety-net spending.

Economists are now able to discern the long-run effects on children of safety-net programs that are fifty years old or older. One such program in the United States is the food stamp program, which dates back to a pilot program launched by President Kennedy when he first took office in 1961. From then through 1974, when food stamp was mandated for all fifty states, food stamps "rolled out" at different times in different counties across America. How would a low-income parent's receiving food stamps have affected their children's wellbeing as adults fifty years later? Let us follow a particular study of the long-run effects of food stamps, a type of study that should soon be available for other safety-net programs as well. Martha Bailey and her co-authors (2020) have blazed a trail worth following.[34]

Bailey and co-authors are now able to trace 17.5 million Americans living in the 2000–2013 era back to their births, or conceptions, thanks to census-type data on their dates and places of birth. Their adult "wellbeing" in 2000–2013 is captured by several outcomes for each individual: the level of schooling attained, whether they are working, their earnings level, criminal record, personal health, survival to year 2012, home ownership, rental value of their home, and indicators of the quality of their neighborhood. The individuals are linked to their places of birth, by county and year, and even month for some tests. The sample of places for initial "exposure to" food stamp availability covers all counties in the contiguous forty-eight states, 1950 through 1980, distinguishing whether or not the food stamp program had already been rolled out. The phrase "exposure to" is key here. For adults alive in the 2000–2013 era, neither they nor we can observe directly whether their household received food stamps back to the time of conception (they were not interviewed *in utero* or in infancy, for a start). Nonetheless, one can trace the shares of households that did receive food stamps in their birth counties back then, and use those shares to infer the likely effects on the share whose parents actually did receive stamps.

The giant sample finds so many significantly positive effects on their adult wellbeing that the Food Stamp program since 1961 has clearly "paid for itself" in the long run, in the broad sense of raising each child's later adult income, quality of life, and life expectancy, while also improving social externalities. Intriguingly, even though the food stamp applies to all age groups, its positive effects stemmed mainly from exposure to food stamp availability in early childhood, and even between conception and birth.

Thus America's food stamp program has paid off as a long-run investment, not just as a short-run humanitarian act. As an implicit loan from society, America's food stamp program has more than repaid the loan at conventional interest rates.

Would the same be true of the other general safety-net programs that have been provided less generously in the United States than in the three comparison countries? There lies the research frontier on the benefits and costs of social assistance to the poor.

CRADLE TO CAREER. Finally, policies directly targeted at children, and new parents, are a related area in which the United States fell short of Canada, New Zealand, and Australia, and indeed fell short of all the

OECD member countries except Mexico and Turkey, as noted in Chapter 9. America's shortfall returns to the spotlight when Table 14.2 compares its support with the levels offered by the other three national governments. All four countries are below the median levels of support among OECD countries, both for paid parental leave and for public funding of pre-primary education. Yet even in this company, the United States offers the least. Washington offers no paid parental leave at all. A minority of US state governments do offer some, but these also fall short of the OECD average, as already noted in Chapter 9. Of the four governments, Canada offers the most support for paid leave, either in terms of the number of weeks covered or in terms of the actual leave payments. As for public funding of pre-primary education, on the other hand, Canada offers none at the federal level. For both types of policies, New Zealand and Australia are ahead of the United States.

There is no apparent economic reason for America's reluctance to support new parents and invest in their pre-school children. All the points from Chapter 9's review of research on such early-childhood policies around the world still apply. The rates of return on such social investments are high, even higher than the good returns on primary, secondary, and higher education. And even at those conventional education levels, Table 14.2 reminds us that the United States is generally behind in its expenditure efforts, and behind in the test-score results.

It should not be difficult to raise American investments in pre-school children, and their working parents, up to the moderate levels invested by the governments of Canada, New Zealand, and Australia. A little nudging should do the job. As for paid parental leave, the Democrats have been urging it for several years, albeit without the same priority as affordable health care. In 2018, even Ivanka Trump and Senator Marco Rubio (R-FL) proposed allowing people to pull forward money from Social Security to pay for family leave in exchange for deferring retirement benefits by a similar period later in life. Their proposing to take the money out of Social Security was, of course, a poison pill in the view of Democrats. Yet paid parental leave is clearly on the negotiating table in Washington.[35] Parental leave programs would cost the taxpayers so little that they could be amply covered by a small part of the emergency money that Washington pumped out to soften the coronavirus recession of 2020.

Why is the early-childhood roof still not fixed after so many years of both rain and sun? Given the obvious merits, and the massive job losses for mothers in the coronavirus slump of 2020, hopefully only a nudge will be needed to mobilize Washington at long last.

Acknowledgments

My thanks must begin with my debt to Michael Watson of Cambridge University Press, for his piloting of the book through the process and for his audience-savvy suggestions on early chapter drafts. He has made the later drafts more accessible for non-specialist readers than they would otherwise have been.

Thanks, too, to the global data presenters, whose numbers and institutional descriptions have proven indispensable for my coverage of developments since 1980, especially the research teams at the OECD, the World Bank, the Asian Development Bank, the Commitment to Equity (CEQ) Institute headed by Nora Lustig at Tulane, and Christian Aspalter's *Handbook* team.

For my fellow economic historians, the pre-1914 experience is updated in Chapters 3 and 4. Thanks to them for what they have written on social topics over these sixteen years. For innumerable connections with the larger body of thought in economic history, I bow to my economic history teammates at the University of California–Davis, which I have dubbed Team Aggie Clio, anchored by its faculty members Gregory Clark, Katherine Eriksson, Chris Meissner, Alan Olmstead, Santiago Pérez, and Alan Taylor. Their seminars and weekly coffee hours have helped to keep the thoughts stirring. The All-UC Group in Economic History was backed generously for many years by the University of California system, and (despite the All-UC name) by Caltech, Chapman University, Santa Clara University, and Stanford University.

Many individuals have helped me clarify my ideas and reduce my mistakes through our conversations, correspondence, and/or interactions at conferences and seminars since 2004. The occasions cannot be listed here. The helpful individuals were, alphabetically, Willem Adema, Guido Alfani, Gayle Allard, Leticia Arroyo Abad, Sir Tony Atkinson, Luis Bértola, Orsetta Causa, Latika Chaudhary, Chiara Del Bo, Mark Dincecco, J. C. Herbert Emery, Stanley Engerman, Sergio Espuelas, David Feeny, Price Fishback, Marc Fleurbaey, Ewout Frankema, Kyoji Fukao, Norman Gall, Irv Garfinkel, Sun Go, Margaret Grosh, Mikkel Hermansen, Alfonso Herranz-Loncán, Philip T. Hoffman, Herweg Immervoll, Robert Inklaar, Yuzuru Kumon, Kathy Lindert, Lin Lindert, Nora Lustig, Debin Ma, David Mitch, Chiaki Moriguchi, Casey Mulligan, Steven Nafziger, Larry Neal, Santiago Pérez, Giovanni Peri, Leandro Prados de la Escosura, Maarten Prak, James A. Robinson, Jean-Laurent Rosenthal, David Samuels, Pablo Sanguinetti, Joel Slemrod, Tim Smeeding, Eugene Smolensky, Kenneth Sokoloff, Masanori Takashima, Daniel Waldenström, Barry Weingast, Jeffrey Williamson, Larry Willmore, Noam Yuchtman, and Eric Zolt.

A garden of downloadable supporting data will grow on my UC Davis home page. For pre-1914 historical data more generally, remember too to revisit the Global Price and Income History website, at http://gpih.ucdavis.edu.

Notes

CHAPTER 1: ENDURING ISSUES

1. While I emphasize what is new within this century, those who have read through my *Growing Public* (Cambridge University Press, 2004) will detect some overlaps in topic and findings between the two books. True enough. Yet no chapters, and only three paragraphs, have been reproduced from it. The topical emphasis has changed, and the evidence comes mostly from sources not available when *Growing Public* was written.
2. The instructive new history can only be nearly global, and not global, because information on social spending is still incomplete and/or untrustworthy for many countries. Nonetheless, there is more than enough new material to offer global lessons.

   To summarize regional patterns, the book sometime bends geography to fit history or current behavior. Thus at times not only France and Turkey, but even Jordan and Portugal are pushed into the "Mediterranean," on behavioral grounds. Finland and Greece are kept out of "Eastern Europe," a region reserved for countries that had been in the Soviet Bloc before 1991. Croatia is viewed as Eastern European, rather than Mediterranean (as I would have done with Montenegro and Albania, had data permitted).
3. These terms are aptly chosen, and sketched theoretically, by Acemoglu, Robinson, and Verdier (2017).
4. Lindert (2004, vol. I, p. 4).

CHAPTER 2: FINDINGS AND LESSONS

1. This formulation is phrased as if "old age" and "retirement" were the same set of years. The reality of partial and full retirements is more complex, of course. Chapters 12 and 13 discuss the implications of my using old-age life spans in place of retirement spans, and average benefits per year of old age in place of benefits per retiree.
2. This is not the only recent book to note that social assistance needs to shift its attention toward children, especially those in poor households. In particular, see Madrick (2019).

CHAPTER 3: WHY POOR RELIEF ARRIVED SO LATE

1. See Olson (1982); Mokyr (1992, 2000); and Acemoglu and Robinson (2012).
2. On spontaneous early agricultural cooperatives, see Kimball (1988). On guilds and related societies, see Richardson (2005) and Van Leeuwen (2012).
3. Tierney (1959); Michielse (1990).
4. Tierney (1959, p. 367).
5. Even earlier, there were a few cities of Northwest Europe that had used small amounts of tax money to fund poor relief. One example was Nuremburg in the 1430s, which devoted 0.9 percent of its municipals expenditures to poor relief (North 2012, p. 147).
6. See Van Leeuwen (2016, pp. 181–193).
7. The 1760 poor relief percentage for the western Netherlands in Table 3.1's 1760 benchmark might have continued until 1795, to judge from the absolute relief expenditures in Amsterdam (Van Leeuwen 2016, pp. 182–184), after which it plummeted under French rule, until stabilizing after 1815. Yet even from 1770 on, the relief shifted from the outdoor aid toward the harsher workhouse regime (De Vries and Van der Woude 1997, pp. 663–664). Using expenditure data from De Vries and Van der Woude and rough estimates of national income, I have elsewhere estimated that by around 1790, relief in the Netherlands amounted to something between 1.46 percent and 1.93 percent of national income (Lindert 1998, p. 106).
8. On their methods of raising revenue and disbursing aid in the eighteenth and early nineteenth centuries, see McCants (1997); Van Leeuwen (2000); and again De Vries and Van der Woude (1997); Van Leeuwen (2016); and Van Bavel and Rijpma (2016).

   An illustration of the mixing of religious and governmental revenue sources is offered for the five top relief institutions of Amsterdam in 1829–1854 (Van Leeuwen 2000, p. 92). The municipal subsidy accounted for 23 percent of all revenue. Yet in the western Netherlands, tax burdens may have been larger (Van Leeuwen 2000, p. 96). The shift toward local taxation was more explicit in the rural part of eighteenth-century Flanders studied in depth by Thijs Lambrecht and Anne Winter (2018). They emphasize that the shift toward taxation was not confined to England, but instead occurred wherever similar socio-economic conditions dictated.
9. Woolf (1986); Lindert (2004, vol. I, pp. 30–45); and Lindert (2014).
10. For a time-series on poor relief in Amsterdam, 1687–1850, see Van Leeuwen (2016, p. 183).
11. As cited by Sidney Webb (1926, p. 121).
12. As translated in Salter (1926, pp. 123–124).
13. Salter (1926, p. 125).
14. For in-depth comparisons of these national fiscal histories and others, see Bonney (1995, 1999); Yun-Casalilla, O'Brien, and Comín (2012); and Dincecco (2011 and 2017).
15. Appendix Tables A.1 and A.2 give the budgetary detail for Tokugawa Japan in 1730 and Mughal India in 1595.

16. Körner (1995, pp. 415–416); Flora and Albers (1983, vol. I, ch. 8); the data sets underlying Dincecco (2011) and, for the Netherlands, Fritschy, 't Hart, and Horlings (2012, p. 47). For Spain, we lack comparable early breakdowns of government expenditure, but Dincecco (2011) shows that total central government revenues were relatively low as a share of GDP, and the narrative histories suggest little developmental investment. Later, after 1870, Italy also achieved higher non-military and non-administrative shares of total central government spending, though the total was still low as a share of GDP.
17. The phrase comes from an essay by Kenneth Schultz and Barry Weingast (1998). The same idea underlies two other prominent generalizations from history: McGuire and Olson's (1996) contrast between the damage done by rapacious roving bandits versus the progress fostered by a secure stationary bandit, and the contrast between extractive and inclusive polities summarized in the tour de force by Daron Acemoglu and James Robinson (2012).
18. In addition to North and Weingast (1988), see DeLong and Shleifer (1993); Hoffman and Norberg (1994); Schultz and Weingast (1998); Dincecco (2011, 2017); Stasavage (2011, 2016); Acemoglu and Robinson (2012); and Bologna Pavlik and Young (2018).
19. For a more detailed statement of the interpretation of the Old Poor Law offered here, with additional evidence, see Boyer (1990, 2018) and Lindert (2004, vol. I, pp. 67–73).
20. The fuller name of the 1834 Poor Law Reform adopted in the same year was the Act for the Amendment and Better Administration of the Laws relating to the Poor in England and Wales (4 & 5 Will. 4 c. 76). It purported to be based on the 1834 Poor Law Report, or *Report from His Majesty's Commissioners for Inquiring into the Administration and Practical Operation of the Poor Laws.*
21. For suggestive applications of the spread-of-voice argument in other countries and other continents, see Lindert (2003) and Lindert (2004, vol. I, pp. 71–86).
22. The extension of the franchise to persons in lower-income ranks was not an exogenous event, of course, and competing theories have offered explanations of it. See, in particular, Acemoglu and Robinson (2000, 2006); Lizzeri and Persico (2004); Ansell and Samuels (2014); and Stasavage (2016). Its economic effects, other than its effects on poor relief, have been explored as well, e.g. by Aidt, Dutta, and Loukoianova (2006); by Aidt and Jensen (2009, 2013); and by Aidt, Winer, and Zhang (2020). This latest study finds no neat fit of the timing of the franchise extensions to the timing of changes in fiscal redistribution.
23. Brundage (1978); Mandler (1987, 1990); Brundage and Eastwood (1990); Boyer (1990, pp. 183–204); and Cody (2000, p. 147).
24. Poor Law Report, p. 197, as cited in Henriques (1967, p. 109).
25. Henriques (1967); Davison (1982); Cody (2000); Levine-Clark (2000); and Zlotnick (2006).
26. Digby (1975); Boyer (2018).
27. Boyer (2018, p. 85). For other evidence on the higher cost of workhouse relief in England, see MacKinnon (1987); Lindert (2004, vol. I, pp. 52–55); and Kiniria (2019, pp. 76–137, 197–209). Similarly, for Amsterdam, Van Leeuwen (2016, p. 193) reports that the cost of indoor relief far exceeded the typical cost of supporting the same persons in their homes.

28. Boyer (2018, pp. 86–92) and Figure 3.1 here.
29. See the regression evidence for 1880–1930 in Lindert (2004, vol. I, ch. 3, and vol. II, ch. 14). In those regressions, poor relief was represented by "welfare and unemployment" spending as a share of national income. Other variables were controlled for, as were heteroskedasticity, censoring of the dependent variable at zero, and the possible endogeneity of GDP per capita. These econometric results carry important caveats, however: they are not backed up with state-of-the-art tests for exclusion restriction or for the exogeneity or power of the first-stage instruments.
30. See, in particular, Peter Baldwin's (1990) interpretation of the pension policy histories of Britain, Denmark, France, Germany, and Sweden, 1875–1975, and the more general comparative historical survey by Flora and Heidenheimer (1981).
31. See Boyer (2018, pp. 164–166, 183–216).
32. As quoted first by Winston Churchill, and then in Boyer (2018, p. 208). Emphasis in the original.

CHAPTER 4: THE DAWN OF MASS SCHOOLING BEFORE 1914

1. This rough measure for England and Wales is reckoned from the 1850 number for the United Kingdom, which was only 0.07 percent. At that time, the rate for England and Wales would have been slightly higher.
2. De Vries and Van der Woude 1997, pp. 314–318. On the larger explanatory power of book production/sales as a development indicator, see Baten and Van Zanden (2008) and Buringh and Van Zanden (2009). For rough sketches of how literacy compared across the countries of Europe before 1800, see Cipolla (1969, esp. pp. 115–116); Graff (1987); and Allen (2003, appendix). The same early modern patterns apply to measures of numeracy as to literacy. On the paths that different countries followed to numeracy in this era, see A'Hearn, Baten, and Crayen (2009).
3. As quoted in Cipolla (1969, p. 47) and Akçomak, Webbink, and Terl Weel (2013, p. 1).
4. Broadberry et al. 2015, pp. 345–364. Note that the emphasis here is on the rise of commerce and the professions, not on the Industrial Revolution. On the literacy rates for different occupations in Norwich 1530–1730, see Cressy (1977). The literature finds little, or even negative, stimulus to literacy from Britain's rise of textiles and mining. For nineteenth-century Prussia, econometric estimates by Becker, Hornung, and Woessmann (2011) confirm the negative association of education with employment in textiles, yet find a positive relationship for other industrial sectors.
5. An econometric literature has now estimated external benefits from education in the late twentieth century. On the civic participation effects of schooling, see Dee (2004) and Milligan, Moretti, and Oreopoulos (2004). On its crime prevention effect, see Lochner and Moretti (2004). Other studies use production-function econometrics to capture the productivity effects of spillovers that leave no specific imprint (e.g. Moretti 2004, in this case referring to higher education). See also the survey by McMahon (2004). The natural-experiment study by Acemoglu and Angrist (2000)

emphasized the low statistical significance of externalities from the extra schooling triggered by compulsory schooling laws. Yet the authors acknowledge that their point estimates still include enough externalities to justify noticeable subsidies, and that their experiment was limited to externalities from secondary education alone.

6. See Smith (1776, pp. 130–134, 420–434, 443). The passage quoted is from p. 443.
7. https://en.wikisource.org/wiki/A_letter_to_Samuel_Whitbread,_Esq._M.P._on_his_proposed_Bill_for_the_Amendment_of_the_Poor_Laws; Source: The Bancroft Library, University of California, Berkeley. Then, in a thought anticipating Milton Friedman's school-voucher proposal, Malthus recommending that "if each child paid a fixed sum (of course very low, and discharged by the rates in the case of orphans and parish poor), the schoolmaster would then have a stronger interest to increase the number of his pupils." A difference is that Malthus called for means-tested targeting, unlike the universality of Friedman's proposal regarding primary education.
8. Butts (1978, pp. 26–28). Virginia did not adopt a statewide school system until 1870, in the Reconstruction era (Kaestle 1983, pp. 8–9 and 198–199). Not all of the American founding fathers shared Jefferson's espousal of tax-based primary schooling. Benjamin Franklin favored subsidies for universities, but was not interested in subsidized education for the poor (Alexander 1980, p. 143).
9. The estimates based on David Mitch's data fall within the range of possible private and social rates of return he staked out (Mitch 1982, 1983–1984, 1992). Professor Mitch suggests that my estimate based on Jason Long's work may have been too pessimistic in assuming that it would take six years of primary school to achieve the kind of wage gains estimated by Long. I am grateful to him for his advice on these estimates.
10. Lindert (2009), Table 5, Row (h) reports the same rates of return as for 1840, but with the adult earnings increments cut in half as if females had zero earnings. This lowers the rates of economic return on schooling, though not by half the rate itself. The result is still a double-digit rate of return – either private or social or fiscal – well above the 4.4 percent rate at which Her Majesty's government could have borrowed.
11. Massie (1761).
12. We cannot extend the same simple indictment back before the late seventeenth century, however. The consol rate was well above 5 percent under the Stuarts and the House of Orange, largely because the throne could (and did) default on its debts before 1688. See Homer and Sylla (1991, chs. 8–9); Clark (1996); Dincecco (2011). Britain and other emerging states were not yet secure enough to take a more modern long-run view of the economics of education subsidies.
13. For a sampling of early modern reasons for rejecting education for the masses, see Kaestle (1976, 1983); Lindert (2004, vol. I, p. 101); and De Mandeville as cited in Ravallion (2015).
14. Hansard, Parochial Schools Bill, HC Deb 13 June 1807, vol. 9 cc. 798–806. Previously cited in Lindert (2004, vol. I, p. 100).
15. For the actual shares of public primary-school spending in GDP, see the smaller number of observations in Lindert (2004, vol. II, Appendix tables C1, C2).

16. For a direct view of France's annual education expenditures in public schools since 1820, in its breakdown by sources of funds, see Carry (1999) and the (Carry-based) Figure 5.5 of Lindert (2004, vol. I, p. 111).
17. See the fuller accounting for German leadership in education in the early nineteenth century given in Lindert (2004, vol. I, pp. 115–122), which drew from the research of Schleunes (1989) and Nipperdey (1977, 1996). The updated econometric studies of the determinants of Prussian education by Becker and Woessmann (2009), and by Becker, Hornung, and Woessmann (2011) exploit the considerable variation within Prussia.
18. Moody (1978, p. 87) as cited in Aghion, Jaravel, Persson and Rouzet (2019). The latter article generalizes the positive effect of military embarrassment on education funding, drawing also on the experiences of Meiji Japan and other governments.
19. On the schooling link, see Engerman, Mariscal, and Sokoloff (2009). On the whole nexus from factor endowments and the inclusiveness of institutions to economic growth and inequality, partly through the supply of different levels of schooling, see Engerman and Sokoloff (2012).
20. For a fuller presentation of the arguments and evidence in this paragraph, see Go and Lindert (2010). On the impressive levels of early education in upper Canada, see Lewis and Urquhart (1999).
21. For a fuller discussion, and a numerical illustration of the possible links between decentralized government and tax support for schools, see Lindert (2004, vol. I, Table 5.4).
22. But not New Zealand, which lacked fiscal autonomy for local governments.
23. On the delayed Dutch and Belgian solutions to the question of funding for religious schools, see De Kwaasteniet (1990, pp. 13–23, 73–161). America followed a secular solution, initially guided by its constitutional separation of church and state, and later reinforced by most states' separate "Blaine Amendments" against tax funding for religious schools in the wake of the Civil War. France opted for secular public schools in the Jules Ferry Laic Laws of 1881 (Moody 1978; Grew and Harrigan 1991). Still, as Mara Squicciarini (2019) has shown, secularization and the development of economic skills was geographically uneven. Catholic teachers in many French localities retained an extra Catholic fervor that biased their teaching away from delivering economically relevant skills during the 1870–1914 period.

CHAPTER 5: PUBLIC EDUCATION SINCE 1914

1. For "today's" (c. 2017) shares of government and private ("household") education expenditures as percentages of GDP, see UNESCO's https://en.unesco.org/gem-report/node/6. For the corresponding shares of government and private expenditures back in the 1860s–1870s, see Lindert (2004, vol. I, pp. 116–117).
2. The fact that GDP per capita is higher in the United States than in most countries might still mean that American children received a greater economic value of tax-financed inputs than children in many other developed countries. Yet as soon as one tries to infer differences in

real inputs of education per child from monetary value comparisons at current prices, the statistical sky darkens. Historians need to launch comparative international research into many dimensions of real inputs per enrolled student or per child of school age for the dark years before about 1990. Two especially helpful indicators would be annual days of school attendance per enrollee, and the number of teachers per 100 children of school age, since 1850. Later in this chapter, we view these dimensions of relative quality for the United States alone, but the international comparisons have yet to be filled in.

3. Lindert (2004, vol. I, pp. 116–117).
4. OECD, *Education at a Glance* (2018, pp. 277–278).
5. Lee and Lee (2016); Chaudhary and Lindert (forthcoming).
6. Mexico's progress paralleled that of Brazil, without the slowdown Brazil experienced in the 1970s. Brazil and Mexico shared the same rapid advance since the 1990s partly because these two countries were both pioneers in conditional cash-transfer programs that paid poor mothers for their children's school attendance. Mexico's version was originally called *progresa*, and later *oportunidades*.
7. The "big time" part of this heading is taken from Chaudhary and Lindert (forthcoming), which in turn borrowed it from Lant Pritchett's (1997) much-cited "Divergence Big Time" article.
8. See King and Hill (1997, pp. 11–20), for example.
9. For the rest of this chapter, the emphasis is on pre-tertiary education, or "schooling."
10. For a listing of the types of IQ test utilized in this literature, see Trahan et al. (2014, pp. 1345–1346).
11. In addition to the works of Flynn cited above, see the summary analyses of Neisser (1998), Trahan et al. (2014) and Pietschnig and Voracek (2015). These studies differ over whether there have been any recent decelerations in the trend toward higher IQ. Trahan et al. (2014) say there has not ever been a deceleration in the rate of IQ gain for any of the countries supplying the relevant data, except for a deceleration around 1982 for historically high-scoring Norway and Denmark (Trahan et al. 2014, p. 1350). Yet Pietschnig and Voracek (2015) say there is a general deceleration over a similar era.
12. Lynn and Vanhanen (2002) have courageously tried to compare IQ averages for over a hundred countries around the world at the turn of the millennium. Yet their analysis rests on too high a ratio of theoretical assumptions to real-world data to be applied here.
13. Gray (2013); Goldin (2001, pp. 273–275).
14. See Flynn (2012, ch. 2 and p. 136).
15. Pietschnig and Voracek (2015, p. 290).
16. See Hanushek and Woessmann (2015, chs. 2, 3, and 8, including the Appendix to ch. 3). Their Table 2.1 (pp. 18–19) lists the main international tests up through 2012.
17. In the 2015 round of PISA, the Chinese-majority world expanded to include an average of two more municipalities and two provinces (Beijing, Shanghai, Jiangsu, and Zhejiang), all of which fit the same pattern of economic boom and exceptionally high-school inputs. As a group, they are still not representative of the whole population of the People's Republic.

18. In particular, see Woessmann (2016) and Hanushek and Woessmann (2015), and their other works cited there. In addition, see my earlier treatment of these issues, citing Woessmann (2002) and Bishop (1996, 1997) among others, in Lindert (2004, vol. I, pp. 155–167).
19. On the longer history of school struggles, see De Kwaasteniet (1985, 1990); Ritzen, Van Dommelen, and De Vijlder (1997); and Hooker (2009, pp. 9–28). On school-choice institutions as of the early twenty-first century, see OECD (2017, pp. 18–19).
20. De Kwaasteniet (1990); Fowler (1992).
21. In Friedman's vision, the payment would be handed to parents as a "voucher" payment, for them to turn over to the school of their choice. While some countries have followed this voucher design, in others the government pays the schools directly, in amounts fixed on a per-student basis. By itself, this distinction between payment-forwarding mechanisms apparently matters less than other system differences. He was right to emphasize the distinction between having the government *run* the schools, and having the government just *pay for* them. While the latter institution gains support from the whole history of education, the case for having government actually own and operate the schools has never been so persuasive. Historically, government-run schools have had three sources: (1) the brain-washing motive preferred by autocracies, (2) the natural economics of having a small rural community start their first schools with local-government supervision, and (3) the desire of the teaching profession to be government-run for easier collective bargaining.
22. Even at the theoretical level, and even with zero costs of switching localities, there are several good reasons why parental choice may not be translated into schools that are effective in promoting students' learning and their later earning power. See Rothstein (2006).
23. SIMCE has been popular, yet opposition from teachers blocked the publication of its results between 1988 and 1995 (Delannoy 2000, pp. 8–9).
24. On the admissions incentives, see Pedigo (2011). This is not to say that the private schools captured the children of the very richest families. There was a legal limit on the amount of topping-up tuitions, so that an extremely rich 7 percent of families opted for unsubsidized high-tuition schools. Nonetheless, the subsidized private schools still sorted out a more affluent student body than those in the strictly public schools.
25. See González, Mizala, and Romaguera (2004); Hsieh and Urquiola (2006); Murnane et al. (2017); Epple, Romano and Urquiola (2017); and OECD (2017, pp. 21–22, and the earlier OECD studies cited there). The econometric study by Hsieh and Urquiola (2006) found no significant gains in learning efficiency, as measured by local communes' average test scores and grade completions between 1982 and 1996.
26. See Choi and Hwang (2017) and Sun and Sohn (2019). They did not test for effects on aggregate average test scores.
27. See Kuosmanen (2014).
28. Those fourteen voucher states at the end of 2016 were Arkansas, Florida, Georgia, Indiana, Louisiana, Maine, Maryland, Mississippi, North Carolina, Ohio, Oklahoma, Utah, Vermont, and Wisconsin.

29. Indiana Department of Education (2019), and its concurrent FAQs link at www.doe.in.gov.
30. Here I draw mainly on the work of Böhlmark and Lindahl (2012, 2015). For alternative summaries that also draw on Böhlmark and Lindahl, see Epple, Romano, and Urquiola (2017, pp. 15–16) and OECD (2017, p. 22).
31. Böhlmark and Lindahl (2012, p. 31) see no connection between the post-1992 rise of independent schools and the decline in Sweden's PISA scores up to 2012. They argue that neither the timing of the two developments nor its spatial distribution in Sweden reveals any link.
32. See, for example, Hanushek (2003) and Hanushek, Peterson, and Woessmann (2013, especially pp. 96–98).
33. Go and Lindert (2010, p. 5). See also Solmon (1975, pp. 94, 134) on rural versus urban attendance days per enrollee in the years 1880 and 1890. Indeed, they were not even expected to attend many days per year, as evidenced by the fact that schools were only open for fewer than half the numbers of days that schools have been open since World War II. On the low number of annual days attended per enrollee, and the days schools tended to be open, see also Goldin, in Carter et al. (2006, Series Bc94–96).
34. Goldin, in Carter et al. (2006, Series Bc12). This gain in teaching inputs, however, was even faster in Western Europe between 1870 and 1930, after which class sizes shrank at about the same rate on both sides of the Atlantic. So on this measure, the United States was not gaining in relative terms.
35. See Hanushek, Peterson, and Woessmann (2013, p. 93) and Hanushek and Woessman (2015, p. 186).
36. For example, Hanushek and Woessmann (2015, p. 23) clearly state: "Most of our estimation relies on an assumption that the average scores for a country tend to be relatively stable over time, and that the differences among countries are a good index of the relative skill differences of the work forces."
37. See Wolf (1977, pp. 34–41).
38. For a diagram of the rise, peak, and decline of US teenagers' test scores since 1940, see Lindert (2004, vol. I, p. 140). There the same timing is observed in the Scholastic Aptitude Tests (SAT), but the SAT is less reliable because the tests were taken only by some who were applying to colleges and universities.
39. See Bishop (1989) on movements in the Iowa scores, Lindert (2004, vol. I, pp. 132–162) on all scores, Hanushek and Woessmann (2015, p. 30) on the NAEP scores.
40. See Lindert (2004, vol. I, p. 128).
41. Eberts and Stone (1986) used previous econometric studies to argue that teachers' unions raised costs significantly, though with little or no effect on student achievement.

    Hoxby (1996) found that teachers' unions reduce student performance. See also Moe's (2011, pp. 275–311) critical recent history of teacher–union fights against the spread of charter schools and related pro-choice reforms. As we shall see in Chapter 7, negative consequences of teacher power were more serious in certain developing countries, most notably India and Mexico, than they were in the United States.

42. See Hoxby (2001, pp. 1210–1223) and Goldin (2001, pp. 286–287). See also Lindert (2004, vol. I, pp. 162–164) on the Californian experience.
43. See Psacharapoulos and Patrinos (2004); Montenegro and Patrinos (2014); Hanushek and Woessmann (2015); Woessmann (2016); Hendren and Sprung-Keyser (2019); and Chaudhary and Lindert (forthcoming).

CHAPTER 6: MORE, BUT DIFFERENT, SOCIAL SPENDING IN RICH COUNTRIES SINCE 1914

1. To add public education's share of GDP, go back to the numbers in Table 5.1 and add these to the shares given in the source link referenced in Figures 6.1 and 6.2.
2. See the updated chronology of the arrival of the Beveridge welfare state (though he disliked that term) in Boyer (2018, pp. 260–285).
3. See, for example, Easterly (1995).
4. Lindert (2003, 2004, vol. I, pp. 179–183, and vol. II, pp. 58–61 and 160–169) explored the effects of the spread of political voice on social spending, exploiting the availability of franchise (voting) data since the mid-nineteenth century for a couple dozen OECD countries. Ansell (2010) has found democratization effects on educational spending worldwide. Go and Lindert (2010) found that counties of the United States that had voting rights spread more broadly also funded primary education more generously. The narrative history by Acemoglu and Robinson (2012) featured the shift from extractive to inclusive political institutions over the centuries and around the world. Ansell and Samuels (2014, pp. 141–170) tested how well different measures of democratization explained social spending, with samples that expanded on those used by Lindert. Acemoglu et al. (2019, pp. 90–92) used a binary yes–no variable for democracy, with robustness checks using subtler measures for sub-samples. Alternative test techniques all confirmed the positive effects of democratization on the tax share of GDP, school enrollments, and child survival, all of them related indirectly to the social-spending budget. Their sample consisted of 184 countries over the years 1960–2010. Not all econometric tests yield direct confirmation of the role of democratization, however. Aidt and Jensen (2013) find the international experience of the nineteenth century yields fragile and ambiguous effects on total government spending.
5. Lott and Kenny (1999); Aidt and Dallal (2008); Kose, Kuka, and Shenhav (2018); and Cascio and Shenhav (2020).
6. Similarly, among OECD countries in 1880–1930, democratization did a poorer job than other variables in explaining international differences in social-spending budget shares, even though democratization was a powerful stimulus to raising those shares over time, from 1880 to 1930 (Lindert 2004, vol. II, pp. 58–61).
7. See Easterly and Levine (1997); Alesina, Baqir, and Easterly (1999); Alesina and Glaeser (2004); and Lindert (2004, vol. II, pp. 66–81). On the negative effect of caste barriers on school funding in British India, see Chaudhary (2009). See also Chapter 11's coverage of

Europe's refugee shocks on expressed attitudes toward the welfare state, drawing on Alesina, Miano, and Stantcheva (2018) and Alesina, Murard, and Rapoport (2019).

8. Lindert (2004, vol. I, pp. 183–186, vol. II, pp. 58–61 and 65–70).
9. See Deaton (2015), and the brief summary in Chaudhary and Lindert (forthcoming).
10. These two quotations are presented in Miller (2008, p. 1289) and in Moehling and Thomasson (2012, p. 76). Alas, the federal Sheppard–Towner Act was killed by 1929, due to the renewed opposition of the American Medical Association, combined with the Daughters of the American Revolution and anti-suffrage groups who feared that such socialized medicine led to Bolshevism. Its effects were shown to be temporary, with the state-level investments in maternal health continuing much as they would have without the federal help (Moehling and Thomasson 2012).
11. Lindert (2004, vol. I, pp. 183–186, and vol. II, pp. 58–61 and pp. 65–70).
12. OECD (2018b). All but four of those forty-two countries shared in that rise, the four exceptions were Denmark, Norway, South Africa, and USA.
13. See Lee and Mason (2011) and Lee (2016), and ntaccounts.org. The NTA team has not yet been able to put values on the inter-generational flows of time use within the household, though it plans to do so in the future. One of their supporting studies, estimating international time-flows in Thailand, is cited here, however.
14. As this comment about grandmothers implies, the net flow of time-giving between the adult generations within the home is probably away from, and not toward, the elderly. A recent study of household time-use in Thailand (Phananiramai 2011) has quantified the relevant time flows by a person's age and gender. An outstanding pattern is that females over 55 are strong net givers of time to others. Anecdotal reporting from China seems to show the same.

CHAPTER 7: IS THE REST OF THE WORLD FOLLOWING A DIFFERENT PATH?

1. Actually, the global diffusion of best-practice recipes has been happening, and will probably continue to do so. The international agencies, especially the World Bank and the regional Development Banks, export their "technical assistance" for the launching and the continual monitoring of social programs. For current best-practice recipes from the World Bank, see Lindert et al. (2019).
2. This modern speed-up in public education has also been noted, and measured with enrollment data, by Goldin (2001, p. 272) and by Clemens (2004).
3. For similar portrayals of countries' recent trade-offs between investing in the young and transferring to the elderly, see Miller (2011, pp. 176–179) and Arroyo Abad and Lindert (2017).
4. A curious pairing of regional outliers consists of Botswana and Serbia. Botswana has the most pro-education and pension-trimming performance of the global South. Serbia showed a similar commitment to education as Botswana, yet with far more

generous pensions per elderly person, unlike the other nations of formerly communist Eastern Europe.

5. Jordan cannot be discussed here for want of empirical detail. The behavior of Venezuela c. 2010 is examined in Chapter 14. Tunisia is not discussed here because of its respectable level of education support.
6. See Bugra and Keyder (2006) and Elveren and Agartan (2017). Elveren and Agartan have aptly labeled the Turkish approach to social spending as an "inegalitarian corporatist" variant on the "conservative corporatist" category in Esping-Andersen's classic (1990, 1999) taxonomy of welfare states.
7. See the 2016 data in OECD's *Society at a Glance*, 2019, http://dx.doi.org/10.1787/888933939218.
8. The Latin American bias was noted a quarter century ago. The World Bank (1994, p. 132), citing an internal 1993 working paper, had already documented the bias in social security coverage (though not yet the amounts transferred) in favor of higher-income quintiles in Bolivia, Brazil, Costa Rica, and Peru in the late 1980s.
9. See the Brazilian 1988 constitution's pension clauses in Constitute Project (2018).
10. Aspalter (2017, pp. 157–159), emphasis in the original.
11. Arnold and Jalles (2014).
12. For comparative overviews of recent experience, see Arroyo Abad and Lindert (2017), on six Latin American countries, Aspalter (2017), Lustig (2018), and the OECD annual *Pensions at a Glance.*
13. See Rimlinger (1971, pp. 245–301) on social spending from the Revolution through the 1960s, and McAuley's (1979) study of Soviet living standards in the 1960s and 1970s.
14. Public education expenditures, still excluded here, also remain lower in China than in Russia and Eastern Europe after communism. From about 1990 to about 2010, China's public education expenditure drifted from 2.5 percent of GDP down to 1.9 percent, while the public education share varied between 2.9 and 4.3 percent in Russia, and between 4.4 and 5.5 percent in Poland, according to UNESCO. China's spending on higher education seems to have expanded considerably since 2010, but we lack reliable estimates for this last decade.
15. Cook (2007, p. 211), Asian Development Bank (2013), and Lustig (2018). Extending still further west in the set of countries that was communist before 1990, Cuba has at times recorded the highest shares of GDP devoted to social spending. Even if one excludes public education spending, its social-spending share reached over 22 percent of GDP in 2008. Its public education shares were also perhaps the highest in the world at 11–14 percent of GDP (Mesa-Laeo 2017). These high ratios speak not only to Cuba's strong commitment to public health and education (in the numerators), but also to the depressed state of the country's GDP (in the denominators).
16. On anti-poverty social assistance in any developing country, including the former Soviet bloc, see the World Bank's SPEED (alias ASPIRE) data set on social protection, at http://datatopics.worldbank.org/aspire/.
17. World Bank (2011); Neuland (2016); https://uk.reuters.com/article/uk-mongolia-imf-idUKKBN18L0AC; www.reuters.com/article/us-mongolia-imf-idUSKBN1Z90NL;

and www.euromoney.com/article/b16b9k4kq8460l/bailed-out-yet-again-mongolia-stares-at-a-brighter-future.

18. For relevant global empirics and natural experiments, see Ansell (2010). Ansell's study greatly expands on, and updates, the sort of comparative evidence presented in Lindert (2003, 2010). For a comparison of the BRIC countries' experience 1880–1930, at the dawn of their mass primary education, see Chaudhary et al. (2012).
19. While the text will interpret the ratio as reflecting elitism in government preferences, one might imagine that the ratio could be raised as an efficient response to higher relative returns on higher education in some settings than in others. This efficiency argument is set aside here, since the pattern shown in Table 7.4 and other evidence is that education subsidies have been tilted most in favor of higher education (i.e. the ratio is highest) in less-developed settings in which the social rates of return have been particularly higher at the primary level than in higher education. See also Chapter 4's discussion of earlier restrictions on mass education.
20. Within continental sub-Saharan Africa, the following ratios are available for c. 2017: Benin 8.1, Burkina Faso 7.7, Burundi 23.4, Côte d'Ivoire 9.5, Democratic Republic of the Congo 10.4, Ethiopia 33.1, Ghana, 9.4, Guinea 13.6, Kenya 6.8, Malawi 12.7, Mauritania 9.0, Mozambique, Niger 10.4, Rwanda 27.8, Senegal 8.0, South Africa 2.6, Swaziland 7.9, Togo 9.6, and Zimbabwe 11.3. Three offshore African nations had lower, more modern, ratios: Cabo Verde 2.3, Comoros 2.6, and Mauritius 0.6.
21. On Latin America's education lag, see, for example, Engerman, Mariscal, and Sokoloff (2009); Frankema (2009); Lindert (2010); and Arroyo Abad and Lindert (2017). Note that this section has argued that more equal mass schooling tends to equalize earnings of adults *for given wage and salary rates.* There is also a macro-channel, working through induced movements in relative wage rates. Extra mass schooling, by raising average educational attainments, bids down the pay premiums of the more highly skilled.
22. In addition to the event studies in Ansell (2010, pp. 75–118), see the global meta-analyses of Kingdon et al. (2014). Similarly, for African nations in the period before and after independence (1980–1996), Stasavage (2005, p. 343) has linked democracy and egalitarian education policies, finding "clear evidence that democratically elected African governments have spent more on primary education, while spending on universities was unaffected by democratization." Two clear specific cases came in the wake of Uganda's 1996 arrival of real multi-party competition and in Malawi's 1994 shift to democracy.
23. As the use of the term "teachers" implies, this section omits any discussion of political clout or economic rents by suppliers of higher education. The magnitudes were probably not as great in the higher education sector, given its smaller size, its keener competition between private and public suppliers, and its international competition. See, however, Ansell's (2010, pp. 164–218) analysis of the political economy of higher education with the main OECD countries.
24. See Grindle's (2004) landmark study of the political economy of education in sixteen Latin American countries, and the survey chapter by Székely and Montes (2006).

Similar results have emerged in statistical studies of Mexico by Hecock (2006) and by Santibañez and Jarillo Rabling (2008).

25. Lanjouw and Stern (1998, p. 182).

CHAPTER 8: EFFECTS ON GROWTH, JOBS, AND LIFE

1. One might ask whether looking at "as much experience as the data permit" might not itself leave a bias. How would the correlations have looked if we could have included all the countries, and all the decades and centuries, that do not supply good data? Actually, the direction of the implied bias caused by our "selecting" the totality of good-data experiences is quite clear. Most of the nations failing to supply good data had little or no social spending, low GDP per person, and slow growth – think Somalia, or Cambodia. The rich non-data-supplying countries might have had large social expenditures – think Oman or Saudi Arabia. Adding all these in would have tilted the correlations between social-spending shares and GDP per capita in a more positive direction. So would the inclusion of the deeper no-data past centuries, with bare-subsistence living and governments with no social budgets – think Dark Ages. Yet it would be wrong for a believer in a positive relationship between social spending and prosperity to invoke these conjectural likelihoods.
2. Alternatively, one could have asked how the *growth of* social spending's share of GDP correlates with the growth of GDP per capita. Again, the result seems to be near zero, and insignificantly negative. See, for example, Kenworthy (2019, pp. 47, 58). For most of the same countries as in Tables 8.1 and 8.2, Kenworthy correlated changes in the social-spending share of GDP and the average rate of economic growth from the period 1950–1973 to the period 1979–2016, with that near-zero result.
3. The likelihood that richer countries generally prefer to pay more taxes for social spending also helps to explain why the effect of social spending on the growth rate looked more negative in the first column of Table 8.1. In a fuller model of the simultaneous feedbacks involving income and social spending, an exogenously higher level of GDP per capita among industrialized countries tends to mean lower subsequent growth, allowing one to misinterpret the negative correlation in that first column as a negative effect of the social spending that also accompanies the higher level of GDP per capita.
4. See Easterly and Rebelo (1993); Kneller, Bleaney, and Gemmell (1999); Lindert (2004, vol. II, ch. 18); Allard and Lindert (2007); and Gemmell, Kneller, and Sanz (2011). The studies by Gemmell, Kneller, and co-authors subdivide government spending into productive spending, including health and education spending, and unproductive spending, including other social transfers. They find that combining the former with indirect taxation (e.g. a value-added tax) positively affects economic growth, whereas the opposite combination of social transfers and direct taxes on income and wealth would have a negative effect. The other two possible combinations yield zero effect. The

net result is non-negative, given that the magnitudes of productive social expenditures (health, education) and indirect taxes are in fact greater than any financing of unproductive transfers with direct taxes.

5. Whereas the original twenty-one countries had a correlation of -0.15 between jobs and (non-education) social spending, the correlation is + 0.28 for the expanded group of forty-four countries. These tests relate only to job-holding. Relating worked per person-year to government size, Bakija (2016, pp. 112–114) finds a slightly positive international pattern, both for levels in the 2004–2013 period and for changes from 1960 to that period, using twenty-three countries' data.
6. The source is the *OECD Employment Database*, www.oecd.org/employment/emp/onlineoecdemploymentdatabase.htm and www.oecd.org/els/emp/lfsnotes_sources.pdf.
7. See Lindbeck and Snower (2001), Allard and Lindert (2007), and the OECD indices of EPLs for "regular employees" since 1985. Similar laws protected jobs in the privileged sectors of Chile as far back as the 1960s, though these protections were largely dismantled by Pinochet (Montenegro and Pagés 2004).
8. For a meta-analysis showing low rates of return on government expenditures to support the unemployed, see Hendren and Sprung-Keyser (2019, and especially pp. 53–56 of their online appendix).
9. See Levine et al. (2005) for a retrospective discussion of the Negative Income Tax experiments. A recent (quasi-experimental) study by Robert Moffitt (2019) went deeper into the heterogeneity of the population of potential welfare recipients. Welfare program data from 1988–1992 yielded estimates how work by single mothers was probably affected by three changes in US tax-and-welfare policy, occurring in 1967, 1981, and 1996. He found that the effects depended on who, and how many, participated in the welfare programs on the eve of each reform. The conventional prediction that a rise in the marginal tax rate would reduce labor supply was borne out when middling shares of the population of single mothers participated in welfare programs (as in the 1970s), but had no significant effect at earlier high rates or later low rates of participation.
10. See the summary of economists' views on the labor elasticities emerging from this literature, as of 1998, in Lindert (2004, vol. I, pp. 230–231).
11. See the recent summary of the effects of CCTs in Millán et al. (2019), and the studies cited there.
12. For evidence on the workability of such earnings subsidies, see Hoynes and Rothstein (2017); and Hoynes, Rothstein, and Ruffini (2017). For a comparison of the marginal tax and subsidy rates for earnings in the United States, the United Kingdom, and Sweden, see Kenworthy (2019, pp. 207–210).
13. Again, see Deaton (2015) on the global escape from high mortality, and Eggleston and Fuchs (2012) on the improvement in senior life expectancy.
14. On the poverty shares relative to median incomes, see OECD (2008, p. 127). The most reliable international comparisons of absolute poverty are found in studies based on the Luxembourg Income Study; see Smeeding (2006), and Scruggs and Allan (2005) for analyses, and www.lisdatacenter.org/our-data/lis-database/ for the underlying numbers.

15. www.transparency.org/files/content/pages/2018_CPI_ExecutiveSummary.pdf.
16. The source is the World Happiness Report https://ourworldindata.org/happiness-and-life-satisfaction. The underlying source of the happiness scores is the Gallup World Poll – a set of nationally representative surveys undertaken in more than 160 countries in over 140 languages. The main life evaluation question asked in the poll is: "Please imagine a ladder, with steps numbered from 0 at the bottom to 10 at the top. The top of the ladder represents the best possible life for you and the bottom of the ladder represents the worst possible life for you. On which step of the ladder would you say you personally feel you stand at this time?" (Also known as the "Cantril Ladder.")
17. Sachs (2006, p. 42).
18. For example, see Lindert (2004, vol. 1, ch. 10).

CHAPTER 9: WHY NO NET LOSS OF GDP OR WORK?

1. The closest thing to econometric support for this conventional hunch is the semi-robust result of Kneller, Bleaney, and Gemmell (1999), and Gemmell, Kneller, and Sanz (2011) to the effect that indirect taxes are better for growth than direct taxes (already cited in Chapter 8). They employed a revealing, but currently unfashionable, non-experimental panel of nations and years drawn from history.
2. This irony has been noted by Steinmo (1993); Wilensky (2002); Kato (2003); and Lindert (2004, vol. I, ch. 10). As the chain of literature implies, the same pattern dates back some time, probably to the great expansion of welfare-state budgets, funded in large part by VAT, across the 1960s. For an update on rates of VAT taxation among the countries covered by OECD data, see OECD (2018a, Figure 1.2).
3. As cited in Jan M. Rosen, "Tax Watch; The Likely Forms of New Taxes," *New York Times*, Dec. 19, 1988, Section D, p. 2.
4. Schenk (2011, pp. 53–56).
5. Rosen, in *New York Times*, Dec. 19, 1988.
6. See Hinrichs (1966).
7. It would appear that Chile has already moved in this direction since 1975, taking almost half its government revenues from the value-added tax as of 2016. The OECD numbers also imply that Chile has a much lower rate of collecting mandatory paycheck contributions than to other Latin American countries. It is not clear, however, how these numbers treat Chile's mandatory individual pension contributions.
8. The structure of alcohol taxation is too complicated for a quick summary here. Yet it too has been subject to higher rates of taxation in the welfare states than in the low-budget countries. For a more complete coverage of sin taxes, including alcohol, in the 1990s, see Lindert (2004, vol. I, pp. 235–245).
9. Frank Ramsey (1927) ably theorized that the rate of taxation on a consumer item would be higher, the lower the price-elasticity of demand for it.

10. See Sousa (2017) on smoking rates and cigarette tax rates. His tax rate data do not place Chile so high above the others as does Figure 9.2 because he has omitted the value-added tax, which is higher in Chile than in any other country.
11. See Reinhardt (2000, p. 77) on Germany vs. US in 1990, and Cutler and Ly (2011, p. 6), using data from Pozen and Cutler (2010), on Canada vs. US in 2002, as reproduced in Table 9.3 below. For additional comparative cost evidence, see Woodlander, Campbell, and Himmelstein (2003) and Hagist and KoTlikoff (2009).
12. This recent usage of the term "family-friendly," as applied to these policies toward childbirth and the first five years of the child's life, should not be confused with the broader "family" category in social-expenditure data, which includes aid to families in need having children of schools age.
13. Olivetti and Petrongolo (2017, pp. 207–209).
14. The correlations with total non-education social spending as a share of GDP among countries in 2016 were:

For parental leave		For pre-primary support	
35 countries	0.13	32 countries	0.32
23 core OECD	0.47	22 core OECD	0.49

15. See Olivetti and Petrongolo (2017, pp. 208–209) and Goldin, Kerr, and Olivetti (2020, pp. 1–2).
16. In addition to the employment studies cited in the text of this section, one study of Danish experience since 2001 explicitly finds negligible damage to firms and co-workers from a paid parental leave entitlement of more than nine months (Brenøe et al. 2020).
17. The fifty-week flattening of the positive employment effect is implied by Olivetti and Petrongolo (2017, esp. pp. 218–220). An earlier study by Thévenon and Solaz (2013, pp. 27–30) had estimated that more paid leave means more female employment up to 100–120 weeks. In either case, the slope is positive across the range of most OECD countries' policies. While the conclusion of positive effects on women's employment remains the prevailing one, micro-level studies of some reforms have not generated positive results. (Olivetti and Petrongolo 2017, pp. 222–224).
18. The effects of job continuity versus job interruption on parents' subsequent pay has been quantified by the studies surveyed in Waldfogel (1998), and later by Goldin and Mitchell (2017, pp. 175–178). The points made in this paragraph also draw on tests reported by Lundberg and Rose (2000); Harkness and Waldfogel (2003); and England et al. (2016). For a recent overview of gender pay gaps and the job-interruption damage for mothers in several countries, see OECD (2018c, pp. 211–251).
19. Fort, Ichino, and Zanella (2020).
20. In contrast to its high-quality schooling for 4-year-olds, Oklahoma's K-12 (primary and secondary) school system has recently slipped to a ranking of forty-fifth to forty-ninth among the fifty states in educational quality, in the wake of its severe budget cuts.
21. Fisher (1917, pp. 9, 14). I am indebted to J. C. Herbert Emery for this reference. As a reading of Emery (2010) makes clear, the compulsory insurance Fisher was

discussing was limited to certain occupations, both in European practice and in his proposals. It was not the universal kind of health insurance adopted in most of the rich countries after World War II.

22. On the fight to make Britain's cities more livable in the nineteenth century, see Williamson (1990). On the constrained campaign for better sanitation and hygiene in America, see Troesken (2004, 2015) and Catillon, Cutler, and Getzen (2018, pp. 19–28). More generally, see Deaton (2015) on the global health revolution.
23. See Starr (1982, pp. 112–127); Hollingsworth (1986); Hollingsworth, Hage, and Hanneman (1990); and Moehling et al. (2019).
24. The underlying price and wage data are presented in Adams (1944), and are downloadable at http://gpih.ucdavis.edu, Main Data set, North America.
25. See www.washingtonpost.com/national/the-clinic-of-lastresort/2019/06/22/2833c8a0-92cc-11e9-aadb74e6b2b46f6a_story.html?utm_term=.1a86dd9e3d7c2833c8a0-92cc-11e9-aadb74e6b2b46f6a_story.html?utm_term=.1a86dd9e3d7c.
26. Starr (1982, p. 334).
27. Starr (1982, pp. 310–334); Thomasson (2002, 2003).
28. On America's pro-elderly bias in health insurance and other social expenditures, see Lynch (2001, 2006), as well as the international contrasts in pensions documented in Chapter 12 below. On the age-discontinuity in relative mortality rates, Eggleston and Fuchs (2012).
29. The source is https://news.gallup.com/poll/8056/healthcare-system-ratings-us-great-britain-canada.aspx.
30. Hollingsworth (1986), and Hollingsworth, Hage, and Hanneman (1990).
31. See Hendren and Sprung-Keyser (2019), and its online appendix.

CHAPTER 10: DO THE RICH PAY THE POOR FOR ALL THIS?

1. Chapter 10 summarizes parts of the author's (2017) longer CEQ Institute Working Paper on the history of fiscal redistribution. For greater detail, download that paper from the CEQ site.
2. The clearest exception is the decline in Sweden's progressive (richer-to-poorer) redistribution between 1993 and 2009, as documented by Bengtsson, Holmlund, and Waldenström (2016).
3. Milanovic, Lindert, and Williamson (2011); Milanovic (2018).
4. See OECD (2008, 2011, 2014) for results and for links to the LIS estimates. The LIS data have also yielded international comparisons for a similar set of countries by Wang, Caminada, and Goudswaard (2012).
5. On Latin American redistribution, see De Ferranti et al. (2004, especially ch. 9); Székely and Montes (2006); Skoufias, Lindert, and Shapiro (2010) and the World Bank studies and databases cited there; and Bértola and Williamson (2017) and its sources.
6. See Lustig (2017, 2018).
7. All of the conclusions derived from this comparison of snapshots draw support from the similar recent comparisons in OECD (2008, 2011, 2014); Wang, Caminada, and

Goudswaard (2012); and Ostry, Berg, and Tsangarides (2014), that last of which draws on the large Standardized World Income Inequality Database (SWIID) of Frederick Solt (2009, 2014). While its use of interpolating and extrapolating assumptions makes the SWIID attractive for trying out hypotheses, I prefer to stick with the OECD and CEQ data sets, which will offer a clearer path of verification in terms of primary data. Readers seeking global income distribution data sets should also consult Branko Milanovic's handy "All the Ginis" database for 1950–2015 (at www.gc.cuny.edu), though it does not offer pairings of pre-fisc and post-ginis for the same country and year for the present purpose of tracing fiscal redistribution.

8. On the likely aggregate magnitudes of top incomes hidden abroad and/or in the form of corporate earnings, see Zucman (2015).
9. Branko Milanovic (2000, pp. 389–390) similarly found that an OECD-oriented sample from the late twentieth century yielded only positive differences between original market-income gini's and disposable-income gini's. In a similar vein, out of seventy-six countries yielding redistribution estimates for the year 2007, only two (Philippines and Belarus) were estimated, or predicted, to have slightly regressive redistributions in Solt's SWIID 4.0. Three others in East Asia were estimated to have zero redistribution, and the remaining seventy-one were estimated to be progressive overall.
10. In fairness, it should be noted that eight of the 108 countries not supplying data to Table 10.1 did supply data that were used by the CEQ group to measure inequality and redistribution – but their measures referred to inequality and redistribution of consumption, not income. The difference in definition, and not any data-hiding on their part, explains their not being included in the numbers tabulated here. Those eight countries are Ethiopia, Ghana, Indonesia, Jordan, Sri Lanka, Tanzania, Tunisia, and Uganda.
11. For earlier emphasis on these economies' equality-without-redistribution pattern, see Kwon (1997); Bourguignon, Fournier, and Gurgnand (1998, 1999); and Jacobs (2000). The available estimates for other East Asian economies also suggest very little progressive redistribution, but start from much greater income inequalities than in Japan, Korea, and Taiwan.
12. Our interpretations differ mainly for two reasons. First, I consider the progressivity of the mid-1990s to have been inflated by the crises then experienced by Finland, Sweden, and Norway, causing a cyclical rise in transfers minus taxes. Second, the OECD authors emphasize a relative measure, equaling the change in gini as a share of the pre-fisc gini, whereas I use only the absolute Reynolds–Smolensky measure.
13. For twenty-one countries supplying the needed data around 2013, the top income tax rate had a correlation of only 0.40 with net fiscal redistribution. The social transfer measure used here is the OECD's SOCX, which excludes expenditures on public education. Studying several countries for the 1980s–2000s, the OECD study *Divided We Stand* (2011, ch. 7) also found that differences in benefits explained more of the overall progressivity than did differences in taxes or social security payroll contributions. The same aggregate correlation was emphasized by Kato (2003) and Lindert (2004, vol. I, chs. 10–11).

14. Using their middling variant with "normal assumptions, except that general government expenditure is allocated by income" (Reynolds and Smolensky 1977, p. 71) yields these percentage gini coefficients:

	RS pre-fisc	RS post-fisc	Implied redistribution
1950	39.1	33.4	5.7
1961	39.8	33.3	6.5
1970	40.0	32.2	7.8

15. The only gap to be filled in the PSZ series before 1962 is to allocate the incomes of those in the bottom 90 percent between a below-median group and a 50–90 group. My assumptions for filling in this point on the Lorenz curve are detailed in Appendix B.
16. Here the term "social transfers" violates a convention of national income and product accounting by including as "transfers" some direct payments for currently produced services such as health care. This is done here, as in Lindert (2004), to have a shorthand name for a concept matching the social-expenditure measure of the OECD. I use the term "social spending" to include the public education spending omitted by the OECD measure. For an alternative history of the American welfare state using a full integration of public education into the overall measure of social expenditures, see Garfinkel, Rainwater, and Smeeding (2010).
17. Saez and Zucman (2019). In technical jargon, this paragraph notes that the trends in impacts on the richest decile and poorest half of the population are sensitive to the choice of income denominators. Figure 10.4(B) shows their fortunes as shares of overall national income. Since 1980, the trends would have looked different had Figure 10.4(B) graphed the fiscal impacts as shares of their class-specific pre-fisc incomes, such as tax rates. The rising inequality of pre-fisc inequality since 1980 means that the class-specific impact ratios would bend upward more since 1980, with more upward movement in the effects on the poorer half and less downward trend against the top decile than shown here.
18. For the long era up to World War I, see O'Brien (1988); Brewer (1989); Daunton (2002a). For the period since World War I, see Daunton (2002b) and the British coverage within Baldwin (1990) and Steinmo (1993).
19. Specifically, they omit any inequality in the benefits of the National Health Service, housing subsidy, rail travel subsidy, and bus travel subsidy. Measuring the incidence of such transfers in kind would raise the progressivity of the final result, especially after World War II. In fact, detailed figures from the Office of National Statistics have allocated such aid-in-kind to disposable-income deciles for 1977–2016, though not for earlier years. In addition to these types of aid-in-kind, the official income distributions also omit public education and school meals and Healthy Start Vouchers, but I deliberately defer education-related subsidies to the next section, to mimic some other studies and to delay consideration of effects from subsidies that occurred deep in the past.
20. For the estimates putting upper and lower bounds on British income inequality for dates between 1911 and 1977, see Lindert (2017, especially the discussion around its Figure 4).
21. See Lindert (1986, 1991).

22. As cited in Eastwood (1994, p. 101).
23. See in particular, O'Brien (1988); O'Brien and Hunt (1993); De Vries and Van der Woude (1997, pp. 110–113); the European chapters of Yun-Casalilla and O'Brien (2012) and Alfani and Di Tullio (2019, pp. 149–180).
24. See the recent summary in Alfani and Di Tullio (2019, pp. 149–180).
25. De Vries and Van der Woude (1997, p. 112), as amplified by Fritschy, 't Hart, and Horlings (2012, p. 60) and by Alfani and Di Tullio (2019).
26. Again see Piketty (2014); Zucman (2015); and Saez and Zucman (2019).
27. For these three economies, as for most others, the gini coefficients based on household surveys have understated inequality at the top. This bias in the gini coefficients has been offset by recent improved measures of top-income-group shares for Japan and Korea (not for Taiwan). In all these cases, however, the available estimates seem to capture a relatively equal distribution within the lower 90 percent ranks, a tentative view supported by comparisons of data on wage inequality (Atkinson 2008).
28. I am not the first to notice this contrast. In the 1970s, the World Bank Study *Redistribution with Growth* lauded Korea and Taiwan, along with Sri Lanka and India, as examples of growth with equity (Chenery et al. 1974; Fei, Ranis, and Kuo 1979). The same theme was taken up again in the 1990s by those viewing the European welfare state from an Asian perspective. See Kwon (1997) and Jacobs (2000).
29. On the rise of Chinese income inequality since 1978, see Piketty, Yang, and Zucman (2017).
30. For comparisons of the inequality (gini coefficient) of disposable incomes worldwide, including mainland China 2002, Japan 2008, Korea, and Taiwan, see Luxembourg Income Study (2017). Hong Kong gini coefficients and income distributions are available 1971–2011 in Hong Kong, Education Bureau (2015). Singapore top-income shares are available 1974–2014 in https://wid.world/country/singapore/. For gini coefficients see Branko Milanovic's All the Ginis site.
31. See Kumon (2019) and the larger historical evidence he cites.
32. On Mexico's wage widening with the opening of trade, see Hanson and Harrison (1999). For a broader multi-country view of the importance of historical timing for the trade-wage link, see Wood (1997) and Lindert and Williamson (2003).
33. The immigration policies of New Zealand, Australia, Canada and some other destination countries, have tended to follow an intermediate course. The gate is quite open for those with high skills or enterprise wealth, yet remains closed for others.
34. See Goldin and Katz (2008, p. 308) and Lindert and Williamson (2016, pp. 208–211).
35. Compare Japan and Korea with other countries in Figure 5.5 above. For a direct contrast between more equal education on Japan, Korea, and Taiwan on the one hand, and the more elitist schooling in Latin America on the other, see Székely and Montes (2006, pp. 594–616).
36. Compare the shares of GDP spent on primary versus higher education (the residual category) in the US, England–Wales, France, and Germany 1850–1910, in Lindert

(2004, vol. II, pp. 153–155.) See also the treatment of American mass education before 1914 in Chapter 4 above.

CHAPTER 11: DO IMMIGRATION TENSIONS FRAY THE SAFETY NETS?

1. Both the *New York Times* article ("The Unpopular Branch") and Coolidge's article ("Whose Country Is This?") were recently pointed out by Okrent (2019).
2. Immigration into Hungary has indeed remained low in the face of the government's tough restrictions. Foreigners accounted for only 1.5 percent of Hungary's total population. The main origin countries continued to be Romania (24,000), China (19,100), and Germany (18,600) (OECD, *International Migration Outlook*, 2018, p. 238).
3. "Denmark's immigration issue," BBC, Feb. 19, 2005.
4. TIME Staff, June 16, 2015. http://time.com/3923128/donald-trump-announcement-speech/.
5. To be charitable to the survey respondents, we could conjecture three possible reasons for their overestimating the share of immigrants who have not finished high school:

   (1) Perhaps their thinking immigrants had not finished high school reflected their knowing that the immigrants had not finished high school *within the host country*. It is well known that immigrants' qualifications downgrade immediately on arrival in the new country, if only because the new host country finds it hard to value educational certification received abroad (Blau and Mackie 2016, p. 158, and the studies cited there).

   (2) Perhaps their views were just out of date, and accurately reflected how little education immigrants *used to* have on arrival. In the United States, for example, they may have missed the fact that in 2017 only 22 percent of the foreign-born have not finished high school because back in 1970, for example, the share arriving with no high-school diploma was in fact as high as 51 percent (Blau and Mackie 2016, p. 68).

   (3) Perhaps they were giving answers about the kinds of immigrant mix matching their *fears*, even though the questions asked about actual immigrants.

6. Even when scholars can take aim at the economic effects of a particular policy proposal, such as Brexit's likely restrictions on immigration, they have had to draw on estimates referring to the aggregate recent mix of immigrants, for want of specifics on which groups would be affected most severely. See Portes and Forte (2017, especially Parts 3 and 4).
7. For an overall survey, see Peri (2016). A pooled international test for twenty-two countries in recent years is offered by Boubtane, Dumont, and Rault (2014). Recent positive summary appraisals of the GDP effects of immigration into the UK are Dustmann and Frattini (2013); Wadsworth et al. (2016); and Portes and Forte (2017). Summaries based on extensive literature are also available in Blau and Mackie (2016, ch. 6) and in Borjas (2019). An especially positive set of results has been obtained by

Sequeira, Nunn, and Qian (2020), who linked immigration positively to main growth indicators for the United States 1850–1920, using county data and instrumenting immigration with railroad access and prior immigration.

8. The revenue gains tend to accrue to central governments more than to state/province and local governments, which tend to bear more of the social-spending costs of new immigrants. Issues of revenue-sharing therefore heat up when immigration speeds up. On the fiscal effects of immigration on sub-national governments, see Blau and Mackie (2016, ch. 9).
9. See the survey evidence in Boeri (2010, pp. 662–668), using the European Social Survey of 2002. Curiously, Boeri finds that the Nordic countries, where immigrants are a relative fiscal burden, believe more that the fiscal contributions of immigrants are positive on balance, whereas countries like Austria, Britain, and Spain believe more in a fiscal drain that does not seem to exist in their cases. Differences in perceptions may drive differences in social policy, rather than vice versa. For 2018 survey evidence on perceptions about immigrants' fiscal effects in six countries, again see Alesina, Miano, and Stantcheva (2018). Yet the same negative effect on attitudes toward the welfare state has also emerged from actual exposure to the less welcome kinds of immigrants (lower skilled, Muslim, etc.) and not just from the misperceptions effect, according to Alesina, Murard, and Rapaport (2019).
10. The text here follows a simulation run by Ronald D. Lee and Timothy Miller (2000). Similar results emerge from simulations run by the OECD, International Migration Outlook (2013), and by the UK's Migration Advisory Committee (2018, ch. 4).
11. Most quantifications of the fiscal effects of immigration concentrate on this short-run, or pay-as-you-go, effect (e.g. Boeri 2010, pp. 656–661; OECD, International Migration Outlook, 2013, pp. 144–160). A strength of the Lee–Miller simulation is that it traces out the longer-run effects that follow from demographic likelihoods. On the other hand, their simulation omits behavioral effects, market-equilibrium effects, and the impacts of different mixes of immigrants. For theoretical and empirical warnings on these other fronts, see Preston (2014).
12. For a meta-analysis of net fiscal impact research on immigrants in the OECD countries, see (OECD, International Migration Outlook, 2013, ch. 3 and appendices). Most of the analysis tends to address the first question, the short-run pay-as-you-go question, of our Table 11.2. For a summary of both short- and long-run effects, with emphasis on the United States, see Blau and Mackie (2016, chs. 7 and 8).
13. Estimates based on data from several countries around the turn of the century yield net fiscal benefits from migrants that tend to be near zero over the short run, with more positive net results than negative ones. See OECD, International Migration Outlook (2013, ch. 3) for the assumptions and time horizons used. Note that the simulations run by Lee and Miller (2000) do not refer to a large refugee influx, since their parameters were drawn from calm time periods.
14. Chancellor Merkel first used the phrase on August 31, 2015, at a press conference following a visit to a refugee camp near Dresden, where local opponents of her refugee policy booed and heckled her. The full sentence she used was "*Wir haben so vieles*

geschafft – wir schaffen das." This can be translated as "We have managed so many things – we will also manage this situation." By September 2016, she had dropped the phrase, and imposed new restrictions on the refugee inflow.

15. An insightful July 2019 report on the continued Swedish debate over the responsibilities of, and responsibly for, Sweden's refugees is found in Goodman (2019).
16. Such studies on pooled samples of political jurisdictions are also subject to econometricians' standard concerns about potential endogeneity bias.
17. To these negative fiscal effects, one can add the slightly negative effect of restricting immigrants on GDP per capita, as discussed by Peri (2016).
18. The only exception to this logical pattern is the lack of clear calls for discrimination against the foreign-born in universal family assistance. On this front, only Britain's UK Independence Party clearly called for discrimination (Ennser-Jedenastik 2018, p. 305).
19. This statement assumes that within the migrants' countries of origin, the desire to emigrate does not independently shift away from the higher education and skills groups toward those with less education and skills. No such trend is evident yet.
20. I am indebted to Santiago Pérez for pointing out that Canada does offset its cherry-picking points system with something more akin to Option 3. Canada's guest worker programs allow temporary immigration of lower-skilled workers with only limited access to Canada's social safety nets.
21. Antecol, Cobb-Clark, and Trejo (2003).

CHAPTER 12: PENSIONS AND THE CURSE OF LONG LIFE

1. This chapter, and the next, will concentrate on public pensions to the retired elderly, which are about half of what the elderly population receives from government in today's more developed countries. The other half is dominated by health-care and health insurance benefits, which also tend to be paid out much more heavily to seniors. Yet health care must be set aside here, mainly because the data on health-care benefits are seldom divided into beneficiaries' age groups. In what follows, I shall use the shorthand "public pensions" to refer to a somewhat larger category of expenditures targeted toward the elderly. That larger category is the OECD's public "old-age" plus "survivor" benefits, of which the OECD's "pensions" are only a part. It still excludes incapacity benefits and health-care benefits, even though a large, but hard to measure, share of these is directed at the elderly. As we noted in earlier chapters, many social-expenditure programs defy sharp divisions between target populations: again, are expenditures aimed at the poor and disabled elderly to be counted as expenditures on the poor, or on the disabled, or on the elderly?
2. Again, see Deaton (2015) and Eggleston and Fuchs (2012).
3. World Bank (1994, p. 139).
4. World Bank (1994, p. 129).
5. The World Bank authors offered no explanation for the offhand remark about negative interest rates.

6. For a concise critique of the Kotlikoff and Burns book, see Krugman (2005).
7. Public pension systems are also supposed to be progressive *within* generations, offering better returns to those who had lower lifetime earnings than others born in the same years. This design feature fits the idea of social insurance. Yet in practice, part of its progressivity is cancelled by the tendency of those with higher lifetime earnings to outlive the poor enough to have longer retirements, thereby collecting the stipulated pensions for more years than do those with lower lifetime earnings.
8. For example, the exact same pattern has been documented by World Bank economists for Costa Rica as of 2012: the pay advantage captured by public-sector employees was greater for the less skilled than for professionals (Oviedo et al. 2015, pp. 104–105).

   Even the American CBO study could not hold all other things equal, however. On one hand, in defense of the claim that the federal workers are not overpaid, one could note that their jobs require them to live in areas where the cost of housing, and the overall cost of living, is higher, as it is in the metropolitan Washington DC area. On the other hand, the CBO was not able to fine-tune its comparisons for the highly educated to take account of differences in markets for different degree subjects. Thus its highly educated federal workers would include a higher share of those with lower private-sector alternatives, such as those with degrees in social work, while the private sector would dominate in the pay and hiring of advanced degrees in engineering and medicine.
9. The remainder of this chapter deals with the more common kind of government-run pension plans, the conventional "social security" insurance program, based on "tax revenues." The other kind, called non-tax compulsory payments (NTCPs) into a government fund, or "provident fund," is discussed in Chapter 13 in connection with Chile and Singapore. The OECD's specialists have cautioned that it is not always clear which payments into government-run pension funds are truly taxes and which are NTCPs (OECD 2018e, para. 9).
10. For an illustration of the complexity of determining the annuity payout schedule, see US Internal Revenue Service (2009, 2019). As will be noted again in Chapter 13, the payroll contributions are indeed taxes, according to the official definitions that the OECD applies to OECD-associated countries. See OECD (2018e, Annex A, p. 164).
11. See Jordà, Schularick, and Taylor (2017, and its online data series), and Jordà et al. (forthcoming).
12. Changing the assumption that contribution reserve funds were invested in bonds would change the results of such an exercise. One alternative, recommended by Monika Queisser and Edward Whitehouse (2006), is that the contributions could have been invested at a riskier portfolio, such as a mix of a 50–50 mix of real estate and equities in the Jordà–Schularick–Taylor data set. Doing so cancels out the net tendency toward (or away from) declining funding shares. Such a risky portfolio seems unrealistic, however. Countries tend not to make such a choice. Also, assuming such high-risk rates of return would actually imply over-accumulation of reserves in most of the data-supplying countries for the periods covered.

13. Note that the groups here are age groups, not groups defined by employment versus retirement. The budgetary logic refers to "the elderly" versus "young adults" or "working-age adults." It does not refer to "retirees," "dependents," or "the employed." This choice is dictated by the need for clarity, both in defining the budget equation here and in fashioning policy formulas like the notional defined contribution system discussed in Chapter 13. The age distribution numbers are clear, and predictable, and hard for politicians to fudge. There are more serious measurement issues with who is "retired" or even with the measurement of life expectancy.
14. This section draws mainly on Margaret McClure's informative and insightful history of New Zealand's social-spending policy swings (McClure 1998, especially chs. 4–6). Also helpful here is Thomson (1996), especially in its quantification of the early postwar swings in age targeting.
15. As quoted in McClure (1998, pp. 213–214).
16. For semantic convenience, "Mediterranean Europe" is stretched to include Portugal and France, as well as Spain, Italy, Greece, and Turkey, both here and in Chapter 7. It excludes the Balkans and Malta, however.
17. The equally dramatic case of Japan is discussed separately in Chapter 14.
18. Again, as in Chapter 8, see Blanchet, Bozio and Roger (2019) on France's senior work incentives.
19. The only other brief retreat in this cost measure occurred during the military Junta (1967–1974), as can be seen in Figure 12.3.
20. www.reuters.com/article/us-greece-mitsotakis/greek-conservative-leader-eyes-eu-vote-victory-pm-post-in-election-by-autumn-idUSKCN1RL1L5, accessed Apr. 9, 2019.
21. Sachs (2015).
22. The Fornero reform's provisions were summarized in (OECD 2017, p. 7). On the subsequent retreat, see www.nytimes.com/2018/06/21/business/economy/greece-europe-bailout.html?hp&action=click&pgtype=Homepage&clickSource=story-heading&module=first-column-region®ion=top-news&WT.nav=top-news.
23. www.reuters.com/article/us-italy-pensions-salvini/italy-deputy-pm-promises-to-dismantle-pension-reform-piece-by-piece-idUSKBN1J90YP, and www.ipe.com/reports/special-reports/top-1000-pension-funds/italy-new-government-prioritises-public-pension-overhaul/10026477.article, both accessed June 27, 2019. We return in Chapter 13 to Italy's struggles with pension reforms in discussing notional defined contribution plans.
24. See Elveren and Agartan (2017, pp. 317–321). To judge their anti-poverty commitments by the shares of GDP devoted to the sum of (family assistance + labor-market policies + unemployment compensation + public housing) in 2013, we can contrast Turkey with three neighbors thus:

Hungary	Italy	Greece	Turkey
4.6%	3.4%	2.8%	0.5%

25. Greece is not listed here because the Macrohistory Database does not include Greece. Nonetheless, Greece was estimated to have a pension deficit equal to 9 percent of GDP as of 2015: https://greekanalyst.wordpress.com/2015/06/12/game-of-ultimatums-the-nonpaper-of-the-greek-government/.
26. Appendix C presents equations that derive the leeway-to-2050 formula from the basic accounting equation.
27. The 1994 starting year for this recent era was chosen, instead of an earlier date, in order to include post-communist countries' experience starting from a year in which they had already achieved some initial recovery from the Soviet breakup of 1989–1991.
28. In early 2019, the Colombian government agreed to postpone planned pension reforms (Reuters.com. 2019. "Colombia to postpone pensions overhaul until next year: minister." World News, January 15). Its shaky attempt to adopt Chilean-style mandatory savings is discussed in Chapter 13.
29. Also in in the favorable-leeway group (C) are these additional formerly communist states: Albania, Belarus, Bosnia-Herzegovina, Kazakhstan, Macedonia, Mongolia, Montenegro, Romania, Serbia, Turkmenistan, and Ukraine. However, the negative-leeway group (A) includes Kyrgyzstan, Moldova, and Uzbekistan.
30. While those rates of return were average rates on the money already spent on public education, the likelihood is that higher average rates are accompanied by higher marginal rates as well. That is, what has consistently paid high returns so far (e.g. public education) would probably reap further high returns if more money were invested in them.
31. This listing of pro-youth omits Jamaica and Guyana, whose support ratios might look misleadingly tilted toward youth in Figure 7.3 above, due to the absence of significant pensions, and not to high rates of support for school-age children.
32. What brought the United States into the pro-elderly spotlight was its inclusion of age-specific measures of health-care benefits. Huge subsidies under Medicare made the difference.
33. The need to include the hard-to-allocate health-care benefits unavoidably limited the sample. The OECD study of nineteen countries did not include any observations on Austria, Greece, Hungary, Iceland, Poland, Spain, or any country from Latin America, Africa, or Asia (other than Japan). The only Eastern European country included among the nineteen was the Czech Republic.
34. This list must exclude some countries that Figure 7.3 had shown to have tilted badly away from public education and toward public pensions, namely Mongolia, Tunisia, Jordan, Tanzania, and Mali. They are excluded here for their lack of data on multiple stress tests. On the other hand, for this chapter's pension emphasis, the list includes Japan, Portugal, and Spain even though their commitments to public education have been relatively strong.
35. Greece is even worse, letting its elderly support advance faster than average incomes. This is largely due, however, to the fact that the austerity enforced since 2010 has

slashed the income (GDP) denominator without yet slashing the privileged-pension numerator as much.

CHAPTER 13: APPROACHES TO PUBLIC PENSION REFORM

1. Some have suggested that there is a fourth pillar, namely relying on family and friends in your old age. That was probably never a reliable and practical form of insurance, except for the richer extended families and gilds in poor societies that lacked financial market alternatives. Today, reliance on extended family and gilds has become obsolete in modern economies, because individuals can draw on financial markets and government safety nets.
2. See Willmore's original paper (2000) and his annotated 2014 version of it, which exposes attempts by international agencies to mute his call for removing the second pillar. See also Saint John and Willmore (2001) and Willmore's (2007) set of lessons for all developing countries.
3. The phrase "bloated and inequitable" is again from Gill et al. (2004, p. 4). For broad verdicts on the history of Latin American pensions and health insurance, see Mesa-Lago (2002); the relevant chapters in Lustig (2018); Arroyo Abad and Lindert (2017); the Latin American chapters in Aspalter (2017), and Chapter 12 above. Recall also that the workplace feature has been a fatal flaw in the evolution of health insurance in the United States since the 1940s, as documented in Chapter 7 above.
4. For more on the problems of the old system, see Mamalakis (1976, pp. 200–201); Cheyre Valenzuela (1988, pp. 27–71); Edwards (1996, pp. 6–8); Acuña and Iglesias (2001, pp. 19–21); Borzutzky and Hyde (2017, pp. 138–140); and especially the Chile, ODEPLAN (1971) report that underlies Table 13.1.
5. See the fiscal sources cited in Arroyo Abad and Lindert (2017).
6. ODEPLAN (1971, p. 359).
7. Like Chile's military regime, Fidel Castro's Cuba exempted its armed forces and state security personnel from the brutal cutbacks inflicted on the civilian population during the crisis of 1990–1993, the "*período especial*" when Soviet aid to Cuba collapsed. As of 1995, as Carmelo Mesa-Lago notes, "the cost of armed forces pensions was equal to the total deficit accumulated by the general pension system that covers most of the labor force" (Mesa-Lago 2017, p. 112).
8. On the continuing debate issues over pensions, and the deficit projections, see Uthoff (2017a, 2017b).
9. For the Lee Kuan Yew interview, see Zakaria (1994, p. 114). The speech by Ong Teng Cheong is cited in Tremewan (1998, p. 78).
10. The conventional tax share of 16.9 percent for Singapore general government is derived from Tables 5.1 and 20.2 of the 2019 *Yearbook of Statistics*. The CPF contributions share of 8.8 percent draws on Tables 5.1 and 19.16 of the same volume.

    The payroll contributions are indeed taxes, according to the OECD official definitions that are applied to OECD-associated countries. See OECD (2018e, Annex A, p. 164).

11. Asian Development Bank (2013, p. 21 of the Technical Report on Singapore).
12. Asher (1999); Asher and Newman (2002); Kwan and Asher (2019). The passage quoted here is from Asher and Newman (2002, p. 57).
13. On the complex work-incentive issues for elderly individuals, see Börsch-Supan and Coile (2018), and the many publications of the related NBER project on aging and retirement.
14. For a detailed account of the political fights in the 1990s that led to the initial compromises on pension cutting and then the launching of the indexing system in 1998, see Anderson (2005). For a summary of the whole package of the 1993 reforms laid down by the Economics Commission (Ekonomikommissionen), see Lindert (2004, vol. I, pp. 264–267).
15. I have over-simplified Sweden's system, which is well described in Kruse (2010) and Swedish Pensions Agency (2019). Instead of an index tied to GDP per working-age adult, Sweden uses two other index factors that yield a similar result. The economic aggregate is wages and salaries per employed person, not GDP per person 18–64. And Sweden backs up its pension stability with an additional trigger that goes off whenever the pension fund's "Balance ratio" BR = capitalized assets / capitalized obligations drops below 1.
16. See Kruse (2010).
17. See Börsch-Supan and Coile (2018) for a comparison of twelve OECD countries' retirement incentives and seniors' apparent responses to them.
18. See Hinrichs (2005) on Germany's reforms between 1957 and 2001, and Bonin (2009, p. 7) on the 2004 reform.
19. As cited in Khan (2001, p. 5).

CHAPTER 14: BORROWING SOCIAL-SPENDING LESSONS

1. Previously quoted in *Financial Times* print edition September 17, 2016, in an "Essay" by James Crabtree.
2. The "cradle to career" phrase is not original here. It has already been used by Gavin Newsom's California gubernatorial campaign in the autumn of 2018.
3. For a deeper methodological exploration of how to choose which history a country could emulate, see King and Zeng (2006, 2007).
4. For the big picture among OECD countries, see the OECD's gender portal at www.oecd.org/gender. For detailed gender-specific pay rates by occupation for many countries, see the ILO's www.ilo.org/ilostat.
5. Note that this section's arguments are presented as though Japan's public pension benefits were funded entirely by current taxpayers on a pay-as-you-go (PAYG) basis, and not from mandatory contributions – that is, they are "first-pillar" benefits, not "second-pillar" benefits. This is close enough to the truth to allow such a simplification. Recall that of sixteen major countries in 2004–2013, Table 12.1 found Japan's benefits to be the least funded (regardless of the portfolio assumption) after one

sets aside the purely PAYG systems of Australia, New Zealand, and Denmark. Similarly, the OECD detailed data on sources of "old-age" benefits in 2013 show that 76 percent of all benefits were in the "public" category instead of from private government-mandated or private voluntary sources.

6. Börsch-Supan and Coile (2018, especially pp. 11–24).
7. If the indexing to expected years in retirement were followed faithfully, would annual pension benefits actually drop in absolute purchasing power? Not if productivity growth matches or exceeds the rate of aging. If the "secular stagnation" nightmare were to come true, and productivity growth fell short of the rate of aging, then yes, annual benefits would fall, along with national income per capita. The elderly would share in the burden of stagnation. But that nightmare seems unlikely over the long run.
8. For the estimates of net emigration since 2015, see www.wilsoncenter.org/publication/venezuelan-emigration-explained, accessed Apr. 22, 2020. For UN population estimates, see https://worldpopulationreview.com/countries/venezuela-population/. An accelerated loss of life in 2017–2019 is documented by Weisbrot and Sachs (2019, pp. 14–16).
9. See Singer and Moleiro (2020) and Kurmanaev and Herrera (2020).
10. The 1958–1998 chronology draws largely on the chapters in Hausmann and Rodríguez (2013), with emphasis on the oil swings, and on Buxton (2014), which uses health-care policy as a vantage point for viewing the policy swings. The movements in GDP per capita were followed with the help of De Corso (2013) through 2012, and the Penn World Tables through 2017. The latter appears to have extrapolated Venezuela's GDP per capita into the 2014–2017 statistical darkness on the basis of international oil prices and Venezuela's oil exports.
11. For a direct debate, with competing data claims, see Rodríguez (2008a, 2008b); Alvarez Herrera (2008); and Weisbrot (2008).
12. Buxton (2014, p. 27).
13. For these contrasts, see Figures 7.1 and 7.2, as well as Table 14.1.
14. See the estimates of fiscal redistribution in Table 10.1.
15. See the World Bank's social-sector sourcebook (Lindert et al. 2019).
16. For a summary of experiences with anti-poverty CCT programs, see Fiszbein et al. (2009).
17. At some point, there would be a political debate over adding a work requirement ("workfare") for able-bodied adults. The merits of a work conditionality would depend on the level of the demogrant and the rest of the tax-transfer system, and thus cannot be addressed here.
18. For the calculations of high foregone returns in Venezuela around 1958, see Lindert (2010, pp. 395–398). For the analogous mistake in Victorian England, see Chapter 4 above.
19. As quoted in Shoup et al. (1959, p. 409).
20. See, for example, https://news.yahoo.com/seniors-block-venezuela-streets-demanding-pension-checks-213439933.html.
21. Venezuela's pension debate is recounted in Pederson and Shekha (2018).

22. See the chronologies in www.abs.gov.au/ausstats/abs@.nsf/94713ad445ff1425c a25682000192af2/8e72c4526a94aaedca2569de00296978!OpenDocument, and in www.aph.gov.au/About_Parliament/Parliamentary_Departments/Parliamentary_Library/pubs/BN/1011/SSPayments1.
23. Specifically, in the period 1998–2015, American public pensions rose by 1.2 percent of GDP, Canada's fell by 0.3 percent of GDP, as did the share in New Zealand, while Australia's share rose only by 0.2 percent of GDP.
24. Early in 2005, in the middle of the period covered here, the administration of President George W. Bush did make an attempt to "touch the third rail" of American politics, proposing cuts in Social Security benefits. Despite his having been re-elected the previous November along with a Republican majority in both houses, this effort was "dead on arrival" in Congress, and his attempt at trimming Social Security was arguably a factor in the Republicans' loss of both houses of Congress in 2006.
25. "Pure" community rating would prohibit insurance rate variations based on demographic characteristics such as age or gender, whereas adjusted or modified community rating allows insurance rate variations based on demographic characteristics such as age or gender. Premiums can vary only with the design of the package (deductibles, percentage of cost reimbursement above the deductible, etc.) and within household structure, still setting aside ages.
26. There are some detailed limits to community rating in the Affordable Care Act of 2010:

    - charging higher premiums for the elderly is possible, but only up to 3:1 (300 percent);
    - gender rating is illegal, and guaranteed issue applies across genders;
    - tobacco use can increase premiums up to a ratio of 1.5:1;
    - households with incomes below 400 percent of the Federal Poverty Level pay lower costs.

27. This phrase appeared in the title of Anderson et al. (2003), and has been repeated in Starr (2018a, p. 54) and in Reinhardt (2019, p. 21). The phrase harkens back to James Carville's widely quoted "It's the economy, stupid" from the Clinton campaign in 1992. Similarly, Hagist and Kotlikoff (2009) have concluded that "Although healthcare spending is growing at unsustainable rates in most, if not all, OECD countries, the U.S. appears least able to control its benefit growth due to the nature of its fee-for-service healthcare payment system."
28. For recent international comparisons showing the extreme pricing of American health care, see US House Ways and Means Committee (2019) and Reinhardt (2019, pp. 13–77).
29. The two examples cited here are from Reinhardt (2000) and Cutler and Ly (2011). For an overview of the price contrasts, see Reinhardt (2019, pp. 41–69). A survey by Stabile and Thompson (2014, p. 514) cautiously agrees that price restraint is probably central to future progress.
30. Starr (2018a, p. 54).

31. See Hoynes and Schanzenbach (2018).
32. See Bitler and Hoynes (2016).
33. On the timing, the inequality, and the inadequacy of US safety nets during the covid-19 crisis in 2020, see Bitler, Hoynes, and Schanzenbach (2020).
34. For a review of similar studies on the long-run effects of American safety-net programs, each having less extensive data than Bailey et al. (2020), again see Hoynes and Schanzenbach (2018).
35. Unfortunately, even the Democrats' versions call for using payroll taxes to cover the costs of paid parental leave. While that is better than mandating that employers pay the individual employee for leave time, it shares the defect of taxing the employment relationship, just like so many of the second-pillar methods of financing pensions discussed in Chapter 13.

References

Acemoglu, Daron and Joshua Angrist. 2000. "How Large Are Human Capital Externalities? Evidence from Compulsory Schooling Laws." *NBER Macroeconomics Annual 2000*: 9–59.

Acemoglu, Daron and James A. Robinson. 2000. "Why Did the West Extend the Franchise? Democracy, Inequality, and Growth in Historical Perspective." *Quarterly Journal of Economics* 115, 4 (November): 1167–1200.

Acemoglu, Daron and James A. Robinson. 2006. *Economic Origins of Dictatorship and Democracy*. Cambridge: Cambridge University Press.

Acemoglu, Daron and James A. Robinson. 2012. *Why Nations Fail*. New York: Crown Publishers.

Acemoglu, Daron, James A. Robinson, and Thierry Verdier. 2017. "Asymmetric Growth and Institutions in an Interdependent World." *Journal of Political Economy* 125, 5: 1245–1305.

Acemoglu, Daron, Suresh Naidu, Pascual Restrepo, and James A. Robinson. 2019. "Democracy Does Cause Growth." *Journal of Political Economy* 127, 1 (February): 47–100.

Ackerby, Stefan. 1998. "Sweden's Pension Reform – An Example for Others?" *Unitas* 70, 4: 26–29.

Acuña R., Rodrigo and Augusto Iglesias P. 2001. "Chile's Pension Reform after 20 Years." World Bank Social Protection Discussion Paper 0129 (December). An earlier version of this paper was published in the book Felipe Larrain and Rodrigo Vergara (eds.), *La Transformacion Economica de Chile*. Santiago: Centro de Estudios Públicos, 2000.

Adams, T. M. 1944. *Prices Paid by Vermont Farmers [1790–1940]. Bulletin 507.* Burlington, VT: Vermont Agricultural Experiment Station.

Aghion, Philippe, Xavier Jaravel, Torsten Persson, and Dorothée Rouzet. 2019. "Education and Military Rivalry." *Journal of the European Economic Association* 17, 2 (April): 376–412.

A'Hearn, Brian, Joerg Baten, and Dorothee Crayen. 2009. "Quantifying Quantitative Literacy: Age Heaping and the History of Human Capital." *Journal of Economic History* 69, 3 (September): 783–808.

Aidt, Toke S. and Bianca Dallal. 2008. "Female Voting Power: The Contribution of Women's Suffrage to the Growth of Social Spending in Western Europe (1869–1960)." *Public Choice*, 134, 3–4 (March): 391–417.

Aidt, Toke S. and Peter S. Jensen. 2009. "The Taxman Tools Up: An Event History Study of the Introduction of the Personal Income Tax." *Journal of Public Economics* 93: 160–175.

Aidt, Toke S. and Peter S. Jensen. 2013. "Democratization and the Size of Government: Evidence from the Long Nineteenth Century." *Public Choice* 157 (December): 511–542.

Aidt, Toke, Jayasri Dutta, and Elena Loukoianova. 2006. "Democracy Comes to Europe: Franchise Expansion and Fiscal Outcomes 1831–1938." *European Economic Review* 50, 2 (February): 249–283.

Aidt, Toke S., Stanley L. Winer, and Peng Zhang. 2020. "Franchise Extension and Fiscal Structure in the United Kingdom 1820–1913: A New Test of the Redistribution Hypothesis." CESifo Working Paper 8114 (February).

Akçomak, I. Semih, Dinand Webbink, and Bas ter Weel. 2016. "Why Did the Netherlands Develop So Early? The Legacy of the Brethren of the Common Life." *Economic Journal* 126, 593 (June): 821–860.

Alesina, Alberto and Edward Glaeser. 2004. *Fighting Poverty in the US and Europe: A World of Difference*. Oxford: Oxford University Press.

Alesina, Alberto, Reza Baqir, and William Easterly. 1999. "Public Goods and Ethnic Divisions." *Quarterly Journal of Economics* 114, 4 (November): 1243–1284.

Alesina, Alberto, Armando Miano, and Stefanie Stantcheva. 2018. "Immigration and Redistribution." NBER Working Paper 24733 (July).

Alesina, Alberto, Elie Murard, and Hillel Rapoport. 2019. "Immigration and Preferences for Redistribution in Europe." NBER Working Paper 22562 (February).

Alexander, John K. 1980. *Render Them Submissive: Responses to Poverty in Philadelphia, 1760–1800*. Amherst: University of Massachusetts Press.

Alfani, Guido and Matteo Di Tullio. 2019. *The Lion's Share: Inequality and the Rise of the Fiscal State in Preindustrial Europe*. Cambridge: Cambridge University Press.

Allard, Gayle J. and Peter H. Lindert. 2007. "Euro-Productivity and Euro-Jobs since the 1960s: Which Institutions Really Mattered?" In Timothy J. Hatton, Kevin H. O'Rourke, and Alan M. Taylor (eds.), *The New Comparative Economic History: Essays in Honor of Jeffrey G. Williamson*. Cambridge, MA: MIT Press, pp. 365–394.

Allen, Robert C. 2003. "Progress and Poverty in Early Modern Europe." *Economic History Review* 56, 3 (August): 403–443.

Alvarez Herrera, Bernardo. 2008. "How Chávez Has Helped the Poor." *Foreign Affairs* 87, 4 (July/August): 158–160.

Anderson, Gerard, Uwe E. Reinhardt, Peter S. Hussey, and Varduhi Petrosyan. 2003. "It's the Prices, Stupid: Why the United States Is So Different from Other Countries," *Health Affairs* 22, 3 (May–June): 89–105.

Anderson, Karen M. 2005. "Pension Reform in Sweden: Radical Reform in a Mature Pension System." In Guiliano Bonoli and Toshimitsu Shinkawa (eds.), *Ageing and Pension Reform around the World: Evidence from Eleven Countries*. Cheltenham: Edward Elgar, pp. 94–114.

Ansell, Ben W. 2010. *From the Ballot to the Blackboard: The Redistributive Political Economy of Education*. Cambridge: Cambridge University Press.

Ansell, Ben W. and David J. Samuels. 2014. *Inequality and Democratization: An Elite-Competition Approach*. Cambridge: Cambridge University Press.

Antecol, Heather, Deborah A. Cobb-Clark, and Stephen J. Trejo. 2003. "Immigration Policy and the Skills of Immigrants to Australia, Canada, and the United States." *Journal of Human Resources* 38, 1 (Winter): 192–218.

Arenas de Mesa, Alberto. 2005. "Fiscal and Institutional Considerations of Pension Reform: Lessons Learned from Chile." In Carolin A. Crabbe (ed.), *A Quarter Century of Pension Reform in Latin America and the Caribbean: Lessons Learned and Next Steps*. Washington, DC: Inter-American Development Bank, pp. 83–126.

Arenas de Mesa, Alberto and Carmelo Mesa-Lago. 2006. "The Structural Pension Reform in Chile: Effects, Comparisons with Other Latin American Reforms, and Lessons." *Oxford Review of Economic Policy* 22, 1: 149–167.

Argentina, Dirección General de Estadística. 1915. *Extracto estadístico de la República Argentina*. Buenos Aires: Compañia Sud-Americana de Billetes de Banco.

Arnold, Jens and João Jalles. 2014. "Dividing the Pie in Brazil: Income Distribution, Social Policies and the New Middle Class." OECD Economics Department Working Papers, No. 1105, OECD Publishing. http://dx.doi.org/10.1787/5jzb6w1rt99p-en.

Arroyo Abad, Leticia and Peter H. Lindert. 2017. "Fiscal Redistribution in Latin America since the Nineteenth Century." In Luis Bértola and Jeffrey G. Williamson (eds.), *Has Latin American Inequality Changed Direction? Looking over the Long Run*. Cham: Springer International Publishing, pp. 243–282.

Asher, Mukul G. 1999. "The Pension System in Singapore." World Bank Social Protection Discussion Paper 9919 (August).

Asher, Mukul G. and David Newman. 2002. "Private Pensions in Asia: An Assessment of Eight Systems." In Organization for Economic Cooperation and Development (OECD), *Regulating Private Pensions Schemes: Trends and Challenges*. Paris: OECD, Private Pensions Series, No. 4, pp. 51–101.

Asian Development Bank. 2013. *The Social Protection Index: Assessing Results for Asia and the Pacific*. Mandaluyong City, Philippines: Asian Development Bank. Building on a series of (2012) Technical Assistance Consultant's Reports for each country covered.

Aspalter, Christian (ed.). 2017. *The Routledge International Handbook to Welfare Systems*. London: Routledge.

Atkinson, Anthony B. 2008. *The Changing Distribution of Earnings in OECD Countries*. Oxford: Oxford University Press.

Bachas, Pierre, Lucie Gadenne, and Anders Jensen. 2020. "Informality, Consumption Taxes, and Redistribution." NBER Working Paper 27429 (June).

Bailey, Martha J., Hilary W. Hoynes, Maya Rossin-Slater, and Reed Walker. 2020. "Is the Social Safety Net a Long-Term Investment? Large-Scale Evidence from the Food Stamps Program." NBER Working Paper 26942 (April).

Baker, Michael, Jonathan Gruber, and Kevin Milligan. 2019. "The Long-Run Impacts of a Universal Child Care Program." *American Economic Journal: Economic Policy* 11, 3 (August): 1–26.

Bakija, Jon. 2016. "Would a Bigger Government Hurt the Economy?" In Jon Bakija, Lane Kenworthy, Peter Lindert, and Jeffrey Madrick (eds.), *How Big Should Our Government Be?* Berkeley: University of California Press, pp. 67–134.

Baldwin, Peter. 1990. *The Politics of Social Solidarity and the Bourgeois Basis of the European Welfare State, 1875–1975.* Cambridge: Cambridge University Press.

Barro, Robert J. and Jong Wha Lee. 2013. "A New Data Set of Educational Attainment in the World, 1950–2010." *Journal of Development Economics* 104: 184–198.

Baten, Jorg and Jan Luiten van Zanden. 2008. "Book Production and the Onset of Modern Economic Growth." *Journal of Economic Growth* 13, 3: 217–235.

Becker, Sascha O. and Ludger Woessmann. 2009. "Was Weber Wrong? A Human Capital Theory of Protestant Economic History." *Quarterly Journal of Economics* 124, 2 (May): 531–596.

Becker, Sascha O., Erik Hornung, and Ludger Woessmann. 2011. "Education and Catch-Up in the Industrial Revolution." *American Economic Journal: Macroeconomics* 3, 3 (July): 92–126.

Benavot, Aaron and Phyllis Riddle. 1988. "The Expansion of Primary Education, 1870–1940: Trends and Issues." *Sociology of Education* 61 (July): 191–210.

Bengtsson, Niklas, Bertil Holmlund, and Daniel Waldenström. 2016. "Lifetime versus Annual Tax Progressivity: Sweden, 1968–2009." *Scandinavian Journal of Economics*, 118, 4: 619–645.

Bergh, Andreas. 2005. "On the Counterfactual Problem of Welfare State Research: How Can We Measure Redistribution?" *European Sociological Review* 21, (4 September): 345–57.

Bértola, Luis and Jeffrey G. Williamson (eds.). 2017. *Has Latin American Inequality Changed Direction? Looking over the Long Run.* Cham: Springer International Publishing. Spanish edition: *La fractura – Pasado y presente de la búsqueda de equidad social en América Latina*, Banco Interamericano de Desarrollo.

Bird, Richard M. 1980. "Income Redistribution through the Fiscal System: The Limits of Knowledge." *American Economic Review* 70, 2 (May): 77–81.

Bishop, John H. 1989. "Is the Test Score Decline Responsible for the Productivity Growth Decline?" *American Economic Review* 79, 1 (March): 178–197.

Bishop, John H. 1996. "Signaling, Incentives, and School Organization in France, the Netherlands, Britain, and the United States." In Eric A. Hanushek and Dale W. Jorgenson (eds.), *Improving America's Schools: The Role of Incentives.* Washington, DC: National Academies Press, pp. 111–145.

Bishop, John H. 1997. "The Effect of National Standards and Curriculum-Based Exams on Achievement." *American Economic Review* 87, 2 (May): 260–264.

Bitler, Marianne and Hilary Hoynes. 2016. "The More Things Change, the More They Stay the Same? The Safety Net and Poverty in the Great Recession." *Journal of Labor Economics* 34, Supplement 1: S403–S444.

Bitler, Marianne, Hilary W. Hoynes, and Diane Whitmore Schanzenbach. 2020. "The Social Safety Net in the Wake of Covid 19." NBER Working Paper 27796 (September).

Blanchet, Didier, Antoine Bozio, Simon Rabaté, and Muriel Roger. 2019. "Workers' Employment Rates and Pension Reforms in France: The Role of Implicit Labor Taxation." NBER Working Paper 25733 (April).

Blau, Francine D. and Christopher Mackie. 2016. *The Economic and Fiscal Consequences of Immigration.* Washington, DC: National Academies Press.

Boeri, Tito. 2010. "Immigration to the Land of Redistribution." *Economica* 77, 308 (October): 651–687.

Böhlmark, Anders, and Mikael Lindahl. 2012. "Independent Schools and Long-Run Educational Outcomes: Evidence from Sweden's Large-Scale Voucher Reform." IZA Discussion Paper 6683 (June).

Böhlmark, Anders and Mikael Lindahl. 2015. "Independent Schools and Long-Run Educational Outcomes: Evidence from Sweden's Large-Scale Voucher Reform." *Economica* 82, 327 (July): 508–551 doi:10.1111/ecca.12130.

Bologna Pavlik, Jamie and Andrew T. Young. 2018. *Medieval European Traditions in Representation and State Capacity Today.* Lubbock, TX: Texas Tech University.

Bonin, Holger. 2009. "15 Years of Pension Reform in Germany: Old Successes and New Threats." Center for European Economic Research (ZEW), Discussion Paper 09-035. ftp://ftp.zew.de/pub/zew-docs/dp/dp09035.pdf.

Bonney, Richard (ed.). 1995. *Economic Systems and State Finance.* Oxford: Clarendon Press.

Bonney, Richard (ed.). 1999. *The Rise of the Fiscal State in Europe (1200–1815).* Oxford: Oxford University Press.

Borjas, George. 2019. "Immigration and Economic Growth." NBER Working Paper 25836 (May).

Börsch-Supan, Axel H. and Courtney Coile. 2018. "Social Security Programs and Retirement around the World: Reforms and Retirement Incentives – Introduction and Summary." NBER Working Paper 25280 (November).

Borzutzky, Silvia and Mark Hyde. 2017. "The Chilean Welfare State System, with Special Reference to Social Security Privatization." In Christian Aspalter (ed.), *The Routledge International Handbook to Welfare Systems.* London: Routledge, pp. 138–154.

Boubtane, Ekrame, Jean-Christophe Dumont and Cristophe Rault. 2014. "Immigration and Economic Growth in the OECD Countries 1986–2006." CESifo Working Paper Series 5392.

Bourguignon, François and Christian Morrisson. 2002. "Inequality among World Citizens, 1820–1992." *American Economic Review* 92, 4 (September): 727–744.

Bourguignon, F., M. Fournier, and M. Gurgnand. 1998. "Distribution, Development and Education: Taiwan, 1979–1994." World Bank Working Paper (May).

Bourguignon, F., M. Fournier, and M. Gurgnand. 1999. "Fast Development with a Stable Income Distribution: Taiwan, 1979–1994," Document de Travail 9921, Centre de Recherche en Économie et Statistique. Paris: Institut National de la Statistique et des Études Économiques.

Boyer, George R. 1989. "Malthus Was Right after All: Poor Relief and Birth Rates in Southeastern England." *Journal of Political Economy* 97, 1 (February): 93–114.

Boyer, George R. 1990. *An Economic History of the English Poor Law, 1750 – 1850.* Cambridge: Cambridge University Press.

Boyer, George. R. 2018. *The Winding Road to the Welfare State: Economic Insecurity and Social Welfare Policy in Britain.* Princeton: Princeton University Press.

Brandt, Loren, Debin Ma, and Thomas G. Rawski. 2014. "From Divergence to Convergence: Reevaluating the History behind China's Economic Boom." *Journal of Economic Literature* 52, 1 (March): 45–123. http://dx.doi.org/10.1257/jel.52.1.45.

Brenøe, Anne A., Serena P. Canaan, Nikolaj A. Harmon, and Heather N. Royer. 2020. "Is Parental Leave Costly for Firms and Co-Workers?" NBER Working Paper 26622 (January).

Brewer, John. 1989. *The Sinews of Power: Money, War, and the English State, 1688–1783.* Boston, MA: Unwin.

Broadberry, Stephen, Johann Custodis, and Bishnupriya Gupta. 2015. "India and the Great Divergence: An Anglo-Indian Comparison of GDP Per Capita, 1600–1871." *Explorations in Economic History* 55 (January): 58–75.

Broadberry, Stephen, Hanhui Guan, and David Daokui Li. 2018. "China, Europe, and the Great Divergence: A Study in Historical National Accounting, 980–1850." *Journal of Economic History* 78, 4 (December): 955–1000.

Broadberry, Stephen, Bruce Campbell, Alexander Klein, Mark Overton, and Bas van Leeuwen. 2015. *British Economic Growth, 1270–1870.* Cambridge: Cambridge University Press.

Brundage, Anthony. 1978. *The Making of the New Poor Law: The Politics of Inquiry, Enactment, and Implementation, 1832–39.* New Brunswick: Rutgers University Press.

Brundage, Anthony and David Eastwood. 1990. "The Making of the New Poor Law Redivivus." *Past & Present* 127 (May): 183–194.

Bugra, Ayse and Çaglar Keyder. 2006. "The Turkish Welfare Regime in Transformation." *Journal of European Social Policy* 16, 3 (August): 211–228.

Buringh, Eltjo and Jan Luiten van Zanden. 2009. "Charting the 'Rise of the West': Manuscripts and Printed Books in Europe, A Long-Term Perspective from the Sixth through Eighteenth Centuries," *Journal of Economic History* 69, 2 (June): 409–445.

Butts, R. Freeman. 1978. *Public Education in the United States from Revolution to Reform.* New York: Holt Rinehart and Winston.

Buxton, Julia. 2014. "Social Policy in Venezuela: Bucking Neoliberalism or Unsustainable Clientelism." Working Paper 2014-16. United Nations Research Institute for Social Development.

Carry, Alain. 1999. "Le compte satellite rétrospectif de l'éducation en France (1820–1996)." *Économies et sociétés: Cahiers de l'ISMÉA*, Série AF, no. 25 (February–March).

Carter, Susan et al. (eds.). 2006. *The Historical Statistics of the United States: Millennial Edition.* 5 volumes. New York: Cambridge University Press.

Cascio, Elizabeth U. and Diane Whitmore Schanzenbach. 2013. "The Impacts of Expanding Access to High-Quality Preschool Education." *Brookings Papers on Economic Activity* (Fall): 127–178, and comments by Caroline Hoxby and Alan B. Krueger, 179–192.

Cascio, Elizabeth U. and Na'ama Shenhav. 2020. "A Century of the American Woman Voter: Sex Gaps in Political Participation, Preferences, and Partisanship since Women's Enfranchisement." NBER Working Paper 26709 (January).

Case, Anne and Angus Deaton. 2020. *Deaths of Despair and the Future of Capitalism.* Princeton: Princeton University Press.

Catillon, Maryaline, David Cutler, and Thomas Getzen. 2018. "Two Hundred Years of Health and Medical Care: The Importance of Medical Care for Life Expectancy Gains." NBER Working Paper 25330 (December).

Chaudhary, Latika. 2009. "Determinants of Primary Schooling in British India." *Journal of Economic History* 69, 1 (March): 269–302.

Chaudhary, Latika and Peter H. Lindert. Forthcoming. "Healthy, Literate, and Smart: The Global Increase in Human Capital since 1870." In Stephen Broadberry and Kyoji Fukao (eds.), *Cambridge Economic History of the Modern World,* volume II: *1870–2010.* Cambridge: Cambridge University Press.

Chaudhury, Nazmul, Jeffrey Hammer, Michael Kremer, Karthik Muralidharan, and F. Halsey Rogers. 2006. "Missing in Action: Teacher and Health Worker Absence in Developing Countries." *Journal of Economic Perspectives* 20, 1 (Winter): 91–116.

Chaudhary, Latika, Aldo Musacchio, Steven Nafziger, and Se Yan. 2012. "Big BRICs, Weak Foundations: The Beginning of Public Elementary Education in Brazil, Russia, India, and China, 1880–1930." *Explorations in Economic History* 49, 2: 221–240.

Chenery, Hollis et al. 1974. *Redistribution with Growth.* London: Oxford University Press.

Cheyre Valenzuela, Hernán. 1988. *La Previsíon en Chile Ayer y Hoy.* Santiago: Centro de Estudios Públicos.

Chile, Oficina de Planificación Nacional (ODEPLAN). 1971. *Plan de la economía nacional, 1971–76; antecedentes sobre el desarrollo chileno, 1960–70.* Santiago: ODEPLAN.

Choi, Jaesung and Jisoo Hwang. 2017. "The Effect of School Choice on Student's Academic Performance." *Hitotsubashi Journal of Economics* 58: 1–19.

Cipolla, Carlo M. 1969. *Literacy and Development in the West.* Harmondsworth: Penguin.

Clark, Gregory. 1996. "The Political Foundations of Modern Economic Growth: England, 1540–1800." *Journal of Interdisciplinary History* 26 (Spring): 563–588.

Clemens, Michael A. 2004. "The Long Walk to School: International Education Goals in Historical Perspective." Center for Global Development Working Paper 37 (March).

Cody, Lisa Forman. 2000. "The Politics of Illegitimacy in an Age of Reform: Women, Reproduction, and Political Economy in England's New Poor Law of 1834." *Journal of Women's History* 11, 4 (Winter): 131–156.

Comín Comín, Francisco. 2012. "Spain: From Composite Monarchy to Nation-State, 1492–1914: An Exceptional Case?" In Bartolomé Yun-Casalilla and Patrick K. O'Brien (eds.), with Francisco Comín Comín, *The Rise of Fiscal States: A Global History, 1500–1914*. Cambridge: Cambridge University Press, pp. 233–266.

Connor, Philip and Neil G. Ruiz. 2019. "Majority of U.S. Public Supports High-Skilled Immigration." Pew Research Center, January 22.

Constitute Project. 2018. *Brazil's Constitution of 1988 with Amendments through 2014*. Translated to English by Keith S. Rosenn. Constituteproject.org, accessed July 4, 2019.

Cook, Linda J. 2007. *Postcommunist Welfare States: Reform Politics in Russia and Eastern Europe*. Ithaca, NY: Cornell University Press.

Cressy, David. 1977. "Levels of Illiteracy in England, 1530–1730." *Historical Journal* 20, 1 (March): 1–23.

Cutler, David M. and Dan P. Ly. 2011. "The (Paper)Work of Medicine: Understanding International Medical Costs." *Journal of Economic Perspectives* 25, 2 (Spring): 3–25.

Dahlberg, Matz, Karin Edmark, and Heléne Lundqvist. 2012. "Ethnic Diversity and Preferences for Redistribution." *Journal of Political Economy* 120, 1 (February): 41–76.

Dahlberg, Matz, Karin Edmark, and Heléne Lundqvist. 2013. "Ethnic Diversity and Preferences for Redistribution: Reply." Research Institute of Industrial Economics (Stockholm), IFN Working Paper 955 (February). www.ifn.se/wfiles/wp/wp955.pdf.

Daniels, Robert V. 1984. *A Documentary History of Communism*. Burlington, VT: University of Vermont Press.

Daunton, Martin. 2002a *Trusting Leviathan: The Politics of Taxation in Britain, 1799–1914*. Cambridge: Cambridge University Press.

Daunton, Martin. 2002b. *Just Taxes: The Politics of Taxation in Britain 1914–1979*. Cambridge: Cambridge University Press.

Davis, Karen, Kristof Stremikis, David Squires, and Cathy Schoen. 2014. "Mirror, Mirror on the Wall: How the Performance of the U.S. Health Care System Compares Internationally." Commonwealth Fund (June). www.commonwealthfund.org/sites/default/files/documents/___media_files_publications_fund_report_2014_jun_1755_davis_mirror_mirror_2014.pdf, accessed Apr. 29, 2020.

Davison, Diane M. 1982. "The Bastardy Controversy of Nineteenth-Century Britain." Doctoral dissertation, Lehigh University. https://preserve.lehigh.edu/cgi/viewcontent.cgi?article=3430&context=etd.

Deaton, Angus. 2015. *The Great Escape: Health, Wealth, and the Origins of Inequality*. Princeton: Princeton University Press.

De Corso, Giuseppe. 2013. "El Crecimiento Económico de Venezuela, desde la Oligarquía conservatora hasta la Revolución Bolivariana: 1830–2012. Una Visión Cuantitativa."*Revista de Historia Económica* 31, 3 (December): 321–357.

Dee, Thomas S. 2004. "Are There Civic Returns to Education?" *Journal of Public Economics* 88, 9–10 (August): 1697–1720.

De Ferranti, David, Guillermo E. Perry, Francisco H. G. Ferreira, and Michael Walton. 2004. *Inequality in Latin America: Breaking with History?* Washington, DC: World Bank.

De Kwaasteniet, Marjanne. 1985. "Denominational Education and Contemporary Education Policy in the Netherlands." *European Journal of Education* 20, 4: 371–383.

De Kwaasteniet, Marjanne. 1990. *Denomination and Primary Education in the Netherlands (1870–1984).* Amsterdam: Instituut voor Sociale Geografie, Universiteit van Amsterdam.

Delannoy, Françoise. 2000. "Education Reforms in Chile, 1980–98: A Lesson in Pragmatism." Washington, DC, World Bank. Country Studies, Education Reform and Management Publication Series Vol. 1, No. 1.

DeLong, J. Bradford and Andrei Shleifer. 1993. "Princes and Merchants: City Growth before the Industrial Revolution." *Journal of Law and Economics* 36 (October): 671–702.

Deng, Kent G. 2012. "The Continuation and Efficiency of the Chinese Fiscal State, 700 BC – 1911." In Bartolomé Yun-Casalilla and Patrick K. O'Brien (eds.), with Franciso Comín Comín, *The Rise of Fiscal States: A Global History, 1500–1914.* Cambridge: Cambridge University Press, pp. 335–352.

De Vries, Jan and Ad van der Woude (1997). *The First Modern Economy: Success, Failure, and Perseverance of the Dutch Economy, 1500–1815.* Cambridge: Cambridge University Press.

Díaz, J., Rolf Lüders, and Gert Wagner. 2010. "La República en Cifras, 2010." EH Clio Lab-Iniciativa Científica Milenio. http://cliolab.economia.uc.cl/BD .html.

Diebolt, Claude. 1997. "L'évolution de longue période du système éducatif allemand xixe et xxe siécles." *Économies et sociétés: Cahiers de l'ISMÉA*, Série AF, no. 23 (February–March): 278–279, 338–341.

Diebolt, Claude. 2000. *Dépenses d'éducation et cycles économiques en espagne: XIXe et Xxe siècles.* Paris: L'Harmattan.

Digby, Anne. 1975. "The Labour Market and the Continuity of Social Policy after 1834: The Case of the Eastern Counties." *Economic History Review* 28, 1 (February): 69–83.

Dincecco, Mark. 2011. *Political Transformations and Public Finances: Europe, 1650–1913.* Cambridge: Cambridge University Press.

Dincecco, Mark. 2017. *State Capacity and Economic Development: Present and Past.* Cambridge: Cambridge University Press.

Dixon, John. 1981. *The Chinese Welfare System, 1949–1979.* New York: Praeger.

Duflo, Esther, Rema Hanna, and Stephen P. Ryan. 2012. "Incentives Work: Getting Teachers to Come to School." *American Economic Review* 102, 4: 1241–1278.

Dustmann, Christian and Tommaso Frattini. 2013. "The Fiscal Effects of Immigration to the UK." Centre for Research and Analysis of Migration Department of Economics, University College London, CDP No. 22/13 (November).

Easterlin, Richard A. 1981. "Why Isn't the Whole World Developed?" *Journal of Economic History* 41, 1 (March): 1–17.
Easterly, William. 1995. Comment on "What Do Cross-Country Studies Teach about Government Involvement, Prosperity, and Economic Growth?" *Brookings Papers on Economic Activity* 2: 419–424.
Easterly, William and Ross Levine. 1997. "Africa's Growth Tragedy: Policies and Ethnic Divisions." *Quarterly Journal of Economics* 112, 44 (November): 1203–1250.
Easterly, William and Sergio Rebelo. 1993. "Fiscal Policy and Economic Growth." *Journal of Monetary Economics* 32 (December): 417–458.
Eastwood, David. 1994. *Governing Rural England: Tradition and Transformation in Local Government, 1780–1840.* Oxford: Clarendon Press.
Eberts, Randall W. and Joe A. Stone. 1986. "Teachers' Unions and the Productivity of Public Schools." *Economic Inquiry* 24 (October): 631–644.
Edwards, Sebastian. 1996. "The Chilean Pension Reform." NBER Working Paper 5811 (November).
Eggleston, Karen N. and Victor R. Fuchs. 2012. "The New Demographic Transition: Most Gains in Life Expectancy Now Realized Late in Life." *Journal of Economic Perspectives* 26, 3 (Summer): 137–156.
Elveren, Adam Yaruz and Tuba I. Agartan. 2017. "The Turkish Welfare State System: With Special Reference to Human Capital Development." In Christain Aspalter (ed.), *The Routledge International Handbook to Welfare Systems.* London: Routledge, pp. 317–331.
Emery, J. C. Herbert. 2010. "'Un-American' or Unnecessary? America's Rejection of Compulsory Government Health Insurance in the Progressive Era." *Explorations in Economic History* 47, 1 (March): 68–81.
Engerman, Stanley L. and Kenneth L. Sokoloff. 2012. *Economic Development in the Americas since 1500: Endowments and Institutions.* Cambridge: Cambridge University Press.
Engerman, Stanley L., Elena V. Mariscal, and Kenneth L. Sokoloff. 2009. "The Evolution of Schooling Institutions in the Americas, 1800–1925." In David Eltis, Frank Lewis, and Kenneth L. Sokoloff (eds.), *Human Capital and Institutions: A Long Run View.* New York: Cambridge University Press, pp. 93–142.
England, Paula, Jonathan Bearak, Michelle Budig, and Melissa Hodges. 2016. "Do Highly Paid, Highly Skilled Women Experience the Largest Motherhood Penalty?" *American Sociological Review* 81, 6 (December): 1161–1189.
Ennser-Jedenastik, Laurenz. 2018. "Welfare Chauvinism in Populist Radical Right Platforms: The Role of Redistributive Justice Principles." *Social Policy & Administration* 52, 1 (January): 293–314.
Epple, Dennis, Richard E. Romano, and Miguel Urquiola. 2017. "School Vouchers: A Survey of the Economics Literature." *Journal of Economic Literature* 55, 2 (June): 441–492.
Esping-Andersen, Gøsta. 1990. *The Three Worlds of Welfare Capitalism.* Princeton: Princeton University Press.
Esping-Andersen, Gøsta. 1999. *Social Foundations of Post-Industrial Economies.* Oxford: Oxford University Press.

Espuelas, Sergio. 2012. "Are Dictatorships Less Redistributive? A Comparative Analysis of Social Spending in Europe, 1950–1980." *European Review of Economic History* 16, 2: 211–232.

Espuelas, Sergio. 2013. "La evolución del gasto social público en España, 1850–2005." Estudios de Historia Económica 63. Banco de España, Madrid.

Fei, John C. H., Gustav Ranis, and Shirley W. Y. Kuo. 1979. *Growth with Equity: The Taiwan Case.* New York: Oxford University Press.

Feigenberg, Benjamin, Steven Rivkin, and Rui Yan. 2017. "Illusory Gains from Chile's Targeted School Voucher Experiment." NBER Working Paper 23178 (February).

Feuerwerker, Albert. 1984. "The State and the Economy in Late Imperial China." *Theory and Society* 13, 3 (May): 297–326.

Fishback, Price V. 2020. "Social Insurance and Public Assistance in the Twentieth-Century United States: 2019 Presidential Address for the Economic History Association." NBER Working Paper 26938 (April).

Fisher, Irving. 1917. "The Need for Health Insurance." *American Labor Legislation Review* 7, 1 (March): 9–26.

Fiszbein, Ariel and Norbert Schady, with Francisco H. G. Ferreira, Margaret Grosh, Nial Kelleher, Pedro Olinto, and Emmanuel Skoufias. 2009. *Conditional Cash Transfers – Reducing Present and Future Poverty.* Washington, DC: World Bank.

Flora, Peter and Jens Albers. 1983. *State, Economy and Society in Western Europe, 1815–1975.* Frankfurt: Campus Verlag.

Flora, Peter and Arnold J. Heidenheimer (eds.). 1981. *The Development of Welfare States in Europe and America.* London: Transaction Books.

Flynn, James R. 1984. "The Mean IQ of Americans: Massive Gains 1932 to 1978." *Psychological Bulletin* 95, 1 (January): 29–51.

Flynn, James R. 1987. "Massive IQ Gains in 14 Nations: What IQ Tests Really Measure." *Psychological Bulletin* 101, 2 (March): 171–191.

Flynn, James R. 2000. "IQ Trends over Time: Intelligence, Race, and Meritocracy." In Kenneth A. Arrow, Samuel Bowles, and Steven Derlauf (eds.), *Meritocracy and Economic Inequality.* Princeton: Princeton University Press, pp. 35–60.

Flynn, James R. 2007. *What Is Intelligence? Beyond the Flynn Effect.* New York: Cambridge University Press.

Flynn, James R. 2008. *Where Have All the Liberals Gone? Race, Class, and Ideals in America.* New York: Cambridge University Press.

Flynn, James R. 2012. *Are We Getting Smarter? Rising IQ in the Twenty-First Century.* Cambridge: Cambridge University Press.

Fort, Margherita, Andrea Ichino, and Giulio Zanella. 2020. "Cognitive and Non-Cognitive Costs of Day Care at Age 0–2 for Children in Advantaged Families." *Journal of Political Economy* 128, 1 (January): 158–205.

Fowler, Frances C. 1992. "School Choice Policy in France: Success and Limitations." *Educational Policy* 6, 4 (December): 429–443.

Frankema, Ewout H. P. 2009. *Has Latin America Always Been Unequal? A Comparative Study of Asset and Income Inequality in the Long Twentieth Century.* Leiden and Boston: Brill.

Friedman, Milton. 1955. "The Role of Government in Education." In Robert A. Solo (ed.), *Economics and the Public Interest.* New Brunswick, NJ: Rutgers University Press.

Fritschy, Wantje, Marjolein 't Hart, and Edwin Horlings. 2012. "Long-Term Trends in the Fiscal History of the Netherlands, 1515–1913." In Bartolomé Yun-Casalilla and Patrick K. O'Brien (eds.), with Francisco Comín, *The Rise of Fiscal States: A Global History, 1500–1914.* Cambridge: Cambridge University Press, pp. 39–66.

Garfinkel, Irwin, Lee Rainwater, and Timothy M. Smeeding. 2010. *Wealth and Welfare States: Is America a Laggard or Leader?* Oxford: Oxford University Press.

Gaston, Noel and Gulasekaran Rajaguru. 2013. "International Migration and the Welfare State Revisited." *European Journal of Political Economy* 29 (March): 90–101.

Gatrell, Peter. 2012. "The Russian Fiscal State, 1600–1914." In Bartolomé Yun-Casalilla and Patrick K. O'Brien (eds.), with Francisco Comín, *The Rise of Fiscal States: A Global History, 1500–1914.* Cambridge: Cambridge University Press, pp. 191–214.

Gemmell, Norman, Richard Kneller, and Ismael Sanz. 2011. "The Timing and Persistence of Fiscal Policy Impacts on Growth: Evidence from OECD Countries." *Economic Journal* 121 (February): F33–F58.

Gill, Indermit S., Truman G. Packard, Juan Yermo, and Todd Pugatch. 2004. *Keeping the Promise of Old Age Income Security in Latin America.* Washington, DC: World Bank (September). https://openknowledge.worldbank.org/handle/10986/10349.

Go, Sun and Peter H. Lindert. 2010. "The Uneven Rise of American Public Schools to 1850." *Journal of Economic History* 70, 1 (March): 1–26.

Goldin, Claudia. 1998. "America's Graduation from High School: The Evolution and Spread of Secondary Schooling in the Twentieth Century." *Journal of Economic History* 58, 2 (June): 345-374.

Goldin, Claudia. 2001. "The Human Capital Century and American Leadership: Virtues of the Past." *Journal of Economic History* 61, 2 (June): 263–292.

Goldin, Claudia. 2006. "Education." In Susan Carter et al. (eds.), *The Historical Statistics of the United States: Millennial Edition.* 5 volumes. New York: Cambridge University Press, vol. B, ch. Bc.

Goldin, Claudia and Lawrence F. Katz. 2008. *The Race between Education and Technology.* Cambridge, MA.: Belknap Press for Harvard University Press.

Goldin, Claudia and Joshua Mitchell. 2017. "The New Life Cycle of Women's Employment: Disappearing Humps, Sagging Middles, Expanding Tops." *Journal of Economic Perspectives* 31, 1 (Winter 2017): 161–182.

Goldin, Claudia, Sari Pekkala Kerr, and Claudia Olivetti. 2020. "Why Firms Offer Paid Parental Leave: An Exploratory Study." NBER Working Paper 26617 (January).

Goldsmith, Raymond W. 1985. *Comparative National Balance Sheets: A Study of Twenty Countries, 1688–1978.* Chicago: University of Chicago Press.

González, Pablo, Alejandra Mizala, and Pilar Romaguera. 2004. "Vouchers, Inequalities, and the Chilean Experience." Center for Applied Economics (CEA) University of Chile (June). www.academia.edu/29631499/.

Goodman, Peter S. 2019. "The Nordic Model May Be the Best Cushion against Capitalism. Can It Survive Immigration?" *New York Times*, July 11. www.nytimes.com/2019/07/11/business/sweden-economy-immigration.html

Graff, Harvey J. 1987. *The Legacies of Literacy*. Bloomington: Indiana University Press.

Gray, Rowena. 2013. "Taking Technology to Task: The Skill Content of Technological Change in Early Twentieth Century United States." *Explorations in Economic History* 50, 3 (July): 351–367.

Green, David A. and W. Craig Riddell. 2019. "Is There a Tradeoff between Ethnic Diversity and Redistribution? The Case of Income Assistance in Canada." IZA Discussion Paper 12098 (January).

Greif, Avner and Murat Iyigun. 2013. "What Did the Old Poor Law Really Accomplish? A Redux." IZA Discussion Paper 7398. Available at SSRN: https://ssrn.com/abstract=2266825.

Grew, Raymond and Patrick J. Harrigan. 1991. *School, State, and Society: The Growth of Elementary Schooling in Nineteenth-Century France*. Ann Arbor: University of Michigan Press.

Grindle, Merilee Serrill. 2004. *Despite the Odds: The Contentious Politics of Education Reform*. Princeton: Princeton University Press.

Gu, Edward X. 2001. "Dismantling the Chinese Mini-Welfare State? Marketization and the Politics of Institutional Transformation, 1979–1999." *Communist and Post-Communist Studies* 34: 91–111.

Hagist, Christian and Laurence J. Kotlikoff. 2009. "Who's Going Broke? Comparing Healthcare Costs in Ten OECD Countries." *Hacienda Publica Espanola/Revista de Economia Publica* 188, 1: 55–72.

Haile, Fiseha and Miguel Niño-Zarazúa. 2018. "Does Social Spending Improve Welfare in Low-Income and Middle-Income Countries?" *Journal of International Development* 30, 3 (April): 367–398.

Hanson, Gordon and Ann Harrison. 1999. "Trade Liberalization and Wage Inequality in Mexico." *Industrial and Labor Relations Review* 52 (January): 271–288.

Hanson, Gordon and Craig McIntosh. 2016. "Is the Mediterranean the New Rio Grande? US and EU Pressures in the Long Run." NBER Working Paper 22622 (September).

Hanushek, Eric A. 2003. "The Failure of Input-Based Schooling Policies." *Economic Journal* 113, 485: F64-F98.

Hanushek, Eric A. and Ludger Woessmann. 2015. *The Knowledge Capital of Nations: Education and the Economics of Growth*. Cambridge, MA: MIT Press.

Hanushek, Eric A., Paul E. Peterson, and Ludger Woessmann. 2013. *Endangering Prosperity: A Global View of the American School*. Washington, DC: Brookings Institution Press.

Harkness, Sara and Jane Waldfogel. 2003. "The Family Gap in Pay: Evidence from Seven Industrialized Countries." *Research in Labor Economics* 1, 22: 369–413.

Hausmann, Ricardo and Francisco R. Rodríguez (eds.). 2013. *Venezuela before Chávez: Anatomy of an Economic Collapse.* University Park, PA: Pennsylvania State University Press.

Hecock, R. Douglas. 2006. "Electoral Competition, Globalization, and Subnational Education Spending in Mexico, 1999–2004." *American Journal of Political Science* 50, 4 (October): 950–961.

Hedberg, P., L. Karlsson, and H. Häggqvist. 2018. "How Does Openness to Trade Really Affect the Welfare State? Evidence from Social Spending in 21 Countries, 1920-2000." Paper presented at the XVIII World Economic History Congress, Boston. Underlying data kindly supplied by Henric Haggqvist.

Hendren, Nathaniel and Ben Sprung-Keyser. 2019. "A Unified Welfare Analysis of Government Policies." NBER Working Paper 26144 (August).

Henriques, Ursala R. Q. 1967. "Bastardy and the New Poor Law." *Past & Present* 37 (July): 103–129.

Hinrichs, Harley H. 1966. *A General Theory of Tax Structure Change during Economic Development.* Cambridge, MA: Harvard Law School of Harvard University.

Hinrichs, Karl. 2005. "New Century – New Paradigm: Pension Reforms in Germany." In Guiliano Bonoli and Toshimitsu Shinkawa (eds.), *Ageing and Pension Reform around the World: Evidence from Eleven Countries.* Cheltenham: Edward Elgar, pp. 47–73.

Hoffman, Philip T. and Kathryn Norberg (eds.). 1994. *Fiscal Crises, Liberty, and Representative Government, 1450–1789.* Stanford: Stanford University Press.

Hollingsworth, J. Rogers. 1986. *A Political Economy of Medicine: Great Britain and the United States.* Baltimore: Johns Hopkins University Press.

Hollingsworth, J. Rogers, Jerald Hage, and Robert A. Hanneman. 1990. *State Intervention in Medical Care: Consequences for Britain, France, Sweden, and the United States 1890–1970.* Baltimore: Johns Hopkins University Press.

Homer, Sidney and Richard Sylla. 1991. *A History of Interest Rates.* Third edition. New Brunswick: Rutgers University Press.

Hong Kong, Education Bureau. 2015. "Income Inequality." www.edb.gov.hk/attachment/en/curriculum-development/kla/pshe/references-and-resources/economics/income_eng.pdf.

Hooker, Mark. 2009. *Freedom of Education: The Dutch Political Battle for State Funding of All Schools Both Public and Private (1801–1920).* USA [no city given]: Llyfrawr (copy borrowed from the University of Arkansas).

Hoxby, Caroline. 1996. "How Teachers' Unions Affect Education Production." *Quarterly Journal of Economics* 111, 3 (August): 671–718.

Hoxby, Caroline M. 2001. "All School Finance Equalizations Are Not Created Equal." *Quarterly Journal of Economics* 116, 4 (November): 1188–1231.

Hoynes, Hilary and Jesse Rothstein. 2017. "Tax Policy toward Low-Income Families." In Alan Auerbach and Kent Smetters (eds.), *Economics of Tax Policy.* New York: Oxford University Press, pp. 183–225.

Hoynes, Hilary and Diane Whitmore Schanzenbach. 2018. "Safety Net Investments in Children." *Brookings Papers on Economic Activity* 1 (Spring): 89–133.

Hoynes, Hilary, Jesse Rothstein, and Krista Ruffini. 2017. "Making Work Pay Better through an Expanded Earned Income Tax Credit." Hamilton Project Policy Proposal 2017–2019 (October).

Hsieh, Chang-Tai and Miguel Urquiola. 2006. "The Effect of Generalized School Choice on Stratification and Achievement: Evidence from Chile's School Voucher Program," *Journal of Public Economics* 90 (November): 1477–1503.

Immervoll, Herwig and Linda Richardson. 2011. "Redistribution Policy and Inequality Reduction in OECD Countries: What Has Changed in Two Decades?" OECD Social, Employment, and Migration Working Paper no. 122. ELSA/ELSA/WD/SEM(2011)7.

Indiana Department of Education, Office of School Finance. 2019. *Choice Scholarships Program Annual Report 2018–2019*, at www.doe.in.gov, accessed Oct. 29, 2019.

Inklaar, Robert, Pieter Woltjer, and Daniel Gallardo Albarrán. 2019. "The Composition of Capital and Cross-country Productivity Comparisons." *International Productivity Monitor* 36 (Spring): 34–52.

Jacobs, Didier. 2000. "Low Inequality with Low Redistribution? An Analysis of Income Distribution in Japan, South Korea and Taiwan Compared to Britain." London School of Economics. Centre for Analysis of Social Exclusion CASE paper 33 (January).

Jordà, Òscar, Moritz Schularick, and Alan M. Taylor. 2017. "Macro-Financial History and the New Business Cycle Facts." In Martin Eichenbaum and Jonathan A. Parker (eds.), *NBER Macroeconomics Annual 2016*, volume 31. Chicago: University of Chicago Press, pp. 213–263.

Jordà, Òscar, Katharina Knoll, Dmitry Kuvshinov, Moritz Schularick, and Alan M. Taylor. Forthcoming. "The Rate of Return on Everything, 1870–2015." *Quarterly Journal of Economics.*

Kaestle, Carl. 1976. "'Between the Scylla of Brutal Ignorance and the Charybdis of a Literary Education': Elite Attitudes toward Mass Schooling in Early Industrial England and America." In Lawrence Stone (ed.), *Schooling and Society: Studies in the History of Education.* Baltimore: Johns Hopkins University Press, pp. 177–191.

Kaestle, Carl. 1983. *Pillars of the Republic: Common Schools and American Society, 1780–1860.* New York: Hill & Wang.

Karaman, K. Kivanc and Sevket Pamuk. 2010. "Ottoman State Finances in European Perspective, 1500–1914." *Journal of Economic History* 70, 3 (September): 593–629.

Kato, Junko. 2003. *Regressive Taxation and the Welfare State: Path Dependence and Policy Diffusion.* Cambridge: Cambridge University Press.

Kenworthy, Lane. 2019. *Social Democratic Capitalism.* Oxford: Oxford University Press.

Khan, Habibullah. 2001. *Social Policy in Singapore: A Confucian Model?* Washington, DC: World Bank Institute.

Kimball, Miles. 1988. "Farmers' Cooperatives as Behavior toward Risk." *American Economic Review* 78, 1 (March): 224–232.

King, Elizabeth M. and M. Anne Hill. 1997. "Women's Education in Developing Countries: An Overview." In E. M. King and M. A. Hill (eds.), *Women's Education in Developing Countries: Barriers, Benefits, and Policies.* Baltimore: Johns Hopkins University Press, pp. 1–50.

King, Gary and Langche Zeng. 2006. "The Dangers of Extreme Counterfactuals." *Political Analysis* 14: 131–159.

King, Gary and Langche Zeng. 2007. "When Can History Be Our Guide? The Pitfalls of Counterfactual Inference." *International Studies Quarterly* 51, 1 (March): 183–210.

Kingdon, Geeta, Angela Little, Monazza Aslam, Shenila Rawal, Terry Moe, Harry Patrinos, Tara Beteille, Rukmini Banerji, Brent Parton, and Shailendra K. Sharma. 2014. "A Rigorous Review of the Political Economy of Education Systems in Developing Countries." Final Report. Education Rigorous Literature Review. Department for International Development. The DFID Research for Development website: http://r4d.dfid.gov.uk/ and the EPPI-Centre website: http://eppi.ioe.ac.uk/.

Kiniria, Maxwell Dryjer. 2019. "Essays on Social Policy in Victorian England." Ph.D. dissertation, Cornell University.

Kneller, Richard, Michael Bleaney, and Norman Gemmell. 1999. "Fiscal Policy and Growth: Evidence from OECD Countries." *Journal of Public Economics* 74, 2 (November): 171–190.

Körner, Martin. 1995. "Expenditure." In Richard Bonney (ed.), *Economic Systems and State Finance.* Oxford: Clarendon Press, pp. 393–421.

Kose, Esra, Elira Kuka, and Na'ama Shenhav. 2018. "Who Benefitted from Women's Suffrage?" NBER Working Paper 24933 (August).

Kotlikoff, Laurence J. and Scott Burns. 2005. *The Coming Generational Storm.* Cambridge, MA: MIT Press.

Kritzer, Barbara E. 2008. "Chile's Next Generation Pension Reform." *Social Security Bulletin* 68, 2. www.ssa.gov/policy/docs/ssb/v68n2/v68n2p69-text.html#chart2.

Krugman, Paul. 1994. "The Myth of Asia's Miracle," *Foreign Affairs* 73, 6 (November–December): 62–78.

Krugman, Paul. 2005. "America's Senior Moment." *New York Review of Books* 52, 4 (March 10).

Kruse, Agneta. 2010. "A Stable Pension System: The Eighth Wonder." In Tommy Bengtsson (ed.), *Population Ageing – A Threat to the Welfare State?* Berlin and Heidelberg: Springer-Verlag, pp. 47–64.

Kumon, Yuzuru. 2019. "Rich Europe, Poor Asia: How Wealth Inequality, Demography and Crop Risks Explain the Poverty of Pre-Industrial East Asia, 1300–1800." Ph.D. dissertation, University of California–Davis.

Kuosmanen, Isa. 2014. "The Effects of School Choice on Segregation of Finnish Comprehensive Schools." Master's thesis, University of Helsinki Faculty of Social Sciences Economics.

Kurmanaev, Anatoly and Isayen Herrera. 2020. "Venezuela's Capital Is Booming: Is This the End of the Revolution?" *New York Times*, Feb. 1, updated Feb. 18.

Kwan, Chang Yee and Mukul G. Asher. 2019. "Signs of Transition and Renewal in Singapore." *East Asia Forum*, January 3. www.eastasiaforum.org/2019/01/03/signs-of-transition-and-renewal-in-singapore.

Kwon, Huck-Ju. 1997. "Beyond European Welfare Regimes: Comparative Perspectives on East Asian Welfare Systems". *Journal of Social Policy* 26, 4: 467–484.

Lambrecht, Thijs and Anne Winter. 2018. "An Old Poor Law on the Continent? Agrarian Capitalism, Poor Taxes, and Village Conflict in Eighteenth-Century Coastal Flanders." *Economic History Review* 71, 4 (November): 1173–1198.

Lanjouw, Peter, and Nicholas Stern. 1998. *Economic Development in Palanpur over Five Decades.* Oxford: Clarendon Press.

Lee, Jong-Wha and Hanol Lee. 2016. "Human Capital in the Long Run" *Journal of Development Economics* 122 (2016): 147–169.

Lee. Ronald D. 2016. "Macroeconomics, Aging, and Growth." In John Piggott and Alan Woodland (eds.), *Handbook of the Economics of Population Aging*, vol. 1A. Amsterdam: Elsevier, pp. 59–118.

Lee, Ronald D. and Andrew Mason (eds.). 2011. *Population Aging and the Generational Economy: A Global Perspective.* Cheltenham and Northampton, MA: Edward Elgar.

Lee, Ronald D. and Timothy Miller. 2000. "Immigration, Social Security, and Broader Fiscal Impacts." *American Economic Review* 90, 2 (May): 350–354.

Levine, Robert A., Harold Watts, Robinson Hollister, Walter Williams, Alice O'Connor, and Karl Widerquist. 2005. "A Retrospective on the Negative Income Tax Experiments: Looking Back at the Most Innovative Field Studies in Social Policy." In Karl Widerquist, Michael Anthony Lewis, and Steven Pressman (eds.). *The Ethics and Economics of the Basic Income Guarantee.* Burlington, VT: Ashgate, pp. 95–108.

Levine-Clark, Marjorie. 2000. "Engendering Relief: Women, Ablebodiedness, and the New Poor Law in Early Victorian England." *Journal of Women's History* 11, 4 (Winter): 107–130.

Lewis, Frank and M. C. Urquhart. 1999. "Growth and the Standard of Living in a Pioneer Economy: Upper Canada, 1826 to 1851." *William and Mary Quarterly*, 3rd series, 56, 1 (January): 151–179.

Lillard, Lee A. 1977. "Inequality: Earnings vs. Human Wealth." *American Economic Review* 67, 1 (March): 42–53.

Lindbeck, Assar and Dennis J. Snower. 2001. "Insiders versus Outsiders." *Journal of Economic Perspectives* 15, 1 (Winter): 165–188.

Lindert, Kathy, Tina George Karippacheril, Ines Rodriguez Caillava, and Kenichi Nishikawa Chavez. 2019. *Sourcebook on the Foundations of Social Protection Delivery Systems.* Washington, DC: World Bank.

Lindert, Peter H. 1986. "Unequal English Wealth since 1670." *Journal of Political Economy* 94, 6 (December): 1127–1162.

Lindert, Peter H. 1991. "Historical Patterns of Agricultural Policy." In C. Peter Timmer (ed.), *Agriculture and the State.* Ithaca: Cornell University Press, pp. 29–83.

Lindert, Peter H. 1994. "The Rise of Social Spending, 1880–1930." *Explorations in Economic History* 31, 1 (January): 1–36.

Lindert, Peter H. 1998. "Poor Relief before the Welfare State: Britain versus the Continent, 1780–1880." *European Review of Economic History* 2 (August): 101–140.

Lindert, Peter H. 2003. "Voice and Growth: Was Churchill Right?" *Journal of Economic History* 63, 2 (June): 315–350.

Lindert, Peter H. 2004. *Growing Public: Social Spending and Economic Growth since the Eighteenth Century*. 2 volumes. Cambridge: Cambridge University Press.

Lindert, Peter H. 2009. "Revealing Failures in the History of School Finance." NBER Working Paper 15491 (November). www.nber.org/papers/w15491.

Lindert, Peter H. 2010. "The Unequal Lag in Latin American Schooling since 1900: Follow the Money." *Revista de Historia Económica* 28, 2: 375–405.

Lindert, Peter H. 2014. "Private Welfare and the Welfare State." In Larry Neal and Jeffrey. G. Williamson (eds.), *The Cambridge History of Capitalism*, vol. II: *The Spread of Capitalism*. Cambridge: Cambridge University Press, pp. 464–500.

Lindert, Peter H. 2017. "The Rise and Future of Progressive Redistribution." Commitment to Equity (CEQ) Institute, Tulane University, Working Paper 73 (October).

Lindert, Peter H. and Jeffrey G. Williamson. 2003. "Does Globalization Make the World More Unequal?" In Michael D. Bordo, Alan M. Taylor, and Jeffrey G. Williamson (eds.), *Globalization in Historical Perspective*. Chicago: University of Chicago Press, pp. 227–270.

Lindert, Peter H. and Jeffrey G. Williamson. 2016. *Unequal Gains: American Growth and Inequality since 1700*. Princeton: Princeton University Press.

Liu, Dazhong (Ta-chung). 1968. "Quantitative Trends in the Economy." In Alexander Eckstein, Walter Galenson, and Liu Dazhong (eds.), *Economic Trends in Communist China*. Chicago: Aldine.

Liu, Dazhong (Ta-chung) and K. C. (K'ung-chia) Yeh. 1965. *The Economy of the Chinese Mainland*. Princeton: Princeton University Press.

Lizzeri, Alessandro and Nicola Persico. 2004. "Why Did the Elites Extend the Suffrage? Democracy and the Scope of Government, with an Application to Britain's 'Age of Reform.'" *Quarterly Journal of Economics* 119, 2 (May): 707–765.

Lochner, Lance and Enrico Moretti. 2004. "The Effects of Education on Crime: Evidence from Prison Inmates, Arrests, and Self-Reports." *American Economic Review* 94, 1 (March): 155–189.

Long, Jason. 2006. "The Socioeconomic Return to Primary Schooling in Victorian England." *Journal of Economic History* 66, 4 (December): 1026–1053.

Lott, John R. Jr. and Lawrence W. Kenny. 1999. "Did Women's Suffrage Change the Size and Scope of Government?" *Journal of Political Economy* 107, 6, Part I (December): 1163–1198.

Lundberg, Shelley and Elaina Rose. 2000. "Parenthood and the Earnings of Married Men and Women." *Labour Economics* 7, 6 (November): 689–710.

Lustig, Nora. 2017. "Fiscal Policy, Income Redistribution and Poverty Reduction in Low and Middle Income Countries." Commitment to Equity Institute Working Paper 54 (January).

Lustig, Nora (ed.). 2018. *Commitment to Equity Handbook: Estimating the Impact of Fiscal Policy on Inequality and Poverty*. Washington, DC: Brookings Institution Press.

Luxembourg Income Study. 2017. www.lisdatacenter.org/download-key-figures /, accessed May 2, 2019.

Lynch, Julia. 2001. "The Age-Orientation of Social Policy Regimes in OECD Countries." *Journal of Social Policy* 30, 3: 411–436.

Lynch, Julia. 2006. *Age in the Welfare State*. Cambridge: Cambridge University Press.

Lynn, Richard and Tatu Vanhanen. 2002. *IQ and the Wealth of Nations*. Westport, CT: Praeger.

McAuley, Alastair. 1979. *Economic Welfare in the Soviet Union: Poverty, Living Standards, and Inequality*. Madison: University of Wisconsin Press.

McCants, Anne E. C. 1997. *Civic Charity in a Golden Age: Orphan Care in Early Modern Amsterdam*. Urbana: University of Illinois Press.

McCloskey, Diedre [Dierdre]. 1976. "English Open Fields as Behavior towards Risk." *Research in Economic History* 1 (Fall): 124–170.

McCloskey, Donald [Dierdre]. 1991. "The Prudent Peasant: New Findings on Open Fields." *Journal of Economic History* 51, 2 (June): 343–355.

McClure, Margaret. 1998. *A Civilised Community: A History of Social Security in New Zealand 1898–1998*. Auckland: Auckland University Press.

McGuire, Martin C. and Mancur Olson Jr. 1996. "The Economics of Autocracy and Majority Rule: The Invisible Hand and the Use of Force." *Journal of Economic Literature* 34, 1 (March): 72–96.

Mackie, Thomas T. and Richard Rose. 1991. *The International Almanac of Electoral History*. Fully revised third edition. London: MacMillan.

MacKinnon, Mary. 1987. "English Poor Law Policy and the Crusade against Outrelief." *Journal of Economic History* 47, 3 (September): 603–625.

McMahon, Walter W. 2004. "The Social and External Benefits of Education." In Geraint Johnes and Jill Johnes (eds.), *International Handbook on the Economics of Education*. Cheltenham: Edward Elgar, pp. 211–259.

Madrick, Jeff. 2019. *The Tragic Cost of Child Poverty*. New York: Knopf.

Mamalakis, Markos. 1976. *Growth and Structure of the Chilean Economy*. New Haven, CT: Yale University Press.

Mandler, Peter. 1987. "The Making of the New Poor Law *Redivivus*." *Past & Present* 117 (November): 131–157.

Mandler, Peter. 1990. "Debate: The Making of the Old Poor Law *Redivivus*." *Past & Present* 127 (May): 194–201.

Massie, Joseph. 1761. *Calculations of Taxes for a Family of Each Rank, Degree, or Class, for One Year*. Second edition. London: T. Payne.

Mesa-Lago, Carmelo. 2002. "Myth and Reality of Pension Reform: The Latin American Evidence." *World Development* 30, 8: 1309–1321.

Mesa-Lago, Carmelo. 2017. "The Cuban Welfare System: With Special Reference to Universalism." In Christian Aspalter (ed.), *The Routledge International Handbook to Welfare Systems*. London: Routledge, pp. 106–121.

Michielse, H. C. M. 1990. "Policing the Poor: J. L. Vives and the Sixteenth-Century Origins of Modern Social Administration." *Social Service Review* 64, 1 (March): 1–21.

Milanovic, Branko. 2000. "The Median-Voter Hypothesis, Income Inequality, and Income Redistribution: An Empirical Test with the Required Data." *European Journal of Political Economy* 16: 367–410.

Milanovic, Branko. 2018. "Towards an Explanation of Inequality in Premodern Societies: The Role of Colonies, Urbanization, and High Population Density." *Economic History Review* 71, 4 (November): 1029–1047.

Milanovic, Branko. 2019. *Capitalism, Alone: The Future of the System that Rules the World.* Cambridge, MA: Belknap Press of Harvard University Press.

Milanovic, Branko, Peter H. Lindert, and Jeffrey G. Williamson. 2011. "Pre-Industrial Inequality." *Economic Journal* 121 (March): 255–272.

Millán, Teresa Molina, Tania Barham, Karen Macours, John A. Maluccio, and Marco Stampini. 2019. "Long-Term Impacts of Conditional Cash Transfers: Review of the Evidence." *World Bank Research Observer* 34, 1 (February): 119–159. https://doi.org/10.1093/wbro/lky005.

Miller, Grant. 2008. "Women's Suffrage, Political Responsiveness, and Child Survival in American History." *Quarterly Journal of Economics* 123, 3 (August): 1287–1327.

Miller, Tim. 2011. "The Rise of the Intergenerational State: Aging and Development." In Ronald D. Lee and Andrew Mason (eds.), *Population Aging and the Generational Economy: A Global Perspective.* Cheltenham and Northampton, MA: Edward Elgar, pp. 161–184.

Milligan, Kevin, Enrico Moretti, and Philip Oreopoulos. 2004. "Does Education Improve Citizenship? Evidence from the United States and the United Kingdom." *Journal of Public Economics* 88, 9–10 (August): 1667–1695.

Mitch, David F. 1982. "The Spread of Literacy in Nineteenth-Century England." Doctoral dissertation, University of Chicago.

Mitch, David F. 1983–1984. "Underinvestment in Literacy? The Potential Contribution of Government Involvement in Elementary Education to Economic Growth in Nineteenth Century England." *Journal of Economic History* 44, 2 (June 1984): 557–566; and the expanded 1983 draft of this article kindly supplied by the author.

Mitch, David F. 1992. *The Rise of Popular Literacy in Victorian England: The Influence of Private Choice and Public Policy.* Philadelphia: University of Pennsylvania Press.

Mitchell, Brian R. (ed.). 1998a. *International Historical Statistics: Africa, Asia & Oceania, 1750–1993.* Cambridge: Cambridge University Press.

Mitchell, Brian R. (ed.). 1998b. *International Historical Statistics: Europe 1750–1993.* Cambridge: Cambridge University Press.

Mitchell, Brian R. (ed.). 1998c. *International Historical Statistics: The Americas 1750–1993.* Cambridge: Cambridge University Press.

Mitsui Bunko. 1989. *Trends of Major Prices in Early Modern Japan.* Tokyo: University of Tokyo Press.

Moe, Terry M. 2011. *Special Interest: Teachers Unions and America's Public Schools.* Washington, DC: Brookings Institution Press.

Moehling, Carolyn M. and Melissa A. Thomasson, 2012. "The Political Economy of Saving Mothers and Babies: The Politics of State Participation in the Sheppard–Towner Program." *Journal of Economic History* 72, 1 (March): 75–103.

Moehling, Carolyn M., Gregory T. Niemesh, Melissa A. Thomasson, and Jaret Treber. 2019. "Medical Education Reforms and the Origins of the Rural Physician Shortage." *Cliometrica* 14 (May): 181–225. https://doi.org/10.1007/s11698-019-00187-w.

Moffitt, Robert A. 2019. "The Marginal Labor Supply Disincentives of Welfare Reforms." NBER Working Paper 26028 (June).

Mokyr, Joel. 1992. "Technological Inertia in Economic History." *Journal of Economic History* 52, 2 (June): 325–338.

Mokyr, Joel. 2000. "Innovation and Its Enemies: The Economic and Political Roots of Technological Inertia." In Mancur Olson and Satu Kähkönen (eds.), *A Not-So-Dismal Science: A Broader View of Economies and Societies*. Oxford: Oxford University Press, pp. 269–300.

Montenegro, Claudio E. and Carmen Pagés. 2004. "Who Benefits from Labor Market Regulations? Chile, 1960–1998." In James Heckman and Carmen Pagés (eds.), *Law and Employment: Lessons from Latin America and the Caribbean*. Chicago: University of Chicago Press, pp. 401–434.

Montenegro, Claudio E. and Harry A. Patrinos. 2014. "Comparable Estimates of Returns to Schooling around the World." World Bank, Education Global Practice Group, Policy Research Working Paper 7020 (September).

Moody, Joseph N. 1978. *French Education since Napoleon*. Syracuse: Syracuse University Press.

Moosvi, Shireen. 1987. *The Economy of the Mughal Empire c. 1595: A Statistical Study*. Delhi: Oxford University Press.

Moosvi, Shireen. 2008. *People, Taxation and Trade in Mughal India*. Oxford: Oxford University Press.

Moretti, Enrico. 2004. "Estimating the Social Return to Higher Education: Evidence from Longitudinal and Cross-Sectional Data." *Journal of Econometrics* 121, 1–2 (July-August): 157–212.

Moriconi, Simone, Giovanni Peri, and Riccardo Turati. 2018. "Skill of the Immigrants and Vote of the Native: Immigration and Nationalism in European Elections 2007–2016." NBER Working Paper 25077 (September).

Muralidharan, Karthik and Venkatesh Sundararaman. 2011. "Teacher Performance Pay: Experimental Evidence from India." *Journal of Political Economy* 119, 1 (February): 39–77.

Murnane, Richard J., Marcus R. Waldman, John B. Willett, Maria Soledad Bos, and Emiliana Vegas. 2017. "The Consequences of Educational Voucher Reform in Chile." NBER Working Paper 23550 (June).

Nakabayashi, Masaki. 2012. "The Rise of a Japanese Fiscal State." In Bartolomé Yun-Casalilla and Patrick K. O'Brien (eds.), with Francisco Comín Comín, *The Rise of Fiscal States: A Global History, 1500–1914*. Cambridge: Cambridge University Press, pp. 378–409.

Neisser, Ulric (ed.). 1998. *The Rising Curve: Long-Term Gains in IQ and Related Measures*. APA Science Volume Series. Washington, DC: American Psychological Association.

Neuland, Simon. 2016. *Universal Social Protection: Universal Old-Age Pensions in Mongolia*. Geneva: United Nations.

Nipperdey, Thomas. 1977. "Mass Education and Modernization: The Case of Germany 1780–1850." *Transactions of the Royal Historical Society*, 5th series, 27: 155–172.

Nipperdey, Thomas. 1996. *Germany from Napoleon to Bismarck: 1800 to 1866*. Princeton: Princeton University Press.

North, Douglass C. and Barry R. Weingast. 1988. "Constitutions and Commitment: The Evolution of Institutions Governing Public Choice in

Seventeenth-Century England." *Journal of Economic History* 49, 4 (December): 803–832.

North, Michael. 2012. "Finances and Power in the German State System." In Bartolomé Yun-Casalilla and Patrick K. O'Brien (eds.), with Francisco Comín Comín, *The Rise of Fiscal States: A Global History, 1500–1914*. Cambridge: Cambridge University Press, pp. 145–163.

O'Brien, Patrick K. 1988. "The Political Economy of British Taxation, 1660–1815." *Economic History Review*, Second Series, 41, 1 (February): 1–32.

O'Brien, Patrick K. and Philip A. Hunt. 1993. "The Rise of a Fiscal State in England, 1485–1815." *Historical Research* 66, 160 (June): 129–176.

OECD. 1985. *Social Expenditure 1960–1990*. Paris: OECD.

OECD. 1992–2018. *Education at a Glance* [annual]. Paris: OECD.

OECD. 2008. *Growing Unequal? Income Distribution and Poverty in OECD Countries*. Paris: OECD.

OECD. 2008–2019. *International Migration Outlook [2008–2019]*. Paris: OECD, annual.

OECD. 2011. *Divided We Stand: Why Inequality Keeps Rising*. Paris: OECD.

OECD. 2014. *All on Board: Making Inclusive Growth Happen*. Paris: OECD.

OECD. 2015. *Health at a Glance 2015*. Paris: OECD.

OECD. 2016. *Education in China: A Snapshot*. Paris: OECD.

OECD. 2017. *School Choice and School Vouchers: An OECD Perspective*. Paris: OECD.

OECD. 2018a. *Consumption Tax Trends 2018 – VAT/GST and Excise Rates, Trends, and Policy Issues*. Paris: OECD.

OECD. 2018b. *Employment/Population Ratio, Age Group 15–64, 1950–2017*. https://stats.oecd.org/Index.aspx?DataSetCode=ALFS_SUMTAB, accessed Aug. 19, 2018.

OECD. 2018c. *Employment Outlook 2018*. Paris: OECD.

OECD. 2018d. "Income Redistribution through Taxes and Transfers across OECD Countries." Economics Department Working Paper 1453 (June). By Orsetta and Mikkel Hermansen.

OECD. 2018e. *Revenue Statistics 2018*. Paris: OECD.

OECD, Programme for International Student Assessment (PISA). 2001–2019. *Programme for International Student Evaluation, 2000 ... 2018* [each triennial issue has a different title]. Paris: OECD. Downloaded from zzwww.oecd.org/pisa/.

Oguchi, Yujiro. 2004. "The Finances of the Tokugawa Shogunate." In Kōnosuke Odaka, Akira Hayami, and Takafusa Nakamura (eds.), *The Economic History of Japan: 1600–1990*, vol. I: *Emergence of Economic Society in Japan, 1600–1859*. Oxford: Oxford University Press, pp. 192–200. HC462.N534513 2003.

Okrent, Daniel. 2019. "When Anti-Immigrant Hatred Was Mainstream." *New York Times*, May 3. www.nytimes.com/2019/05/03/opinion/sunday/anti-immigrant-hatred-1920s.html.

Olivetti, Claudia and Barbara Petrongolo. 2017. "Economic Consequences of Family Policies: Lessons from a Century of Legislation in High-Income Countries." *Journal of Economic Perspectives* 31, 1 (Winter): 205–230.

Olson, Mancur. 1982. *The Rise and Decline of Nations*. New Haven, CT: Yale University Press.

Orszag, Peter T. and Joseph E. Stiglitz. 2001. "Rethinking Pension Reform: Ten Myths about Social Security Systems." In R. Holzmann and J. Stiglitz (eds.), *New Ideas about Social Security: Toward Sustainable Pension Systems in the 21st Century.* Washington, DC: World Bank, pp. 17–56.

Ostry, J., A. Berg, and C. Tsangarides. 2014. "Redistribution, Inequality, and Growth." IMF working paper SDN/14/02 (April).

Oviedo, Ana, Susana M. Sanchez, Kathy A. Lindert, and J. Humberto Lopez. 2015. *Costa Rica's Development: From Good to Better.* Washington, DC: World Bank.

Pallares-Miralles, Montserrat, Carolina Romero, and Edward Whitehouse. 2012. "International Patterns of Pension Provision II: Worldwide Overview of Facts and Figures." World Bank Social Protection & Labor Discussion Paper 1211 (June).

Pamuk, Sevket. 2012. "The Evolution of Fiscal Institutions in the Ottoman Empire, 1500–1914." In Bartolomé Yun-Casalilla and Patrick K. O'Brien (eds.), with Francisco Comín Comín, *The Rise of Fiscal States: A Global History, 1500–1914.* Cambridge: Cambridge University Press, pp. 304–331.

Pederson, JoEllen and K. Russell Shekha. 2018. "Attitudes toward Public Pensions in Chile, Uruguay, and Venezuela: Testing Self-Interest and Political Ideology Theories in Latin American Countries." *International Social Work* 61, 2: 183–198.

Pedigo, David. 2011. "Privatization and Educational Inequality in Chile." *Santiago Times* Wednesday, November 30.

Peri, Giovanni. 2016. "Immigrants, Productivity, and Labor Markets." *Journal of Economic Perspectives* 30, 4 (Fall): 1–30.

Phananiramai, Mathana. 2011. "Incorporating Time into the National Transfer Accounts: The Case of Thailand." In Ronald Lee and Andrew Mason (eds.), *Population Aging and the Generational Economy: A Global Perspective.* Cheltenham and Northampton, MA: Edward Elgar, pp. 528–541.

Pietschnig, Jakob and Martin Voracek. 2015. "One Century of Global IQ Gains: A Formal Meta-Analysis of the Flynn Effect (1909–2013)." *Perspectives on Psychological Science* 10, 3: 282–306.

Piketty, Thomas. 2014. *Capital in the Twenty-First Century.* Translated by Arthur Goldhammer. Cambridge, MA: Belknap Press.

Piketty, Thomas, Emmanuel Saez, and Gabriel Zucman. 2016. "Distributional National Accounts: Methods and Estimates for the United States." NBER Working Paper 22945 (December), including its links to online appendices. www.nber.org/papers/w22945.

Piketty, Thomas, Li Yang, and Gabriel Zucman. 2017. "Capital Accumulation, Private Property, and Rising Inequality in China, 1978–2015." NBER Working Paper 23368 (April), and published in *American Economic Review* 109, 7 (July 2019).

Portes, Jonathan and Giuseppe Forte. 2017. "The Economic Impact of Brexit-Induced Reductions in Migration." *Oxford Review of Economic Policy* 33, Issue suppl. 1 (March 1): S31–S44, as a pdf file (working paper) accessed via www.niesr.ac.uk, June 15, 2018.

Pozen, Alexis, and David M. Cutler. 2010. "Medical Spending Differences in the United States and Canada: The Role of Prices, Procedures, and Administrative Expenses." *Inquiry* 47, 2: 124–134.

Preston, Ian. 2014. "The Effect of Immigration on Public Finances." *Economic Journal* 124, 580, Feature Issue (November): F569–F592.

Pritchett, Lant. 1997. "Divergence, Big Time." *Journal of Economic Perspectives* 11, 3: 3–17.

Psacharapoulos, George and Harry Anthony Patrinos. 2004. "Returns to Investment in Education: A Further Update." *Education Economics* 12, 2 (August): 111–134.

Queisser, Monika and Edward Whitehouse. 2006. "Neutral or Fair? Actuarial Concepts and Pension-System Design". OECD Social, Employment and Migration Working Papers 40 (December), http://dx.doi.org/10.1787/351382456457.

Ramsey, Frank P. 1927. "A Contribution to the Theory of Taxation." *Economic Journal* 37: 47–61.

Ravallion, Martin. 2015. *The Economics of Poverty: History, Measurement, and Policy.* Oxford: Oxford University Press. Part 1.

Reinhardt, Uwe E. 2000. "Health Care for the Aging Baby Boom: Lessons from Abroad." *Journal of Economic Perspectives* 14, 2 (Spring): 71–84.

Reinhardt, Uwe E. 2019. *Priced Out: The Economic and Ethical Costs of American Health Care.* Princeton: Princeton University Press.

Reynolds, Morgan and Eugene Smolensky. 1977. *Public Expenditures, Taxes, and the Distribution of Income: The United States, 1950, 1961, 1970.* New York: Academic Press.

Richards, John F. 2012. "Fiscal States in Mughal and British India." In Bartolomé Yun-Casalilla and Patrick K. O'Brien (eds.), with Francisco Comín Comín, *The Rise of Fiscal States: A Global History, 1500–1914.* Cambridge: Cambridge University Press, pp. 410–441.

Richardson, Gary. 2005. "The Prudent Village: Risk Pooling Institutions in Medieval English Agriculture." *Journal of Economic History* 65, 2 (June): 386–413.

Rimlinger, Gaston V. 1971. *Welfare Policy and Industrialization in Europe, America, and Russia.* New York: John Wiley & Sons.

Ritzen, Jozef M. M., Jan van Dommelen, and Frans J. de Vijlder. 1997. "School Finance and School Choice in the Netherlands." *Economics of Education Review* 16, 3 (June): 329–335.

Rodríguez, Francisco. 2008a. "An Empty Revolution: The Unfulfilled Promises of Hugo Chávez." *Foreign Affairs* 87, 2 (March/April): 49–62.

Rodríguez, Francisco. 2008b. "Rodríguez Replies." *Foreign Affairs* 87, 4 (July/August): 160–162.

Rothstein, Jesse. 2006. "Good Principals or Good Peers: Parental Valuation of School Characteristics, Tiebout Equilibrium, and the Incentive Effects of Competition among Jurisdictions." *American Economic Review* 96, 4 (September): 1333–1350.

Sachs, Jeffrey D. 2006. "Welfare States, beyond Ideology." *Scientific American* 295, 5 (November): 42.

Sachs, Jeffrey D. 2015. "A Way Out for Greece." www.project-syndicate.org/commentary July 3, 2015.

Saez, Emmanuel and Gabriel Zucman. 2019. *The Triumph of Injustice: How the Rich Dodge Taxes and How to Make Them Pay.* New York: W. W. Norton.

Saint John, Susan and Larry Willmore. 2001. "Two Legs Are Better than Three: New Zealand as a Model for Old Age Pensions." *World Development*, 29, 8: 1291–1305.

Saito, Osamu and Masanori Takashima. 2016. "Estimating the Shares of Secondary- and Tertiary-Sector Outputs in the Age of Early Modern Growth: The Case of Japan, 1600–1874." *European Review of Economic History* 20: 368–386.

Salter, F. S. 1926. *Early Tracts on Poor Relief*. London: Methuen.

Santibañez, Lucretia and Brenda Jarillo Rabling. 2008. "Conflict and Power: The Teachers' Union and Education Quality in Mexico." *Well-Being and Social Policy* 3, 2: 21–40. www.researchgate.net/publication/288192152_Conflict_and_power_The_teacher%27s_union_and_education_quality_in_Mexico.

Schenk, Alan. 2011. "Prior U.S. Flirtations with VAT." In Tax Analysts (US firm), *The VAT Reader: What a Federal Consumption Tax Would Mean for America*. Arlington, VA: Tax Analysts, pp. 52–63.

Schleunes, Karl A. 1989. *Schooling and Society: The Politics of Education in Prussia and Bavaria 1750–1900*. New York: Berg and St. Martin's Press.

Schneider, Eric C., Dana O. Sarnak, David Squires, Arnav Shah, and Michelle M. Doty. 2017. "Mirror, Mirror 2017: International Comparison Reflects Flaws and Opportunities for Better U.S. Health Care." (July). www.commonwealthfund.org/.sites/default/files/documents/media files publications fund report 2017 jul schneider mirror mirror 2017.pdf.

Schreurs, Gerardus Joseph. 2019. "Government Institutions and Economic Development in Tokugawa Japan: A Tale of Systems Competition." Doctoral dissertation, Hitotsubashi University.

Schultz, Kenneth A. and Barry R. Weingast. 1998. "Limited Governments, Powerful States." In Randolph M. Siverson (ed.), *Strategic Politicians, Institutions, and Foreign Policy*. Ann Arbor: University of Michigan Press, pp. 15–49.

Scruggs, Lyle and James Allan. 2005. "The Material Consequences of Welfare States: Benefit Generosity and Absolute Poverty in 16 OECD Countries." Luxembourg Income Study Working Paper 409 (April).

Sequeira, Sandra, Nathan Nunn, and Nancy Qian. 2020. "Immigrants and the Making of America." *Review of Economic Studies* 87, 1 (January): 382–419.

Shammas, Carole. 2015. "Did Democracy Give the United States an Edge in Primary Schooling?" *Social Science History* 39, 3 (Fall): 315–338.

Shoup, Carl S. et al. 1959. *The Fiscal System of Venezuela*. Baltimore: Johns Hopkins University Press.

Singer, Florantonia and Alonso Moleiro. 2020. ""El espejismo de la normalidad en Caracas." *El País*, Caracas, January 20.

Skoufias, Emmanuel, Kathy Lindert, and Joseph Shapiro. 2010. "Globalization and the Role of Public Transfers in Redistributing Income in Latin America and the Caribbean." *World Development* 38, 6: 895–907.

Smeeding, Timothy. 2006. "Poor People in Rich Nations: The United States in Comparative Perspective." *Journal of Economic Perspectives* 20, 1 (Winter): 69–90.

Smith, Adam. 1993 (1776). *An Inquiry into the Nature and Causes of the Wealth of Nations*. Edited by Kathryn Sutherland. New York: Oxford University Press.

Smolensky, E., W. Hoyt, and S. Danziger. 1987. "A Critical Survey of Efforts to Measure Budget Incidence." In H. M. van de Kar and B. L. Wolfe (eds.), *The Relevance of Public Finance for Policy-Making: Proceedings of the 41st Congress of the International Institute of Public Finance, Madrid, 1985.* Detroit: Wayne State University Press, pp. 191–205.

Sng, Tuan-Hwee and Chiaki Moriguchi. 2014. "Asia's Little Divergence: State Capacity in China and Japan before 1850." *Journal of Economic Growth* 19, 4 (December) 439–470.

Sokhey, Sarah Wilson. 2017. *The Political Economy of Pension Policy Reversal in Post-Communist Countries.* Cambridge: Cambridge University Press. E-book.

Solmon, Lewis. 1975. *Capital Formation by Expenditures on Formal Education 1880 and 1890.* New York: Arno Press.

Solt, Frederick. 2009. "Standardizing the World Income Inequality Database." *Social Science Quarterly* 90, 2: 231–42.

Solt, Frederick. 2014. "The Standardized World Income Inequality Database." frederick-solt@uiowa.edu., accessed Oct. 2, 2014.

Sousa, Gregory. 2017. "Countries That Impose the Highest Taxes on Cigarettes." WorldAtlas, Apr. 25, 2017, www.worldatlas.com/articles/countries-that-impose-the-highest-tax-on-cigarettes.html, accessed Jan. 10, 2020.

Squicciarini, Mara P. 2019. "Devotion and Development: Religiosity, Education, and Economic Progress in 19th-Century France." CESifo Working Paper 7768 (July).

Stabile, Mark and Sarah Thomson. 2014. "The Changing Role of Government in Financing Health Care: An International Perspective." *Journal of Economic Literature* 52, 2 (June): 480–518.

Starr, Paul. 1982. *The Social Transformation of American Medicine.* New York: Basic Books.

Starr, Paul. 2018a. "A New Strategy for Health Care." *The American Prospect* (Winter): 51–57.

Starr, Paul. 2018b. "Rebounding with Medicare: Reform and Counter-Reform in American Health Care." *Journal of Health Politics, Policy, and Law* 43, 4 (August): 708–730.

Stasavage, David. 2005. "Democracy and Education Spending in Africa." *American Journal of Political Science* 49, 2 (April): 343–358.

Stasavage, David. 2011. *States of Credit: Size, Power, and the Development of European Polities.* Princeton: Princeton University Press.

Stasavage, David. 2016. "Representation and Consent: Why They Arose in Europe and Not Elsewhere." *Annual Review of Political Science* 19: 145–162.

Steinmo, Sven. 1993. *Taxation and Democracy: Swedish, British and American Approaches to Financing the Modern State.* New Haven, CT: Yale University Press.

Sun, Jung Oh and Hosung Sohn. 2019. "The Impact of the School Choice Policy on Student Sorting: Evidence from Seoul, South Korea." *Policy Studies.* https://doi.org/10.1080/01442872.2019.1618807.

Swedish Pensions Agency. 2019. *Orange Report: Annual Report of the Swedish Pensions Agency 2018.* Stockholm: SPA.

Symeonidis, Georgios. 2016. "The Greek Pension Reform Strategy 2010–2016." World Bank, Social Protection and Labor Discussion Paper 1601 (July).

Székely, Miguel and Andrés Montes. 2006. "Poverty and Inequality." In Victor Bulmer-Thomas, John H. Coatsworth, and Roberto Cortés-Conde (eds.), *The Cambridge Economic History of Latin America*, vol. II: *The Long Twentieth Century*. Cambridge: Cambridge University Press, pp. 585–646.

Takayama, Noriyuki, Yukinobu Kitamura, and Hiroshi Yoshida. 1999. "Generational Accounting in Japan." In Alan J. Auerbach, Laurence J. Kotlikoff, and Willi Leibfritz (eds.), *Generational Accounting around the World*. Chicago: University of Chicago Press, pp. 447-469.

Thévenon, O. and A. Solaz. 2013. "Labour Market Effects of Parental Leave Policies in OECD Countries," OECD Social, Employment and Migration Working Papers 141, OECD Publishing. http://dx.doi.org/10.1787/5k8xb6hw1wjf-en.

Thomasson, Melissa A. 2002. "From Sickness to Health: The Twentieth Century Development of U.S. Health Insurance." *Explorations in Economic History* 39, 3: 233–253.

Thomasson, Melissa A. 2003. "The Importance of Group Coverage: How Tax Policy Shaped U.S. Health Insurance." *American Economic Review*, 93, 4 (September), 1373–1384.

Thomson, David. 1996. *Selfish Generations? How Welfare States Grow Old*. Cambridge: White Horse Press.

Tiebout, Charles M. 1956. "A Pure Theory of Local Expenditures." *Journal of Political Economy* 64, 5 (October): 416–424.

Tierney, Brian. 1959. "The Decretists and the 'Deserving Poor.'" *Comparative Studies in Society and History* 1, 4 (June): 360–371.

Trahan, Lisa H., Karla K. Stuebing, Jack M. Fletcher, and Merrill Hiscock. 2014. "The Flynn Effect: A Meta-Analysis." *Psychological Bulletin* 140, 5 (September): 1332–1360.

Tremewan, Christopher. 1998. "Welfare and Governance: Public Housing under Singapore's Party-State." In R. Goodman, G. White, and H. Kwon (eds.), *The East Asian Welfare Model: Welfare Orientalism and the State*. London: Routledge, pp. 77–105.

Troesken, Werner. 2004. *Water, Race, and Disease*. Cambridge, MA: MIT Press.

Troesken, Werner. 2015. *The Pox of Liberty: How The Constitution Left Americans Rich, Free, and Prone to Infection*. Chicago: University of Chicago Press.

United Kingdom, Migration Advisory Committee. 2018. EEA Migration into the UK: Final Report (September). https://assets.publishing.service.gov.uk/government/uploads/system/uploads/attachment_data/file/741926/Final_EEA_report.PDF.

United Nations, Department of Economic and Social Affairs, Population Division. 2015. "World Population Prospects: The 2015 Revision." DVD Edition.

US Congressional Budget Office. 2017. *Comparing the Compensation of Federal and Private-Sector Employees, 2011 to 2015*. Washington, DC: GPO.

US House Ways and Means Committee. 2019. *A Painful Pill to Swallow: U.S. vs. International Prescription Drug Prices*. Washington, DC: GP. https://waysandmeans.house.gov/sites/democrats.waysandmeans.house.gov/files/documents/U.S.%20vs.%20International%20Prescription%20Drug%20Prices_0.pdf.

US Internal Revenue Service. 2009. *Actuarial Valuations, Version 3A*. Publication 1457 (Rev. 5-2009).

US Internal Revenue Service. 2019. www.irs.gov/retirement-plans/actuarial-tables.

Uthoff, Andras. 2017a. "Do Competitive Markets of Individual Savings Accounts and Health Insurance Work as Part of the Welfare State?" In José Antonio Ocampo and Joseph Stiglitz (eds.), *The Welfare State Revisited*. New York: Columbia University Press, ch. 12.

Uthoff, Andras. 2017b. "El debate sobre la reforma previsional necesaria en Chile." *El Cotidiano*, 204 (July–August): 77–85.

Van Bavel, Bas and Auke Rijpma. 2016. "How Important Were Formalized Charity and Social Spending before the Rise of the Welfare State? A Long-Run Analysis of Selected Western European Cases, 1400–1850." *Economic History Review* 69, 1 (February): 159–187.

Van Leeuwen, Marco H. D. 2000. *The Logic of Charity: Amsterdam, 1800–1850*. Translation of his *Bijstand in Amsterdam, ca. 1800–1850* by J. Arnold. Basingstoke: Macmillan.

Van Leeuwen, Marco H. D. 2012. "Guilds and Middle-Class Welfare 1550–1800: Provisions for Burial, Sickness, Old Age, and Widowhood." *Economic History Review* 65, 1: 61–90.

Van Leeuwen, Marco H. D. 2016. "Overrun by Hungry Hordes? Migrants' Entitlements to Poor Relief in the Netherlands, 16th–20th Centuries." In Steve Hindle and Anne Winter (eds.), *Migration, Settlement and Belonging in Europe, 1500–2000: Comparative Perspective*. New York: Berghahn Publishers, pp. 173–203.

Wadsworth, Jonathan, Swati Dhingra, Gianmarco Ottaviano, and John van Reenen. 2016. "Brexit and the Impact of Immigration on the UK." Brexit Analysis No. 5, Centre for Economic Performance. http://cep.lse.ac.uk/pubs/download/brexit05.pdf.

Waldfogel, Jane. 1998. "Understanding the 'Family Gap' in Pay for Women and Children." *Journal of Economic Perspectives* 12, 1 (Winter), 137–156.

Wang, Chen, Koen Caminada, and Kees Goudswaard. 2012. "The Redistributive Effect of Social Transfer Programmes and Taxes: A Decomposition across Countries." *International Social Security Review* 65, 3: 27–48.

Wang, Ya Ping and Alan Murie. 1999. *Housing Policy and Practice in China*. New York: St. Martin's Press.

Webb, Sidney. 1926. "Preface" to F. S. Salter, *Some Early Tracts on Poor Relief*. London: Methuen, pp. vii–xii.

Weisbrot, Mark. 2008. "An Empty Research Agenda: The Creation of Myths about Contemporary Venezuela." Center for Economic and Policy Research, Issue Brief (March). www.cepr.net.

Weisbrot, Mark and Jeffrey Sachs. 2019. "Economic Sanctions as Collective Punishment: The Case of Venezuela." Center for Economic and Policy Research, Report (April 25).

Wilensky, Harold. 2002. *Rich Democracies: Political Economy, Public Policy, and Performance*. Berkeley: University of California Press.

Williamson, Jeffrey G. 1990. *Coping with City Growth during the British Industrial Revolution.* Cambridge: Cambridge University Press.
Willmore, Larry. 2000. "Three Pillars of Pensions? A Proposal to End Mandatory Contributions." United Nations DESA Discussion Paper 13 (June 2000), plus his annotated 2014 version at larrywillmore.net, accessed Jan. 25, 2020.
Willmore, Larry. 2007. "Universal Pensions for Developing Countries." *World Development* 35, 1: 24–51.
Woessmann, Ludger. 2002. *Schooling and the Quality of Human Capital.* Berlin: Springer-Verlag.
Woessmann, Ludger. 2016. "The Importance of School Systems: Evidence from International Differences in Student Achievement." *Journal of Economic Perspectives* 30, 3 (Summer): 3–32.
Wolf, Richard M. 1977. *Achievement in America: National Report of the United States for the International Education Achievement Project.* New York: Teachers College Press.
Wood, Adrian. 1997. "Openness and Wage Inequality in Developing Countries: The Latin American Challenge to East Asian Conventional Wisdom." *World Bank Economic Review* 11 (January): 33–57.
Woodlander, Steffie, Terry Campbell, and David U. Himmelstein. 2003. "Costs of Health Care Administration in the United States and Canada." *New England Journal of Medicine* 349, 8 (August 21): 768–775.
Woolf, Stuart. 1986. *The Poor in Western Europe in the Eighteenth and Nineteenth Centuries.* New York: Methuen.
World Bank. 1994. *Averting the Old Age Crisis.* New York: Oxford University Press.
World Bank. 2011. "Mongolia – Policy Options for Pension Reform." Human Development Unit, East Asia and Pacific Region, Report No. 68526-MN (January 20).
Yun-Casalilla, Bartolomé and Patrick K. O'Brien (eds.), with Franciso Comín Comín. 2012. *The Rise of Fiscal States: A Global History, 1500–1914.* Cambridge: Cambridge University Press.
Zakaria, Fareed. 1994. "Culture in Destiny: A Conversation with Lee Kuan Yew." *Foreign Affairs* 73, 2 (March–April): 109–126.
Zhang, Xing Quan. 1998. *Privatisation: A Study of Housing Policy in Urban China.* New York: Nova Science Publishers.
Zlotnick, Susan. 2006. "'The Law's a Bachelor': Oliver Twist, Bastardy, and the New Poor Law." *Victorian Literature and Culture* 34: 131–146.
Zucman, Gabriel. 2015. *The Hidden Wealth of Nations.* Chicago: University of Chicago Press.

Index